Read this book online today:

With SAP PRESS BooksOnline we offer you online access to knowledge from
the leading SAP experts. Whether you use it as a beneficial supplement or as
an alternative to the printed book, with SAP PRESS BooksOnline you can:

- Access your book anywhere, at any time. All you need is an Internet connection.
- Perform full text searches on your book and on the entire SAP PRESS library.
- Build your own personalized SAP library.

The SAP PRESS customer advantage:

Register this book today at *www.sap-press.com* and obtain exclusive free trial
access to its online version. If you like it (and we think you will), you can choose to
purchase permanent, unrestricted access to the online edition at a very special price!

Here's how to get started:

1. Visit *www.sap-press.com*.
2. Click on the link for SAP PRESS BooksOnline and login (or create an account).
3. Enter your free trial license key, shown below in the corner of the page.
4. Try out your online book with full, unrestricted access for a limited time!

Your personal free trial **license key**
for this online book is: u3pd-79s6-5ymb-hq4z

Data Modeling in SAP NetWeaver® BW

 **PRESS**

SAP PRESS is a joint initiative of SAP and Galileo Press. The know-how offered by SAP specialists combined with the expertise of the Galileo Press publishing house offers the reader expert books in the field. SAP PRESS features first-hand information and expert advice, and provides useful skills for professional decision-making.

SAP PRESS offers a variety of books on technical and business related topics for the SAP user. For further information, please visit our website: *www.sap-press.com*.

Mike Garrett
Using Crystal Reports with SAP
2010, 500 pp.
978-1-59229-327-8

Jim Brogden, Heather Sinkwitz, Mac Holden
SAP BusinessObjects Web Intelligence
2010, 583 pp.
978-1-59229-322-3

Ingo Hilgefort
Reporting and Analytics with SAP BusinessObjects
2009, 655 pp.
978-1-59229-310-0

Larry Sackett
MDX Reporting and Analytics with SAP NetWeaver BW
2009, 380 pp.
978-1-59229-249-3

Frank K. Wolf and Stefan Yamada

Data Modeling in SAP NetWeaver® BW

Bonn • Boston

Galileo Press is named after the Italian physicist, mathematician and philosopher Galileo Galilei (1564–1642). He is known as one of the founders of modern science and an advocate of our contemporary, heliocentric worldview. His words *Eppur se muove* (And yet it moves) have become legendary. The Galileo Press logo depicts Jupiter orbited by the four Galilean moons, which were discovered by Galileo in 1610.

Editor Eva Tripp
English Edition Editor Erik Herman
Translation Lemoine International, Inc., Salt Lake City, UT
Copyeditor Mike Beady
Cover Design Graham Geary
Photo Credit iStockphoto/Jan Pietruszka
Layout Design Vera Brauner
Production Editor Kelly O'Callaghan
Assistant Production Editor Graham Geary
Typesetting Publishers' Design and Production Services, Inc.
Printed and bound in Canada

ISBN 978-1-59229-346-9

© 2011 by Galileo Press Inc., Boston (MA)
1st Edition 2011
1st German edition published 2010 by Galileo Press, Bonn, Germany

Library of Congress Cataloging-in-Publication Data
Wolf, Frank K.
 [Datenmodellierung in SAP NetWeaver BW. English]
 Data Modeling in SAP NetWeaver BW / Frank K. Wolf, Stefan Yamada.
   p. cm.
 ISBN-13: 978-1-59229-346-9 (alk. paper)
 ISBN-10: 1-59229-346-8 (alk. paper)
 1. SAP NetWeaver BW. 2. Data warehousing. 3. Business intelligence—Data processing. I. Yamada, Stefan. II. Title.
 QA76.9.D37W65 2011
 005.74—dc22

                                                                        2010022841

Contents at a Glance

Contents

7   Modeling the EDW 231

10 Data Modeling for Planning Applications 403

11 Optimizing Data Retention 447

12 Specific Data Modeling Issues in BW Projects 471

1 Introduction

Analysis-oriented information systems are used to support planning and strategic processes. They provide enterprises with current and historical data. Analysis-oriented information systems are frequently based on a data warehouse in which relevant data is collected, formatted, and made available. The core of a data warehouse is a (usually relational) database.

With SAP® NetWeaver Business Warehouse (BW), SAP provides a solution that includes all of the required components for setting up a data warehouse architecture. In addition to the basic technology for data retention, the system provides all of the essential components for evaluating the data stored in BW, that is, reporting tools, data mining methods, and an option for a portal connection. One essential feature when compared to other solutions is SAP's Business Content, which includes preconfigured sample solutions for various business areas. **SAP NetWeaver BW**

Although BW supplies predefined content, a BW implementation is basically an individual solution. This is necessary, because users' requirements and preferences are as diverse as their business models and corporate cultures. Moreover, BW content is developed continuously. The modification of business strategies, the mapping of new business processes, or quite simply the emergence of new analytical problems all result in — and indeed require — the further development of content mapped in BW to ensure the goal of supplying an enterprise with relevant information.

Before it can be stored in BW, the content is systematically structured (into a data model) on the basis of the technical relevance of the content that is supposed to be mapped. This structure in turn determines the available options for data analyses. Besides the evaluation options for content and restrictions resulting from the data model, further criteria that can affect the data model's quality have to be considered, such as the performance of the data retrieval (report execution) and the time and effort involved in making modifications to the model (flexibility of **Data model** modifications), both defining the acceptance and therefore the success of a BW implementation. These aspects are essentially determined by the data model, which has been created for mapping the content.

Maturity model Your enterprise's or organization's experience with analysis-oriented information systems will be just as varied as the requirements you place on the content in the BW system. A solution is often developed gradually (see Figure 1.1), from a simple reporting solution, to more complex Excel-based analyses, to solutions that are based on a department-related dataset (so-called data marts) or, in a further step, on a company-wide, integrated dataset (the data warehouse). It can be frustrating at this point (see the gap in Figure 1.1) if, for example, you notice that it takes too long to implement technical requirements or load data, or if you find that the acceptance of the BW system in the company is at risk, which stalls further development of the system.

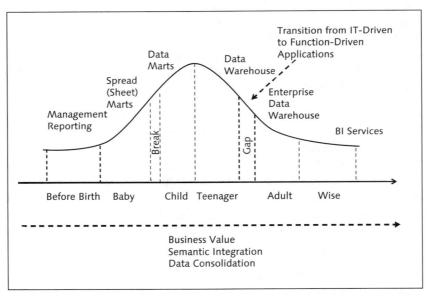

Figure 1.1 Phases in the Business Intelligence (BI) Maturity Model (TDWI, 2007)

When introducing a BW system, you don't need to start from scratch and learn everything the hard way. Business Content makes it easier for you to reconcile and integrate content. DataSources and basic modules of the Business Content's data model (characteristics and key data) are often integrated in the implementation.

As of Release 7.x, BW provides technologies that enable the development of an architecture facilitating the integration of user departments and the consideration of their interests within the overall architecture. This helps you bridge the gap more efficiently and develop a "mature system" that has the necessary support within the user departments.

At the core of the implementation of requirements is the data model — whether it is on a logical level as the basis for reconciliation and discussion with the user department or as a high-performing physical model that supports data loading (staging) and data retrieval (reporting). Moreover, new technologies, such as Nearline Storage (NLS) for outsourcing data or Business Warehouse Accelerator (BWA) for high-performing data retrieval, must also be integrated at the physical model level. The integration of these technologies requires a coherent architecture of the data model. It becomes clear that the issue of data modeling in BW is very complex and not limited to the consideration of conventional modeling types for data-warehouse systems (for example, the star schema, a denormalized type of data storage). The physical mapping of the data store even takes a back seat to some extent, because the BW system generates these structures. Instead, the optimization of the architecture, especially the formation of so-called layers, assumes particular significance. These layers help you standardize the development and ensure a high degree of flexibility with regard to modifications to the data model.

1.1 Target Audience

This book addresses those who need to know how to design and develop new content in BW or how to optimize existing content. The emphasis is on growth-oriented modeling and the design of an extensible data model. This means you can benefit from this book if you've started with a small implementation at first, but also if you want to gradually optimize the data modeling of an existing system and use new technologies.

For BW consultants and developers (internal and external), this book is a good starting point for familiarizing yourself with data modeling. Besides the conventional data modeling concepts, you also get to know the specific characteristics of the BW data model and a reference architecture, which helps you standardize and design a future-oriented model.

Consultants and developers

User department
employees

This book also addresses employees of user departments responsible for defining and communicating (new) requirements. On the one hand, the methods for logical data modeling are useful when describing requirements; on the other hand, the explanations on the reference architecture in this book provide knowledge about methods every project member should be acquainted with. The explanations on Business Content and the modeling examples also teach you how to efficiently model data using Business Content.

Decision makers
and project leads

The sections on reference architecture are of particular interest for decision makers and project leads who want to address these critical issues and consider them in their departments or projects.

1.2 Structure of the Book

This book first provides the necessary background information on data modeling in general and on the BW data model in particular.

Knowing the individual modules of the data model, this book discusses the concepts of the reference architecture introduced by SAP, the Layered, Scalable Architecture (LSA). This architecture describes multiple layers with different tasks. Each of these tasks requires an appropriately adapted data model. After covering these special features, the theory is applied to concrete case studies from real life. The topics "data modeling for planning applications," "optimization of data retention for planning applications," and "special aspects of data modeling" round off the book.

This book is divided into the following chapters:

Chapter 2, Basic Principles of Data Modeling, describes the required conceptual principles of data modeling. It introduces modeling methods and discusses the logical, conceptual, and physical level of a BW data model.

Chapter 3, Overview of SAP NetWeaver BW and SAP BusinessObjects, provides an overview of the diversity of reports and evaluations that can be implemented on the basis of SAP NetWeaver BW. The tools introduced in this chapter are the interface between data model and user. In addition to SAP Business Explorer (BEx) front ends, you also get to know SAP BusinessObjects.

Chapter 4, Structure of a BW Data Model, details the various types of DataProviders that are used to store and provide data in SAP NetWeaver BW.

Now that you're familiar with the individual modules of the BW data model, **Chapter 5**, Reference Architecture for Data Modeling, addresses the structure of an architecture in which the individual DataProviders are organized in layers. In this context, you have to distinguish between two areas: the area in which data is formatted in such a way that you can easily use them for various analysis contexts (Enterprise Data Warehouse (EDW) Layer) and the area that provides analysis datasets for specific issues (Reporting Layer). These two areas place completely different requirements on the data modeling types that are discussed in Chapters 7 and 8.

Business Content is covered in **Chapter 6**, Business Content. Business Content refers to predefined content that is related to specific business application fields. This chapter provides numerous tips on how to efficiently develop your own solutions using Business Content.

Chapter 7, Modeling the Enterprise Data Warehouse, provides details on the specific modeling aspects of the EDW Layer. Besides data integration and storage, the chapter also describes transformations that are used to process data in BW. The implementation of process chains and a loading process control round off this chapter.

The essential goal of the data warehouse is to provide data in such a way that it can be queried with a high performance. To do this, a special layer, the Reporting Layer, is modeled. Because reporting requirements can change frequently, in addition to the performance, flexibility is also a critical goal for the modeling of the Reporting Layer. Chapter 8 deals with data modeling in the Reporting Layer.

Chapter 9, Case Studies, applies the newly acquired knowledge to two concrete case studies. The first case study describes the layered, Scalable Architecture (LSA), where the respective data model is developed and implemented step by step. The second case study discusses the use of Business Content with examples of various representative application cases.

With BW-integrated planning, SAP has created a planning solution that is based directly on a BW data model and also writes to such a data model. Some alternative modeling options are possible here. Chapter 10, Data Modeling for Planning Applications, discusses the corresponding issues.

In **Chapter 11**, Optimizing Data Retention, you learn how to secure your investments in the BW data model for the long term, make them more economical, and adjust them to new requirements.

Chapter 12, Data Modeling in BW Projects, summarizes some BW-specific data modeling aspects.

After a brief outlook in **Chapter 13**, the **Appendix** provides a selection of useful information: abbreviations, transaction codes, programs, function modules, includes, tables, posting keys, literature, and a glossary.

1.3   How to Use This Book

For readers who want to enter the world of data modeling, Chapter 2 introduces the basic principles of data modeling.

If you're already acquainted with the theoretical principles of data modeling in data warehouse environments but you're new to SAP NetWeaver BW world, Chapter 3 provides an overview of the modeling tool, of the Data Warehousing Workbench, and of the BW reporting tools. Alternatively, you can start with Chapter 4 and directly turn to the structure of the BW data model. Chapters 7 (structure of the EDW Layer) and 8 (structure of the Reporting Layer) detail further data modeling aspects, particularly with regard to the layer architecture introduced in Chapter 5. Depending on your fields of interest, you can read Chapter 6, Chapter 10, and Chapter 12. Chapter 11 provides tips for optimizing and remodeling data retention and data modeling.

If you already have experience with working in BW and are looking for architecture or data modeling improvements, you should read the explanations on the LSA, SAP's reference architecture, described in Chapter 5. In addition, the descriptions of the specific modeling topics in Chapters 7 and 8 provide detailed information about the topics relevant for you. You can read Chapter 10 and Chapter 11.

Readers who specifically deal with the implementation of new technologies and want to analyze their effects on data modeling can directly start with the respective chapters, that is, Chapter 10 regarding the integration of planning applications and Chapter 11 regarding NLS solutions and remodeling. Chapter 8 also addresses BWA. However, you should read Chapter 5 on the LSA first. This architecture lays the foundation for a flexible integration of new technologies with the existing solution.

It was very important to us to include our wealth of experience gained in numerous BW projects. Therefore, Chapter 6 and the case studies in Chapter 9 introduce many application cases from real life and their modeling. Chapter 12 discusses the special features of BW project management. If you face the challenge of having to map specific topics in BW, these explanations can be invaluable— and considerably accelerate the processing of projects.

To make it easier for you to work with this book, we use specific icons to highlight certain sections:

The tips marked with this icon provide recommendations from real life, which will make your work easier. **[+]**

Notes marked with this icon contain information on critical requirements or effects you should always take into account. **[«]**

This icon refers to examples that explain the topic discussed in more detail and are supposed to illustrate how to use the individual functions in your enterprise. **[Ex]**

1.4 Acknowledgments

Numerous colleagues and friends contributed to the successful completion of this book. They answered questions, provided tips, and were valuable discussion partners — every one of them deserves a big thank-you.

Sincere thanks are also due to Eva Tripp at SAP PRESS, who supported this book project all of the way, from concept to completion. Her effective and great collaboration was a valuable contribution to the realization of this book project.

Above all, we'd like to thank our families. Numerous weekends and evenings, our wives, Dr. Makiko Wolf and Juri Yamada, had to do without their husbands, and our children, Hannah Marie, Paul Yoshi, Kakuei, and

Kento, without their fathers. They tolerated this with patience and still gave us the necessary support and confidence to finish this book.

Frank K. Wolf
frank.wolf@triple-a.de

Stefan Yamada
stefan.yamada@gmail.com

This chapter describes the basic principles of data modeling: characteristics of a data warehouse, data models, and modeling methods. The main focus is always on the relevance to SAP NetWeaver Business Warehouse (BW).

2 Basic Principles of Data Modeling

Data modeling is one of the biggest challenges for setting up a data warehouse. In an operational system (such as SAP Enterprise Resource Planning (ERP), SAP Advanced Planning and Optimization (APO), or SAP Customer Relationship Management (CRM)), the data model only needs to provide data for the respective application. Furthermore, technical aspects, such as the normalization of the database schema or system performance, are of significance in operational systems. In a BW project, however, the data model is part of the application itself and therefore of particular interest — even from a functional point of view. You have to determine which detail level must be considered, whether characteristics are historically true or must be evaluated with current references, and so on. In interviews with the user department, the question which data model is useful for the user ultimately takes up much space even if only individual reports are discussed with the user superficially. After all, SAP NetWeaver BW is not a collection of reports, but a powerful tool for providing data models that enable effective and efficient reporting.

This chapter first presents the special features of SAP NetWeaver BW as a data warehouse. Then you'll learn about the division into the conceptual, logical, and physical layers, which is common in data modeling. This chapter discusses two presentation methods and then outlines the critical topics from all three layers that are required for modeling analytical applications. The basic principles are presented independent of the BW system; however, the special features of BW will also be addressed.

2.1 SAP NetWeaver BW as a Data Warehouse (DWH) System

Many enterprises collect and store data without being able to combine it in a reasonable way. In a DWH — a data storage area, so to speak — data is combined in a structured way by bringing it together from operational systems (for instance, SAP ERP), and cleansing and providing it consistently for reporting (see Figure 2.1). SAP NetWeaver BW is SAP's DWH solution.

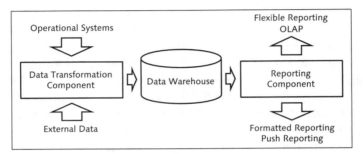

Figure 2.1 General Overview of a DWH

BW — like other DWH systems — differs fundamentally from an operational system. The operational SAP system is primarily optimized for transaction processing and not for analytical applications. The special characteristics of a DWH system include the following:

▶ Topic orientation

▶ Integration

▶ Time base

Topic orientation   In an operational system, the focus of every development, which can usually be considered relatively isolated, is on an application, a program, or a transaction; in BW the development is topic oriented. The DWH is sorted by topics that are suited for the analysis of key figures for supporting decisions (for instance, product or customer), but not by operational processes. For example, you evaluate all information on a customer: order history, sales, payment history, vendor relationships, order entry, invoicing, accounts receivable, and accounts payable. The operational system, however, is organized in applications (for example, sales or accounting). Therefore, the DWH has a higher integration level with other systems than operational systems.

To enable this comprehensive view of data, it is necessary to standardize the data from the different operational systems. This integration is usually done using mapping rules (for instance, a method to go from a customer number in system A to the corresponding customer number in system B). You may need mapping tables to determine how key values must be transcoded. You may also have to standardize texts, master data, hierarchies, and key figures, particularly units of measure and currencies.

Integration

Due to the high integration, changes at one location can affect large parts of the entire system and consequently trigger a domino effect. The high level of integration is also a challenge for transports in the BW system that should not be underestimated.

The time base is another essential difference between BW and operational systems: An operational application usually focuses on the current status; in BW, however, the past also plays a crucial role. Depending on the respective issue, there are different views of the past. A key account manager is mainly interested in the customer currently assigned to him. If his supervisor wants to appraise him, he needs the historical view (that is, the system also displays sales with customers that the employee currently doesn't attend to). These time aspects play a major role in BW. It must be possible to consider different requirements in the data model. Moreover, in DWH systems you usually keep a longer history than in operational systems. Therefore, consistency emerges as the fourth property — besides topic orientation, integration, and time base.

Time base

In comparison to the DWH solutions of other providers, SAP NetWeaver BW exhibits some differences: Most DWH solutions have a stronger database orientation, and other DWH solutions have more freedom when using specific technologies of various database manufacturers. The strong relationship to the operational SAP systems (both organizational and technical) is an essential benefit of SAP NetWeaver BW compared to other DWH systems.

So the difference between BW projects and other data warehouse projects is the close link to the SAP landscape; BW projects distinguish themselves from other SAP projects by the three special characteristics of a DWH: topic orientation, integration, and time base.

2.2   Conceptual, Logical, and Physical Data Model

You distinguish between a functional/conceptual (semantic), logical, and physical level of the data model. The benefit of this three-part division is that you consider the functional/conceptual level, the logical definition of the data model, and the physical implementation independent of each other. The following briefly discusses the three levels of the data model:

▸ **Conceptual level**
Purely functional and without reference to specific BW objects

▸ **Logical level**
Link between the functional and the physical modeling

▸ **Physical level**
InfoProviders, that is, primarily InfoCubes, DataStore objects (DSOs), and InfoObjects (Chapter 4, Structure of a BW Data Model, provides a description of these terms)

Conceptual model The conceptual model involves the purely functional description of the reporting requirements without reference to a concrete implementation in BW or another system. For an analytical application, this means that you must describe all key figures and dimensions required. For these descriptions you are provided with ADAPT as a special presentation method for analytical systems; this method is presented in Section 2.3.2, ADAPT Model.

Logical model A logical model is a presentation that is organized independent of its physical representation, but toward the implementation of a specific technology (for instance, the relational schema for relational databases). The logical model is the link between the conceptual model and the physical implementation. For the implementation of a DWH system using a relational database, the logical model marks the decision for a concrete modeling schema (for instance, the star schema, see Section 2.5.2, Star Schema).

When you use BW, you not only decided on the relational schema, but you can only make very specific system-technical settings in logical data modeling (see Chapter 4). Therefore, it doesn't necessarily make sense to document these settings using complex diagrams. Chapter 12, Section,

12.2.4, Data Model in the Technical Concept, discusses the meaning of the logical data model in the BW project.

The physical model is the actual implementation of data objects in the BW system. Chapter 4 and Chapter 5, Reference Architecture for Data Modeling, discuss the physical model. Chapter 4 describes the individual (physical) objects in the BW system, and Chapter 5 outlines the general considerations on the overall architecture. Here, not only functional requirements, but the specifications of information technology (IT), particularly Enterprise Data Warehouse (EDW) strategy, naming conventions, Business Content usage, performance strategy, and so on, play a role.

Physical model

Before discussing special data modeling topics for analytical systems, let's look at the description methods, ER and ADAPT.

2.3 Modeling Methods

This section introduces two modeling methods: the ER model according to Chen and the ADAPT model according to Bulos. Section 2.4, Conceptual Multidimensional Modeling, discusses the concepts and problems of multidimensional modeling.

The conceptual level of a multidimensional data model appears to be less complex at first glance. For conceptual and logical models, you don't often use special presentation methods, but lists or a simple star diagram (for example, in Microsoft PowerPoint®) for documentation. The reason for this is that no default method has emerged yet for multidimensional modeling. The use of methods like ADAPT is simple and ensures a better understanding between users and developers.

Physical data modeling in BW primarily refers to the data flow and the layers required. In most projects, there is no graphical presentation of the physical data model because the physical implementation is automatically performed by the system during the activation of BW object such as an InfoCube.

2.3.1 ER Model

ER stands for Entity Relationship model. The purpose of the ER model is to describe the relationships between the various data objects during

ER model according to Chen

data modeling. It comprises a graphical presentation of the data content and structures and is supposed to build a bridge between users and developers in data modeling and to support the designing of the DWH.

The ER model particularly consists of entities, attributes, and relationships:

▶ **Entity**
Entities are objects from the real world that can be uniquely identified. Entities are shown as rectangles. Examples of entities are employee, customer, order, project, and so on.

▶ **Attribute**
Attributes (or characteristics) entail properties of entities. Attributes are shown as ovals; key characteristics are underscored.

▶ **Relationship**
Relationships are shown as diamonds whose ends are connected with the rectangles (entities).

Figure 2.2 illustrates an ER model.

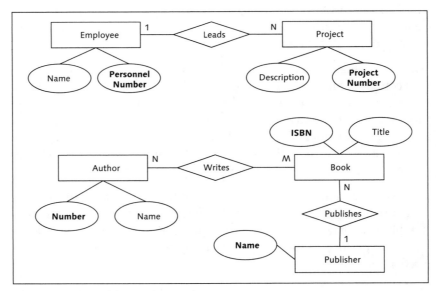

Figure 2.2 ER Model According to Chen

ER models are particularly helpful to describe the data basis in operational systems. In principle, it is also possible to describe a multidimensional data model using the ER model, but this doesn't make sense because there are no special constructs for its description (that is, aggregation levels (calculation levels) or calculation rules).

Although the method, which was presented by Chen in 1976, is not particularly suited for multidimensional modeling, there is no way around it because it is virtually the standard for conceptual data modeling. However, besides the presentation form according to Chen, there are additional notations available (for instance, IDEF1X).

Meaning of the ER model for BW

ER models are the ideal technology to describe source data in a very comprehensible way. Moreover, you can use ER models to describe InfoSet definitions.

2.3.2 ADAPT Model

The ADAPT method is a data modeling method that is designed for multidimensional modeling. Therefore, this section provides a detailed description and it is frequently referenced throughout the book.

The ADAPT model, which was presented by Bulos in 1996, is a description approach whose focus is on multidimensional data models. Hahne (2005) relates this approach explicitly to BW. At its core, ADAPT consists of nine icons; sometimes additional icons are used. For example, Hahne presents icons for all technical settings that are possible in the BW model; this impairs the clarity of diagrams. If you use too many different icons, the diagrams appear to be overloaded and are difficult to understand.

This section describes the most important icons and their use. Dimensions and key figures are the two critical elements of conceptual modeling. The ADAPT method supports the description of these two elements. Table 2.1 shows the central icons that are used in the ADAPT method.

Dimensions and key figures

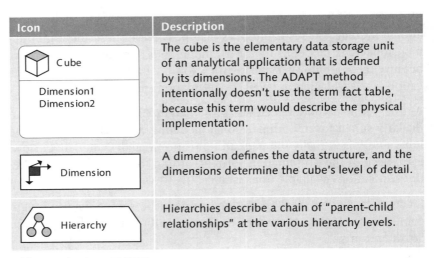

Icon	Description
Cube Dimension1 Dimension2	The cube is the elementary data storage unit of an analytical application that is defined by its dimensions. The ADAPT method intentionally doesn't use the term fact table, because this term would describe the physical implementation.
Dimension	A dimension defines the data structure, and the dimensions determine the cube's level of detail.
Hierarchy	Hierarchies describe a chain of "parent-child relationships" at the various hierarchy levels.

Table 2.1 The Core ADAPT Icons

Table 2.2 shows the APAPT icons for describing a dimension.

Icon	Description
{○} Member	A member or dimension element is an independent characteristic within a dimension.
{△} Level	A level is within a hierarchy.
◇ Attribute	An attribute is used to further describe a dimension element.
{ } Scope	A scope refers to a subset of a dimension.

Table 2.2 Icons to Describe a Dimension

Table 2.3 lists model and context as additional icons.

Icon	Description
$f()$ Model	A model is the description of mathematical operations which, in turn, describe the derivation of a key figure.
Context	A context is a subset of a cube which, in turn, is defined by subsets (scopes) of dimensions.

Table 2.3   Additional Icons

You must connect the individual icons with lines. In this context, ADAPT distinguishes different connection types, which are shown in Table 2.4.

Icon	Description
◀—	A line with a single arrow describes a loose relationship.
◀◀—	A line with a double arrow describes a strict relationship.
↻	An open circle with an arrowhead describes a recursive relationship.
◀◀▶▶	A line with double arrowheads in both directions describes an n:m relationship.

Table 2.4   ADAPT Connection Types

In addition to the connection types, you can also use relationship types. These are shown in Table 2.5.

Icon	Description
⬭⬭	The *or relationship* allows for overlappings.
⊗	The *exclusive or* says that all subsets are disjunct.
⌒⌒	The *partial or* means that the union of subsets doesn't correspond to the entirety.
⌒×	The *partial exclusive or* indicates that the union of disjunct subsets doesn't correspond to the entirety.

Table 2.5   Relationship Types

Figure 2.3 illustrates a simple cube model. Because a larger model would become very unclear in a diagram, it often makes sense to create diagrams for individual dimensions.

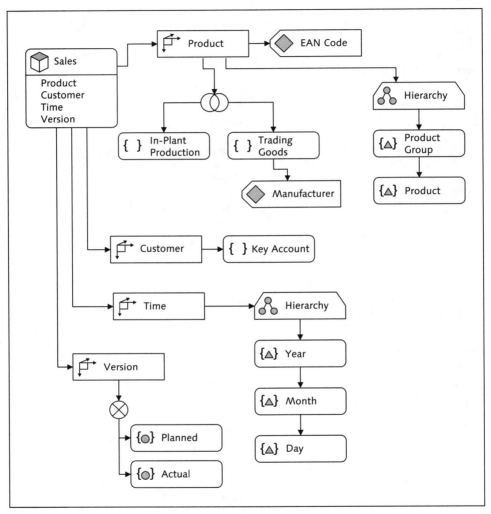

Figure 2.3 Example of an ADAPT Diagram

The following section discusses the individual questions of multidimensional data modeling.

2.4　Conceptual Multidimensional Modeling

Data modeling for analytical applications — such as the BW system — usually involves multidimensional modeling, that is, the modeling of multidimensional data structures.

In most cases, a cube is used as the symbol. The cube edges present the different dimensions and the cells of the cube stand for the values, for example, a key figure (see Figure 2.4). Needless to say, this is not a three-dimensional cube but a hyper-dimensional cube. Hence the commonly used name, HyperCube.

Data cubes

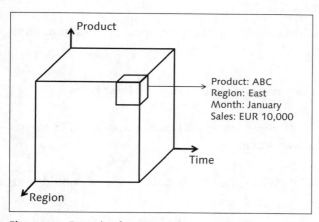

Figure 2.4　Example of a HyperCube

The reporting tool provides a view of the data cube that is as flexible as possible. In this context, a two-dimensional table is a simple view of the cube, for example.

The following terms are used to describe navigation in the different views:

Navigation in multidimensional data structures

- ▶ **Slice and dice**
  Slice describes the projection of a two-dimensional table from the data cube, and dice involves the filtering to a partial sub-cube.
- ▶ **Drill-down**
  Drill-down is the option to insert flexibly detailed characteristics in a report.

▶ **Roll-up**
With roll-up, you can hide levels of detail and display data only at a higher aggregation level.

▶ **Drill-through**
With drill-through, you can access the document level; ideally, you can navigate directly to the operational system.

▶ **Drill-across**
With drill-across, you can navigate to another report for the same selection (for instance, along the logistics chain).

Programs that support these functions are also referred to as Online Analytical Processing (OLAP) tools.

At all three levels of data modeling, there are special topics in multidimensional modeling:

▶ **Conceptual**
Structure and characteristics of dimensions and key figures

▶ **Logical**
The basic models of multidimensional data models, such as star schema and snowflake schema

▶ **Physical**
MOLAP and ROLAP systems (see Section 2.6, Physical Multidimensional Modeling)

The following section presents the most important aspects of multidimensional modeling and describes their relevance in the BW system.

2.4.1 Dimensions

Document data In an operational system, data occurs at the document level, and you must format the document data in an aggregated form to enable meaningful support. In analytical systems, the data is usually not stored at the lowest level, but only with the characteristics required in reporting. The document data is added within the scope of updating. In this context, dimensions refer to logically related characteristics and their interrelations. The structure of elements within a dimension is referred to as hierarchy. The lowest level is usually referred to as the level of basic elements or as the leaf level. Higher levels can be referred to as hierarchy levels or consolidation levels.

The following presents some elementary types of dimensions:

▸ **Flat characteristic structure**
A flat structure is a set of equal characteristic values for which a hierarchical structure cannot or is not supposed to be formed.

▸ **Balanced tree and forest structure**
You have a balanced, or more precisely, a height-balanced structure if the length of the shortest path of two leaves to the root node is always identical. If there is only one root node in the entire hierarchy, this is a tree structure; but if there are more root nodes, you have a forest structure.

The time dimension is usually interpreted as a balanced structure, that is, year/quarter/month/day.

▸ **Unbalanced tree and forest structure**
You have an unbalanced structure if the length of the shortest path of two leaves to the root node is not always identical. Unbalanced structures are often found in organizational structures.

▸ **Parallel hierarchies**
In most cases, you can model parallel hierarchies meaningfully. For organizational structures, hierarchies are often only an intentional business sequence of characteristics. For example, the structure, region/ customer group/product, is just as possible as any other combination.

▸ **Heterarchies**
In a heterarchy, you can assign individual nodes multiple times. It is also possible to assign allocation records to the individual connections in such a structure, which would make sense in evaluating corporate group structures, for example.

The hierarchy concept in BW is very comprehensive and can support virtually all possible scenarios. For instance, you can make multiple assignments in BW hierarchies, chargeable nodes can be at different levels, and nodes within a hierarchy can be different characteristics.

A conceptual hierarchy doesn't necessarily need to be modeled as a hierarchy from a technical point of view. Navigation attributes and characteristics of a (logical) dimension also present a hierarchy conceptually.

[»]   **Dimensions in the Conceptual Model**

Don't confuse dimensions in the conceptual sense with dimensions in the physical BW model. In the physical model, that is, in the data model for an InfoCube, completely different considerations are important, particularly with regard to performance. However, the conceptual and the logical model should correspond to the MultiProvider model and have a logical structure.

2.4.2   Key Figures

Besides dimensions, key figures are an important topic in conceptual multidimensional modeling. Key figures are stored in the fact table together with dimensions. Dimensions determine the organization and structure of a fact table, and key figures are quantitative values that enable mathematical operations.

Key Figure Model versus Account Model

During conceptual modeling, you must decide the amount of key figures to be defined (width of the fact tables). Characteristics with only a few values can basically be modeled both as characteristic dimensions and as key figures. For example, instead of value types (that is, planned, actual, and so on) you can also model key figures for planned and actual.

Account model

Particularly in financial accounting, it is not possible to model all key figures as a static structure; instead, key figures present groupings of individual accounts. For these groupings, you usually use hierarchies; this ensures that definitions in SAP ERP and BW are synchronized. Due to the high significance of key figure modeling in financial accounting, the term account model is frequently used for this approach.

Key figure model

In contrast to the account model, as many key figures as possible are modeled in the key figure model (also groupings of characteristics). Both approaches are difficult to manage in their extreme forms. A pure account model is flexible, but it requires knowledge about the required restrictions. A pure key figure system is easy to understand, but it features little flexibility in case of changes. Because the key figures in the key figure model describe groups of characteristic attributes, this is often referred to as grouped key figures.

If such grouped key figures are not stored physically but calculated in reporting, these are called restricted key figures. Time key figures are frequently used examples of grouped key figures. Some very common examples are: previous year, current month, Year-to-Date (YTD). If such values are calculated in reporting, transaction data of 24 months must be read in December. Alternatively, you could also store the values of the previous or the current year as physical key figure values in the fact table. Such key figures are more difficult to manage for flexible reporting, but they can be beneficial for a more static reporting application, like formatted reports or dashboards. In this example, only data for one month must be read.

Restricted key figures

Stock and Flow Quantities

Most key figures are either stock or flow quantities.

Flow quantities are key figures of recurring transactions, for instance, costs, sales, and revenues.

Stock and flow quantities

Stock quantities, however, are values that can be determined for fixed key dates. Inventory stock values, financial account balances, and headcount are typical stock quantities. Flow quantities are period-related and stock quantities are key date-related. Calculation of stock quantites about a period are always made at a point in time, usually the last day of the period.

In BW, you must technically specify for each key figure whether it is a cumulative (flow quantity) or noncumulative value (stock quantity), which has a similar meaning as stock and flow quantities. The technical implementation as a noncumulative value involves various disadvantages. Technically, you can also model stock quantities as cumulative values. Here, it is possible to update the opening balance in the first month (for example, data transfer upon system implementation) and subsequently all stock changes; this procedure is typical for balance sheet key figures. Snapshots are another alternative; this means that you write all data every month, for example. This method is frequently used in the personnel area or for statistical key figures in Controlling (CO). Stock quantities cannot be summed via the time axis.

Number Key Figure (Factless Fact Table)

Some key figures don't directly refer to a quantitative value, but count the occurrence of a relationship. Therefore, a corresponding fact table doesn't require key figures, but only dimensions. Consequently, other books (for example, Adamson, 1998) also use the term, factless fact table. There are two different types of number key figures:

▶ **Event count**
An event relationship has occurred, for example, in visit statistics.

▶ **Coverage analysis**
This entails a comparison of all possible combinations with the event relationship value, for example, considering which product has not been sold in which subsidiary in which month.

You usually need to calculate number key figures in aggregated form on a specific dimension. This means that you calculate the number of sold (different) products or the number of doctors that a medical representative visited instead of considering only the number of events, that is, the number of sales per product or the number of visits to doctors. From the logical and technical perspective, this calculation method is more difficult to model than a simple number of events. To do this, it makes sense to use an exception aggregation.

For practical reasons, in BW you may not model factless fact tables but key figures with the number 1. This means that the system doesn't count the result rows, but you are provided with a fully additive key figure whose handling is simple. For example, you can use the additive key figure as a basis to set up aggregates. The 1ROWCOUNT key figure is always automatically available for InfoObjects and DSOs.

[»]   **1ROWCOUNT and Slow-Moving Items**

In reporting in all "flat" InfoProviders, that is, in master data reporting via InfoObjects and for DSOs, the 1ROWCOUNT key figure exists virtually. The number of records in the InfoProvider is important, but it is not available in the data model. Under the term, list of slow-moving items, at *help.sap.com*, you learn how you can implement a coverage analysis in BW reporting.

Valuation as a Key Figure

In some areas, for example, in quality management and in Human Resources (HR) management, valuations play a critical role. Valuations always refer to a concrete object, for example, to a product, a vendor, or an employee. Therefore, valuations can also be modeled as an attribute very easily. It may make sense to form levels instead of scale values. Frequently, special aggregation rules apply to valuations; these rules consider the importance of an individual valuation within an overall valuation. The time aspects of a valuation key figure can also differentiate from the time aspects of other key figures. This is the case, for example, if you want a valuation to remain valid until a more recent valuation is available.

Time Key Figures

Time key figures are another group of key figures. Time key figures also have some specific features. There are three different types of time key figures:

▶ **Real times**
for example, working times in hours and minutes

▶ **Comparisons of two points in time (or date fields)**
for example, the number of days between invoicing and incoming payment

▶ **Countback or countforward of inflows and outflows for a stock quantity**
for example, the scope of the warehouse stock of product X for production

Time comparisons can often require complex lookups in different tables, because the times to be compared occur in different process steps. Frequently, you must solve a 1:n or n:m relationship in this context, for example, the processing time of an order up to the delivery of goods.

Countback calculations can involve very intensive development, which, in turn, depends on the calculation accuracy required. The simplest calculation is the comparison of an annual key figure and the current inventory, for example. It is needless to say that seasonal fluctuations are not considered in this context, and this calculation would respond very slowly (for instance, increase of receivables and warehouse stocks during a sudden economic downturn). It is therefore better to calculate the countback as a calculation of shorter periods of time, for instance, monthly inflows and outflows any time recently. The complexity of the calculation increases depending on how many months are supposed to

Countback
calculations

be taken into account (this depends on the average ratio of the respective stock value and inflows and outflows).

Calculated Key Figures

Calculated key figures mainly involve differences, percentage calculations, and relations of two or more individual key figures, for instance, planned/actual comparison (difference) or market share (relation).

The best way to implement calculated key figures is usually in reporting. If calculated key figures are stored physically, they can often only be aggregated with some effort. For calculations that require a lot of system resources and for which you require virtual key figures, for example, it can definitely make sense to store calculations physically. In such cases, calculation results can be retained physically for all aggregation levels required. However, a disadvantage of this procedure is that the flexibility of reporting is impaired because the aggregation level in the report must always be known. Ideally, you make a preliminary calculation for the computing-intensive parts of a complex key figure and design it in such a way that you ensure a flexible aggregation behavior.

Additivity and Calculation Level of Key Figures

When you model key figures, you must also consider the additivity of the respective key figure. Additivity means that the total of key figure values of multiple characteristic values equals the key figure value of the total of these characteristic values. This means, for example, that the sales of January added to the sales of February equals the sales of January and February. Normally, key figure values are added; so they are fully additive.

Additive key figures
Flow quantities are additive without restrictions; for all other types of key figures you must consider specifics with regard to additivity, particularly with regard to the time dimension. Not all key figures are fully additive. Note that the most critical key figures, such as profit, sales, and costs, are additive key figures.

Non-additive key figures
Non-additive key figures are characterized by the fact that you cannot sum individual values across any dimension. Calculated key figures are often non-additive. However, the parts of calculated key figures are usually fully additive. For example, you cannot sum relation key figures (for instance, sales share of new customers), but you can sum individual

parts (for instance, sales generated by new customers and total sales). In reporting, the calculation is usually performed conclusively; so calculation is possible at any level.

Semi-additive key figures can be summed across individual dimensions, but not across all dimensions. In most cases it is not possible to form sums via the time dimension, because noncumulative key figures are non-additive on the time dimension; on other dimensions, however, they are normally additive.

Semi-additive key figures

Aggregation behavior is a term similar to additivity. Aggregation behavior in an OLAP system determines how data is supposed to be condensed. Besides summation, aggregation can also be calculated as minimum, maximum, average, sum, number, and so on (aggregation function). Aggregation behavior is the system setting that you must make to consider additivity of a key figure.

Aggregation behavior

Aggregation Behavior in BW

In BW, you differentiate standard aggregation and exception aggregation. In this context, semi-additive key figures have the standard aggregation, *summation,* and an exception aggregation, for instance, average, via the time dimension.

[«]

Besides additivity, the calculation level also plays an essential role.

Calculation level

Some key figures can only be calculated at the document level, for example, the delay in payment for an invoice in days. Alternatively, you can define the reference level functionally, for instance, the number of overtime hours based on the hours greater than 40 per person per week.

Up to BW Release 3.5, you have the option to define calculated key figures as a before aggregation. The calculation is then performed at the lowest data record level in the physical InfoCube model. This means that it might be important whether the data is compressed or not, and you also need to physically store the data in an InfoCube (for information on the InfoCube data model see Chapter 4). In practical use, this means that you need to compress the data immediately after every data load to use this function reasonably. It is surely due to this circumstance that before aggregation is no longer available as of BW Release 7.0.

Aggregation at the lowest level, up to Release 3.5

[»] **Technical Implementation of the Conceptual Properties**

The technical settings in SAP BW don't necessarily have to follow the conceptual properties. For example, stock quantities can be modeled in different ways. Besides conceptual properties, performance considerations play a role.

Table 2.6 summarizes the different categories of key figures and their additivity behavior.

Key Figure Type	Additive	Non-additive	Semi-additive	Level-Specific Calculation	Example
Flow quantity	X				Sales
Stock quantity			X (time)		Warehouse stock
Number	X				Visits
Number, aggregated			X		Customers visited
Valuation	(X)	(X)	(X)	(X)	Appraisal points
Posted time	X				Absence times
Time comparison	X			X	Processing time
Countback		X			DSO
Difference	X				Planned/actual
Quota		X			Gross margin
Complex calculation		X			Relative market share

Table 2.6 Aggregation Behavior of Conceptual Key Figure Categories

2.5 Logical Multidimensional Modeling

The following presents the basic structures of logical modeling and describes its influence on the logical data model of BW.

2.5.1 Flat Reporting Structure

A flat reporting structure is the simplest form of an analytical data model: A table contains all of the characteristics that can be used for evaluation and all key figures. Therefore, all characteristics available for evaluations must be included in the table. This table is highly denormalized, which means that there are a lot of fields in the table that are interdependent (that is, redundant) functionally. Table 2.7 shows a simple example of a flat structure.

Product	Customer Number	Customer Name	Month	Sales	Quantity

Table 2.7   Table of a Flat Reporting Structure

Whereas tables are normalized for transactional systems, the denormalization ensures a performance advantage for evaluating data. A major disadvantage of a flat structure is the fact that because all characteristics must be added to a table a very long key develops. The key number and the table width are limited in most systems: Tables in the basic SAP system, for example, can only contain 16 keys. This limitation is a major restriction of the SAP ERP reporting systems, Logistics Information System (LIS) and Enterprise Information System (EIS).

Denormalization

Because all of the characteristics are directly stored in the reporting table and no additional master tables are provided, all of the reports only show the historical view. In reporting systems that use flat structures, the reporting tables are rebuilt from time to time if a current view is required. Aggregated values can only be stored in additional tables (that is, in additional flat reporting structures).

Flat structures for reporting tables don't play a significant role in BW. For example, reporting on DSOs (without navigation attributes and master data ID (SID) generation) involves reporting on a flat structure. Most application cases with regard to reporting on DSOs, however, are reports at the detail level. In exceptional cases, you can store highly aggregated reports on a 1:1 basis in a DSO, for example, to exclude retroactive changes for Financial Accounting (FI) reports.

2.5.2 Star Schema

The star schema was developed to create a data model for analytical applications that can be easily implemented in relational databases, that is, in the relational schema.

Fact and
dimension table

In the star schema, you store key figures in a central fact table. Characteristics are not stored directly as keys, but as separately generated dimension keys. These dimension keys, in turn, are the keys of the dimension tables, which contain all of the characteristics of a dimension. Figure 2.5 shows a star schema based on a simple model that contains customer, product, and time.

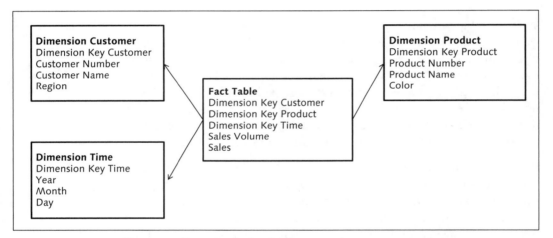

Figure 2.5 Example of a Star Schema

When you model dimensions, it is not necessary to structure them logically by area. In the ideal case (from a technical perspective), however, the characteristics should depend on one another functionally, more precisely, from the characteristic that describes the highest details level. This is usually the case for attributes of a characteristic (at least if you only consider the current view), which is why you still achieve an logical combination of characteristics in most cases.

Slowly changing
dimensions

Characteristic values can change; that's how slowly changing dimensions emerge. The term, slowly changing dimensions, summarizes different methods to collect changes in dimension tables and possibly store the history. The advantage of the star schema is that you can handle slowly changing dimensions more flexibly because the key of the dimension table is not the characteristic key but an artificially generated dimension key.

There are three types of slowly changing dimensions:

▶ **Type 1:** Unchangeable attributes; changes usually involve error corrections, and the old values are not relevant for reporting.

▶ **Type 2:** Attributes that can effectively change from time to time, whereas the old assignment usually remains relevant for historical data and the new assignment applies to data (for example, the region of a customer) as of the time of the change.

▶ **Type 3:** A completely new structure is implemented, where the old data must be analyzable based on the new structure and the new data based on the old structure.

You can implement all three types in the star schema. For type 1, you must correct the dimension table. For this correction, a remodeling function for dimension tables is available in BW. For type 2, you generate a new entry for the same characteristic in the dimension table. This entry then receives the newly generated key (SID, see Section 2.5.6, BW Star Schema). This is the normal case in the BW system. For type 3, you must create a new characteristic in the same dimension, which is often the case in the sales area (for example, sales region 2005, sales region 2010, and so on) — this is possible in the star schema. In BW, you have additional options; external hierarchies are particularly suitable here (see Chapter 4, Section 4.2.3, External Hierarchies).

One benefit of the star schema is that you can use very short keys (for instance, a 4-byte integer) as generated dimension keys instead of very long, meaningful characteristic keys, which ensures performance advantages.

Dimension key

Normalized master data is not provided in the star schema, that is, all attributes must exist in the dimension tables. In BW, this corresponds to storing attributes in dimensions. Provided that you don't reorganize a dimension (for example, by remodeling the dimension table or via frequent reorganization of fact table and dimension table), the data model of the star schema semantically corresponds to the historical view of transactional data.

In real life, reloading an InfoCube in BW happens more frequently than remodeling dimension tables. The dimension tables don't necessarily have to be deleted when you delete and reorganize the fact table; then, however, the old entries no longer required would not be automatically deleted in the dimension tables.

It is also possible to store aggregated values in the star schema. For storing aggregated values, you must add a characteristic for level to all dimensions with aggregated values to prevent multiple aggregations. However, this approach is not useful for very large data quantities because a high-performance access to aggregated data is possible but difficult, because this data is also available in the same fact table.

Star schema and BW
The star schema is the basic data model for almost all analytical systems that are implemented using relational databases. Therefore, it is also the basic model for InfoCubes in BW. For more information on the star schema of BW, refer to Section 2.5.6 and Chapter 4, Section 4.4.1, Physical Data Model.

2.5.3 Galaxies

In the classical star schema, you store all key figures in one fact table. Not all transactions (facts) that are supposed to be evaluated together have the same characteristic attributes and levels of detail. As a result, not all dimension characteristics are always available and the dimension tables with unnecessary zero values grow. A good example is planning data, because it never has the same level of detail as the actual data: In most cases, you plan on a monthly basis and not on a daily basis. You only plan for a rough product group, but not for thousands of product codes. And you only plan for a customer group, but not for all individual customers. Therefore, if you store actual and planning data in the same InfoCube, this results in considerable modeling disadvantages. Up to BW Release 1.2b, users had to store all key figures that were supposed to be displayed in the same query in the same InfoCube.

In this context, the distribution of key figures to multiple fact tables is referred to as a galaxy (see Figure 2.6) in general literature (for instance, Chamoni, 1998).

Galaxies in BW
In BW, you create multiple InfoCubes for different key figures. You can use these InfoCubes via MultiProviders. However, it is not possible to use a common dimension in BW here.

46

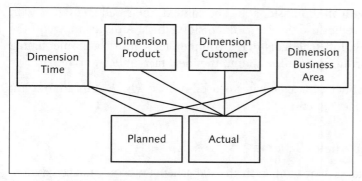

Figure 2.6 Example of a Galaxy

2.5.4 Fact Constellation Schema

You can store aggregated data in the star schema by adding multiple levels to the dimension tables. The relatively simple implementation is an advantage. A disadvantage is that the fact table and the dimension table become even bigger and fast access to the aggregated data may not be ensured. This problem is supposed to be resolved with the fact constellation schema.

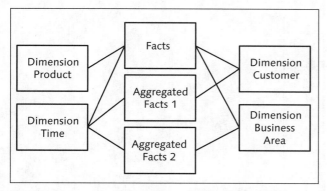

Figure 2.7 Example of a Fact Constellation Schema

The fact constellation schema comprises additional fact tables to which aggregated values are outsourced. This is illustrated in Figure 2.7. This results in separate tables that you can access quickly because they only contain aggregated data and are therefore much smaller than a large fact table with all dimensions. In this context, the small fact tables with aggregated values use the same dimension tables. A disadvantage of the fact constellation schema is that a complex logic must be implemented in the reporting application to find the ideal fact table.

Fact constellation schema in BW A similar model with aggregates is used in BW, where you cannot omit the "large" fact table.

2.5.5 Snowflake Schema

The snowflake schema enhances the star schema with normalized dimension tables. The term normalization is less strict in this context than in the context of transactional databases.

Figure 2.8 shows this normalization based on an example. The result is a splitting of dimension tables into level-specific dimension tables that you can use very effectively for queries with aggregates, for example, in the fact constellation schema. The normalization of dimensions also results in additional master data tables that enable a current view of the characteristic attributes.

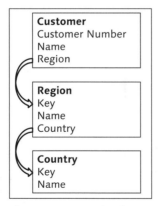

Figure 2.8 Normalized Dimension Tables

Snowflake and BW BW doesn't use a snowflake schema in the actual sense, but separate denormalized master data to enable reporting with the current assignment.

2.5.6   BW Star Schema

BW uses an enhanced form of the star schema, which is described in more detail in the following section.

The InfoCube is the most important data model in BW for reporting (see Chapter 4, Section 4.4, InfoCubes). From a logical data modeling perspective, this basically involves a star schema with denormalized master data. Figure 2.9 shows this basic form.

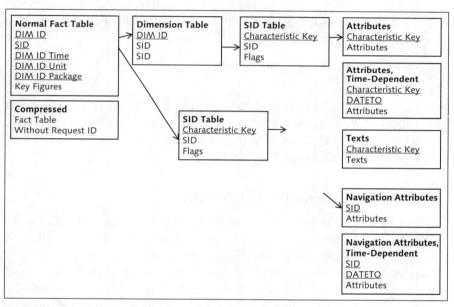

Figure 2.9   BW Star Schema

There are two fact tables: the "normal" table (F table) and a compressed table (E table). The facts are loaded from the F table into the E table via compression. This deletes the request ID and possible zero records. A fact table has up to 16 key fields or dimensions, of which three are predefined: time, unit (currency or unit of measure), and package. The remaining 13 dimensions can be designed as required. For each dimension you generate a dimension table with an artificial key, the DIM ID. Additional artificial master data keys (SID) are stored in the dimension table. Via the SID table you can navigate to the characteristic keys, which you need to display attributes and texts. You determine the master data tables for navigation attributes directly via the SID. You also have the option of creating line item dimensions; here you store the SID directly in the fact table, which ensures a more efficient access to data. However, a line item dimension can only contain one characteristic.

Attributes of attributes are not provided in the InfoCube model and must be stored redundantly in the superordinate master data, if required. This means that master data must be modeled denormalized. The SID of the navigation attribute tables is imported either via the dimension table or directly via the fact table for line item dimensions. Characteristics in the dimension tables generally enable a historical view of data, and the navigation attributes enable a current view.

To simplify things, external hierarchies, aggregates, and BWA indices were omitted here.

Logical data model
of the InfoCube
In general, the analytical data model in BW involves a star schema enhanced with denormalized master data. Unlike the snowflake schema, the master data enhancement is used to enable the current view of transactional data and not to form aggregate tables.

2.5.7 Operational Data Store (ODS)

ODS is a separate database for reporting purposes, similar to a data warehouse. Like a DWH, an ODS is an independent system that is supposed to relieve an operational system from reporting tasks. The ODS usually provides data from multiple upstream systems. A data cleansing and consolidation is implemented here. Like a DWH, an ODS is periodically provided with data. The nature of the data is different, however, because an ODS contains detail data that is available for complex analyses this way. In the DWH, data is usually provided for many years. But in an ODS data is only relevant for a short period of time. Examples of typical ODS data include connection data of telecommunications providers or cash register receipt data of retailers.

Also, in the layer model of Chapter 4, the ODS is modeled as a separate layer. Note, however, that this approach is usually not used: BW is not optimized for this purpose; for example, it lacks a function to handle longer text fields.

ODS in BW
SAP has already used the term, operational data store, twice for different tables in BW. Prior to Release 2.0a, today's Persistent Storage Area

was called ODS. After that and up to Release 3.5, today's DSO was called ODS. The reason why the term ODS is no longer used is that technical literature refers to the ODS as the approach described previously and not a special table form.

2.6   Physical Multidimensional Modeling

Data is usually saved in relational databases. These are optimized for transaction processing in operational systems. However, there have been approaches for multidimensional databases. Multidimensional databases also implement the conceptual cube model as a physical data model.

With regard to the physical modeling, it was discussed for a long time whether it would be better to use multidimensional databases instead of relational databases. In multidimensional databases, you don't use tables but multidimensional data structures. Multidimensional Online Analytical Processing (MOLAP) refers to the use of a multidimensional database for an OLAP application. A very good reporting performance is the decisive advantage of the MLOAP approach. The disadvantage of multidimensional databases is that they must manage higher quantities of empty cells and that the growth of these structures increases exponentially with the number of dimensions. Another disadvantage is that the standard query language of databases (SQL) doesn't work with multidimensional databases and therefore proprietary approaches are used in most cases.

MOLAP versus ROLAP

Relational Online Analytical Processing (ROLAP) refers to the use of a relational database for OLAP applications.

In BW, the MOLAP approach was supported temporarily in Release 3.5 using Microsoft SQL Server for aggregates. Today, the performance benefits, which the MOLAP approach had, can be achieved with other technical means, particularly with BWA indices. Therefore, MOLAP approaches no longer play a role in the SAP NetWeaver BW environment.

2.7   Conclusion

The conceptual model should be created independent of the system properties and only describe the real world. The ADAPT method is particularly suitable here. The technical descriptions of dimensions, in particular, can be presented well with this method. Conceptual modeling is part of the technical concept. In addition to dimensions, you must also describe all key figures in the conceptual model.

Conceptual modeling can be implemented individually, whereas the logical data model is predefined by the BW data model to a large extent. Due to the high significance of MultiProviders for the reporting area, creating a detailed model is recommended.

In physical data modeling, the main question is about data flow and the objects required; this is the subject of Chapter 5, Reference Architecture for Data Modeling.

This chapter presents SAP NetWeaver Business Warehouse (BW)
as the central key area of SAP NetWeaver. You'll get to know the
versatile usage options of SAP NetWeaver BW and get an over-
view of the various tools, including the applications and reports
that you can create using the tools.

3   Overview of SAP NetWeaver BW and SAP BusinessObjects

This chapter provides an overview of SAP NetWeaver BW and the two front-end tools, SAP Business Explorer (BEx) and SAP BusinessObjects.

This book essentially discusses the modeling of InfoProviders in the BW system. All modeling efforts are aimed at achieving good results in the upper layers when you create queries in the Query Designer and use queries in the various reporting tools. To get an idea of how the tools work and to be able to better assess the requirements on data modeling that result from reporting requirements, this chapter presents the various reporting tools.

Section 3.1, SAP NetWeaver, discusses the SAP NetWeaver technology, and Section 3.2, Overview of SAP NetWeaver BW7.x, outlines SAP NetWeaver BW, a central component of SAP NetWeaver. The various front-end components are based on BW; these are subdivided into the original front ends of SAP BEx Suite, SAP NetWeaver Visual Composer, and the new front ends of SAP BusinessObjects, which were added with the acquisition of Business Objects (see Section 3.3, SAP BusinessObjects).

3.1   SAP NetWeaver

With SAP NetWeaver, SAP offers a technological infrastructure to design heterogeneous and complex system worlds that can be integrated more easily. Within the scope of SAP NetWeaver, you are provided with implementation tools to develop new applications flexibly and with a component orientation. An application is no longer self-contained, but it consists of flexibly linked services that can easily be relinked and connected with the outside world (see Section 3.1.1, Service Orientation). But SAP NetWeaver is not limited to the integration of SAP platforms: You can also integrate third-party applications and frameworks with the system landscape. Using the SAP NetWeaver portfolio you can implement various integration requirements. Section 3.1.2, Key Areas of SAP NetWeaver, describes the central areas of SAP NetWeaver.

3.1.1 Service Orientation

Service The basic idea with regard to service orientation in software development is that an application is no longer supposed to be considered as a self-contained monolithic block. Instead, the application is split into reusable and independent services. Each service can be called from the outside, that is, from various applications or processes. To enable this, the service must have standardized and open interfaces.

Because SAP also provides functions of, for example, SAP ERP as a service, this means that you can access parts of an application as required by combining services to form a new application. The same applies to third parties that now have the chance to combine SAP applications with their special solutions and therefore provide new solutions.

The implementation of service orientation doesn't entail a general waiver of centralization, because services can be provided centrally to then integrate them decentrally. Master data is consolidated, harmonized, and managed centrally, for example. The synchronized data is then distributed via the decentralized integration of the services provided.

Service orientation enables a simplified support of business processes in which you work beyond system boundaries. Upstream and downstream enterprises of the value chain can access (released) parts of own processes and therefore be directly connected.

SOA In the SAP environment, Service-Oriented Architecture (SOA) is the term used for this new approach in software development.

3.1.2　Key Areas of SAP NetWeaver

SAP NetWeaver as an application platform forms the basis for developing, distributing, and implementing applications and enables their integration.

The concept of integration is not limited to the technical level, because the platform serves as the basis for the integration of processes, of information, and ultimately of employees — even beyond enterprise boundaries.

Integration

Figure 3.1 shows the key areas of SAP NetWeaver that refer to concrete solution components. With these components you can implement various integration requirements, which are presented in the following sections.

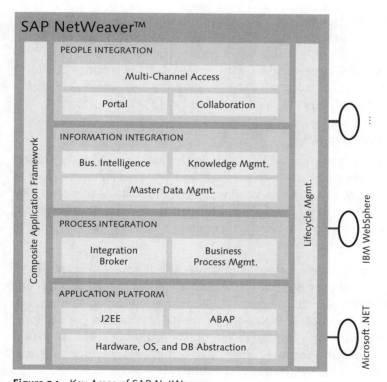

Figure 3.1　Key Areas of SAP NetWeaver

People Integration

Homogeneous user interface
For their daily work, users must access a variety of different services (represented by applications and application modules). Despite the multitude of applications, access to central applications and information is supposed to be homogeneous and be operated as uniformly as possible. Besides access to structured data, access to unstructured data (such as documents, articles, drawings, emails) is supposed to be possible as well. Structured data entails data that is typically stored in (relational) databases. For example, this includes the data basis, for example, of SAP ERP, and BW itself. Access to the systems is supposed to be possible via different end devices, that is, not only PCs and laptops but also mobile end devices (multichannel access). Furthermore, it is a requirement of this integration level to also enable and support collaboration in groups (teamwork).

SAP NetWeaver Portal
The technologies, which are required for the integration at the user level, are essentially provided by SAP NetWeaver Portal. SAP NetWeaver Portal provides a uniform interface for accessing back-end systems and processes and it is closely linked with Knowledge Management (KM) to enable access to unstructured data. The portal's structure is role-oriented and combines all services that a user requires in one user interface.

Information Integration

Semantic integration
The integration of information refers to the merging and synchronization of information. Data is generated in all parts of an enterprise. Due to different implementations in various applications, data usually cannot be evaluated comprehensively without further processing. An integration, that is, a presentation of data that is similar in meaning, is a prerequisite here (semantic integration).

SAP NetWeaver BW
BW provides options to load data from various sources, to transform (format) it, and provide it in a data model that is optimized for reporting. Moreover, you can use special technologies that can further accelerate queries. The tool, SAP NetWeaver Business Warehouse Accelerator (BWA), even lets you implement an online analysis Online Analytical Processing (OLAP) for a very large data volume. In addition, unstructured data can also be made available (KM).

Integration of master data
The integration of master data plays a special role. The topic of master data integration is also a central topic for data modeling in BW. The SAP

56

NetWeaver Master Data Management (MDM) tool is a product that is specialized in the consolidation, harmonization, management, and distribution of master data. It closely collaborates with BW so that a data exchange can be set up in both directions.

Process Integration

Process integration ensures that you can design business processes across systems. Within the scope of process integration, you define standardized interfaces that harmonize data formats and communication. This way, you can combine the individual services with one another. From process components, you gradually compose applications that map and support entire business processes. SAP NetWeaver Process Integration is the technical basis of the components of this integration layer (integration broker and business process management).

Standardized interfaces

Application Platform

The application platform in SAP NetWeaver describes the technical and platform-independent infrastructure and development environment. It provides all services for developing, distributing, and executing applications.

Lifecycle Management

Lifecycle management includes all services and technologies that are used to manage the software and application lifecycle. The spectrum ranges from component installation, to management (monitoring and performance) in operation, to archiving, upgrading, and support. In particular, the handling of aging data is an important topic from a BW perspective (see Chapter 11, Section 11.1, ILM).

SAP Composite Application Framework (CAF)

SAP CAF lets you create composed applications. The tools of CAF support the business process–oriented combination of services (orchestration of services) into applications. This involves a model-oriented approach according to which applications are modeled graphically instead of programmed and according to which the system can use the lower-level application layers to derive and generate the entire program code from the model thanks to the metadata available.

3.2 Overview of SAP NetWeaver BW 7.x

BW Release 7.x comprises a complete data warehouse solution that includes all of the components required to extract, transform, and save data and to enable analyses based on this data.

BW function areas

The function areas covered by BW include the following, among others:

- Functions for loading data (extraction, transformation, loading)
- Objects for filing and storing data
- Modeling tools (metadata management)
- Tools for administration, customizing, modeling, control, and monitoring
- Reporting tools

Components of the integrated BW architecture

Figure 3.2 provides an overview of the individual components of the integrated BW architecture. The components range from the areas of extraction ❶, to modeling and data retention within BW (❷ and ❸), to reporting tools (❹ through ❼). SAP NetWeaver Portal is the central environment in which reports are displayed as the "product" of BW. If required, you can use additional technologies, such as BWA, to accelerate queries ❽.

If you compare Figure 3.2 with the SAP NetWeaver integration areas of Figure 3.1, you can see that BW presents a central interface between the business processes as a data source and the information provision in the portal.

Closed loop

Here, the information flow is not unidirectional, because information from BW is used to support decisions and ultimately to develop an enterprise strategy that is implemented in the form of business processes. Suitable measurement values enable you to track the implementation of the selected strategy. The collection and evaluation of data is then performed in BW again. This way, you obtain a closed loop.

Reporting and analysis

Today, data is primarily evaluated by creating reports (standard and ad hoc reports) or through analyses (OLAP, data mining). In this type of information provision, a clear distinction is still made between operational and planning business processes. The user must be active in an information role assigned to him to obtain the information required. Besides reports for detailed analyses, cockpits provide essential key figures in a clear and easily comprehensible way so that you can readily detect (erroneous) developments. The reporting and analysis tools presented in Section 3.2.3 through 3.2.7 and 3.3.1 through 3.3.4, respectively, all have a specific purpose for the creation of reports and cockpits and analyses.

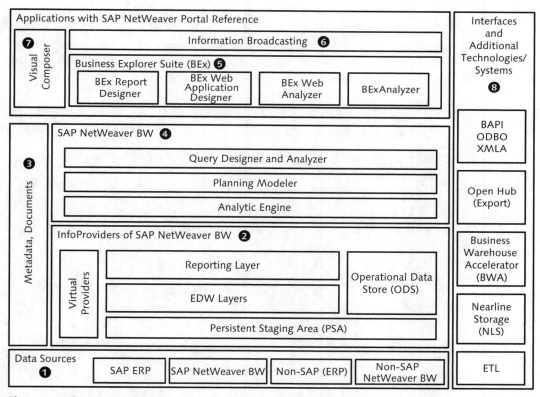

Figure 3.2 The Integrated Data Warehouse Architecture of SAP NetWeaver BW

It is useful to provide each business process (that is, operational business processes as well) with additional information. This requires a close link of the functionality for implementing business processes with the components for retrieving information. SOA supports the option to create such applications. By combining operational transactions with the

Integration of operational and planning world

BW components, you can create dashboards that not only support planning decisions but also the decision quality of operational processes. SAP
NetWeaver Visual Composer, which is presented in Section 3.2.9, SAP
NetWeaver Visual Composer, is an example of an environment creating
such integrated applications.

3.2.1 Administration and Metadata Management

The Data Warehousing Workbench (in older releases: Administrator
Workbench) is the central application in BW that you can use to structure a data model and create transformation rules and data transfer processes (see Figure 3.3). You start the Data Warehousing Workbench via
Transaction RSA1.

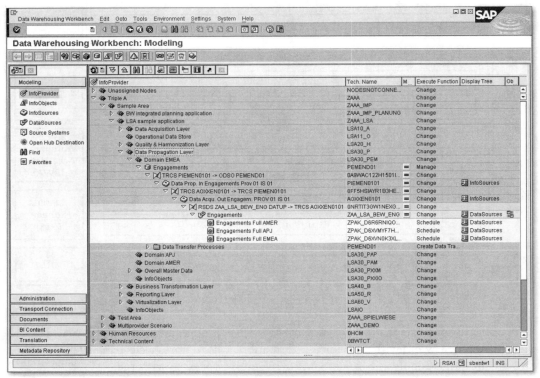

Figure 3.3 Data Warehousing Workbench — "Modeling" View (InfoProvider)

In principle, you use the Data Warehousing Workbench to perform the following activities:

Functionality of the Data Warehousing Workbench

- ▶ Administration (for instance, monitoring of load processes)
- ▶ Collecting and transporting objects
- ▶ Uploading and categorizing documents
- ▶ Transferring objects from Business Content (see Figure 3.4)

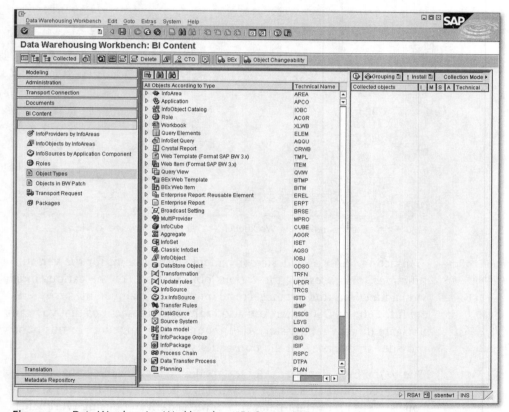

Figure 3.4 Data Warehousing Workbench — "BI Content" View

In addition, you can also translate objects here and obtain an overview of all of the objects mapped in the repository sorted by category and model affiliation (see Figure 3.5).

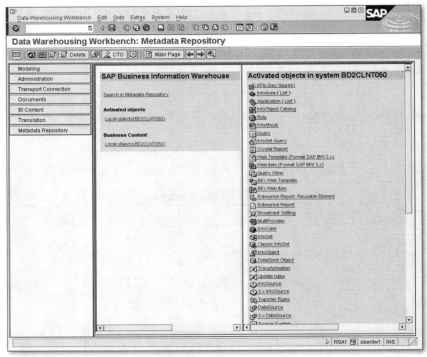

Figure 3.5 Data Warehousing Workbench — "Metadata Repository" View

Contents of the modeling view

Transaction RSA1 provides a convenient starting point for the versatile functions for processing the various object types. For the various individual functions (for instance, create InfoObject, maintain hierarchy, create InfoCube or DSO) there are also individual transactions that you can navigate directly (and faster) to, if required. The appendix of this book provides an overview of the transactions.

Due to the high significance of the modeling view in this book, the following section discusses it in more detail. There are various subareas that you can select. The right-hand area of the Data Warehousing Workbench is used to display the various object types (content area); you can select the respective object type in the area on the left. For example, the INFO-PROVIDER object type is selected in Figure 3.3. Accordingly, the content area shows all InfoProviders arranged by InfoAreas.

"Modeling" area

You use the MODELING area of the Data Warehousing Workbench to structure a BW data model. You can process the following objects:

You use *InfoProviders* to save or merge data. InfoProviders include InfoObjects, DataStore Objects (DSOs), InfoCubes, MultiProviders, and InfoSets. DSOs and InfoCubes are used to save data, whereas MultiProviders and InfoSets define specific views of the physical data models.

InfoObjects are the central modules of the BW data model. You can use InfoObjects that contain master data to describe complex business objects. A simple InfoObject without master data ultimately describes a simple table field.

InfoSources as a flat structure describe a unit of related data. This data usually refers to a specific business transaction, a group of similar business transactions (in the case of transaction data), or to data of an InfoObject (in the case of master data).

DataSources as a flat structure describe a set of logically related fields that are offered for transfer into the BW system.

Source Systems are systems that are known as data providers in BW. These can include SAP ERP systems, other BW systems, flat files, and other systems/databases.

The display for InfoProviders and InfoObjects is in a tree structure, which is arranged by InfoAreas. The display of InfoSources and Data-Sources is also in a tree structure. This is referred to as an application component hierarchy. You can create both the InfoAreas and application components yourself. Their definition is also part of the Business Content. Most customers, however, create their own InfoAreas and application components.

Moreover, you can create an Open Hub Destination in the Data Warehousing Workbench, search for objects, and save objects as favorites (references).

In the Data Warehousing Workbench, you can use its components to build a complete data flow. Figure 3.6 shows the components of a BW 7.0 data flow. ❶ describes the transformation from an (external) data source into an InfoProvider of BW. ❷ shows that this InfoProvider in turn is used as a data source and can be transformed into another data target (InfoProvider). The Data Transfer Processes (DTPs) control the selection and update of data. Figure 3.3 shows the result of such a modeling in the modeling view of the Data Warehousing Workbench.

Structure of a data flow

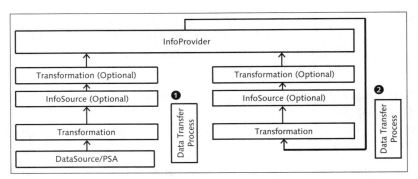

Figure 3.6 Schematic Diagram of an SAP NetWeaver BW 7.0 Data Flow

BW up to
Release 3.5

Up to BW Release 3.5, another concept with transfer and update rules was used; InfoSources had a different, central role in this model. In BW 7.x, you can also work with these old modeling elements; but you will implement new developments in the "new world." If your system still includes data flows that are modeled based on the old pattern, you can process these in Transaction RSA1. Alternatively, you can access the old version of Transaction RSA1; this transaction is still available in Transaction RSA1OLD.

3.2.2 Overview of Reporting and Analysis Using SAP NetWeaver BW

You can access the analysis and the analysis of the data stored in BW using one of the following reporting tools:

► BEx product
► SAP BusinessObjects reporting tool
► Third-party tool

BEx Suite

BEx Suite products include the following:

The *BEx Query Designer* is used to create queries on the basis of BW. The queries created with this tool form the basis for the other tools that present the data provided by the queries in different forms and that serve different analysis purposes.

The *BEx Analyzer* is an Excel® add-in that is used for reporting and analysis. The data delivered by a query is embedded directly in Microsoft Excel and can be processed there. Besides the Excel functions, this Excel add-in also provides OLAP analysis functions. From Microsoft Excel, you can readily navigate to the BEx Query Designer to process the query.

Using the *BEx Web Application Designer* (WAD) you can embed queries in the web interface to publish it there (for example, in the portal). This is a desktop application for processing the definition of web templates. These web templates can be published in SAP NetWeaver Portal. The templates' design can be simple (one query, one table) or more comprehensive (multiple embedded queries/tables), and they can include advanced, integrated functions (for example, calling of planning functions).

The *BEx Web Analyzer* enables the execution of queries on the web and provides OLAP navigation functions for ad hoc evaluations. In principle, this is the same analysis function because it can be provided via explicitly created web templates — presented in a standard template that is offered by SAP for ad hoc analyses.

The *BEx Report Designer* is used for the formatted output of data provided by queries. Here, you can make formattings, generate group totals, and place specific fields in the report for output. The result can be presented on the Web and as PDF files.

The *BEx Information Broadcaster* enables the distribution of reports within the enterprise. The distribution can be controlled by user, event, and time.

Figure 3.7 shows an overview of the various BEx Suite products.

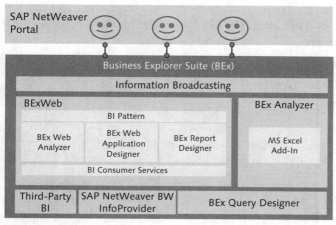

Figure 3.7 SAP BEx Suite

Meaning of SAP
NetWeaver Portal

The integration of tools with SAP NetWeaver Portal has been very close since Release 7.0. The use of web reports and the Broadcaster requires SAP NetWeaver BW Portal or the installation of the Java stack. Sections 3.2.3 through 3.2.9 present the different front ends of BEx Suite and the Visual Composer.

SAP
BusinessObjects

Due to the reporting and analysis front ends of SAP BusinessObjects, the number of available tools has increased. SAP continuously advances the integration of the products. Presumably not all front ends of BEx Suite will be further developed in the long term because there are overlaps in functionality. The maintenance, however, will be guaranteed for a long period of time. Section 3.3 discusses the SAP BusinessObjects front ends for reporting and analysis in more detail.

Interfaces

You can also connect third-party front ends with BW. The following interfaces are supported:

▶ The ODBO interface (OLE DB for OLAP)
▶ The OLAP–Business Application Programming Interface (BAPI)
▶ The XML for Analysis (XMLA) interface

The interfaces are based on Multidimensional Expressions (MDX), a query language developed by Microsoft for multidimensional analyses. The ODBO interface has been available since SAP BW 1.2 and is based on Microsoft's interface specification OLE DB for OLAP. Later on, the interface has been enhanced by further functions. The OLAP-BAPI interface developed by SAP is platform-independent. Since SAP BW 2.0, it has been available to third parties for connecting their products. XMLA is a Simple Object Access Protocol (SOAP)–based, standardized programming interface used for data access to OLAP providers.

3.2.3 BEx Query Designer

You use the BEx Query Designer to create queries, that is, data selections. When you create a new report, you select an InfoProvider on which the query is supposed to be based. To adapt the report later on, it is useful to create the report based on a MultiProvider or on an InfoSet.

Query definition

Figure 3.8 shows the query definition view in the BEx Query Designer. In area ❶ on the left, you can view all of the key figures, characteristics, and attributes of the InfoProvider based on which you create the query. You add these objects to your report via drag and drop. You can drag the characteristics and key figures into the Rows ❷ or Columns ❸. The combination of row and column characteristics defines the drill-down (that is, the level of detail of the display) as it is shown when you execute the report. The user can change the display by navigating in the report. You can add further characteristics, which can be accessed during analysis, to the Free Characteristics ❹.

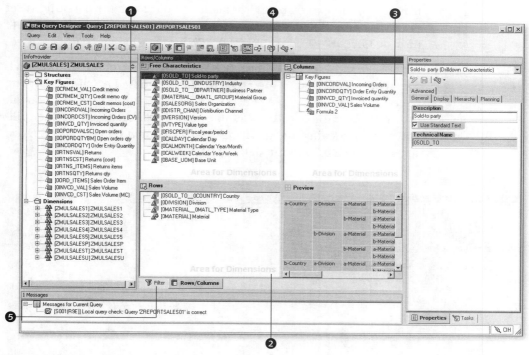

Figure 3.8 BEx Query Designer

In addition, you define filters to limit the query and add variables if the user is supposed to select the filter criteria during report execution (Filter tab ❺). You can add additional calculations via the definition of restricted and calculated key figures and the report-internal enhancement of the key figure structure.

You use a query that was created in the BEx Query Designer in various front ends. In the simplest case, it is just executed and the report result is shown on the Web. The query also serves as a data source for web reports and web cockpits, and for the BEx Analyzer and the Report

Query usage

Designer. You can also form BusinessObjects universes that are based on BEx queries. The following sections describe the individual reporting tools.

3.2.4 BEx Web Analyzer

When you run a query created with the Query Designer, this is automatically done in a web environment. If your system has not been set otherwise, the system automatically displays a standard web template provided by SAP (0ANALYSIS_PATTERN).

Figure 3.9 shows an executed BEx Web Analyzer report ❶. The environment enables you to run an OLAP analysis based on the underlying query, and you can implement the usual navigation steps (drill-down, drill-across). You navigate by adding free characteristics ❷ to the drill-down and removing others, change the drill-down sequence, and move across hierarchies. You can define filters and hide key figures.

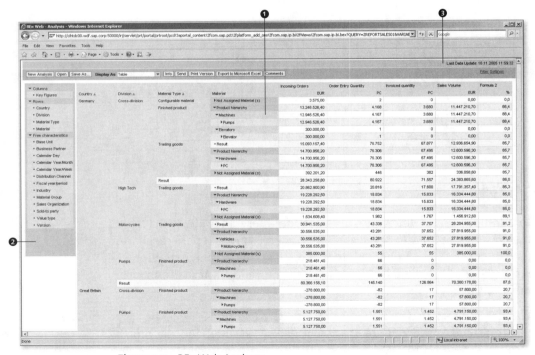

Figure 3.9 BEx Web Analyzer

You can export (for example, as a PDF document and to Microsoft Excel) and print report results ❸. Moreover, you can open other queries from the BEx Web Analyzer and use it as a cross-query analysis tool.

3.2.5 BEx Analyzer

As an alternative to the Web, you can also integrate the BEx query with an Excel workbook. This is where you use the Excel add-in, BEx Analyzer. Besides navigating in the data (OLAP analysis, see Figure 3.10), you have the option of implementing additional calculations using Excel functions.

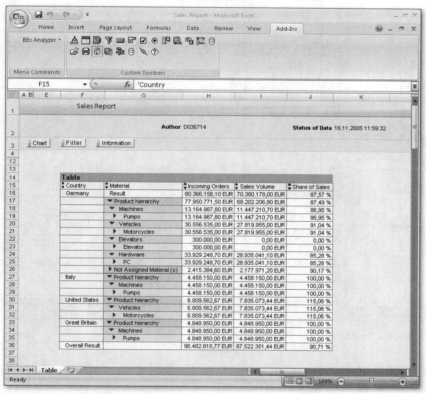

Figure 3.10 Data Analysis in the BEx Analyzer

3.2.6 BEx WAD

The BEx WAD (see Figure 3.11) is a tool that you can use to design a web interface in which you can embed your analyses (queries) for display. The presentation options for data range from simple tables (with or without navigation option) to various charts. Furthermore, you are provided with predefined components that are used for displaying filter and selection fields or intended for map display, exceptions, and so on.

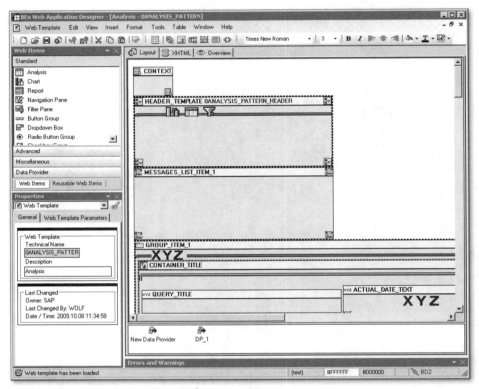

Figure 3.11 BEx WAD — Definition View

Standard web template

The BEx Web Analyzer described in Section 3.2.4, BEx Web Analyzer, uses the same analysis environment as the WAD. There you use a template defined by SAP (0ANALYSIS_PATTERN) that you can also open in the WAD. Remember, don't change the original or create a backup copy before you make any changes.

The application range of the BEx WAD is manifold. It ranges from simple templates, which, for example, display a table with a heading and enable an OLAP analysis, to more complex web cockpits (see Figure 3.12).

OLAP to web cockpit

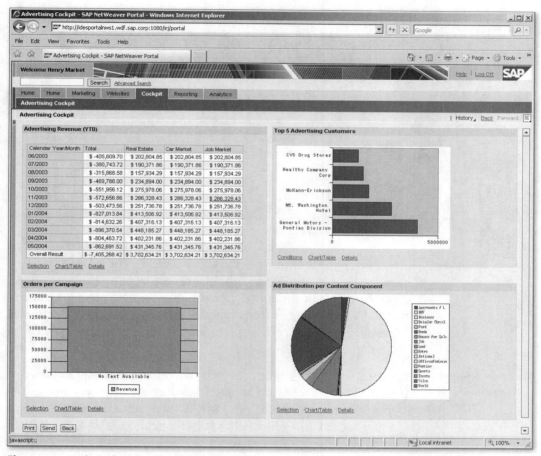

Figure 3.12   Web Cockpit Created with BEx WAD

3.2.7   BEx Report Designer

The BEx Report Designer (see Figure 3.13) opens advanced options to further edit query results with regard to layout and formatting. The report result can be displayed on the Web or provided as a PDF document, which can be printed easily.

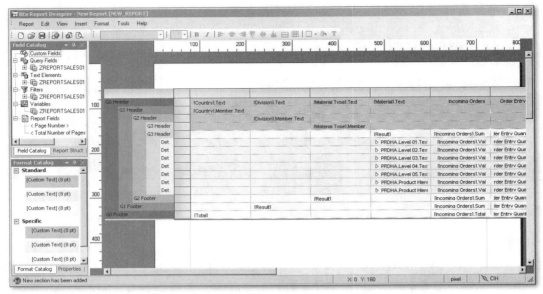

Figure 3.13 BEx Report Designer

Definition

The hierarchy levels of the query are automatically copied as such to the Report Designer and provide an initial report layout (see Figure 3.14). You can further edit the initial view by adding or removing hierarchy levels and so on. Objects (for example, texts), which are added to the headers or footers, are each displayed in the respective area level in the executed report.

Merging of multiple data sources

You can also integrate multiple queries in a BEx report. You can then format the results of the individual queries, which are displayed one below the other. Thanks to the high flexibility for positioning data elements and texts you can also generate cockpit-like reports as an alternative to formatted lists.

Reports are inflexible due to the fact that new query objects can only be added by copying the query again (whereas the existing formatting and grouping cannot be copied automatically).

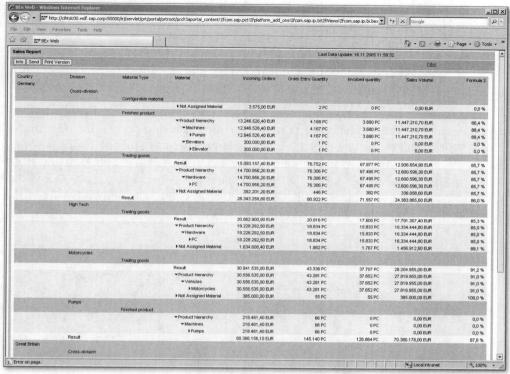

Figure 3.14 BEx Report Designer — Executed Report

3.2.8 BEx Broadcaster

Using the Broadcaster you can precalculate (that is, execute automatically based on your access authorizations) and distribute web templates, queries, query views, reports, and workbooks. It is possible to send alternative precalculated documents (for instance, workbooks and PDF files) or online links to data. You can distribute documents to email recipients or to the portal. In addition, you can print the report documents.

The settings can also involve automatic sending, which can be done periodically or if data has changed in an InfoProvider.

3.2.9 SAP NetWeaver Visual Composer

With SAP NetWeaver Visual Composer, SAP provides a powerful development and integration tool. The goal of SAP NetWeaver Visual Composer is to create applications that are composed of heterogeneous application components.

Graphical modeling
In this tool, modeling is performed exclusively via a graphical user interface; programming is not required. The graphic models include all of the information necessary to generate the executable programming code automatically.

Visual Composer model
Such a model consists of one or more starting points. In the example shown in Figure 3.15, a query is executed ❶ and the result is sorted alphabetically in ascending order and displayed as a table ❷. If you select a row in this table, the system starts the dependent queries ❸ and displays the query results as a graphic ❹. The model shown is part of the application illustrated in Figure 3.16.

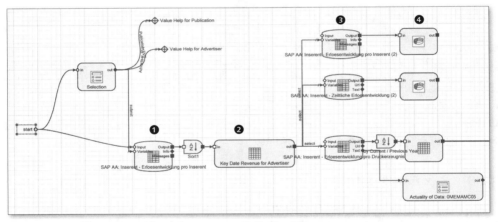

Figure 3.15 Visual Composer — Definition View

SAP NetWeaver Composer is integrated with the portal. All services provided by the systems that are connected with the portal can be integrated with the model.

Analytical applications
For example, it is possible to integrate BW queries with a Visual Composer model and display the data provided by the queries (as a table or chart). However, the functionality is not limited to the display of information, because data can be processed (sorted, merged, and so on) in a data flow step by step before it is displayed. In this context, the services mentioned can be located in different systems. For example, you can transfer data from administration systems (for instance, SAP NetWeaver

BW) to operational systems (for instance, SAP ERP) and vice versa. This way, you can easily develop an application that combines a process-oriented operational flow with the necessary analytical components. In doing so, you pass the respective "context" as characteristic keys via the data flow.

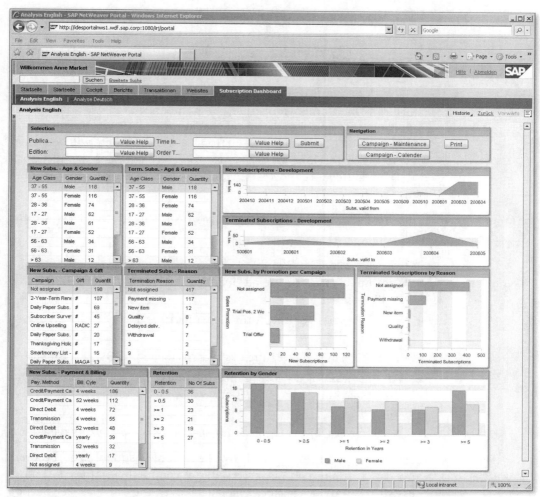

Figure 3.16 Sample Dashboard from Visual Composer

The majority of the models are applications in which the analytical part prevails. Figure 3.16 shows such an example. It is a web cockpit (dashboard) in which you select characteristics similarly as for a query. When

Dashboards

75

you execute the web cockpit with the corresponding parameterization, the system supplies numerous lists and graphics with corresponding values. The tables are interactive, that is, the system filters the dependent objects for the corresponding value when you select a specific row and refreshes the screen objects. You can easily integrate services with such a model; these services display time-critical detail information from SAP ERP.

3.3   SAP BusinessObjects

In early 2008, SAP acquired Business Objects, an analysis software manufacturer. Due to this acquisition, the number of available analysis and reporting front ends has increased considerably. SAP advances the gradual integration of products. Not all front ends of BEx Suite will be further developed in the long term because there are overlaps in functionality. The maintenance, however, will be guaranteed for a long period of time.

Reporting tools
The most important reporting tools of SAP BusinessObjects are the following:

▶ InfoView as a reporting portal

▶ Web Intelligence for the ad hoc web reporting (Section 3.3.1, Web Intelligence)

▶ Crystal Reports for the formatted reporting (Section 3.3.2, Crystal Reports)

▶ Crystal Xcelsius for creating dashboards (Section 3.3.3, Xcelsius)

▶ SAP BusinessObjects Live Office for integrating the report contents with Microsoft Office (Section 3.3.5, SAP BusinessObjects Live Office)

▶ SAP BusinessObjects Explorer for searching and analyzing data

Universes as semantic layers
Besides the question of which front-end tool is supposed to be used, how data is supposed to be accessed is of central importance. SAP BusinessObjects provides a special metadata layer, the universe (see Section 3.3.4, SAP BusinessObjects Universes). But this is not the only option for accessing SAP systems; for BW, however, this is the main access path. Figure 3.17 provides an overview of the various access paths.

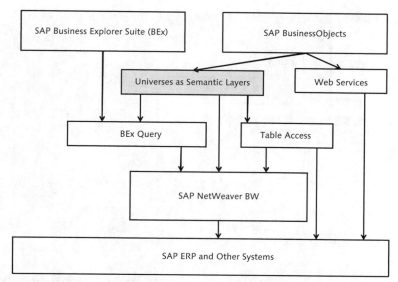

Figure 3.17 The Universe and Alternative Access Paths

With regard to the BW system, you can create the universe either based on a MultiProvider (or an InfoCube, which is not recommended) or based on a BEx query. The more favorable path depends on which contents you want to provide in the universe and how your BW reporting is structured. Compared to the DataProvider solution, the BEx query has the benefit that you can provide the various restricted and calculated key figures and the structure elements of the query environment in the universe.

Basis of the universe

The universe and the various SAP BusinessObjects front ends, which are presented in the following sections, form the basis for reporting.

3.3.1 Web Intelligence

Web Intelligence enables the end user to create ad hoc reports (see Figure 3.18). Here, the end user accesses a combination of characteristics and key figures that was prepared previously (in the form of a universe, see Section 3.3.4). The data is selected via a query (selection of characteristics and key figures using filters) and you can display it in a table or as a graphic, group it, and evaluate it ad hoc in various ways. Programming knowledge is not required here. The reports are provided in the Info-View and can also be converted in Microsoft Office and PDF files.

Ad hoc evaluations

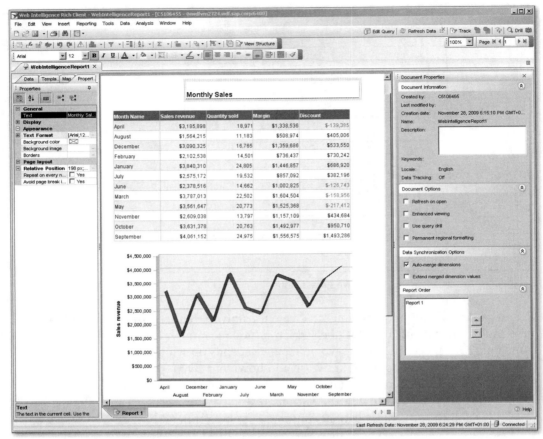

Figure 3.18   Web Intelligence

3.3.2   Crystal Reports

Formatted
reporting

Crystal Reports focus on the formatting and presentation of data; for example, you can design forms that are exact to the pixel. The presentation of complex contexts in Controlling (CO) is one application area of Crystal Reports. Data access is not restricted to BW; various data sources can be connected. Figure 3.19 shows the definition view of a Crystal Reports report.

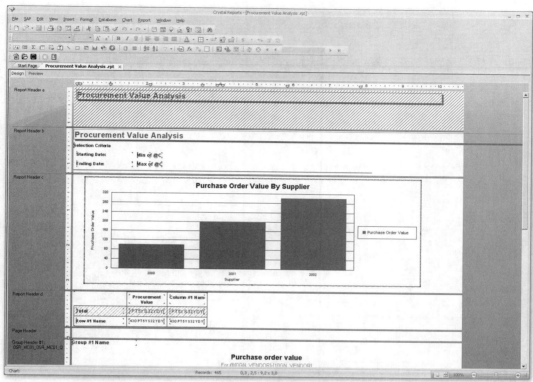

Figure 3.19 Crystal Reports — Definition View

3.3.3 Xcelsius

Xcelsius provides the option to develop simple to complex cockpits (dashboards; see Figure 3.20). You can then publish them in the portal or present them in Microsoft Office or as PDF documents. The offline analysis of data is supported by Xcelsius. The user interface integrates Microsoft Excel so that you have an environment that you're familiar with — at least to a certain extent.

Cockpits/
dashboards

The applications generated with Xcelsius are implemented with Adobe Flash technology, which enables dynamic visualization effects. For example, you can integrate switches and sliders whose status you can change. Dependent visualization objects (for instance, charts) automatically adjust to the value defined by the user.

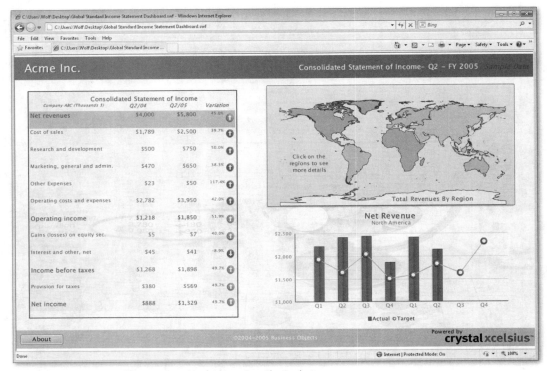

Figure 3.20 Xcelsius — Sample Cockpit

3.3.4 SAP BusinessObjects Universes

Originally, SAP BusinessObjects was developed as a query tool based on relational databases. To provide fields and their contents conveniently to users, the tables that are relevant for the users in an analysis context were linked via a join and the relevant contents were made available in a tree structure (the universe). You can rename and regroup fields in this tree structure.

Metadata view This option is still available today. When you access BW, the definition of the universe is done via an InfoProvider or a query. Joins don't need to be created here, because all of the relevant objects are already summarized in the InfoProvider. The options for filtering, renaming, and regrouping are also available here. Because you copy a lot of content — particularly for the definition of a universe on an InfoProvider — you usually need to postprocess the universe before end users can work with it reasonably (see Chapter 8, Section 8.5.1, SAP BusinessObjects Universes on the Basis of SAP NetWeaver BW). So a universe corresponds to another metadata layer between InfoProvider and the end user. Figure 3.21 shows a universe view.

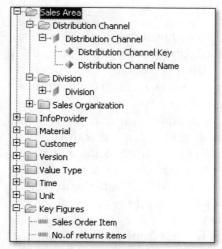

Figure 3.21 Excerpt of a Sample Universe

3.3.5 SAP BusinessObjects Live Office

Live Office enables you to integrate ad hoc analyses from Web Intelligence, formatted reports from Crystal Reports, and universes directly with Microsoft Word®, Excel, and PowerPoint. The reports' appearance corresponds to the definition made in the original applications. The special benefit of this integration is that the data can be refreshed. You can also parameterize the refresh so that it is implemented at regular intervals, for example. This enables a simplified reuse of Office documents without having to continuously redefine their contents.

3.3.6 SAP BusinessObjects Explorer

SAP has provided SAP BusinessObjects Explorer as another attractive front end. Users can search for terms and then obtain context-related relevant results. Then they can drill down in the information and follow an analysis path step by step that they consider interesting. In this process, the system exhibits an intelligent behavior and automatically selects a

Intelligent search

suitable presentation form (for instance, a bar or pie chart). Here, the search abstracts from the underlying sources. Users search for technical terms and then follow alternative paths provided by the system. Here, the system also presents the relations that result from the analysis of a large underlying data quantity — this involves a scalability of up to one billion data records!

BW Accelerator   To enable the execution of such a query online in real time, the software was combined with the memory-based database, SAP NetWeaver BWA (see Chapter 8, Section 8.2.6, BWA). BWA is based on a special indexing of data sources and metadata. These indices are loaded into the main memory and enable a free association of data. This increases the performance considerably and enables you to explore the data. By contrast, the aggregates of an OLAP cube are always optimized with regard to specific queries. When you perform an OLAP analysis without SAP BusinessObjects Explorer or BWA, it is likely that the user can successfully make some navigation steps and then suddenly fall into the unpredictable "trap," where he has to wait for a long time to get a response from the system. By contrast, the response time behavior of the system using BWA is calculably fast. The speed gains result from the fact that all necessary index data is retained in the main memory and that the query is executed in parallel.

3.4   Conclusion

Already in BEx Suite, the BEx Query Designer plays a central role. The queries developed form the basis of all BEx Suite analysis tools. The various front ends all have their specific uses. The Report Designer has not become widely accepted yet. Besides the restricted functionality (in comparison to Crystal Reports), it has the major disadvantage that changes to reporting requirements, which require new InfoObjects or key figures, result in a new creation of the report. The portal is the preferred medium, but Microsoft Excel is also supported.

The product range is considerably enhanced via the SAP BusinessObjects front-end tools. The new products fill the gaps that may occur in formatted reporting. The universe is the central interface for accessing BW data. Among other options, universes can be created based on queries and InfoProviders. The basic difference between the two access types is in the scope of objects provided (calculated and restricted key figures are only available via the query access) and the dependence of data model changes. Data model changes are supposed to entail an adaptation effort for report objects that is a little as possible. It is therefore recommended to define universes — just like queries — only on MultiProviders (and not directly on physical DataProviders) or based on queries, which in turn should be defined based on a MultiProvider. The clear benefit of the query as an interface is that restricted and calculated key figures and structure elements are available. Therefore, the Query Designer expands its position as an interface between data model and reporting in the enhanced product range.

SAP BusinessObjects lets you create reports on the basis of a wide variety of data sources, like BW. A uniform access via the portal and Microsoft Office is possible. These are good prerequisites to achieve the goal of information or user integration that is defined in the context of SAP NetWeaver.

So it is necessary to establish a stable data architecture within BW, which provides a suitable basis for using various reporting tools. Only if the essential information is available with a central coordination and the basic part of reporting and analyses can be implemented easily on this basis, can you manage and integrate additional flexible evaluation requests using the existing access flexibility of the reporting tools.

In this chapter, you will learn about the basic elements of an SAP NetWeaver Business Warehouse (BW) data model.
Here, we will limit our discussion to DataProviders, which store or retrieve data.

4 Structure of a BW Data Model

This chapter will provide basic information about the structure of a BW data model. When modeling data, you can choose between a variety of different BW objects. Each of these objects and their variants has specific uses that you need to know to make the best possible modeling decision. In this chapter, we will describe the implementation and basic properties of objects or methods that can store data (InfoObjects, DataStore Objects (DSOs), and InfoCubes) or retrieve data (RemoteCubes and Real-Time Data Acquisition).

In Section 4.1, InfoObjects, we will introduce InfoObjects as *the* basic building blocks of a BW data model. You will learn about simple characteristic InfoObjects and InfoObjects that are used to store master data (attributes, texts, and hierarchies). We will take a closer look at master data in Section 4.2, Master Data in SAP NetWeaver BW.

InfoObjects are the basis for all other InfoProviders. DSOs physically store data while optimized InfoCubes store flat data and are used for reporting, in particular. DSOs will be discussed in Section 4.3, DataStore Objects, and InfoCubes in Section 4.4, InfoCubes.

One disadvantage associated with data that is physically stored in SAP NetWeaver BW is that it needs to be loaded (staged) first, which delays data retrieval. In Section 4.5, Providers for Real-Time Data Access, we will take a look at VirtualProviders, which make it possible to access data in (almost) real time.

4.1 InfoObjects

InfoObjects are the basic building blocks of a BW data model. They can have a simple structure and describe a simple field (for example, for storing a postal code). However, they can also map a complex business object and its master data (texts, attributes, and hierarchies) (for example, for mapping the *Business Partner* object whereby the postal code part of an address can be modeled as an attribute).

Significance of InfoObjects
InfoObjects are the elements used to create DataProviders. InfoCubes, DSOs, MultiProviders, and InfoSets are therefore based on InfoObjects that have already been created. InfoObjects themselves can also be used as DataProviders. They enable you to create master data reports that can access characteristic attributes.

InfoObject types
The following are the various types of InfoObjects:

▸ **Characteristic InfoObjects**
Characteristic InfoObjects can have various data type values, namely characteristic values. This value quantity describes permitted values for an evaluation group (for example, customer, customer group, profit center, fiscal year, country, region, and so on). In addition to a key field that identifies the InfoObject, the InfoObject can have additional texts and descriptive attributes. The characteristics describe criteria according to which the key figures of a DataProvider can be evaluated. Similarly, the InfoObject is an independent unit that can also be an InfoProvider, in other words, the data basis for reports.

▸ **Key figure InfoObjects**
Key figure InfoObjects are used to store numerical values that can be evaluated in reports. Here, you must distinguish between key figures for quantities, amounts, and numbers of items.

▸ **Unit or currency InfoObjects**
Unit or currency InfoObjects add a unit of measure or currency to key figure InfoObjects.

▸ **Time characteristics**
Time characteristics are special characteristics that can be used to establish a time base (for example, calendar year, quarter, calendar month, or calendar day).

▸ **Technical InfoObjects**
Technical InfoObjects are specific to SAP NetWeaver BW and describe

various aspects. For example, the technical characteristic *Request number* is created when you load data. This characteristic is an ID that can be used to detect which data has been loaded together (in a request). You cannot modify technical characteristics, nor can you explicitly use them to build data models.

Table 4.1 summarizes the various InfoObject types and provides a Business Content example of each.

InfoObject Type	Description	Examples
Characteristic	▶ Data type must be selected upon creation ▶ Key and, if necessary, additional texts and attributes ▶ Maps the evaluation criteria in the data analysis	Profit center (0PROFIT_CTR) Material (0MATERIAL)
Key figure	▶ Data type must be selected upon creation ▶ Describes the numerical values that are evaluated by means of analyses	Amount (0AMOUNT) Quantity (0QUANTITY)
Unit	Adds a unit (for example, hour, meter, or crate) or currency (for example, EUR, USD, etc.) to the key figures	Unit (0UNIT) Currency (0CURRENCY)
Time characteristic	The time base required by almost all datasets	Calendar year (0CALYEAR) Calendar day (0CALDAY) Fiscal year (0FISCYEAR)
Technical characteristic	Provided by SAP Cannot be modified	Request ID (0REQUID) Change run ID (0CHNGID)

Table 4.1 InfoObject Types

Business Content (see Chapter 6, Business Content) provides a range of predefined InfoObjects. The technical name of all Business Content InfoObjects begins with 0. You can also create your own InfoObjects. However, they must not begin with 0.

In the following sections, we will describe the various InfoObject types and their maintenance in the system in more detail. The dialog box for InfoObject maintenance is in the MODELING area of the Data Warehousing Workbench (see the Data Warehousing Workbench description in

Chapter 3, Section 3.2.1, Administration and Metadata Management). Alternatively, you can call Transaction RSD1 to access the maintenance screen for characteristics or Transaction RSD2 to access the maintenance screen for key figures.

4.1.1 Characteristics

Most InfoObjects in a BW implementation are characteristics. Generally, the information is more descriptive than key figures alone.

The maintenance screen for characteristics is divided into various tabs, each of which is grouped into various areas.

General Tab

On the GENERAL tab (see Figure 4.1), you can select the data type of the InfoObject, specify settings for its basic behavior, and view administrative information.

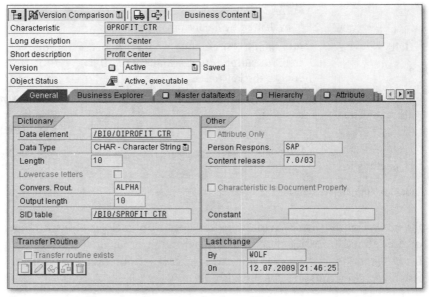

Figure 4.1 InfoObject Maintenance — the General Tab

Dictionary   In the DICTIONARY area, you select the DATA TYPE (NUMC, CHAR, and so on), the LENGTH of the data type (a maximum of 60 characters), whether lowercase letters are permitted, and, if necessary, a conversion routine (CONVERS. ROUT.). You cannot make any entries in the DATA ELEMENT, OUTPUT LENGTH, and SID TABLE fields. These values are automatically determined by the other entries made here.

In the TRANSFER ROUTINE area, specific source text (source code) is defined as a transfer routine for the InfoObject. This source code is automatically integrated into all transformation rules in which the InfoObject is used.

Transfer routine

If the ATTRIBUTE ONLY indicator is set in the OTHER area, the InfoObject cannot be added as a characteristic to an InfoCube in subsequent modeling, nor can it be used as a navigation attribute. The CHARACTERISTIC IS DOCUMENT PROPERTY indicator defines whether or not the values of the relevant characteristic will be selected as a reference size when integrating documents (and comments) into reporting. If you define a constant value, each data record that contains the relevant object can only contain this value. This may be useful in compounding, for example, if the compound object from Content can only have one value globally in a customer data model. The PERSON RESPONS. or CONTENT RELEASE fields contain SAP Business Content objects or the version of the Content object that you have installed. If you have created your own objects, you can select and define a user that will be responsible for each object.

Other

The LAST CHANGE area contains not only information about the last person to change/activate the object but information about when this change was made (date and time).

Last change

When you create an InfoObject, you must commit to a particular data type and data type length. For the data type, you can choose a maximum of 60 characters and numbers. The data type describes the type of characteristic values associated with a particular InfoObject.

Finding InfoObjects

Selecting the Type of Characteristic Values Associated with an InfoObject

[+]

If possible, define the InfoObjects in such a way that the characteristic values have the characteristics of IDs that uniquely identify the objects in reality. If possible, you should never change the values in this key. Exceptions to this rule are possible, but should be applied with caution.

In addition to the key, you can use attributes and short, medium, or long texts to describe the object. You can model each of these as time-dependent texts and attributes.

Example   We now wish to use an example to illustrate the significance of this modeling rule. Let's assume that you create a data model and add an ACCOUNT InfoObject to this model. However, you do not select an ID as a characteristic value of the InfoObject. Instead, you add a description. Later on, you notice that you wrongly gave an account the name *Expenses* and now wish to change this to *Costs*. Because all of the data already loaded into the datasets was posted to the *Expenses* characteristic value, it would be extremely time-consuming to modify this description because you would have to retransfer and transform the data. Another disadvantage associated with this solution is that you would not be able to demonstrate the system's multilingual capability. However, when you select an ID during data modeling and then model the description as text, you can simply load the new values as new text and make it available in multiple languages. If you model the text as time-dependent text, the old value is retained in addition to the current value.

If you are using an SAP ERP system, the distinction between the ID and text is clear in most cases. Moreover, a characteristic value for the ACCOUNT InfoObject is already supplied as an account number. In the case of external sources or user-defined DataSources, you must take care to distinguish between the ID and text.

Business Explorer Tab

When you create an InfoObject, you can define its reporting properties. These properties define, for example, whether a key or text will be displayed in the report, which text length will be selected, and which characteristic values will be available for selection during filtering (see Figure 4.2). Please note that the settings only describe one standard behavior. You can override some of the settings when you define the report. Furthermore, many of the settings at the level of the InfoProvider into which the InfoObjects are integrated can be defined differently than those specified in the InfoObject.

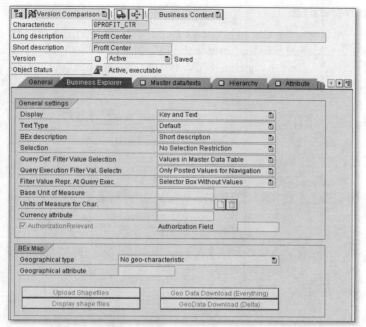

Figure 4.2 InfoObject Maintenance — the Business Explorer Tab

In the GENERAL SETTINGS area, you can define how the object will be displayed in a particular report (for example, whether the key or text will be displayed). You can also select the text type here (short, medium, or long). Other settings refer to the scope of the values displayed when you define the filter (on the one hand, when creating the definition in Business Explorer (BEx) and, on the other hand, in the report that is executed).

General settings

The BASE UNIT OF MEASURE and UNITS OF MEASURE FOR CHAR. input fields enable you to use the InfoObject's master data (via a unit attribute) to control the conversions for quantity key figures in BEx. To facilitate higher-performance access to the data required for the conversion, the system automatically generates a corresponding quantity DSO, which you cannot edit directly. However, if you make changes to the data model, you may have to regenerate the quantity DSO. In accordance with the unit of measure conversion, you can use the CURRENCY ATTRIBUTE to select the InfoObject attribute that you want to use in the currency conversion.

Master Data/Texts Tab

With master data   You use the WITH MASTER DATA checkbox (see Figure 4.3) in the area of the same name to define whether or not the InfoObject will contain master data. If you activate the checkbox, the system automatically displays the ATTRIBUTES tab, where you can add attributes in a second step.

Figure 4.3   Creating an InfoObject — the Master Data/Texts Tab

You can use the MSTDATAMAINT WITH AUTHORIZATION CHECK flag to control the extent to which master data maintenance will be restricted to certain values (flag activated) or the extent to which it will suffice to grant authorization for master data maintenance for the entire InfoObject (flag deactivated).

Referential integrity   When you load data, the system checks its referential integrity against existing characteristic values by default. However, if you define a DSO in the DS OBJECT FOR CHECK field, the system checks the values contained in this DSO. The InfoObject itself and all compound characteristics must be modeled as key values in the DSO that you have defined.

In accordance with the procedure for attributes, you can use the WITH TEXTS checkbox in the WITH TEXTS area to ensure that not only the key but also texts will be used to represent the InfoObject values. You can define short texts (20 characters), medium texts (40 characters), and long texts (60 characters). In addition to the text length, you can also define whether multiple languages will be mapped and whether it will be possible to change the texts over time.

With texts

Now let's take a look at the MASTER DATA INFOSOURCE • DATA TARGET • INFOPROVIDER • MASTER DATA READ ACCESS area. The INFOSOURCE WITH DIRECT UPDATE checkbox is activated if you define an application component in the APPLICATION COMPONENT input field. You can then use transfer rules to update the master data of the InfoObject directly (without having to create an update rule). If you define an application component here, the InfoObject in the INFOSOURCES modeling view is inserted in the appropriate place in the InfoSource tree. At this point, you can assign a DataSource and therefore a source system to the InfoObject. In Release BW 3.0A and later, you can perform a flexible master data update. In other words, you can use update rules to update data into various data targets in a flexible manner (InfoCubes, DSOs, and InfoObjects). Here, one InfoSource can supply several data targets.

Data retrieval

However, CHARACTER. IS INFOPROVIDER indicates that the data of the InfoObject itself (texts and attributes) will be made accessible to reporting or that it will be possible to update this data into other data targets. You cannot use the checkbox to activate this property directly. Instead, you must enter an InfoArea.

Character. is InfoProvider

You can use CHARACTERIST. IS EXPORT DATA SOURCE to generate an export DataSource, so that you can update the texts, attributes, and hierarchies of the InfoObject into other BW systems.

You can use MASTER DATA ACCESS to define your own implementation for the purpose of reading master data. This way, you can display reporting data as master data that is not stored in the actual master data tables of the InfoObject.

Hierarchy Tab

Hierarchy
When you activate the WITH HIERARCHIES checkbox (see Figure 4.4), you activate the HIERARCHY PROPERTIES area where you can specify additional settings for the hierarchy properties.

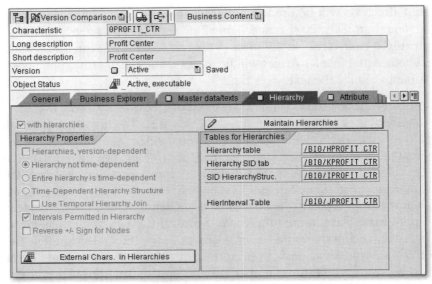

Figure 4.4 Creating an InfoObject — the Hierarchy Tab

Tables for hierarchies
If hierarchies are provided for a characteristic, the system generates special tables that store information about each hierarchy. The TABLES FOR HIERARCHIES area contains references to all relevant hierarchy tables. You can create the hierarchy manually or you can load it from the source system or via a flat file. In reporting, hierarchies enable you to display data in aggregated form across various hierarchy levels and, if necessary, drill down to the details. Usually, the characteristic that contains the hierarchy is displayed, with its values, at the most detailed level.

Hierarchy properties
In the HIERARCHY PROPERTIES area, you choose whether the hierarchy will be held in versions and whether the entire hierarchy or its structure will be time-dependent.

Characteristics in hierarchy
The EXTERNAL CHARS. IN HIERARCHIES button makes it possible to define InfoObjects whose characteristic values can be accessed when you define a hierarchy. Let's assume that you manually define a hierarchy that dis-

plays countries at a certain level. You could then select, for example, the InfoObject 0COUNTRY as an external characteristic for the hierarchy. In this case, however, you really only save yourself the time and effort associated with entering characteristic values for each individual country. Alternatively, you can enter the nodes as text nodes. However, you have to create each node individually in hierarchy maintenance. Always check the use of external characteristics because this will improve the readability of the data model.

You can use the MAINTAIN HIERARCHIES button to navigate directly to hierarchy processing. You cannot influence the tables in which the hierarchy data is stored, but you can double-click the technical table identifiers defined on the HIERARCHIES tab in the TABLES FOR HIERARCHIES area to easily navigate to the table definition or table content.

Maintain hierarchies

Figure 4.5 provides an example of a hierarchy that was defined on the basis of the *Age* characteristic. The hierarchy divides the characteristic values of the *Age* characteristic (0–99) into certain age classes. Sparse value ranges, namely the under 20 and 70+ value ranges, are summarized as < 20 years and >= 70 years, while each age group between these two value ranges spans a ten-year period.

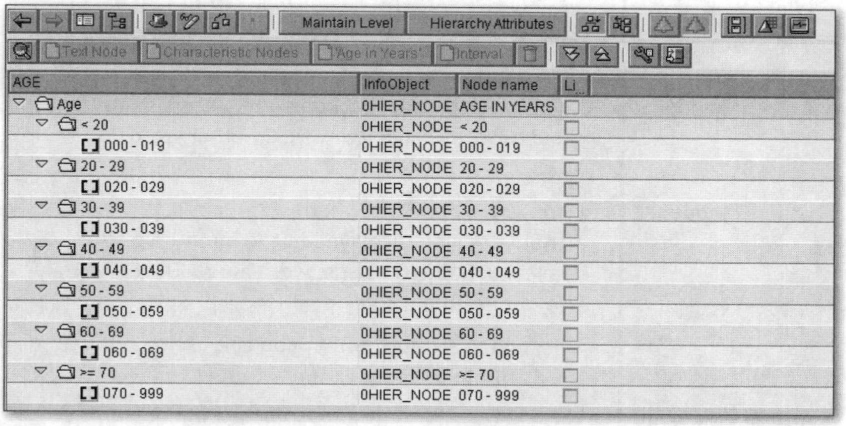

Figure 4.5 Hierarchy Definition for the Age InfoObject

Attribute Tab

On the ATTRIBUTE tab, you can define other InfoObjects as attributes (see Figure 4.6). When the InfoObject is in EDIT mode, you can add existing InfoObjects to the list. You make the corresponding selection either by knowing the object name and entering it directly, using the input help F4 to make a selection, or switching to the ASSIGNED DATASOURCE ATTRIBUTES view and selecting an object from a DataSource assigned to the InfoObject.

Attribute
maintenance

If you add a new InfoObject as an attribute, you can also specify some settings immediately. For example, you can decide whether you want to use the attribute for display purposes only or also for navigation, or whether the attributes will be time-dependent. Furthermore, you can specify a new name if you select an object as a navigation attribute. Later, in reporting, the navigation attribute will be displayed with this name.

Table 4.2 explains the significance of each of the columns in the ATTRIBUTES: DETAIL/NAVIGATION ATTRIBUTES table.

Column Name	Significance
Attribute	Technical name of the InfoObject inserted as an attribute.
Long description	Description of the InfoObject inserted as an attribute.
Type	Describes whether it is a display attribute (DIS) or a navigation attribute (NAV) — the default setting is DIS.
Time-dependent	If you activate this checkbox, the system stores changes to this characteristic, in other words, they are not lost.
F4 help sequence	Here, you can define whether and at what point the attribute will be displayed in the input help. Not displayed: Value 0; Displayed: Value > 0. The value also defines the display position.
Navigation attribute on/off	This field has a button that you can use to activate the attribute as a navigation attribute.
Author.-relevant	This checkbox is relevant for navigation attributes. If you activate this checkbox, the system performs a check to determine whether the user is authorized to access certain characteristic values of this attribute.

Table 4.2 Overview of All of the Fields in Attribute Maintenance for InfoObjects

Column Name	Significance
Characteristic texts	This checkbox is relevant for navigation attributes. If you activate this checkbox, the InfoObject text is transferred as the name of the navigation attribute. If you want to overwrite the name in the next field, you must deactivate this checkbox.
Navigation attribute descr.	Here, you can assign your own name to the navigation attribute. In reporting, the navigation attribute will be displayed with this description. The same applies to the short text (next field).
Navigation attribute short	Here, you can enter a short text that will be displayed in reporting.
Navigation attribute name	The name of this field is somewhat confusing because the technical ID of the navigation attribute is displayed here. This technical ID comprises the technical ID of the InfoObject itself and the technical ID of the InfoObject of the navigation attribute.
DType	The DATA TYPE (DTYPE) and LENGTH fields are not ready for input and display the format of the relevant attribute.
Length	See DTYPE.

Table 4.2 Overview of All of the Fields in Attribute Maintenance for InfoObjects (Cont.)

You can use the NAVIGATION ATTRIBUTE INFOPROVIDER button to enhance the InfoObjects available to reporting. If you define the InfoObject itself as an InfoProvider, its attributes will describe the InfoObjects available to reporting. You can now enhance this view by displaying additional navigation attributes for all navigation attributes (two-step navigation attribute access).

Compounding Tab

Generally, you can enter a characteristic value of an InfoObject only once. Compounding lets you break this rule because compounding enhances the key — only the entire key must be unique. On the COMPOUNDING tab, you implement compounding by entering all of the InfoObjects that you need to create a unique key.

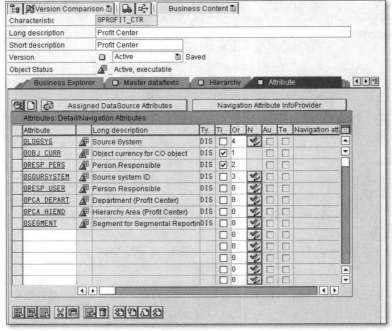

Figure 4.6 Creating an InfoObject — the Attributes Tab

Let's illustrate this with a specific example. In Figure 4.7, the object 0CO_ AREA is compounded to the object 0PROFIT_CTR. Therefore, multiple profit centers can have the same ID if they belong to different controlling areas. Compounding enables the compound characteristic to be added to the key (concatenated object key). The behavior changes accordingly when you load data.

Loading master data on a source system basis

A special case of compounding is when you use the MASTER DATA LOCALLY FOR SOURCE SYS. checkbox to enhance the key in such a way that it results in compounding to the standard InfoObject 0SOURSYSTEM, which describes the source system. This way, the same characteristic values in different systems are no longer overwritten. However, this procedure is only useful if the same characteristic values in different systems refer to different objects, but a new assignment (to establish uniqueness) would require too much time and effort.

Carefully weigh the pros and cons of using compounding. If you define several compound objects for an InfoObject, this may have an adverse effect on performance. In addition, it is no longer easy to remove compounding once it has been defined. In each case, all of the data belonging to the relevant InfoObjects must be deleted before a changeover.

You should therefore only use compounding if the semantics of the data to be loaded actually require it. If you simply want to model a hierarchical relationship, you do not need compounding. Instead, you should use hierarchies.

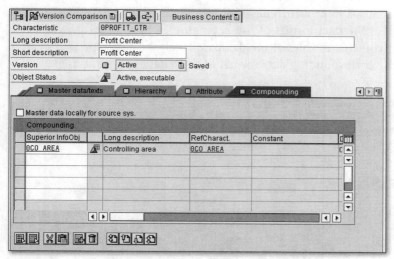

Figure 4.7 Creating an InfoObject — the Compounding Tab

4.1.2 Key Figures

A key figure is used to quantify the measurable size of a state or process. Key figures are essential components of a BW data model. For example, a report always has at least one key figure, which is evaluated according to various criteria (characteristics/attributes).

In BW, you can specify various settings when you create a key figure:

▶ You must select the key figure type.

▶ For amounts and quantities, you must select a fixed currency or unit of measure, or you must define an InfoObject that describes the (variable) currency or unit.

> ▸ You can define the behavior of the key figure, especially the aggregation behavior.

> ▸ As is the case with characteristics, the key figure maintenance screen is also divided into various tabs.

Type/Unit Tab

Data type
On the TYPE/UNIT tab, you can select the data type and, if necessary, a unit of measure or a currency unit (see Figure 4.8). Here, the data type describes the data format of the key figure as you, the user, will see it. When you create tables at the database level, the data type is converted into the corresponding data format of the database system used.

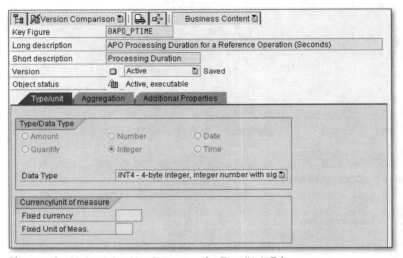

Figure 4.8 Maintaining Key Figures — the Type/Unit Tab

Key figure types
BW distinguishes between a range of key figure types (see Table 4.3). For most of these key figure types, please note that you can choose different data types for the implementation. For example, you can map a (currency) amount as a DEC or FLTP data type. In both cases, you must also select a unit/currency. Depending on the data type selected, the implementation varies in terms of mapping precision and therefore in terms of the key figure's memory consumption.

Key Figure Type	Data Type	Description	Key Figure with Unit (U)/ Currency (C)
Amount	CURR	Currency field, stored as DEC	C
	FLTP	Floating point number with 8-byte precision	C
Quantity	QUAN	Quantity field, points to a unit field with the format UNIT	U
	FLTP	Floating point number with 8-byte precision	U
Number	DEC	Computed or amount field with decimal point and sign	—
	FLTP	Floating point number with 8-byte precision	—
Integer	INT4	4-byte integer, whole number with sign	—
Date	DEC	Computed or amount field with decimal point and sign	—
	DATS	Date field (yyyymmdd), stored as CHAR (8)	—
Time	DEC	Computed or amount field with decimal point and sign	—
	TIMS	Time field (hhmmss), stored as CHAR (6)	—

Table 4.3 Key Figure and Data Type Combinations

Key figures of the AMOUNT type are always currencies. Therefore, the system prompts you to enter a fixed currency or to select an InfoObject for the currency reference. If you use a key figure with a fixed currency to post data to a data target, the currency must be converted in an upstream step. If you define an InfoObject for the currency, you can post different currencies. The InfoObject is then used as an additional characteristic that describes the currency that has been posted. Standard InfoObjects frequently used this way include, for example, 0CURRENCY (currency key), 0LOC_CURRENCY (local currency), and 0DOC_CURRENCY (document currency). If you post different currencies to an InfoProvider, the currency conversion must occur in reporting.

Currencies

Key figures of the QUANTITY type, and their defined units, behave in a similar manner. Similar to amounts, the unit must be predefined or it must have a flexible configuration, which is achieved by defining a unit InfoObject (for example, 0UNIT).

Quantities

Floating point
numbers

Please note the following special feature associated with using key figures of the FLOATING POINT NUMBER (FLTP) data type. There may be some rounding differences as a result of the numerical arithmetic used. Floating point key figures generally behave differently than decimal key figures (DEC). For example, the system may store the value 1.4340999999999998E+07 internally when you post the value 1.4341E+07. The difference here is negligible. However, the result may be confusing if it concerns key figures that have a certain recognition effect in reporting. This may be the case, for example, if you enter a round planned value in a planning application, but this is stored in disaggregated (distributed) form. If aggregation is repeated in reporting, the system no longer displays the exact source value. Later in this section, we will discuss the OTHER tab where you will learn how to minimize rounding differences.

Aggregation Tab

Standard
aggregation

You define the aggregation behavior of a key figure in the AGGREGATION input field on the AGGREGATION tab (see Figure 4.9). When you create a new key figure (except in the case of the DATS and TIMS data types), Summation (SUM), which is the most frequently used setting, is preconfigured here. In addition to Summation, you only have the following two standard aggregation behaviors: Maximum (MAX) and Minimum (MIN). You must use these for the DATS and TIMS data types, for example, because CHARACTER fields that are unsuitable for arithmetic operations are used to map these data types internally.

Exception
aggregation

In addition to the standard aggregation behavior, you must specify an exception aggregation behavior. If no other selection is made, the system automatically copies the standard behavior (Summation or Maximum) to the EXCEPTION AGGREGAT. input field. Therefore, exception aggregation is not used if you do not explicitly define a different aggregation behavior.

The following exception aggregation rules are available to you:

▶ **Average**
When you drill down according to the reference characteristic, the average column value is specified in the results row. There are various ways to calculate the average value. Furthermore, the calculation does not always have to consider zero values. A weighting can also occur according to the number of days or work days.

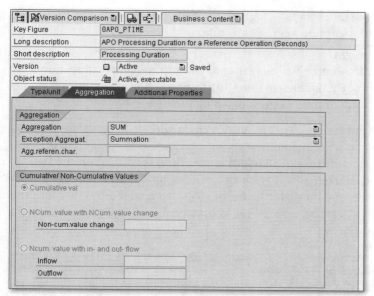

Figure 4.9 Maintaining Key Figures — the Aggregation Tab

▸ **Counter**

All values are counted. You can also choose to include or exclude zero values.

▸ **First Value/Last Value**

The first/last value, which is based on the reference characteristic, is displayed. This setting is useful, for example, for time characteristics as reference characteristics.

▸ **Maximum/Minimum**

The maximum or minimum, which is based on the reference characteristic, is displayed as the result.

▸ **Standard Deviation**

The standard deviation is displayed as the result of aggregation by a characteristic.

▸ **Variance**

The variance is displayed as the result of aggregation by a characteristic.

▸ **Summation**

The total is created here. Because you can also select Maximum or

Minimum as a standard aggregation behavior, Summation is also useful as an exception aggregation rule.

▶ **No Aggregation**
Depending on the various criteria, you can prevent aggregation from occurring. Hierarchies require this setting if, for example, you do not want summation to occur along a hierarchy.

Reference characteristic

You must always specify a reference characteristic (AGG.REFEREN.CHAR.) for exception aggregations. Exception aggregation is applied on the basis of this characteristic and standard aggregation is applied on the basis of all other characteristics. To use exception aggregation, the corresponding characteristic must not be in the drill-down of a query because this will result in aggregation by the characteristic (in accordance with the defined rule).

[Ex] **Determining the Last (Latest) Headcount Value**

Imagine that you have a data model for evaluating headcount. The dataset valid for each month is loaded for each month. The time characteristics are based on the loading date, and the additional characteristics of the model provide more detailed information about the employee (employee group, department, gender, and so on). If you create the *Number of Employees* key figure without exception aggregation, it will produce incorrect values because a total will be displayed by mistake if aggregation is not restricted to a particular month, but occurs across several months. Therefore, the same employee is counted more than once. However, it would be correct, for example, if the system were to display the last headcount to be loaded (December's headcount) instead of the total. You can achieve this particular behavior by creating a LAST VALUE exception aggregation with the reference characteristic Calendar Month (0CALMONTH) for the key figure. Alternatively, the AVERAGE exception aggregation would also produce a useful aggregation result.

[Ex] **Counting the Number of Countries with Sales > 0**

Let's assume that you have already implemented an InfoCube with sales figures that show the worldwide sales achieved for your products. In reporting, you could now use exception aggregation to define a new key figure that counts the number of countries in which you have achieved sales > 0. A COUNT ALL VALUES <> 0 exception aggregation based on the 0COUNTRY characteristic (or your own country object) is sufficient here.

The aggregation behavior settings for a key figure have different effects on the loading behavior and reporting. While the setting for the standard aggregation behavior affects both aforementioned areas, exception aggregation is only used in InfoCube-based reporting. Whenever the Online Analytical Processing (OLAP) processor aggregates data, the exception aggregation rule is also considered after standard aggregation.

Using exception aggregation

As shown in the previous example for counting countries in which sales are generated, you can use the setting for the key figure InfoObject itself to vary the aggregation behavior in reporting by creating newly calculated key figures. We will discuss this aspect in further detail in Chapter 8, Section 8.3.2, Exception Aggregation.

All of the exception aggregation settings discussed previously are based on cumulative values. Values must also be posted for each reporting period for which values are to be displayed. In most cases, the values can be added up. In some cases, however, as we have already seen, exception aggregation must be used to achieve a correct aggregation behavior.

Cumulative and non-cumulative values

The *Number of Employees* key figure described in the previous example for determining the current headcount is not actually a cumulative value, but is nevertheless modeled as such. In other words, you can use the exception aggregation settings to ensure correct behavior and to model this key figure in BW as a cumulative value.

However, you can also model real noncumulative values (as an alternative to the cumulative value) on the AGGREGATION tab. There are two alternative types of modeling

Real non-cumulative key figures

- ▶ **Noncumulative with noncumulative change**
  When you activate NCUM. VALUE WITH NCUM. VALUE CHANGE, the key figure itself becomes the noncumulative key figure. In this case, you must also define a second key figure that describes inflows and outflows as cumulative values.

- ▶ **Noncumulative with inflow and outflow**
  When you activate NON-CUMULATIVE WITH IN- AND OUT- FLOW, the key figure itself also becomes a non-cumulative key figure. In this case, you must also define two other key figures, one that describes the inflow as a cumulative value and one that describes the outflow as a cumulative value.

The noncumulative key figure and the defined cumulative values must have the same key figure type. The units of the key figures must also concur. When you select cumulative values, the system proposes permitted selections.

The key figures for the noncumulative change or for inflows and outflows are modeled as normal cumulative values. Summation is both their standard aggregation behavior and exception aggregation behavior. The noncumulative key figures themselves have summation as their standard aggregation behavior. For reporting, however, the system automatically defines exception aggregation, thus preventing noncumulative key figures from being added up over time.

A reporting scenario using real noncumulative key figures can only be mapped using an InfoCube. This is due to the special application logic described next.

Functions of non-cumulative key figures

Starting with a marker that describes the current noncumulative, forward/backward calculations based on the noncumulative changes in the cumulative value determine a noncumulative that is valid at any time. The time base under which the current, valid final noncumulative is stored is known as the high date (12/31/2009). You can achieve high-performance access to this final noncumulative. A forward/backward calculation, on the other hand, is more laborious. For this reason, you must update the value for the current noncumulative on a regular basis. This is done by compressing the InfoCube.

Alternative implementation options

There are three alternative modeling options for noncumulative key figures, namely the two aforementioned models for mapping real noncumulative key figures and the option to use a cumulative value with exception aggregation. The model you choose depends on the scenario to be mapped. We recommend using real noncumulative key figures for areas in which noncumulatives do not completely change on a regular basis. Classic examples include warehouse stock in retail or headcount mapping. However, even SAP does not use noncumulative key figures in this context in the Standard Content. Cumulative values with exception aggregation are used instead. The advantage of this is that the model can have a simple structure because the noncumulative for each month is loaded in a request and is easy to manage. One disadvantage associated with this procedure is that the data volume (fact table) to be stored is comparably higher.

Reference characteristics

You must select reference characteristics for the noncumulative key figures. However, their selection is not arbitrary because exactly one time base must be established. You can also define other technical reference characteristics. You can specify the relevant settings under MAINTAIN ADDITIONAL NON-CUMULATIVE PARAMETERS.

In addition to defining reference characteristics, you must maintain a validity table for an InfoCube that has noncumulative key figures (Transaction RSDV). This is only possible if you have not yet loaded any data into the InfoCube. However, if this is the case, you must use the program RSDG_CUBE_VALT_MODIFY to modify the validity table.

Validity table

Additional Properties Tab

On the ADDITIONAL PROPERTIES tab (see Figure 4.10), you can specify settings for reporting. You can also indicate whether the key figure under consideration is a key figure InfoObject from the Standard Content and, if necessary, view the person responsible and the date and time when the last change was made.

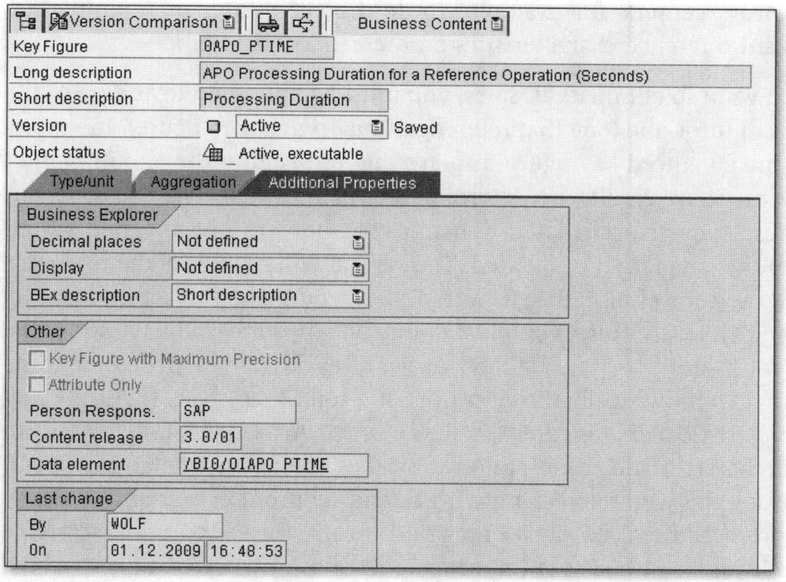

Figure 4.10 Maintaining Key Figures — the Additional Properties Tab

You can use the KEY FIGURE WITH MAXIMUM PRECISION property to ensure that the OLAP processor works internally with packed numbers (and not with floating point numbers). Here, packed numbers have 31 digits. In

Key figure precision

the case of packed numbers, two decimal places are represented in one byte. Because the 16th byte also contains the plus/minus sign, only 31 digits can be used. You can achieve greater precision with packed numbers than with floating point numbers. Rounding differences, in particular, are therefore avoided.

Just like characteristics, you have the option of selecting the ATTRIBUTE ONLY property for key figures. If you select this property, the key figure can only be used as a display attribute, and not for modeling InfoCubes.

Elimination Tab

If you have created your key figure with reference to another key figure, the system displays an additional tab called ELIMINATION (see Figure 4.11). In this context, elimination means that the posted key figure values will never be considered in certain constellations in the analyses. This function is essentially used to eliminate IC sales, that is, sales between two profit centers, for example. To do this, you enter the elimination-relevant reference characteristics on the ELIMINATION tab.

Elimination of IC sales

If you want to eliminate IC sales, you must add another key figure to the relevant InfoCube (one that references the original key figure). In reporting, the enhanced key figure displays the results after the elimination of IC sales. These results are determined dynamically by the OLAP server. Because they are calculated dynamically, they are not assigned values when the data target is updated. The system will not know the reference to be used for eliminating IC sales unless you make the settings on the ELIMINATION tab. Here, you must define one or more characteristic pairs. You must also specify whether you want each characteristic pair to be eliminated individually (ELIMINATION OF EACH CHARACTERISTIC PAIR) or all characteristic pairs together (ELIMINATION OF ALL CHARACTERISTIC PAIRS). Each characteristic combination describes the activity relationship. If, for example, we are working with a sending profit center and a receiving profit center, you must enter both profit centers as a characteristic pair. In this context, it is important that these two InfoObjects, which describe a characteristic pair, are created as referencing InfoObjects.

For example, the two InfoObjects 0PROFIT_CTR (Profit Center) and 0PART_PRCTR (Partner Profit Center) in the Standard Content are suitable for creating a characteristic pair. Moreover, both InfoObjects in the characteristic pair must be contained in the InfoCube that will be used to eliminate IC sales. Figure 4.11 shows how you must add these two InfoObjects to the key figure definition. You can also configure other characteristic pairs. However, you must create the relevant InfoObjects as referencing InfoObjects.

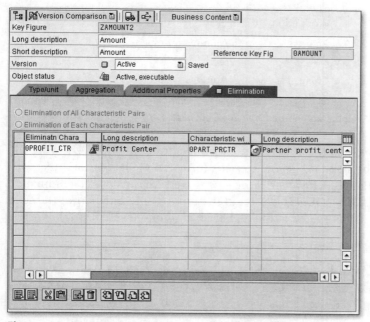

Figure 4.11 Maintaining Key Figures — the Elimination Tab

Let's take a look at an example of an enterprise that has the organizational structure shown in Figure 4.12. Furthermore, let's assume that this example is based on the data contained in Table 4.4. Both the *Pharma Production* profit center and the *Chemistry Production* profit center have IC sales with Administration.

Example

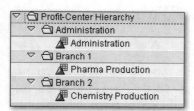

Figure 4.12 Sample Hierarchy for the Elimination of IC Sales

Data Record Seq. No.	Profit Center 0PROFIT_CTR	Partner Profit Center 0PART_PRCTR	Sales 0AMOUNT
1	Pharma Production	–	100
2	Chemistry Production	–	100
3	Pharma Production	Administration	30
4	Chemistry Production	Administration	50

Table 4.4 Sample Data for the Elimination of IC Sales

If you consider the evaluation example shown in Table 4.5, you will see that the standard key figure *Sales* (0AMOUNT) has an incorrect total value (EUR 280). However, if the key figure with the defined elimination of IC sales (ZAMOUNT) is used in the report, only one part of the sales (EUR 80) is eliminated at the higher level (group level) (see Table 4.1).

Hierarchy Level	Profit Center Hierarchy	Sales 0AMOUNT	Sales with Elimination ZAMOUNT
0	Entire Company	$ 280	$ 200
1	Administration	$ 0	$ 0
2	Administration	$ 0	$ 0
1	Division 2	$ 130	$ 130
2	Pharma Production	$ 130	$ 130
1	Division 3	$ 150	$ 150
2	Chemistry Production	$ 150	$ 150

Table 4.5 Sample Result for the Elimination of IC Sales

4.1.3 Currencies and Units

As explained in Section 4.1.2, Key Figures, you must select a currency or unit when you create amount or quantity key figures. You can define the currency or unit as a fixed value or you can retain it as a variable. Variable means that you must define an InfoObject that describes the relevant currency or unit.

All currency InfoObjects in the system reference the standard object 0CURRENCY and all unit InfoObjects reference 0UNIT. Therefore, when you create a new currency or unit InfoObject (see Figure 4.13), you must determine whether it concerns a currency or unit. The system then automatically defines a suitable referencing InfoObject.

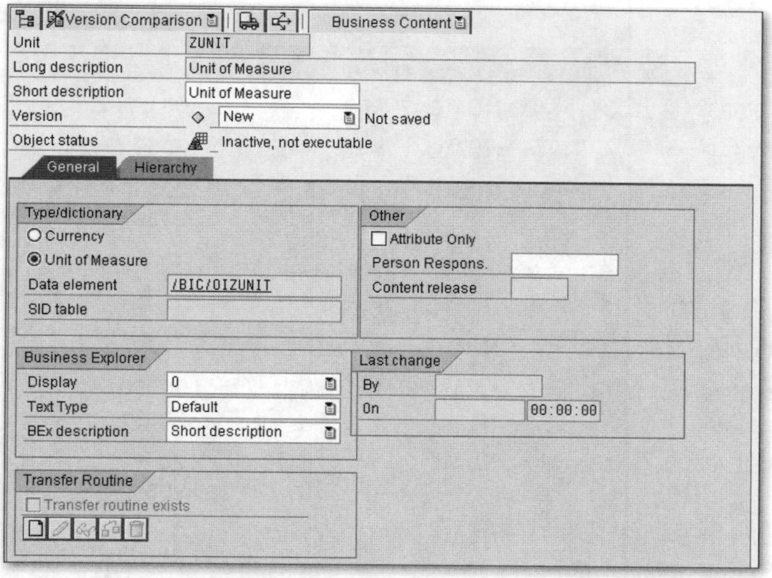

Figure 4.13 Creating a New Unit InfoObject

The 0CURRENCY and 0UNIT InfoObjects define which currencies and units are available in the system. You can add other currencies and units to the SAP Customizing Implementation Guide (IMG) (Transaction SPRO) via the menu path SAP NetWeaver • General Settings.

Table 4.6 contains a list of sample currencies and units.

Currency (0CURRENCY)	Units (0UNIT)
EUR (Euro)	CM2 (square centimeter)
USD (US Dollar)	BOX (box)
JPY (Japanese Yen)	PAL (pallets)
etc.	etc.

Table 4.6 Sample Currencies and Units

4.1.4 Times

In addition to characteristics and units, time characteristics are essential key fields in an InfoCube. The data in almost all datasets has a time base: sales per month, annual headcount, a key date reference for master data, and so on. The SAP system provides the standard time InfoObjects listed in Table 4.7.

Name	Key	Length	Type	Format	Example
Posting period	0FISCPER3	3	NUMC	PPP	001, 002, ...16
Fiscal year	0FISCYEAR	4	NUMC	YYYY	2009
Fiscal year/period	0FISCPER	7	NUMC	YYYYPPP	200901 ... 200916
Fiscal year variant	0FISCVARNT	2	CHAR	CC	K4
Half year	0HALFYEAR1	1	NUMC	H	1, 2
Calendar year	0CALYEAR	4	NUMC	YYYY	2009
Calendar year/ month	0CALMONTH	6	NUMC	YYYYMM	200901 ... 200912
Calendar year/ quarter	0CALQUARTER	5	NUMC	YYYYQQ	200901 ... 200904
Calendar year/ week	0CALWEEK	6	NUMC	YYYYWW	200901 ... 200953
Calendar month	0CALMONTH2	2	NUMC	MM	01 ... 12
Calendar day	0CALDAY	8	DATS	YYYYMMDD	20090101 ... 20091231
Quarter	0CALQUART1	1	NUMC	Q	1 ... 4
Week day	0WEEKDAY1	1	NUMC	D	1 ... 7

Table 4.7 Standard Time Characteristics

Standard time characteristics
When you use standard time characteristics, you benefit from the fact that the system provides predefined conversion routines for staging and predefined variables for reporting. Therefore, you do not have to implement these yourself. In InfoCube modeling, a special dimension is reserved for time characteristics. However, it is not possible to add InfoObjects to another dimension.

When you model InfoCubes, you should always take standard time characteristics into account. For example, you need the InfoObject 0FIS-CPER or 0CALMONTH to partition the fact table (see Chapter 8, Section 8.2.4, Partitioning). Partitioning is one way to improve InfoCube performance.

You can also create your own InfoObjects and add time/date content. However, the system does not recognize these as real-time characteristics. Therefore, you cannot add them to a time dimension. If necessary, you must create your own suitable conversion routines and implement the time control in reporting.

User-defined time characteristics

4.2 Master Data in SAP NetWeaver BW

In Section 4.1.1, Characteristics, we described the options available to you when creating InfoObjects, along with the basic modeling alternatives available for InfoObjects.

The master data of an InfoObject is particularly significant during data modeling. Master data includes texts, attributes, and hierarchies, each of which we will describe in the following sections.

4.2.1 Texts

Texts add an easy-to-understand name to the characteristic values of an InfoObject. Because the characteristic values frequently only comprise a numeric key, texts are extremely important in reporting because they interpret the content of an InfoObject. In the settings for an InfoObject, you can define texts in multiple languages.

You can create short (20 characters), medium (40 characters), or long texts (60 characters). Depending on the reporting requirement, you can select a suitable length in reporting.

To make the search easier, avoid using lowercase letters in the characteristic values of an InfoObject. However, both uppercase and lowercase are commonly used in text descriptions.

Uppercase and lowercase

When you specify the relevant settings, you can define the texts in different languages. The system then automatically displays the content of a report in the logon language of the user logged on to the system.

Multilingual capability

Technically speaking, the language dependency is implemented by adding a LANGU field with the values G, E, J, etc., to the key of the table that contains the texts.

Time dependency of texts

A characteristic value should always describe the same real object. For example, the name of a candy bar may change, but it should nevertheless be possible to interpret it as the same product throughout the entire hierarchy. You can achieve this by using a time-dependent text. Technically speaking, the time dependency is achieved by adding the DATETO date field to the key of the table that contains the texts. Figure 4.14 shows the structure of a time- and language-dependent text table that has short and medium texts.

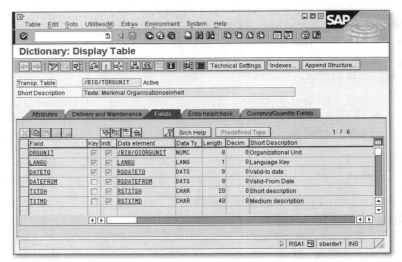

Figure 4.14 Text Table for the InfoObject 0ORGUNIT

However, modeling whereby the name is not modeled as text, but as a characteristic value, would be unfavorable in our candy bar example. In this case, there would be a break, and it would no longer be possible to recognize that it concerns the same product.

Table 4.8 shows the language- and time-dependent data of the organizational unit with the key 1000. It is apparent that a valid and, if need be, empty data record (if no text exists) is created for each point in time between the low date (January 01, 1000) and high date (December 31, 9999). In this case, only one short and one medium text exist. In the case of the Japanese texts, only the medium text has been translated into Japanese. The short text, on the other hand, has been entered in English. Such variations are therefore possible.

ORGUNIT	LANGU	DATETO	DATEFROM	TXTSH	TXTMD
1000	G	12/31/1993	01/01/1000		
1000	G	12/31/9999	01/01/1994	San Francisco, USA	Plant San Francisco (USA)
1000	E	12/31/1993	01/01/1000		
1000	E	12/31/9999	01/01/1994	San Francisco Prod	San Francisco Production Site
1000	F	12/31/1993	01/01/1000		
1000	F	12/31/9999	01/01/1994	San Francisco	Division San Francisco (ALL)
1000	J	12/31/1993	01/01/1000		
1000	J	12/31/9999	01/01/1994	San Francisco Prod	ハンブルグ製造プラント

Table 4.8 Sample Language- and Time-Dependent Texts

In InfoObject maintenance, you can display the text table of a characteristic on the MASTER DATA/TEXTS tab by double-clicking the name of the text table in the TEXT TABLE field. Alternatively, you can call the transaction for database table maintenance (Transaction SE11). In this case, however, you must know the name of the text table, which is derived from the technical name of the InfoObject (in accordance with the schema shown in Table 4.9).

	Standard InfoObject	User-Defined InfoObject
Techn. name of the InfoObject	0<8 characters>	<1letter><8 characters>
Text table name	/BIO/T<8 characters>	/BIC/T<1letter><8 characters>

Table 4.9 Naming Convention for Text Tables

4.2.2 Attributes

The role that a characteristic InfoObject assumes in a BW data model may be that of a simple field or that of a more complex object with texts, attributes, and hierarchies.

If you create a new characteristic InfoObject, the WITH TEXTS and WITH MASTER DATA properties are activated by default. If you do not want to use any texts or master data, you should deselect the relevant property. A characteristic InfoObject without texts and master data comprises only its key, without any further descriptive information.

Many characteristic InfoObjects have a more complex structure. Entities such as customers, vendors, cost centers, organizational units, and so on have a range of attributes that describe the characteristic InfoObject in more detail. If you activate the WITH MASTER DATA option, the SAP NetWeaver BW data model provides you with the option of defining attributes for characteristic InfoObjects. These attributes are other characteristic InfoObjects or key figure InfoObjects, which, in turn, may contain master data (in the case of characteristic InfoObjects), such as attributes.

Once you have configured the settings for an InfoObject, you must save and activate it. During activation, the system generates (creates) the table structures used to store the InfoObject data. In addition to the WITH MASTER DATA or WITH TEXTS basic setting, the following settings determine the structure and scope of the tables generated:

► Time dependency of attributes

► Navigation attributes

► Compounding

The following sections describe each of these settings in more detail.

Time Dependency of Attributes

If you enhance the modeling of an InfoObject by adding an attribute, the system generates a master data table with an additional column when you activate the InfoObject. When you load master data, this column is filled with values, and when you reload master data for the same characteristic value, the old value is overwritten, which means that only one attribute value can be assigned. Because a time-based delimitation is not possible when you load master data, you can no longer identify when an attribute value changed and which value the attribute had before it was changed.

However, you can control whether or not each individual attribute will be time-dependent. To do this, you must activate the TIME-DEPENDENT checkbox on the ATTRIBUTES tab in the DETAIL/NAVIGATION ATTRIBUTES view.

Table 4.10 contains sample time-dependent master data. It concerns an employee (0EMPLOYEE) with personnel number 1031. Mr. Mark Meier was employed on January 01, 1994, as a non–pay scale employee (pay scale group AT). At that time, the system created two data records: an empty record, which is valid from January 01, 1000 (low date), until December 31, 2003, and a data record that contains all relevant attributes for the employee, with the valid-from date January 01, 1994, and the valid-to date December 31, 9999 (high date). On December 31, 2001, the salary paid to Mr. Mark Meier changed in the SAP ERP system from Deutsche Mark to Euro. This change was also transferred to BW. As a result of the attribute change run, the validity of the data record, which was valid at that time until the high date, was delimited and a new data record, beginning on January 01, 2002, was created. Another change occurred on January 01, 2004, when Mr. Mark Meier started to work with a capacity utilization rate of just 50%.

Sample time-dependent master data

Employee	Valid to	Valid from	Organizational unit	Position	Entry date	Rate of cap. utilization	Pay scale group	Annual salary	Currency	Name
1031	12/31/1993	01/01/1000								
1031	12/31/2001	01/01/1994	50000148	50011879	01/01/1994	100	AT	72,000.00	DM	MARK MEIER
1031	12/31/2003	01/01/2002	50000148	50011879	01/01/1994	100	AT	36,813.02	EUR	MARK MEIER
1031	12/31/9999	01/01/2004	50000148	50011879	01/01/1994	50	AT	18,406.51	EUR	MARK MEIER

Table 4.10 Time-Dependent Attributes for the Example 0EMPLOYEE

All attributes of the standard InfoObject 0EMPLOYEE are time-dependent. Therefore, a new time-based delimitation occurs for each change transferred to BW. In other words, an employee's entire history is mapped in his master data. In principle, you can perform an evaluation on any evaluation key date. The employee data valid on that particular date will be displayed.

Time-dependent vs. non-time-dependent attributes

To obtain the display shown in Table 4.10, go to InfoObject maintenance for the 0EMPLOYEE object, select the MASTER DATA/TEXTS tab in the MASTER DATA TABLES area, double-click the table name /BIO/MEMPLOYEE in the MASTER DATA TABLE VIEW field, and display the content of the view. This is actually a view rather than the tables themselves. The background to this is that BW stores the attributes in two tables. One table contains the non-time-dependent attributes (that is, the time-constant attributes) and one contains the time-dependent attributes. One advantage associated with this distribution is that not all time-constant attributes have to be stored redundantly (in each time slice). A view that consolidates both tables is always created automatically and is used to facilitate easier access to the attributes.

Navigation Attributes

Display attributes

The attributes of an InfoObject are automatically classified as display attributes once they have been added to the ATTRIBUTES tab. Such attributes can be displayed in reporting (in addition to the characteristic value of the InfoObject), thus making it possible to vary the sequence and display (text or key). However, navigating through a report that you have executed (drill down, filtering, and so on) occurs solely on the basis of the characteristic values of the InfoObject, and not on the basis of the display attributes.

Navigation attributes

If you also want to use attributes for navigation purposes, you must switch from DISPLAY to NAVIGATION. You must also activate this property at the InfoProvider level (DSO, InfoCube, and MultiProvider). As a result, you can use such a navigation attribute in reporting for filtering purposes and then, regardless of the InfoObject that contains the attribute, navigate as if it concerned another characteristic InfoObject of the InfoProvider.

By classifying an attribute as a navigation attribute, additional master data tables are created. Performance would be inadequate if the original master data tables were used for navigation purposes.

Compounding

When you compound an InfoObject on the COMPOUNDING tab, the InfoObjects listed there are added to all relevant master data tables as additional keys.

Referencing InfoObjects

When you create an InfoObject, you can specify whether you want to create it as a referencing InfoObject. If you select this option, you create the new InfoObject with characteristic values, master data, and texts that are identical to those of the referenced object.

However, this new InfoObject still has a certain degree of flexibility:

▶ You can change the following settings: ATTRIBUTE ONLY, CHARACTERISTIC IS DOCUMENT PROPERTY, and CONSTANT.

▶ You can change some of the general BEx settings (for example, the display, text type, and description in BEx and the filter display).

▶ You can activate the authorization check.

▶ You can define other attributes as navigation attributes or select other descriptions for these attributes.

However, you cannot change the settings for the hierarchy, existing attributes, and compounding. In this regard, modeling of the referencing InfoObject is the same as modeling of the referenced InfoObject.

A typical example of using reference InfoObjects is the standard business partner InfoObject (0BPARTNER). A business partner assumes various roles: vendor, sold-to party, bill-to party, and so on. This leads to a requirement whereby several InfoObjects with different names will be used in reporting. At the same time, however, modeling will be simplified and only one business partner InfoObject and its attributes will be modeled. All of this can be achieved using referencing InfoObjects.

Example

Table 4.11 lists some sample reference InfoObjects. Please note that all of these InfoObjects reference the business partner object. You can define the properties of the InfoObjects immediately or in the context of the aforementioned degree of flexibility (similar to the object 0BPARTNER). It always concerns one business partner that assumes various roles.

InfoObject	Name
0SLL_PPAYE	Payer
0SLL_PRECP	Recipient
0SLL_PSEND	Sender
0SLL_PSHTP	Ship-to party
0SLL_PSOTP	Sold-to party
0SLL_PULCO	Ultimate consignee
0SLL_PVEND	Vendor

Table 4.11 Sample Reference InfoObjects (Business Partner)

4.2.3 External Hierarchies

External hierarchies enable you to group characteristic values according to certain criteria (hierarchical). When they are used in reporting, the key figure values are aggregated across the various levels of the hierarchical structure in accordance with the characteristic value assignments. Figure 4.15 shows a hierarchy for the InfoObject 0COUNTRY, which classifies the characteristic values (DE, AT, CH, and so on) according to region.

The right-hand side of Figure 4.15 shows a report for the *Number of Employees* key figure. The values are aggregated across the levels in the hierarchy. In the report, you can still configure whether and to what extent you want to expand the hierarchy structure in the standard view. You can always dynamically expand and collapse individual nodes in the report or open the entire structure up to a certain hierarchy level.

Aggregation This sample hierarchy is relatively simple because it describes just one level that could still be built across many more hierarchy levels. A top node was also omitted here. Reporting resources are used to create the total displayed in the executed report. Alternatively, you could also add an additional hierarchy level to the hierarchy definition. This level would comprise one node and describe the top level.

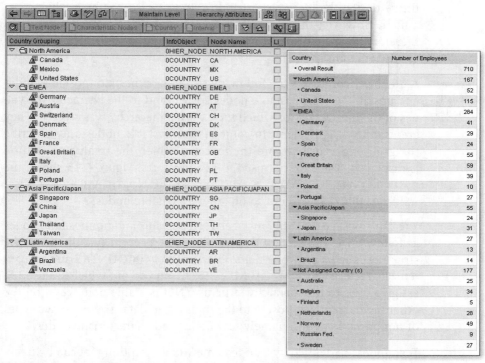

Figure 4.15 Country Hierarchy Based on the Country InfoObject (0COUNTRY)

When you look at the figure, you see that six countries (including Australia and Belgium) are not assigned to the hierarchy. The NOT ASSIGNED COUNTRY(S) node is not explicitly part of the country hierarchy, but is automatically added to the executed report. This node shows (data-driven) all characteristic values of 0COUNTRY for which an assignment could not be found in the hierarchy. For Australia and Belgium, this means that they must be added to the hierarchy structure. To do this, Belgium must be classified as another node under EMEA. For Australia, you must first create a node at the REGION level and then insert Australia below this node. The 177 employees under NOT ASSIGNED indicate that there is a data quality issue. Because these employees are not assigned to any country, the transaction data does not contain a characteristic value for the object O0COUNTRY (the field is empty). You must now check to see if the employee data in the source system needs to be supplemented or whether there is an issue with a transformation in SAP NetWeaver BW. You can also hide the NOT ASSIGNED COUNTRY (S) node by changing

Node "not assigned"

the setting in the hierarchy attributes. In this case, the hierarchy acts as a filter. However, this carries the risk of reporting incorrect totals. It is therefore better to display the node and actively use it for data/hierarchy quality assurance.

Text and characteristic nodes

A hierarchy comprises the following two node types: nonpostable nodes and postable nodes. Postable nodes correspond to the characteristic values of the InfoObject for which the external hierarchy was created. They are used to assign values. In contrast, nonpostable nodes only describe the grouping and therefore the levels at which the totals information is displayed. They are not used to assign values. Figure 4.15 shows the postable nodes CA, MX, US, DE, and so on. NORTH AMERICA, EMEA, ASIA PACIFIC/JAPAN, and so on are nonpostable nodes.

You can envisage the difference between postable and nonpostable nodes as follows: The transaction data displayed in a report (via the hierarchy structure) knows only one field/object, namely 0COUNTRY and its content/characteristic values CA, MX, US, DE, and so on, which are used to assign values to the hierarchy structure. Nonpostable node keys, on the other hand, are never posted to the transaction data. There are two types of nonpostable nodes, namely text nodes and characteristic nodes.

Text nodes are defined by a node name and description that can be freely selected. For example, you can simply create new text nodes in hierarchy maintenance (see Figure 4.16) and use them as the organizational criterion in the hierarchy definition.

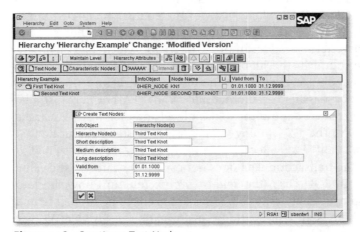

Figure 4.16 Creating a Text Node

Characteristic nodes, on the other hand, correspond to the characteristic values of another InfoObject. If you want to add characteristic nodes to a hierarchy definition, you must first use the EXTERNAL CHARS. IN HIERARCHIES button on the HIERARCHY tab to add the relevant InfoObject in InfoObject maintenance. You can then use the CHARACTERISTIC NODES button in hierarchy maintenance to add characteristic values to the characteristic. Figure 4.17 shows a sample hierarchy whose structure is based on characteristic nodes. The individual pharmaceutical products are grouped according to the preparation (for example, Pharmazol) and then, in turn, according to a higher-level indication group (for example, Pharmazolitika).

Product Hierarchy	InfoObject	No	LI
▽ 🗀 All Articles	0HIER_NODE	ALL	☐
▽ 🏛 Gastronomika	DPHINDI	INDI1	☐
▽ 🏛 Asthmanol	DPHPREP	INDI...	☐
🏛 Asthmanol 350ML	DPHREFNR	000...	☐
▷ 🏛 Gastronom	DPHPREP	INDI...	☐
▽ 🏛 Pharmazolitika	DPHINDI	INDI2	☐
▽ 🏛 Pharmazol	DPHPREP	INDI...	☐
🏛 Pharmazol 100 10ML, 5AMP	DPHREFNR	000...	☐
🏛 Pharmazol 150mg	DPHREFNR	000...	☐
🏛 Pharmazol 40 10ML, 5AMP	DPHREFNR	000...	☐
🏛 Pharmazol 40 10ML, 1AMP	DPHREFNR	000...	☐
🏛 Pharmazol F.P. 1ML, 5PTR	DPHREFNR	000...	☐
🏛 Pharmazol F.P. 1ML, 20PTR	DPHREFNR	000...	☐
🏛 Pharmazol F.P. 1ML, 5PTR	DPHREFNR	000...	☐
🏛 Pharmazol F.P. 3ML, 5PTR	DPHREFNR	000...	☐
🏛 Pharmazol F.P. 3ML, 10PTR	DPHREFNR	000...	☐
🏛 Pharmazol F.P. 3ML, 5PTR	DPHREFNR	000...	☐
▷ 🏛 Pharmazin	DPHPREP	INDI...	☐
▷ 🏛 Muskolytika	DPHINDI	INDI3	☐
▷ 🏛 Herzolinika	DPHINDI	INDI4	☐

Figure 4.17 Using Characteristic Nodes in a Hierarchy

The advantage of characteristic nodes over text nodes is that any update after a change, for example, in the description of a characteristic node (in our example, an indication group value or a preparation value), is also automatically transferred to the hierarchy structure. Therefore, you do not have to manually adjust the hierarchy. If the characteristic nodes have time-dependent texts, a suitable text is always used, depending on the key date selected in reporting.

Advantages of characteristic nodes

A schematic diagram of Figure 4.17 is provided in Figure 4.18. The uppermost node is known as the root node or hierarchy root. The individual hierarchy levels appear below this node. Level 1 describes the indication group and Level 2 describes the preparation level. Each preparation is

Characteristics of hierarchies

available in different forms of presentation (the actual products), which are displayed at Level 3.

The hierarchy definition shown in Figure 4.18 has the following characteristics:

▸ The hierarchy is balanced, that is, each leaf (in other words, the product) is equidistant from the root.
▸ The postable nodes are only inserted at the lowest level.
▸ The hierarchy has a root, which is a text node.
▸ Each level comprises the characteristic values of an InfoObject.

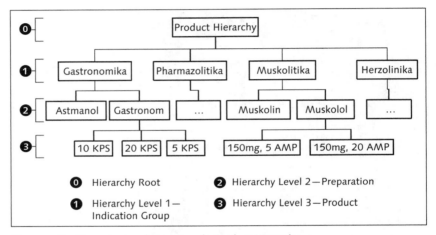

Figure 4.18 Hierarchy Levels in a Sample Product Hierarchy

However, the structure does not have to satisfy these rules. For example, the following flexibility exists:

▸ You can model the branches of the hierarchy at various depths.
▸ You can also insert leaves/postable nodes at various levels.
▸ You can insert text nodes under characteristic nodes and, in general, combine text nodes and characteristic nodes freely.

However, some configurations do not provide a meaningful result. Therefore, each hierarchy branch should have at least one postable node on the lowest level if only nonpostable nodes are above it. Otherwise, assigning a value to this branch is not possible.

In the examples discussed previously, the postable nodes were added to the hierarchy structure as individual characteristic values. As a result, any new characteristic value added at a later time is not yet assigned to the hierarchy. In reporting, the values posted to the relevant characteristic value would be displayed under NOT ASSIGNED until the hierarchy is maintained. The characteristic node must be added to an appropriate place in the hierarchy. However, instead of a single value, you can also define hierarchy intervals (see Figure 4.5). This is particularly useful in conjunction with characteristic keys, which are organized into number ranges. Instead of a hierarchy node that describes a single value, a hierarchy interval node is inserted. If characteristic values are added later, the system will automatically display the posted values in an appropriate place.

Hierarchy intervals

On the HIERARCHY tab in InfoObject maintenance (see Figure 4.4), you can specify settings for hierarchy versions and for the time dependency of the hierarchy or its nodes. These settings are valid for all hierarchies that you create for an InfoObject.

You can create multiple hierarchies for an InfoObject (see Figure 4.19), even if version dependency has not been configured.

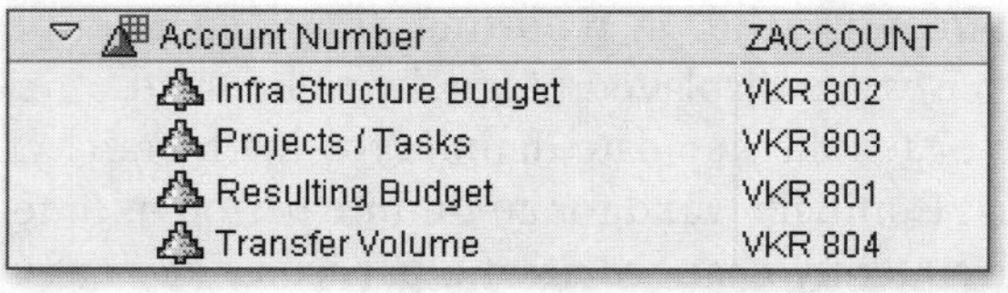

Hierarchy versions

▽ ⬛ Account Number	ZACCOUNT
⬠ Infra Structure Budget	VKR 802
⬠ Projects / Tasks	VKR 803
⬠ Resulting Budget	VKR 801
⬠ Transfer Volume	VKR 804

Figure 4.19   Several Alternative Hierarchies for an InfoObject

Each hierarchy has a unique name. Therefore, you cannot create a second hierarchy of the same name. However, you can use version dependency to ensure that you can create several versions for each hierarchy. In this case, the technical names of the hierarchies are identical, so the hierarchies are distinguished by their versions.

For hierarchies, there may also be a need to display different hierarchies/ hierarchy structures on different evaluation key dates. Two time dependency variants exist for hierarchies, namely time dependency for the entire hierarchy and time dependency for the hierarchy structure.

Time dependency

Entire hierarchy is
time-dependent

If the entire hierarchy is time-dependent, you must specify a validity interval (valid from, valid to) when you create the hierarchy (see Figure 4.20).

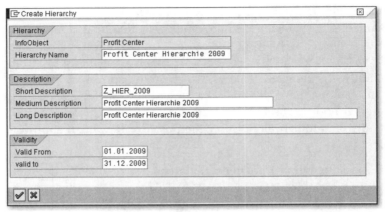

Figure 4.20 Creating a Hierarchy with the Entire Hierarchy is Time-Dependent Property

You can also create several hierarchies of the same name, but the validity intervals must not overlap with each other. However, there may be periods in which no hierarchy is valid. In reporting, time dependency for the entire hierarchy causes the displayed hierarchy to be valid for a particular query key date or for the key date defined for the hierarchy. In practice, a hierarchy that is initially valid for an infinite period of time (December 31, 9999) is frequently changed as of a particular key date. If the new hierarchy is not completely different to the old hierarchy, it may be useful to create the new hierarchy as a copy of the old hierarchy. You can specify a new validity interval for the copied hierarchy and then make the necessary adjustments. Do not forget to delimit the old hierarchy before you copy it. To do this, follow the GOTO • HEADER DATA menu path, and close the validity period in the VALID TO field. In principle, however, you can define completely different hierarchies for each key date.

Time-dependent
hierarchy structure

If the basic structure of the hierarchy is retained, and if only minor changes are made to the hierarchy over time, you should choose a time-dependent hierarchy structure. In such cases, each individual hierarchy node has its own validity interval. Therefore, in reporting, only nodes that are valid on a query or hierarchy key date are displayed within the hierarchy.

One interesting option in conjunction with time-dependent hierarchy structures is the use of temporal hierarchy joins. In reporting, this join lets you display the relevant hierarchy structure for a time interval. Therefore, the display is not restricted to one key date because all nodes that are or were valid during the time interval (at least for a short period) are displayed. If, for example, an organizational hierarchy changes and the report does not use temporal hierarchy joins, you must decide whether you want to display the hierarchy at the start, end, or at any other time during the period under consideration. Accordingly, a hierarchy is displayed before or after the structural change. However, this may be inadequate for a report whose transaction data refers to a period. A temporal hierarchy join can help here as it lets you display a suitable hierarchy for the entire reference period. Therefore, both the transaction data that refers to the hierarchy's old structure and the transaction data that refers to the hierarchy's new structure are assigned accordingly. If you want to use a temporal hierarchy join, you must specify not only the setting on the HIERARCHY tab for the InfoObject but also a key date derivation type, which you then configure in the report (see Figure 4.21).

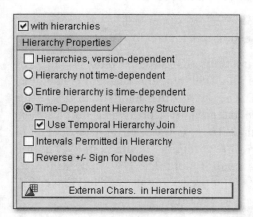

Figure 4.21 InfoObject Setting for Using the Temporal Hierarchy Join

Please note that you may need to delete existing hierarchies when you subsequently change the hierarchy settings for the InfoObject. This is the case, for example, if you have to change from ENTIRE HIERARCHY IS TIME-DEPENDENT to TIME-DEPENDENT HIERARCHY STRUCTURE. Because the hierarchy property is defined centrally for the InfoObject, you must choose a value.

As is the case with attributes and texts, the hierarchies are available for all referencing InfoObjects. They are always created and maintained for the referencing characteristic. For example, customer hierarchies are created for the InfoObject 0CUSTOMER and automatically available in all business partner reference objects (sold-to party, vendor, and so on).

4.3   DSOs

The InfoObjects discussed in Section 4.1 are the building blocks for creating various InfoProviders in SAP NetWeaver BW. The same applies to creating DSOs. DSOs describe a flat data structure that comprises InfoObjects. This is comparable with a database table that contains various fields. However, depending on the DSO type, the system may generate several tables to provide the functions associated with that particular DataStore type.

The following DataStore types are available:

▶ Standard DSO (see Section 4.3.1, Creating DSOs)

▶ Write-optimized DSO (see Section 4.3.3, Write-Optimized DSO)

▶ DSO for direct update (see Section 4.3.4, DSO for Direct Update)

Standard DSOs have special functions that support data staging. For example, a standard DSO is the only DSO type that lets you create delta information. Write-optimized DSOs, on the other hand, do not have this function. Therefore, data can be loaded more quickly. The simplest type of DSO is a DSO for direct update. Here, you can write data directly to the DSO (for example, using an ABAP program) in the same way as you can write data directly to a transparent table. The DSO makes the data available to reporting or other further processing in SAP NetWeaver BW (directly and without any further activation).

Sections 4.3.2 to 4.3.4 will describe each of the DSO types in more detail while the next section, Section 4.3.1, will provide an overview of how to create DSOs.

4.3.1 Creating DSOs

You create a new DSO by navigating to the INFOPROVIDER view in the Data Warehousing Workbench, right-clicking the InfoArea under which you want to create the new object, and selecting CREATE DSO from the context menu. You will now see the dialog box shown in Figure 4.22. Here, select a technical name ❶ and descriptive name ❷ for your DSO. If you want to use an existing DSO as a template, you can specify it under ❸. Then choose CREATE ❹ to switch to the view in which you can edit the structure of the DSO (shown in Figure 4.23). Here, you can add InfoObjects to the DSO structure and specify additional settings for the DSO.

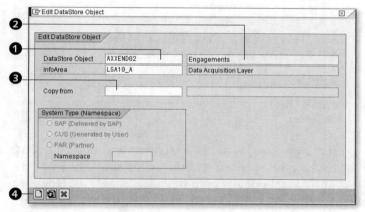

Figure 4.22 Dialog Box for Creating a DSO

When you create a new DSO, it does not contain any InfoObjects. You must now define a suitable key for the new DSO and, if necessary, add more data fields (see Figure 4.23).

Adding InfoObjects

If you know the technical name of the InfoObject you want to add, you can enter it directly by selecting the INFOOBJECT DIRECT INPUT menu option in the context menu for the key fields ❶ or data fields ❷. In the list input that now opens, you can also easily copy, for example, lists of InfoObjects from specification documents, so that you do not have to select the InfoObjects individually. Alternatively, you can also select the InfoObjects from a characteristics catalog ❸. As an alternative to the characteristics catalog, you can also access InfoSources and other Info-Providers, and then transfer the InfoObjects that they contain.

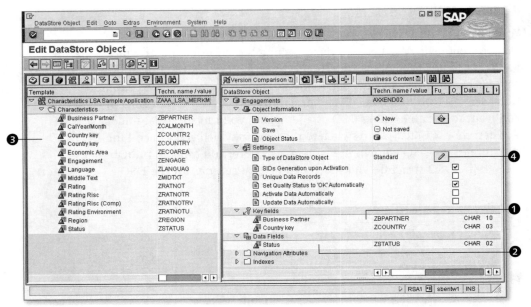

Figure 4.23 Editing a DSO

Specifying settings

Depending on the purpose of your modeling, you can select the DSO type under SETTINGS and then select additional options. When you create a new DSO, the system initially proposes a standard DSO. However, you can subsequently select another type. To do this, access the tree view of the DSO in EDIT mode and select the pencil button, which is used to edit the DSO type ❹. In the next dialog box, determine which DSO type you need (see Figure 4.24).

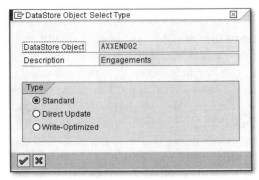

Figure 4.24 Selecting a DSO Type

Under SETTINGS, you can also specify the following additional settings:

▶ If you deactivate SIDs GENERATION UPON ACTIVATION, you can load data more quickly. However, the system's reporting performance may suffer because the SID values have to be regenerated at query runtime.

▶ The UNIQUE DATA RECORDS setting can improve performance (data activation). However, this setting is only useful if all newly loaded data has a new key combination.

▶ SET QUALITY STATUS to 'OK' AUTOMATICALLY, ACTIVATE DATA AUTOMATICALLY, and UPDATE DATA AUTOMATICALLY are load control settings, but they are only relevant in conjunction with the old 3.x loading procedure with InfoPackages. Replicate the corresponding functions under 7.x in process chains.

4.3.2 Standard DSO

As shown in Section 4.3.1, DSOs are created in the context menu of an InfoArea. Once you have created the relevant DSO, it must be filled with content, that is, you must add InfoObjects. During modeling, a distinction is made between a data part and a key part.

When you define the key, consider the requirements of the entity to be mapped. The key describes the characteristic/InfoObject combination that uniquely identifies a data record to be mapped. You can use a maximum of 16 characteristic InfoObjects to create the key.

Key fields

All of the characteristic InfoObjects that are not relevant for the key are added to the data fields. Furthermore, key figures can only be added as data fields. If you load data into a standard DSO, additional data records are only added if a new key combination is loaded. However, loading a record with the same key causes the system to overwrite or aggregate the content. Alphanumeric data fields are always overwritten here. In the case of numeric fields, the key figure setting determines whether the content will be aggregated or overwritten.

Data fields

A standard DSO does not comprise just one table. Instead, the system generates one table for active data, that is, for the data currently available to reporting, one table for newly added data, which is first transferred to active data when it is activated, and the change log.

New data, active data

Activation queue Standard DSOs not only enable you to transfer changes from new data into active data, they also enable you to create delta information by comparing the old and new content. In the context of data activation, the new data is also frequently known as the activation queue.

Figure 4.25 shows the individual substeps involved in loading data into a standard DSO. Data can be loaded in parallel from various sources ❶. Therefore, various delta processes can be used in parallel. The activation queue (new data) stores the data to be activated ❷. During the activation process, change log information is generated ❹ and, if SID generation is active in the DSO settings, SID values are also created for all new characteristic values ❺. Furthermore, the active data itself is also adjusted accordingly ❸. You can use the change log to source additional InfoProviders with delta information ❻. To do this, you must define a transformation that uses the standard DSO as its source. Once the data is activated, it is deleted from the new data.

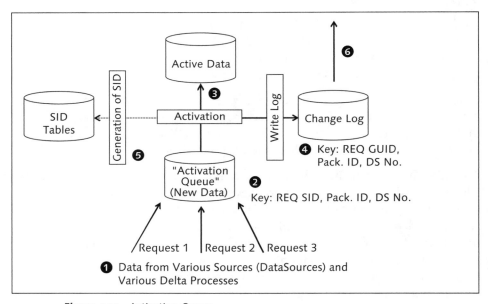

Figure 4.25 Activation Queue

The key for the activation queue (new data) bears the SID of the request number and the package ID in the key. This ensures that the activation process can run in parallel, without changing the sequence in which the changes occur.

When you define a DSO, you specify which InfoObjects describe the key. The key has a substantial effect on how the DSO behaves when you load data. Let's assume that you load data that describes the color and quantity of a material sold. If you do not add the color to the key, the COLOR field is updated (overwritten) when you load a data record that has the same material number but a different color. Figure 4.26 shows this behavior for the material numbered 2.

Significance of the key

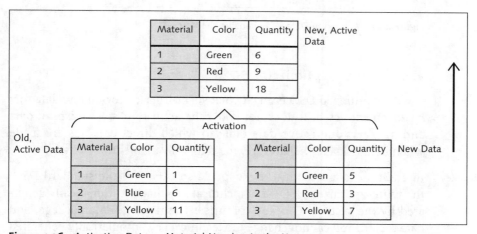

Figure 4.26 Activating Data — Material Number in the Key

If you want to store the various attributes of an InfoObject (master data of an InfoObject) in a DSO, this generally means that you want to overwrite the attributes. In the case of time-dependent master data, you must also add a date (usually the valid-to date) to the key to map various validity periods. Figure 4.27 shows the behavior associated with activating data if the color is also modeled as part of the key. In this case, another data record is transferred to the active data and the color blue is not overwritten.

The various delta processes that a DSO can process are described in Chapter 7, Section 7.2, Defining Inbound Interfaces.

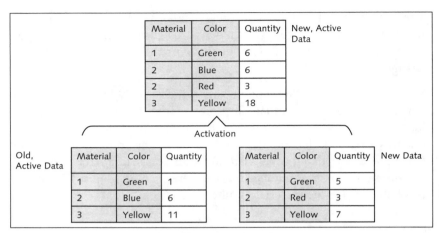

Figure 4.27 Activating Data — Enhancing the Key

4.3.3 Write-Optimized DSO

A write-optimized DSO is a DSO that specializes in storing raw data that has been extracted. It does not know the activation mechanism of data and only has one active data table to which direct postings are made when data is loaded. Therefore, the data is available immediately.

Technical key
In addition to a semantic key, which also exists for the standard DSO, the write-optimized DSO has a technical key that is automatically generated by the system. This key comprises the request, data package, and data record. You cannot change the technical key automatically generated by the system. This prevents the data records from being overwritten by subsequent data records. In addition, the write-optimized DSO has a semantic key, which is also used by standard DSOs. For this semantic key, the system automatically generates a unique secondary index that prevents you from being able to load the same key value twice. You can deactivate this check by selecting the NO CHECK ON UNIQUENESS OF DATA option. In this case, you can repeat the check in a downstream loading step, if required (for example, when loading data into a standard DSO).

Even though the write-optimized DSO does not know any delta mechanism, it can transfer delta data records from the source to a downstream DSO. You must add the field 0RECORDMODE to the write-optimized DSO. This field is used to transfer delta information.

Write-optimized DSOs are primarily used in conjunction with pass-through scenarios. Because there is no activation time, the data can be quickly "loaded through." Because the write-optimized DSO is fully integrated into the data flow and enables you to archive data, it has specific advantages over the DSO for direct update and over PSA tables. Furthermore, write-optimized DSOs fully and accurately map the change history. This is an important criterion in some analysis contexts. However, in such contexts, always remember that the use of write-optimized DSOs may increase the volume of data in the system. You should therefore only use write-optimized DSOs in justified exceptional cases.

Pass-through

4.3.4 DSO for Direct Update

Unlike standard DSOs and write-optimized DSOs, DSOs for direct update are not fully integrated into the data flow. Even though you can use DSOs for direct update as a source in the data flow, they require a user-defined ABAP routine, a predefined function module, or the Analysis Process Designer (APD) to update them.

APD

The APD is an application for creating and executing analysis processes. It primarily accesses staged data already contained in InfoProviders. Here, you can deploy analysis methods such as regression analysis, the decision tree, and cluster analysis. Data can be read and then written back into InfoObjects and DSOs.

[«]

Data activation is not necessary in a DSO for direct update. The data is written directly to the active data table, which means that it is also immediately available to reporting. DSOs for direct update also have a semantic key, which the system checks when updating the data.

DSOs for direct update are the only DSOs suitable for generating or changing data via a (user-defined) ABAP program. When developing your own programs, you can access the following Remote Function Call (RFC)–enabled function modules, which have lock management and can be called across different systems:

Function modules

- RSDI_ODSO_INSERT_RFC
- RSDI_ODSO_UPDATE_RFC
- RSDI_ODSO_MODIFY_RFC
- RSDI_ODSO_DELETE_RFC

As their names suggest, you can use these function modules to insert, update, modify, and delete data.

4.3.5   Summary Comparison of DSOs

DSOs are highly flexible. They are primarily used to store transaction data. However, they can also be used to store master data when performing a flexible master data update into DSOs.

Even though their structure is not optimized for analysis purposes, you can use DSOs to create reports. However, you should only do this if, due to the low volume of data, you do not expect to experience long runtimes or if you want to perform a one-time evaluation. In the case of recurring evaluations that will be made available to a large user group, you should always transfer the data into InfoCubes.

Areas of application for DSOs

In particular, you use DSOs when:

- You want to store data in close proximity to the source system
- You want to cleanse and consolidate data in several steps
- You need to store results temporarily
- You want to store data for later use (if possible, in a nonspecific manner)

In addition to providing access via reports (and the disadvantages cited earlier), DSOs are also frequently used in conjunction with analysis processes (for example, in the APD). Both read and write access is possible here. However, the characteristics of these analyses differ from those for reporting to a wide user group in that you do not necessarily have to provide a special analysis dataset.

Unlike InfoCubes, DSOs have a simple structure, which facilitates easy access via an ABAP program. In the context of data updates, DSOs are suitable for storing reference values, among other things. They can easily be read this way. A program can be used to fill DSOs for direct update with data. Such data can then be written directly to the active data table.

In Chapter 7, Modeling the Enterprise Data Warehouse, and in the first case study in Chapter 9, Case Studies, we will discuss the use of DSOs when modeling the various layers in the Layered, Scalable Architecture (LSA) (see Chapter 5, Reference Architecture for Data Modeling).

In the next section, we will take a look at InfoCubes, which are the focal point of data retention in the Data Warehouse because they represent the actual basis for reporting. Furthermore, the quality of their implementation heavily influences the extent to which the Data Warehouse will achieve acceptance.

4.4 InfoCubes

OLTP/OLAP

Decision support systems require a data basis for their analytical functions. If a database forms the basis for a business administrative system (such as SAP ERP), its design features are different and, due to its structure, it is an unsuitable basis for decision support systems. Business administrative systems are known as Online Transaction Processing (OLTP) systems, because they are designed to provide optimum support to business transactions. In contrast, the Data Warehouse has the task of creating a data basis for decision support systems and processes. Various applications, ranging from simple standard reports and online analyses to special analyses and data mining evaluations, are provided on this data basis. Online analysis, in particular, places high demands on the data model because it requires the system's response time behavior to be such that smooth data navigation is possible even if the data is highly aggregated or a large volume of data needs to be accessed. In contrast to OLTP, systems or tools used to perform online analyses are known as OLAP systems (see Chapter 3, Overview of SAP NetWeaver BW and SAP BusinessObjects). Furthermore, the technology used to support the analysis of BW data is known as OLAP technology.

OLAP server

The OLAP server is a component of the BW server. It mediates between the end user and the database by making multidimensional, staged data available to front-end tools (both BW and third-party front-end tools). If possible, the data is stored in the main memory and read from the database, if required.

The purpose of OLAP is to grant the user high-performance access to data in such a way that he can explore the data and then drill down or filter it "on the fly."

Data cube
Only the InfoCube data model is optimized in terms of high-performance reading of large volumes of (transaction) data. Therefore, this model is extremely significant for data modeling in the Reporting Layer (see Chapter 8, Data Modeling in the Reporting Layer). The term InfoCube (data cube) has established itself as a metaphor for OLAP-compatible datasets. The cube symbolizes the ability to obtain different views of the same dataset by taking account of different characteristics/dimensions and then analyzing the model's key figures.

In the next section, we will describe an InfoCube implementation and explain the steps involved in InfoCube modeling.

4.4.1 Physical Data Model

Star schema
The special needs of an OLAP system require special modeling for data retention. Star schema modeling is a classic way to implement an OLAP-enabled data model in a relational database. Here, descriptive tables are arranged in a star formation around a central fact table. The fact table describes the key figures and their direct assignment to all essential entities while the dimension tables describe these entities in greater detail and provide additional information. Because the fact table describes the actual business transactions and the dimension tables only provide explanatory information, the fact table has considerably more entries than the dimension tables. A high-performance data query can be achieved here because the query's selection criteria make it possible to preselect the relevant entity key values on the small database tables (dimension tables). Therefore, they are joined to the large fact table for relevant data records only. This advantage is lost if, due to unsuitable modeling, one or more dimension tables become larger than the fact table. All in all, a star schema is suitable when modeling data that will have high-performance read access. Due to the high level of denormalization, the data model is unsuitable for systems that have frequent change transactions (OLTP systems).

Enhanced star schema
In BW, the system also maps InfoCubes to a relational table schema. However, a pure star schema is not used here. SAP describes the type of modeling implemented here as an enhanced star schema. The star schema is enhanced in the sense that the dimension tables themselves do not contain the master data information. Instead, this information is stored in separate tables known as master data tables.

4.4.2 Modeling an InfoCube

Just like all other InfoProvider types, you can create InfoCubes in the
context menu of the InfoArea to which you want to assign the Info-
Cube. You can enter the technical name ❶ and descriptive name ❷ of the
InfoCube in the dialog box shown in Figure 4.28. If you want to create
an InfoCube that is very similar to an existing InfoCube, you can use a
template to create the new InfoCube ❸. Furthermore, you can choose ❹
between a standard InfoCube (for reporting) and a real-time InfoCube
(for planning applications, see Chapter 10, Data Modeling for Planning
Applications). Create all of the InfoCubes that you want to use in reporting as standard InfoCubes because planning InfoCubes do not provide
high-performance support to reporting (different data indexing).

Creating an
InfoCube

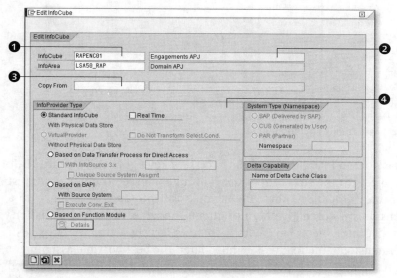

Figure 4.28 Dialog Box for Creating an InfoCube

The other InfoCube types BASED ON DATA TRANSFER PROCESS FOR DIRECT
ACCESS, BASED ON BAPI, and BASED ON FUNCTION MODULE are special
cases in which the InfoCube is not physically used as a data store, but
rather a program logic makes the data available (for more information,
see Section 4.5.1, Direct Access with Virtual Providers).

Virtual
InfoProviders

If you select an InfoCube as a template, both the properties and the structure of the template are transferred. However, if you do not use a template to create a new InfoCube, it is empty at first, that is, it does not yet have any content that is based on key figures and characteristics (see ❶ in Figure 4.29).

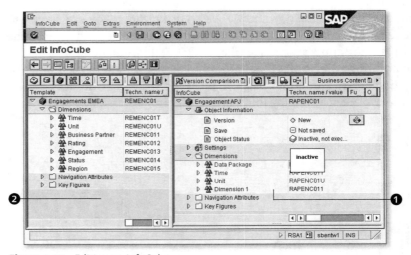

Figure 4.29 Editing an InfoCube

Modeling
The task of modeling is to add the necessary key figure and characteristic InfoObjects to the structure of the InfoCube. Please note that you must group the InfoObjects into dimensions. All InfoObjects assigned to a dimension are stored together in a dimension table. Because the relationships that InfoObjects have with each other largely determine the size of the dimension table that will be filled later, the best possible assignment is instrumental in the performance of the data model (see the detailed description in Chapter 8, Section 8.2.1, Modeling).

Adding InfoObjects
In principle, there are two ways to add InfoObjects to dimensions during InfoCube modeling. If you know the technical names of the InfoObjects, you can call INFOOBJECT DIRECT INPUT in the context menu for the relevant dimension. In the list input, you can enter one or more technical names of InfoObjects directly or you can select them from this entire list. Alternatively, you can select a view of an InfoObject catalog, InfoSource, or another InfoProvider in the template area ❷ and, from there, select

the InfoObjects that you need for the InfoCube definition. You drag and drop to transfer the data.

InfoCubes provide high-performance support to data queries. The first step here is modeling in the form of an enhanced star schema and automatic indexing of the corresponding tables. However, you should avail of the following options for designing a higher-performance cube:

Queries/higher-performance InfoCube design

► Modeling small dimension tables (see Chapter 8, Section 8.2.1)

► Creating aggregates (see Chapter 8, Section 8.2.2, Aggregates)

► Compression (see Chapter 8, Section 8.2.3, Compression)

► Partitioning (see Chapter 8, Section 8.2.4, Partitioning)

► Suitable parameterization of the OLAP cache (see Chapter 8, Section 8.2.5, OLAP Cache)

► Use of the Business Warehouse Accelerator (BWA), if necessary (see Chapter 8, Section 8.2.6, SAP NetWeaver BWA)

Queries are not defined directly on InfoCubes. As we will show in Chapter 8, Section 8.4, Virtual Layer, it is useful to build the queries exclusively on a Virtual Layer, that is, on a layer that cannot store any data itself and only defines views of the dataset.

Even if you want the data to be available in real time, that is, immediately after you post a business transaction, there may not be time to create a physical dataset for reporting. In the next section, we will discuss this issue and the specialized InfoProviders or mechanisms you can use.

4.5   Providers for Real-Time Data Access

Up-to-date data is required for certain decision processes that are generally of a tactical nature. In this context, you tend to require small, up-to-date datasets rather than a comprehensive data history.

In principle, you can also load a "normal" InfoProvider (DSO or Info-Cube) at short intervals. Furthermore, you can automate the staging process and repeat it on short notice. This procedure may still be manageable for daily loads, for example. However, if shorter intervals are required and if, in the case of real-time data access, the data must be made available in the shortest possible time (for example, load processes that may have to take place every minute), this is not feasible because:

- For the most part, the necessary extraction and processing times of nonscheduled extractors and transformations are higher than what could be realized by the necessary loading frequency.

- In the case of very short loading cycles, the BW system would generate a large overhead in terms of log entries. This would complicate system administration considerably and also give rise to a data volume issue with the log entries.

- The administrator would no longer be able to handle the number of requests to DataProviders.

If you need to access data in (almost) real time, various alternative modeling options are available to you. One option is to use special InfoProviders, known as VirtualProviders, to achieve direct access to source system data (see Section 4.5.1). This turns all thoughts of a Data Warehouse upside down because the data is analyzed directly in the source system, in other words, it is not transferred to the BW system.

Another option is the concept of Real-time Data Acquisition (RDA), which was introduced in BW 7.0 (see Section 4.5.2, Real-Time Data Acquisition). Here, a special mechanism is used to transfer the data to the BW system and then make the data available to reporting in the form of "normal" InfoProviders.

4.5.1 Direct Access with VirtualProviders

VirtualProviders are special types of InfoProviders. From a Query Designer perspective, there is no distinction between them and the "normal" InfoProviders that contain data. However, if you execute a query, the source system data is accessed directly and any additional master data you require is read in the BW system.

Transaction data/ master data — You can use VirtualProviders for transaction data and master data. For transaction data, you create a special InfoCube. Two of the following alternative implementations are usually used to facilitate direct access to source system data (see Figure 4.30):

- VirtualProviders with a staging connection

- VirtualProviders with a Business Application Programming Interface (BAPI)

- VirtualProviders based on a function module (service InfoCube)

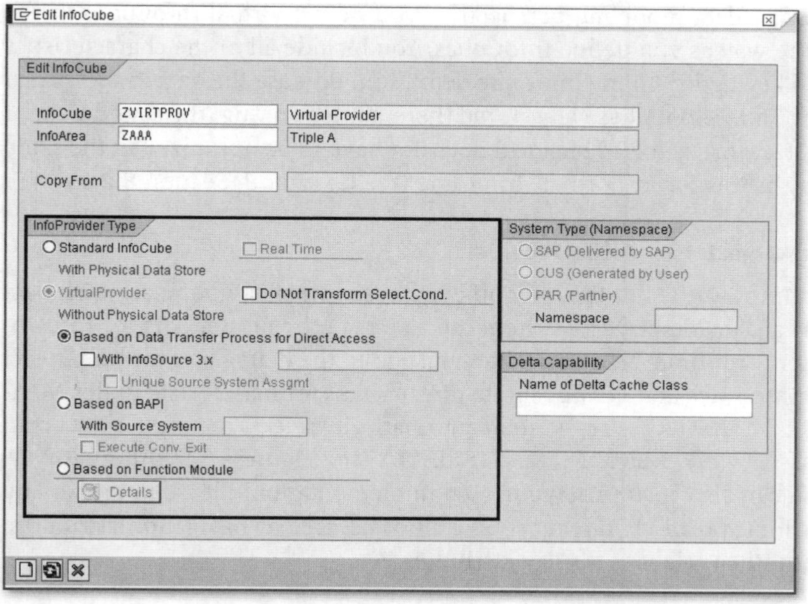

Figure 4.30 Defining VirtualProviders (InfoCubes)

VirtualProvider (InfoCube) with a Staging Connection

In the case of virtual InfoCubes with a staging connection, the transaction data is queried at query runtime. The data (characteristics and key figures) is read directly from the DataSource in the source system. As is the case with "normal" InfoCubes, the master data of the characteristics is read from the physical master data tables stored in the BW system.

Not every DataSource is suitable for defining a virtual InfoCube. For example, many of the DataSources that have a delta process are unsuitable for connections to VirtualProviders. The SAPIDIRECT adapter is used to read the DataSource to be connected, which must be defined accordingly in BW.

DataSource

The BW system can use transformations to process the data supplied by the DataSource. If errors occur during the data transfer, any data that contains errors is filtered out without the system issuing any error messages. Therefore, a certain risk is associated with interpreting such reporting data. You can use multiple DataSources to connect multiple sources to virtual InfoCubes.

Transformation

Data model

From a data modeling perspective, you define virtual InfoCubes in the same way as you define InfoCubes. You include all of the characteristics and key figures in the InfoCube definition. Because the data in the virtual InfoCube is not physically stored there, dimensioning (the assignment of characteristics to dimensions) does not have to be optimized in the same way as it is for a "normal" InfoCube (see Chapter 8, Section 8.2.1).

InfoObject as a VirtualProvider

Virtual master data access

An InfoCube is not the only object that a system can populate with data (via a DataSource). The system can also read the master data for InfoObjects at runtime. To do this, you must go to the dialog box for InfoObject maintenance and define remote direct access for master data under MASTER DATA/TEXTS. The system automatically selects the master data read class CL_RSR_REMOTE_MASTERDATA (see Figure 4.31). Alternatively, you can also customize your own implementation. Please note that any attributes read via direct access cannot be used as navigation attributes, but rather solely as display attributes.

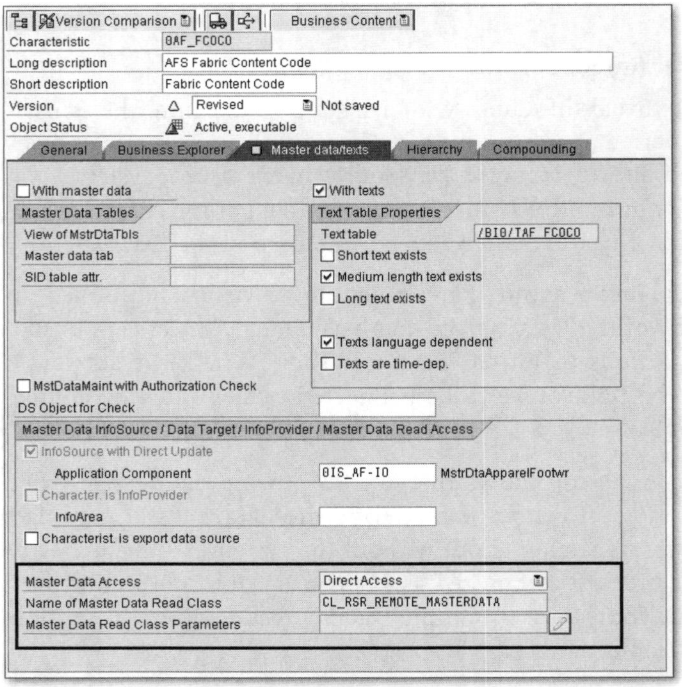

Figure 4.31 Defining Direct Master Data Access

VirtualProvider (InfoCube) with BAPI

This type of InfoCube does not contain any data itself. Unlike a virtual InfoCube with a staging connection, the data at query runtime is not read using a DataSource, but using a BAPI (BAPIs are standardized methods for SAP BusinessObjects, that is, they are ultimately programs), thus making it possible to connect third-party source systems (for example, market data databases). A data transformation is no longer possible here. Therefore, a BAPI must supply the data in the required form.

In the case of virtual InfoCubes with a BAPI, the InfoCube is, once again, created in the same way as when you define a "normal" InfoCube. Furthermore, the distribution of characteristics to dimensions does not need to be optimized.

**VirtualProvider (InfoCube) Based on a
Function Module (Service InfoCube)**

Similar to virtual InfoCubes with BAPIs, service InfoCubes enable you to implement the retrieval of transaction data for an InfoCube based on a function module. The implementation that occurs is independent of extraction and staging, and it is particularly useful if the analysis requirements are so specific that they cannot be implemented using BW system resources alone (transformation, InfoCube, exception aggregation, and report logic).

In the case of virtual InfoCubes based on a function module, the virtual InfoCube is, once again, created in the same way as when you define a "normal" InfoCube. Furthermore, the distribution of characteristics to dimensions does not need to be optimized.

4.5.2   RDA

RDA is a new toolkit that was introduced with BW 7.0. RDA makes it possible to provide operational data in the BW system in (almost) real time (real-time data procurement). The data is loaded into BW at regular intervals (even during the day) and made available there in a DSO.

RDA provides new design options for operational/tactical reporting. The dividing line that clearly existed previously (whereby operational reporting occurs in SAP ERP and analyses are made available in BW) no longer exists. Reports can now also be made available in the BW system as soon as they are posted. Because the time delay associated with RDA is less than one minute, SAP recommends that you use it if you require up-to-date data several times a day, that is, every hour or every minute.

RDA can be implemented in SAP source systems (ERP and BW). In this case, the connection is established using a real-time-capable DataSource (via the BW service Application Programming Interface (API)). Other source systems can be connected via a Web service (known as the push procedure).

SAP source systems

The DataSources provided for a real-time connection to the BW system must be marked as real-time-capable. SAP has already made this classification for any Content DataSources supplied by SAP. A source system that can deliver the relevant delta queue in real time is a prerequisite for real-time-capable DataSources. In the case of generic DataSources, you must check and configure these properties yourself if you want to use them in a real-time scenario.

Many of the steps associated with establishing a real-time connection are comparable with normal delta extraction. For example, you must initialize the delta process first and then be able to execute delta load processes periodically.

DataSource for RDA

Using a DataSource for RDA is just one possibility. The DataSource can also be used for traditional delta extraction. You must therefore set the adapter in the DataSource to REAL-TIME EXTRACTION FROM AN SAP SYSTEM, so that you can no longer simultaneously use the DataSource for traditional delta extraction.

RDA load control

In addition to the DataSource for RDA, you need an InfoPackage that supports RDA, so that you can control the extraction. However, you can only create the InfoPackage if you have already initialized the delta process and created a data transfer process (DTP) (of the type DTP FOR REAL-TIME DATA ACQUISITION). Once you have initialized the delta process, a background job (daemon) takes over the load control (execution of the InfoPackage and DTP for RDA). Figure 4.32 illustrates the functionality.

The daemon retrieves the data from the delta queue in the source system at regular intervals ❶ and makes it directly available in the active data (and change log) of the DSO ❷. You therefore no longer need to activate the data because it is immediately available to reporting.

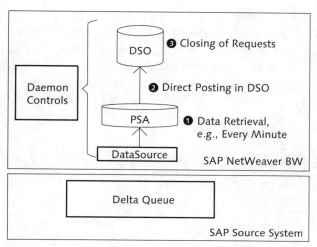

Figure 4.32 Process Steps Controlled by the Daemon

When the threshold value is reached (number of data records or the time interval), the daemon must close all open requests (for PSA, DTP, and the change log) and make the subsequently loaded data available in new requests. This decouples the number of data transfers from the number of requests available in the DSO ❸. Therefore, the number of data transfers remains manageable.

The data provided in the DSO in real time is immediately available to reporting. If the data is used to answer operational/tactical questions, and if the data volume is restricted, it is generally acceptable to store the data in a non-query-optimized DSO. In the introduction to the LSA in Chapter 5, we will see that a specialized Data Warehouse Layer, known as the Operational DataStore Layer, is used to provide such data.

DSO layer

However, if you want to integrate the data provided via RDA into analytical reporting, you need to enhance the analysis data model. Please note that only a small part of the data required for a query is stored in a DSO (for example, 1%) and the rest of the data (for example, 99%), which possibly has the same structure, is stored in query-optimized form. InfoCubes are particularly useful here. Aggregates or, better still, a BWA index should be used to optimize access. Because the transactional delta provided via RDA cannot be provided in an InfoCube in real time (and in the BWA index, for example), you would need at least one additional MultiProvider for cross-data reporting and a mechanism for transferring

Hybrid Provider

data from the DSO to the InfoCube. A new DataProvider type, known as the Hybrid Provider, is planned for future BW versions. It will combine write-optimized real-time datasets with read-optimized BWA datasets (see Figure 4.33). The concept is described in Plattner (2007, p. 34) as follows: "Hybrid Provider ensures actuality of information by combining data already stored in a read-optimized BWA store with the latest transactional delta from OLTP."

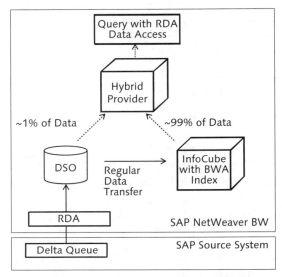

Figure 4.33 Using a Hybrid Provider for Integrated Access to RDA Data

This architecture will enable you to not only make RDA data available in isolated form for specific operational evaluations, but to integrate it seamlessly into analytical reporting.

4.6 Conclusion

BW provides a variety of different DataProviders and each form of data storage has a specific area of use.

DSOs are used for step-by-step data staging. Even though they store the data in a flat structure, they provide more functions than a simple table. Standard DSOs implement a mechanism for activating data and generating delta information. However, DSOs only rarely provide a suitable basis for reports.

InfoCubes are the basis for reporting. They store the data in a query-optimized form. In addition to InfoCubes that physically store data, you can use VirtualProviders, which describe a structure but do not retain any data. Do not confuse VirtualProviders with MultiProviders, which define an overall view of the dataset (see chapter 8, Section 8.4.1, MultiProvider in the Virtual Layer). In addition to the RDA mechanism, VirtualProviders let you access data in real time.

In BW, master data is the central pillar of the data model. It is therefore important to reconcile and harmonize data across all data models.

SAP's Layered, Scalable Architecture (LSA) is a reference architecture for Business Warehouse (BW) implementations. The LSA concept makes it possible to have a standardized procedure even when an implementation is oriented toward a particular target group or specific customer.

5 Reference Architecture for Data Modeling

In Chapter 4, Structure of a BW Data Model, we introduced you to various DataProviders, which are the building blocks of a BW data model and can be combined in a flexible manner to satisfy your requirements. The number of possible data model implementations is also correspondingly high, which prompts us to ask the following question: What are the criteria for a good data model?

The goals you wish to pursue are clear: You want to fully satisfy your current requirements and you want to implement a high-performance solution. All of this provides the basis for user acceptance of your BW implementation and, ultimately, its success.

Requirements are subject to continuous change: New content is added, certain topics become very important while others become less important, your enterprise is restructured, and so on. Your BW implementation will only be effective in the long term if it can adapt to ever-changing requirements. To this end, you must find an architecture that will grow with future requirements.

There are a number of accentuated approaches to modeling Data Warehouse solutions. Two important approaches are multidimensional modeling by Kimball (see Kimball, 2002) and the Corporate Information Factory (CIF) by Inmon (see Inmon, 2001). Rarely are the ideas contained in these approaches implemented in their purest form. In practice, the designs differ greatly and each one depends on the development history of the relevant implementation, along with the enterprise's ever-changing requirements.

SAP has designed its own data model, known as the LSA. This reference architecture is the culmination of SAP's many years of experience with large BW implementations.

In the next section, we will introduce you to the LSA and, in Section 5.2, Naming Conventions, we will discuss some naming conventions that are closely related to this architecture. Finally, in Section 5.3, Information Integration as a Prerequisite for Cross-Sectional Evaluations, we will discuss the fact that the architecture must ensure that the data is merged (integrated) efficiently, especially if a BW implementation has multiple source systems.

5.1   LSA

Layered, Scalable Architecture

SAP has developed a reference architecture known as the LSA, which considers the requirements of large Data Warehouse implementations (for example, the need for high system availability (24/7) and data retrieval in (almost) real time) while taking large volumes of data and an ever-changing environment into consideration. These underlying conditions require a high degree of standardization and automation in system development, maintenance, operation, and administration. In this section, you will see that the topics considered here are also important for smaller BW systems.

Because the LSA is a reference architecture, you must decide which topics are relevant for you. When making your decision, you must consider your environment, requirements, and preferences. The reference architecture helps you to think of absolutely everything, especially questions that, in our experience, only come to light when the system has been in operation for some time and has grown in size.

LSA landmark building blocks

The central building blocks of the LSA are known as landmark building blocks. They describe the following topics, which will fundamentally determine the architecture of your subsequent implementation, and upon which a decision must be made before you start the implementation.

- ▶ Layers and the data model
- ▶ Domains
- ▶ Data integration

You can also avail of the following assistant building blocks, which will enhance the aforementioned landmark building blocks:

LSA assistant building blocks

- Data quality processes
- BW landscape
- Extraction, Transformation, Load (ETL)
- Storage/archiving
- Organization and procedure
- Development/operating concepts

The assistant building blocks do not influence the architecture to the same extent as the topics covered by the landmark building blocks. However, you should still examine the importance of each of these topics for your BW implementation at an early stage.

In the following sections, we will take a detailed look at two fundamental topics, namely layer creation and domain creation. We will then discuss some of the topics covered by the LSA landmark building blocks.

First, let's consider how you can use the LSA specifications to achieve your own project specifications.

5.1.1   Procedure when Developing a Customer-Specific LSA

An LSA is not implemented directly on the basis of the SAP reference documentation. First, you must apply the SAP specifications to your own enterprise and project, state your preferences, and then use these to define your own derived standards. LSAs derived this way are known as customer LSAs (in contrast to SAP reference LSAs). You can interpret the SAP reference LSA as a best practice proposal. If you deliberate and evaluate all of the topics in the SAP reference LSA when you start to derive your own customer LSA, they will help you to consider, at a very early stage, some aspects of the architecture that may not cause problems until the system has been in operation for several years. Any necessary adjustments could then be extremely time-intensive and costly.

Customer LSA

If you are starting a BW implementation from scratch, the SAP reference LSA will afford you the opportunity to define standards from the outset. However, please remember that the initial stages of the implementation may involve a slightly greater effort because you will take the entire architecture into consideration. When deriving the customer LSA

Defining standards

standards, you must consider the topics from a broader perspective than would have been necessary if you were to implement known requirements. Furthermore, provisions must be made for services whose added value will not pay off until later.

Figure 5.1 shows the steps you should take when implementing an LSA. First of all, familiarize yourself with the architecture and the various topics to be considered. Then, learn about modeling alternatives and their consequences in terms of your own objectives. Finally, decide which parts of the architecture you want to deploy. Step by step, you will create a customer LSA that is a subset of the LSA reference architecture.

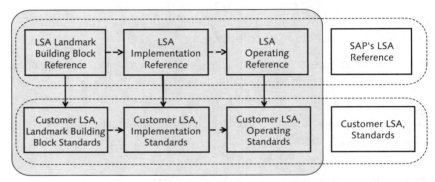

Figure 5.1 Deriving a Customer LSA from SAP Reference Specifications (Source: SAP NetWeaver RIG BI EMEA)

The layers and the services offered by the layers are at the very heart of this consideration. In the next section, we will describe the layer model.

5.1.2 Layer Model of the Reference Architecture

Each of the seven Data Warehouse layers described in the layer model undertakes certain tasks within a Data Warehouse architecture. In this context, each layer provides certain services that, in turn, can be used by other layers.

Reference/
customer LSA

The reference LSA describes the following layers (listed from bottom to top, that is, from data source to data target):

1. Data Acquisition Layer

2. Corporate Memory (Layer)

3. Quality and Harmonization Layer

4. Operational Data Store (Layer)

5. Data Propagation Layer

6. Business Transformation Layer

7. Reporting Layer (Architected Data Mart Layer)

8. Virtualization Layer (MultiProvider)

Figure 5.2 shows you how the individual layers are built upon each other. The gray layers belong to the Enterprise Data Warehouse (EDW) layers (see Chapter 7, Modeling the Enterprise Data Warehouse), which are characterized by the fact that they are modeled regardless of any particular analysis application and therefore create the most generally applicable view of the data. The lightly colored layers, on the other hand, are application-specific. They are also known as the Architected Data Mart (ADM) because any modeling that takes place here is based on special reporting and analysis requirements. The datasets are "constructed" (architected) using these requirements. Special modeling rules must be observed when modeling the Reporting Layer (which is the central layer of the ADM). In particular, query-optimized, easy-to-adjust data models are required here. Chapter 8, Data Modeling in the Reporting Layer, will provide information about data modeling in the Reporting Layer.

Distinction between EDW and ADM

If you consider the way in which data flows through the layers in Figure 5.2, some alternative paths are conceivable. The standard path is from the source system via the Data Acquisition Layer to the Data Propagation Layer ❶. In a second step ❷, the data is transferred to the Reporting Layer. The Quality and Harmonization Layer and the Business Transformation Layer are not skipped here. Rather, they are logical layers in which the data is processed, but not physically stored. Alternatively, the data can be loaded from the Data Acquisition Layer into the Corporate Memory, so that it is permanently stored there ❸. It must also be possible to transfer the data from the Corporate Memory back into the normal data flow ❹. However, if the data is transferred from the Data Acquisition Layer into the Operational Data Store Layer ❺, the data does not usually undergo further processing as part of the regular staging process. Instead, it is deleted again after a period of time.

Typical load processes

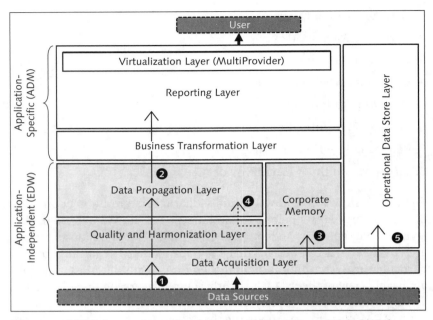

Figure 5.2 LSA Reference Layer Model (Source: SAP NetWeaver RIG BI EMEA)

Reference
architecture

Do not let the relatively high number of layers deter you from using the LSA. Physical data retention is not mandatory for all layers. The reference architecture introduces all of the relevant topics, but you will decide the number of layers to be implemented immediately or later, if necessary. The Quality and Harmonization Layer and the Business Transformation Layer, in particular, do not need to retain data. The same applies to the uppermost layer, known as the Virtualization Layer, which only defines one data view, but does not store any data itself.

In the following sections, we will take a closer look at the individual layers.

Data Acquisition Layer

The Data Acquisition Layer is the inbound layer for data in BW. This layer receives the data in its raw form, that is, exactly as it is supplied by the source system, and it stores the data until it undergoes further processing. The main goal of this procedure is high data throughput, so that the load processes take the least possible time.

If you are at the start of your BW project, you will not yet regard load process runtimes as an important criterion. You will primarily want high-performance reports and load processes that run overnight. However, the more your BW system grows and the more content and services that are provided, the more relevant this topic will become. This is especially true if your BW users are spread across various countries or even continents and, as a result, only a small window of time is available for load activities.

Please note that the Data Acquisition Layer is not intended for creating historical records. If this were the case, the data would have to be loaded via a DataStore Object (DSO) or Persistent Staging Area (PSA) object that stores a lot of data. However, it is exactly this large volume of data that would thwart the load process. It is also important to not only store the data in its raw form but to create a historical record for the data. However, this is the task of another layer, known as the Corporate Memory.

One of the goals of the Data Acquisition Layer, which, at first glance, appears to be harmful to performance, is to make the data available to the BW system in as comprehensive a manner as possible (enhanced inbound layer). In other words, when you implement the interface for the source system, you should add not only the fields that are needed to fulfill your current reporting requirement, but if possible, all of the fields that could be relevant in the foreseeable future. Frequently, however, this does not happen because it would generally take too much time to fully ascertain future information requirements or it would not be possible to adequately specify them. Alternatively, you can add all potentially relevant fields belonging to one extraction context (subject area). Rely on your gut instinct and, if in doubt, add too many rather than too few fields. You will now argue that a lean BW system that comprises only essential data and therefore performs better would be more useful here. However, we wish to show you that our approach will not unduly harm performance.

To benefit from the advantages associated with the enhanced inbound layer, you do not necessarily have to load the data into the upper layers. It is sufficient to enhance the Data Acquisition Layer and to record a history (history management) in the Corporate Memory.

History management is not of equal importance to every source system. Some source systems themselves can also supply historical data. In such cases, you do not lose any information. However, if the source system does not have this feature, history management is necessary in the BW system if you want to enhance data models retroactively and populate them with historical data.

Importance of the
Corporate Memory

If you follow the recommendation of not using the Data Acquisition Layer to record a history, the regular load process will not be adversely affected by any extra fields that you load. However, the use of the Corporate Memory Layer is a prerequisite here.

Data protection

If personal data, in particular, comes into play, your data protection officers will heavily criticize and maybe even forbid the notion of "transferring everything just in case we need it in the future." From an architecture perspective, however, some arguments favor a data transfer beyond the current reporting requirement. Authorizations are important in this context because you can use them to protect the Data Acquisition Layer or Corporate Memory against unauthorized access. Furthermore, the user should only be able to access the layer intended for report creation (Virtual Layer) and, once there, only view the data that he requires to fulfill his tasks. In particular, any areas with personal data, especially retention data, can also be protected in the backend. Here, choosing appropriate naming conventions is an important prerequisite for assigning customized authorizations (see Section 5.2).

Technical
implementation

When you implement a Data Acquisition Layer, you can use the PSA or write-optimized DSOs, for example. When you load data from the Data Acquisition Layer into higher levels, please note that you can improve load performance significantly by using parallel load processes. We will explain this in greater detail when we discuss domain creation in Section 5.1.3, Domains.

Corporate Memory (Layer)

Corporate Memory
in its raw form

The Corporate Memory is a separate layer in the LSA. It is used to permanently store data in the form in which it was loaded, thus creating a "Corporate Memory." Because the main data flow from the data source to the reports should have the best possible high-performance design, it makes sense not to implement this service by using the DataProviders that pass through here, but to provide this service in a separate layer.

The data does not undergo any special staging before it is stored in the Corporate Memory. The only useful exception here is the addition of the data origin (source system and, if necessary, the load time). You add this information in the Data Acquisition Layer and then transfer it to the Corporate Memory.

Why should you store the data persistently in its raw form? Is it not enough to "refine" the data and to permanently store the result? The answer to these questions is that this procedure can be perfectly adequate, but only if the derivation and calculation rules do not change in the long run. Most of the time, however, this is not the case because you want to create a BW architecture that you can also use in the future to respond to new requirements in a flexible manner. New requirements could mean, for example, that changes must be made to the harmonization, conversion, and calculation processes that run in the main load process. If a significant amount of processing is necessary (for example, the derivation of partial keys), and the data is no longer available to you in its original form, you can no longer rebuild the datasets in the upper levels. Frequently, the source system is unable to supply the data correctly and to have a history of this data. Without the Corporate Memory, you can only benefit from the changes as soon as they are implemented. Furthermore, remember that even if the source system could supply new data from past periods, the importance/quality of this data would generally differ to what the Corporate Memory could supply.

Importance of having a history

Importance of Having a History

In August, the following information was recorded in the ERP Human Resources (HR) system: Miss Mueller got married on June 03, 2008, and changed her name to Mrs. Meier. If you load your BW system at the end of each month, the dataset in the Corporate Memory will still show Miss Mueller for the month of June instead of Mrs. Meier. However, if you use a new extraction to rebuild the dataset, it will already show Mrs. Meier as being married in June, which is probably what you want in this case. However, depending on which source system is the basis for your reporting, and how important historical stability is to you, you may need to retain the history of the loaded data in the BW system. You may also need to comply with certain legal regulations.

Corporate Memory modeling is closely related to Data Acquisition Layer modeling. If the Data Acquisition Layer requires extensive modeling as a result of the aforementioned arguments, you must also model the Corporate Memory extensively. If you have built the Corporate Memory as

Reconciling modeling with the Data Acquisition Layer

a historically correct, secure basis for all relevant characteristic values, it is easy to retroactively add fields to the above layers and fill them, if required. Adding further characteristics and key figures to reporting is the most frequently requested enhancement (see Section 5.1.5, LSA and Flexibility when Making Changes).

External data storage

If the relational database underlying the BW system has a large volume of data, this tends to impact negatively on performance. In BW, you can deploy various techniques to reduce this volume. In the Corporate Memory Layer, in particular, it is possible to store the data externally in Nearline Storage (NLS) and to even archive it there. This way, the data does not "clog" the relational database, but can still be accessed at short notice.

Quality and Harmonization Layer

Improving data quality

The data that the source system supplies in its raw form is only suitable for analysis in limited circumstances. Generally, the data is initially staged in a Data Warehouse. However, this is not about changing data to obtain a special analysis view (this is the task of higher-level application-specific views) but about staging the data in such a way that it can be provided in the next level, the Data Propagation Layer, as integrated, uniform, and qualitative, high-quality data. Many processing steps can be involved here. The Data Propagation Layer is extremely important if you want to merge data from various source systems. It may be necessary to interpret new field content to achieve a common view. If necessary, mapping tables and lookup tables can be used to convert characteristic keys.

Using InfoSources for virtual modeling

Frequently, the Quality and Harmonization Layer does not need to physically retain the data. The technical options available in BW enable you to use InfoSources to create defined layer interfaces. Often, you can forgo the additional storage of data. The raw data is available to you in the source layer and the "refined" data is available in the target layer. Therefore, sufficient data is available, especially for the purposes of quality assurance. If anomalies arise when data is reconciled for the first time during productive operation, you can use debugging in a second step to check the layer logic and, if necessary, analyze the interim results.

Mapping tables and lookup tables

When you use the mapping tables and lookup tables, you should think about using validity information (history management). Unlike the interim results provided by the Quality and Harmonization Layer, you should immediately persistently store the content of these tables and create a historical record for the content because the set of rules for "refining" data may change during the lifecycle of a Data Warehouse.

The importance of the Quality and Harmonization Layer will vary depending on your project/enterprise and whether the data to be implemented is master data or transaction data. The transformation rules, the formula editor, and the option to program start/end routines and expert routines in ABAP are competent tools that will enable you to design a powerful Quality and Harmonization Layer. If they do not suffice, you can also use ETL tools such as SAP BusinessObjects Data Integrator.

Extraction, Transformation, Load (ETL)

Data Propagation Layer (Propagator)

Staged, harmonized, and consistent data is persistently stored in the Data Propagation Layer and available there for transfer/further processing. This means that this layer is not generally used directly in reporting. Instead, it forms the data basis for populating analytical applications/ADMs with data, thus making it possible to quickly build new or enhance existing analysis datasets on the basis of the data in the Data Propagation Layer. Both the existence and design of this layer have a significant influence on the success of the entire BW implementation.

The data provided in the Reporting Layer is sufficient from the perspective of the application. High-performance reporting can only be achieved if the data is limited to essential data only. User acceptance of the system suffers greatly if additional requirements cannot be fulfilled within a short period of time. Furthermore, without a broad Data Propagation Layer that includes a history, you will have to return, at the very least, to the Corporate Memory, possibly even to the source system to adjust the load processes. Because you will most likely have to specify and implement new harmonization rules, this is considered to be a "minor" project. Also, note the following: The more layers affected by a change, the more laborious the transport of modified objects via the system landscape (because it is particularly prone to errors).

Data basis for analysis datasets

An important topic associated with the Data Warehouse is the handling of master data that changes over time. To obtain a historically stable view, transaction data is enriched with master data. This can be done by populating an analysis dataset. However, this is not ideal. It is much better to prepare the Data Propagation Layer in such a way that the data is already enriched. When you build multiple datasets, reading at the

Enrichment via master data

analysis level does not have to occur repeatedly (and therefore potentially differently). Instead, it only occurs once when the data is written to the Propagator. The main benefit of this procedure is that you handle the analysis datasets in a more volatile manner and, if necessary, you can fully reload the dataset from the Propagator. If the data is not enriched until the analysis datasets are loaded, the master data history mapped to the transaction data is lost or you have to transfer it to a second dataset and reload it again, which is rather cumbersome. Even though the remodeling function (see Chapter 11, Optimizing Data Retention) makes things easier, it cannot always prevent you from having to create a new dataset, depending on the change to be made to the model.

Harmonizing delta processes

The DataPropagator is also the correct place to harmonize the delta process. You can only load Cubes if you have an additive delta. If different source systems supply different deltas, you can derive an additive delta in the Data Propagation Layer (by using standard DSOs).

Central location for reconciliation of requirements

The Propagator makes it easier to reconcile information technology (IT) with the user department. If you want to implement a new analytical application or a new ADM, the Propagator is the layer that you should use as the source. If data is missing despite generous modeling of the Propagator, you must reconcile the requirement with the Propagator. You do not necessarily have to discuss master data history management for every single project. This layer helps to give user departments responsibility (with certain limitations) for your data models (in the sense of an ADM) and, at the same time, it helps to centralize activities that would make sense to execute only once, that is, centrally (data procurement, harmonization, and history management), thus avoiding unnecessary redundancies.

DataSource-specific data storage

The Propagator is supposed to populate the Reporting Layer with data in an optimal manner. The fastest and most reliable way for the Propagator to do this is to store the data according to DataSource rather than merging it. Therefore, domain creation is also a relevant topic for the DataPropagator (see Section 5.1.3). This type of modeling ensures that, in the event of an error, the entire load process is not stopped and at least some of the data can be loaded into the Reporting Layers.

Benefit of Domain Creation in the Data Propagation Layer [Ex]

Let's assume that your BW implementation has five data marts that contain profit center data. After month end, you want the fastest possible evaluations (decentralized) to occur on the basis of each data mart. The relevant data comes from five source systems (one system for each company). In the month under consideration, a problem occurred when updating the data from a source in the BW system (for example, because important reference data was missing). If you group the DataSources together in the Data Propagation Layer or in a deeper layer, the entire update fails. However, if we separate the sources up until the Data Propagation Layer, at least four companies can be populated with data and can then perform the necessary evaluations. Parallel load processes save you time when loading data. Therefore, a central BW instance can gain considerable acceptance among individual companies.

There may also be application scenarios in which the data is intentionally merged (for example, because you have to use an integrated view only). However, please note that, by doing so, you voluntarily take away any flexibility that may exist.

The granularity of the data in the Data Propagation Layer generally corresponds to the granularity of the data supplied by the DataSource. Aggregates are created downstream in the Reporting Layer, thus preventing a loss of information, which could hinder the flexible use of this data at a later time.

Granularity

Business Transformation Layer

The Business Transformation Layer is the bridge between the generally applicable, modeled Propagator on one side and the Reporting Layer on the other. The task of the Business Transformation Layer is to supply the data in the format expected by the Reporting Layer.

If reporting takes place for aggregated data, it is the task of the Business Transformation Layer to aggregate this data. If you require special application-specific calculations, these are performed in the Business Transformation Layer. In some cases, several physical datasets in the Data Propagation Layer are merged to form one physical dataset in the Reporting Layer. However, this is the exception rather than the rule. Try to model the data in such a way that only MultiProviders are used to merge the data. In this case, the data is separated up to the Reporting Layer and is then merged via the virtual view of a DataProvider. An accurate analysis

Aggregation, derivation, merging

of the requested reports is important here because all of the characteristics used for navigation and filtering purposes exist in all of the physical datasets involved and therefore must be enriched, if necessary.

Modeling the Business Transformation Layer

DSOs (usually standard DSOs) are used to model the Business Transformation Layer. InfoSource modeling is also possible. The considerations described previously for the Quality and Harmonization Layer are similar to those that apply here. However, we cannot give a general recommendation because the implementation strongly depends on the requirements of the analysis application.

Reporting Layer (Architected Data Mart Layer)

The data available in the Reporting Layer is staged in such a way that it directly fulfills the requirements of the analysis application. Many different applications can access the data. They include reporting and Online Analytical Processing (OLAP) tools, and dashboards and data mining applications.

Performance

When modeling the Reporting Layer, it is not necessary to provide the widest possible data basis to grow with future requirements because this is the task of the Data Propagation Layer. The task of the Reporting Layer is to provide high-performance access to the data in such a way that optimum support is provided to special application-specific requirements.

Specialized analysis datasets

Furthermore, when modeling the data model, you should not be tempted to use a dataset to map as many existing requirements as possible. For example, it is useful to store the data in varying forms of granularity, so that you can accelerate queries that do not require detailed data. Alternatively, you can create aggregates for your InfoCubes. Because they aggregate the data, there are fewer data records, which then makes it possible to accelerate queries.

Not every application requires aggregated data. Many a detailed evaluation accesses the detailed data directly in list form. Therefore, DSO objects also play a role in the Reporting Layer.

Sublayer of the Reporting Layer

Figure 5.3 shows the Reporting Layer, including a separate sublayer. If necessary, you can also add more layers. When you break down the layers of the Reporting Layer, you see special sublayers for each of the differentiation criteria discussed previously.

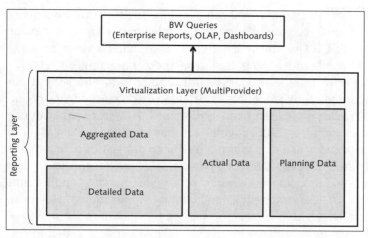

Figure 5.3 Breakdown of the Reporting Layer

The Reporting Layer stores data for as long as necessary. Sometimes, for example, the detailed data does not have to be available in the long term. In general, if data from past periods is only accessed occasionally, it can be stored externally in an NLS system. If you have a Propagator that maps a history, you more easily run the risk of deleting data that you could relatively easily reload from the Propagator. This also simplifies the decision in relation to remodeling measures for the Reporting Layer, which essentially contribute to making the Reporting Layer a continuously high-performance layer.

Management

The Virtual Layer is usually the basis for report creation. Depending on your requirement, you can define specialized views of the Reporting Layer data in the Virtual Layer. This is particularly important when differentiating between authorizations at the InfoProvider level.

MultiProvider

Due to the importance of the Virtual Layer, it is frequently shown as a standalone layer in the LSA (see Figure 5.3). For this reason, we will provide a detailed description of the Virtual Layer in the next section.

Virtual Layer

We recommend that you only create queries on MultiProviders (this is common practice in reality). Within the layer model, MultiProviders create a virtual, uppermost layer that does not store any data. Because this layer enables you to exchange the queries underlying physical data

Flexibility

models in a flexible manner, you can avoid having to create new query objects or maintain existing query objects whenever changes are made to the data model. Due to the large number of dependencies between reporting objects (and objects based on these reporting objects, for example, enterprise reports, dashboards, and so on), you should not underestimate the time and effort associated with such changes. In general, MultiProviders are used to analyze several datasets together in one query. For example, a MultiProvider can have a standardized view of planning data and actual data without having to merge this data into one physical dataset. The separation of planning data (budget) and actual data is the usual modeling approach when you model planning applications (see Chapter 10, Data Modeling for Planning Applications). However, this is just one possible reason for storing the data in two (or more) physically separate datasets.

Parallelism
It is useful to create smaller datasets and initially merge them virtually, regardless of the logical breakdown achieved this way. The OLAP processor divides a query on a MultiProvider into several subqueries that can be executed in parallel on the InfoProviders involved. This may improve performance even though the OLAP processor must also merge the partial results. Dataset segmentation also has many other advantages (for example, simplified administration).

Operational Data Store (Layer)

Ultimately, the purpose of all of the LSA levels discussed previously is to populate the reporting level with data, to create a flexible framework, and to ensure that data is supplied. The data analysis in the Reporting Layer is generally based on aggregated data.

Providing granular data at short notice
In special application scenarios, however, it may be necessary to make large volumes of granular data available at short notice. Once evaluated, this data can generally be deleted again. This means that some essential LSA services are irrelevant. There is no history management in the Corporate Memory, no data staging, no data enrichment, and no aggregation in optimized analysis datasets.

Frequently, the source system (or the Data Acquisition Layer) is the data source for the Operational Data Store (ODS). However, it is also possible that the data to be analyzed comes from one of the other layers (for example, from the Corporate Memory or from an interim staging step). The data is made available for ad hoc evaluations only for a short period of time and is then deleted again. One example that is frequently cited is the analysis of Point of Sale (PoS) data.

Frequently, the technical object, that is, the DSO, is known as an ODS Object because this was the common name for DSOs before NetWeaver Release 7.0 (until SAP introduced the term DSO to avoid any confusion). However, the ODS Layer has nothing directly to do with these objects.

DSO versus ODS

5.1.3 Domains

One of the goals of modeling in accordance with the LSA principles is to make the data available in the Data Propagation Layer in (almost) real time (and therefore also in the Reporting Layer). For this reason, mapping of the Corporate Memory was excluded from the main data flow and placed in a separate layer, thus preventing data from being written to and read from unnecessarily large datasets. If possible, additional avoidable, physical data stores are also omitted from the main data flow.

Data throughput

Parallel data loading is another way to accelerate data loading. Performance is particularly good if different data sources and targets are read or written. For this reason, it is useful to have parallel data threads, at least up to the DataPropagator level. The data to be loaded must be partitioned in an appropriate manner. Often, partitioning is already predefined in such a way that you load (similar) data from various source systems.

Parallelism

In addition to faster loading, another advantage associated with parallel processing is that, if an error that prevents a thread from being loaded into the DataPropagator occurs during a load cycle, it will only affect a subset of the data. Therefore, the data in the remaining (n-1) thread can be made available to reporting despite the error.

Availability

To partition the main data flow into various parallel threads, the data to be loaded must be partitioned into various disjunctive subsets (in other words, without any overlaps). This is known as domain creation whereby a subset is created as a domain.

Domains

There are many different ways to partition data: according to the subsidiaries of a corporate group, according to region, according to division, and so on. If you do not find any "natural" way to partition the data in your application scenario, you can partition the data "artificially," for example, according to certain number intervals. However, do not choose

Criteria for creating domains

too many domains because each domain means that you have to create an additional object thread for the data update. The objects in the thread nevertheless have the same structure because the same kind of data is updated. Figure 5.4 shows you how domain creation affects the architecture. The Data Acquisition Layer is only broken down if the domains have already been created as a result of partitioning the DataSources (for example, because the data creates a domain for each source system). The breakdown is usually reflected right up to the Reporting Layer. In reporting, you can use the MultiProviders to merge data that had previously been consistently separated. If, due to special requirements, you deliberately want to physically merge data in the Reporting Layer, you can do this, but this should not be the norm.

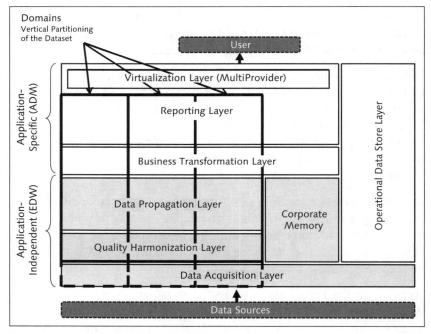

Figure 5.4 Creating Domains in the LSA

Modeling an update between layers is an interesting aspect here. If you work with domains, you work with load threads that comprise identically structured InfoProviders (usually DSOs) and transformations for each domain. You cannot avoid having DataProviders that have the same structure. A breakdown of data was, after all, our goal. However, when you choose a particular form of modeling, you can easily combine identical transformation rules into one transformation rule. This is very beneficial because some source code corrections or enhancements can be made centrally in one place. You will learn more about this topic in Chapter 7, Section 7.5, Transformations.

Up to now, we have only considered the breakdown of the main data flow into domains from a technical perspective. From a technical/content perspective, however, there are also some important reasons for separating the data from various source systems. The EDW concept seeks, among other things, to merge and harmonize data from different sources (for example, from subsidiaries within a corporate group) in one central location. This is necessary to facilitate cross-sectional evaluations. However, some information is lost (for example, information that would have been necessary for subsidiary evaluations within a group). If you only store one central view in the DataPropagator, the Data Warehouse may no longer be able to sufficiently handle the local requirements. However, if the source system data of each subsidiary can be quickly loaded through the layers of a central Data Warehouse, and can therefore also take account of local requirements, you will obtain an architecture that satisfies these local requirements, thus avoiding the need to have a separate system that contains another dataset not based on the EDW layer of a central BW system. However, if reporting is built as an ADM on the basis of the data in the DataPropagator, the data will pass through a central instance and nevertheless provide an individual reporting-specific view (wherever it is required), thus preventing a costly parallel development on various different systems.

EDW/data mart

Importance of Domains for the Architecture

[+]

The LSA pursues the goal of an evolutionary EDW. Domain creation helps to implement local Business Intelligence (BI) services without losing sight of the comprehensive EDW view.

Layer creation and domain creation are two key topics within the LSA landmark building blocks. We now wish to introduce you to some interesting topics associated with the LSA assistant building blocks.

5.1.4   LSA Assistant Building Blocks

There are also various topics within the LSA assistant building blocks that you should consider when deriving a customer LSA. The relevance of each individual point can vary greatly depending on the customer or project.

Data Quality Processes

The operational system directly influences the quality of the data to be loaded into the Data Warehouse. If this is insufficient, you can consider using a data quality assurance tool. Quality assurance tools fall into three categories. A strict distinction is not possible here, but each tool can usually be assigned to one of these categories. The three categories are:

▶ Auditing

▶ Cleansing

▶ Migration

Audit   Auditing tools ensure that the data satisfies certain requirements. Such requirements are defined as (business) rules that are checked by the tool. Usually, this type of "ruling" already occurs in the source system (SAP ERP). For this reason, we can assume that you do not require an additional tool when, for example, SAP ERP is the data source. In principle, any gaps in data validation (for example, in customer developments) should be closed by enhancing the checks at the point where the data is created.

Cleansing   Cleansing tools are used to cleanse data. This usually occurs during staging in a Data Warehouse. In a BW system, data staging programs can be incorporated into a data update. This usually concerns customer developments. If a particular project or customer needs to implement extensive data cleansing, it may be necessary to acquire a special tool for this purpose.

System Landscape

Any decision concerning the number of Data Warehouse systems to be used and how to restrict the usage of each is part of the LSA. The question concerning which system landscape to implement is even more complex in the case of additional technologies such as NLS and SAP NetWeaver BW Accelerator (BWA) (see Chapter 8, Section 8.2.6, SAP

NetWeaver Business Warehouse Accelerator), so a well-founded reference procedure model is helpful here. For example, the decision in relation to whether an existing Data Warehouse will also include HR data also poses some fundamental questions regarding data protection and authorizations.

ETL

The volume of data that must be loaded from third-party systems (non-SAP systems) varies depending on the project or customer. The higher the volume of third-party system data, and the more the data needs to be cleansed and staged, the greater the need to consider using a special ETL tool. In addition to the numerous third-party tools available, SAP has a tool known as SAP BusinessObjects Data Integrator in its portfolio.

Migration tools are used to transfer data from one database/dataset into another. Here, the data is initially transferred to an internal data structure where it undergoes further processing before being forwarded to the target. Each time data is staged in a Data Warehouse, it pursues the same processing objectives. In special situations, for example, when merging and reconciling master data, it may be useful to use specialized tools.

In SAP's product portfolio, the SAP BusinessObjects tools for data integration also support you when connecting non-SAP systems and let you implement both ETL and data quality assurance processes.

ETL

Migration

Integration

Storage

The following new technologies have been available since Release BW 7.0: NLS and BWA. Traditionally, the Data Warehouse data is stored in tabular form in a relational database, which may result in longer report runtimes if the volume of data increases. Even though you can use, for example, segmentation to counteract these long report runtimes, the total volume of data can adversely affect performance. The external storage of data by means of archiving or the NLS can help here. In contrast to archiving, the NLS still permits online access to the data. In BWA, the aggregate tables are not stored in a relational database. Rather, a special index permits fast, random access to the multidimensional dataset.

Organization and Procedure

The LSA also considers organizational aspects, for example, the goal of firmly embedding and communicating BW/BI within an enterprise. This is all the more important because the goals associated with an EDW architecture can only be achieved if their implementation is pursued in a sustainable manner.

To ensure fast processing and implementation, the user department must agree on a procedure for formulating and implementing new requirements for the BW system.

The layers of the LSA contribute to rapid implementation of such requirements. We will discuss this further in the next section.

5.1.5   LSA and Flexibility When Making Changes

Let's assume that your user department has a (rather simple) wish, namely, it wants to add a characteristic InfoObject (field) to a certain report. What needs to be done to implement this requirement and how can the aforementioned layer model contribute to implementing this requirement on short notice?

Changing a report

In the simplest scenario (when you want to add only one new InfoObject to an existing report), a rapid implementation is usually possible. Generally, a power user in the user department can quickly make the adjustment. Depending on whether or not changes to reports are permitted in the production environment, you may need to factor in the time required to transport the report adjustment.

Changing a MultiProvider

Because the report is implemented on the MultiProvider Layer, the InfoObject might not have been added to the MultiProvider. If the underlying data models in the Reporting Layer contain the InfoObject, you must incorporate it into the MultiProvider definition, so that you can adjust the report. In this case, the development department will have to provide additional support when implementing the requirement. All in all, however, the adjustment is made relatively quickly.

Loading a new Analytical Layer

However, if one or more datasets do not contain the InfoObject in the Reporting Layer, it must be added to the data models and updates, the model changes must be transported, and the data must be reloaded. If the Propagation Layer is modeled extensively and if the InfoObject is available here in the relevant dataset or datasets, you can delete the DataProviders in question from the Analytical Layer and reload the data from the Data Propagation Layer (including the history). In addition to the model changes to be transported, this scenario also requires you to reload the data. Such activities require more time, but are implemented relatively quickly when the data is modeled in accordance with the principles of the LSA.

The scenario is completely different if the data is not available in the Data Propagation Layer. If you at least find the basic data in the Corporate Memory, you can be sure that you will also be able to (retroactively) provide the data in the Propagator if you rework the entire load thread. However, if you have to make numerous reconciliation efforts to adjust the various EDW levels (which have a cross-application design), the process can become quite tedious. In any case, the changes affect considerably more objects and, as a result, the technical adjustment and transport activities are extremely time-consuming.

Populating the DataPropagator from the Corporate Memory

The adjustment takes on a completely different quality if you ascertain that the relevant context is not stored in the Corporate Memory or that, at the very least, in an effort to save time and costs, an InfoObject was not added to the ODS (presumably because its integration into the Data Acquisition Layer was overlooked at some point). If the source system is no longer able to supply data from past periods, you cannot populate the new InfoObject with data until the enhancement has been implemented. In any case, it will take some time to implement the requirement. If necessary, you will have to consult with a source system expert, enhance the extraction and, last but not least, enhance the implementation of all layers in the BW system. All of this requires not only a great deal of implementation and transport effort, but the change must also be reconciled with various locations.

Adjusting the extraction

These descriptions show that when a BW implementation follows the principles of the LSA, the DataPropagator, in particular, but also the Corporate Memory, are important layers that make it possible to have a flexible Analytical Layer. This is a prerequisite for user acceptance of the system.

Importance of the Propagator and Corporate Memory

The length of time required for the implementation is heavily influenced by various individual factors. These times vary greatly depending on the reconciliation effort associated with planning and implementation. If you only consider the development activity, a developer who is familiar with the topic and model, and has the necessary authorizations to fully implement the adjustment in person, is much faster at completing the activity than would be the case, for example, in an organization that is strongly based on the division of labor. For this reason, the times provided in Table 5.1 are merely examples.

Prerequisite	Activity	Estimated Duration
InfoObject is in a MultiProvider in the Analytical Layer	Add InfoObject to the report	Three minutes to one day (due to the transport)
InfoObject is in the dataset in the Analytical Layer	Add InfoObject to the MultiProvider and the report	One day (it must always be transported)
InfoObject available in a historical record in the Data Propagation Layer	Enhance the data models in the Analytical Layer, adjust the report, and load the data	Two to seven days, depending on complexity, if possible, the adjustment can only occur on the weekend
InfoObject available in a historical record in the Corporate Memory	Enhance the Quality and Harmonization Layer and the Data Propagation Layer, enhance the data models in the Analytical Layer, adjust the report, and load the data	Several days to several weeks
InfoObject only available by enhancing the extraction	Reconciliation, enhance the extractor, adjust all EDW levels, enhance the data models in the Analytical Layer, adjust the report, and load the data	Heavily dependent on the application scenario and the organization; if a reconciliation process is required first, the implementation may be delayed by days or weeks

Table 5.1 Effort Associated with Enhancing a Report

5.2 Naming Conventions

Naming conventions can help to achieve an architecture specification. Each new implementation project must deal with naming conventions because they form part of the project specifications. If, for example, naming conventions reflect the layer model and domains, these standards are incorporated into the relevant project. Naming conventions must also be reconciled with the authorization concept because the technical names of the DataProviders, planning components, queries, and web templates are later used to grant authorizations. Keys should be created in a systematic fashion to support the assignment of authorizations for namespaces. Figure 5.5 shows the mutual dependencies that exist between the system architecture, roles and authorizations, and naming conventions.

Importance of naming conventions

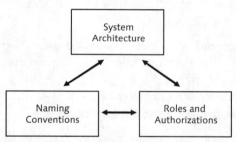

Figure 5.5 Dependencies between the System Architecture, Naming Conventions, and Roles and Authorizations

Let's assume that you have decided to introduce a layer architecture that is based on the LSA. You now need to define the naming conventions for your project.

As you saw in Section 5.1.3, domain creation can, in principle, affect all layers. We therefore recommend that you include data partitioning according to layer and domain in your classification of technical names. Sometimes, the MultiProviders and the Data Acquisition Layer are not differentiated according to domain because MultiProviders usually merge data from several domains, and because domains are missing from the Data Acquisition Layer if they are not supplied by the source system(s) and if the data is first partitioned in the BW system. In these cases, a meaningful standard value can be used to fill the position intended for the layer.

Layer and domains

In addition to assigning objects to a layer and domain, you most definitely want to assign them to the (source system) process, (source) application, or DataSource. The process, in particular, provides for an effective naming convention because it is also geared toward the assignment of authorizations to processes.

Object type Frequently, object types are also coded (for example, C for Cube, D for DSO, and M for MultiProvider). In the Data Warehousing Workbench, however, the object types can also be recognized without this convention. Often, the layer ID is usually enough to restrict the authorization for access to detailed data (DSO), the Reporting Layer (frequently the Cube), and MultiProviders (Virtual Layer). If you want to further differentiate between the authorizations within the Reporting Layer, it may be useful to differentiate according to object type or other criteria (for example, a differentiation according to planning data and actual data or according to other types of segmentation).

Cannot be standardized Here, we can merely offer suggestions. When all is said and done, the naming convention is based on your customer-specific requirements, which are derived from your chosen architecture, especially the authorization concept. Naming conventions can only ever be defined in close cooperation with the people responsible for the authorizations.

Sample naming convention Table 5.2 contains sample naming conventions for InfoProviders. Please note that you should include the Quality and Harmonization Layer and the Business Transformation Layer in your naming convention if you (initially) do not intend to physically store data at these levels because you may still need these layers when implementing new requirements in the future.

Please note that the naming convention shown in Table 5.2 only provides for eight characters. Therefore, you obtain one valid naming convention for all DataProviders. A ninth character is still available for InfoCubes and MultiProviders. However, because you can create aggregation levels (see Chapter 10) on these InfoCubes and MultiProviders, but they also require nine characters, one possible procedure is to generally restrict DataProvider names to eight characters and to use the ninth available character to differentiate between aggregation levels (for example, through sequential numbering). Apart from the ninth differentiating character, the aggregation levels can have the exact same name as the DataProvider on which they are defined.

Length (from ... to)	Sample Values	Explanation
(1,1)	A — Data Acquisition M — Corporate Memory Q — Quality and Harmonization P — DataPropagator B — Business Transformation R — Reporting V — Virtual Layer	Single-character abbreviation for the layers of the architecture
(2,2)	1, 2, 3, 4, 5, 6, 7, 8, 9, 0 A to Z X — Cross-sectional	Domains, for example, organizational breakdown (at a high organizational level)
(3,4)	AA — Asset Accounting FI — Financial Accounting CO — Controlling MM — Logistics HR — Human Resources TC — Technical Content XX — Cross-sectional	Process/module/function
(5,5)	D — DSO C — Cube T — Transactional Cube R — RemoteCube M — MultiProvider I — InfoSet	Object type
(6,7)	01 to 99	Sequential number
(8, 8)	0 to 9 and A to Z	Segmentation, for example, to separate the dataset according to year

Table 5.2 Sample Naming Conventions for InfoProviders

You must also define corresponding naming conventions for other object types. For example, many customers define queries and web templates in such a way that their technical names start with the technical names of the Provider on which they are defined. We recommend that you use an Excel table to describe the naming conventions and the objects created

Excel table for describing the naming conventions

177

according to each convention. In each project, this table can be used as a template for defining project-specific objects.

Table 5.3 lists those object types for which you must define naming conventions. Pay attention to the various key lengths.

Object Type	Length	Object Type	Length
InfoAreas	30	InfoSources	30
InfoProviders except DSOs (BasisCubes, MultiProviders, RemoteCubes, Transactional Cubes, InfoSets)	9	DataSources	30
DSOs	8	Process chains	30
Application components	30	Aggregates	20
InfoObject catalogs	20	Queries	30
InfoObjects	9	Workbooks	generated
InfoObject hierarchies	30	Templates	30
InfoSources	30	Aggregation levels	9
DataSources	9	Planning objects	varied

Table 5.3 Object Types and Naming Conventions

InfoObjects   Because an InfoObject can also assume the role of an InfoProvider (that contains master data), it would be conceivable to name InfoObjects in accordance with the naming convention shown in Table 5.2. However, we don't think this is useful because separate InfoObjects would have to be created for each layer and domain. In general, InfoObjects that contain master data are first made available in the Reporting Layer and therefore are supposed to be used, if possible, at cross-enterprise or, at the very least, cross–data mart level.

Business Content   Frequently, DSOs, Cubes, and MultiProviders are not transferred from Business Content to customer projects without undergoing some changes. Standard InfoObjects, on the other hand, are more frequently integrated into customer data models. Over time, the standard system is more or less adjusted to customer requirements (more attributes, other displays, and so on), which means that a time-consuming reconciliation is necessary when new data is transferred from the Content. In the case of implementation projects that start from scratch, this can be avoided by transferring the standard objects to a customer-specific namespace. We believe that using Content InfoObjects as a template for creating other objects (by selecting CREATE WITH TEMPLATE) has proven itself, especially if we already know that adjustments will be necessary. However, the strategy of not using standard objects and transferring them into a Z namespace, for example, can also pay off because we can never know for sure which objects will need to be adjusted in the future. In the simplest scenario, the naming convention for such objects can ensure that, for example, ZCUSTOMER is created on the basis of 0CUSTOMER and interpreted as a central customer-specific InfoObject for the *Customer* object. It is not absolutely necessary to explicitly choose the letter Z but we recommend that you do so because it is a good way to convey the importance of the central object. Unless proven otherwise, there is only one BW-wide object that begins with Z. If other (local) objects are required, they can be supplemented later. The role of the Z object will then continue to be that of mapping a central overview, thus clearly distinguishing it from other local views.

The preceding procedure for transferring Content is not always useful. It can nevertheless have some merit in the case of more complex InfoObjects (for example, with master data). However, you must remember to also consider many dependent objects (attributes, attributes of attributes, and compounding) and then, in each case, ask whether you want to transfer the relevant object definition or leave it as a standard object. It is not possible to make a clear distinction here. However, you can observe the following rules of thumb: You will use objects that play a special role in BW, for example, time characteristics (such as 0CALMONTH and 0FISCPER), (currency) units (0CURRENCY, 0UNIT), key figures (for example, 0AMOUNT), and technical objects exactly as they were delivered. However, you will transfer important technical objects such as customer (business partner), material, organizational unit or employee to the Z namespace in accordance with the philosophy outlined previously. Everything else is a gray area that you will have to carefully consider

Rules of thumb

yourself. Here, you will generally only transfer objects that contain master data and, because of their importance, are potential candidates for later adjustments. In the case of "basic" objects such as the postal code, street, name, telephone number, and so on, there is generally no reason to create a further object.

5.3 Information Integration as a Prerequisite for Cross-Sectional Evaluations

In its basic form, information integration is the (logical) fusion of heterogeneous information from various sources into one overall homogenous picture.

Schema integration In the case of a Data Warehouse, the data is extracted, staged, and stored in a separate database. Queries are performed directly against this database (or against a dependent data mart). Integration involves analyzing the various database schemas in the source systems and mapping them to one common schema in the Data Warehouse. This can be a very tedious yet necessary process (to obtain an overall homogenous picture).

Other data sources for structured data In most cases, the Data Warehouse does not contain all of the available structured datasets. Therefore, the data you need to answer certain questions is not available directly and, above all, this data is not yet integrated into the overall picture. If you still want to develop these additional data sources (for example, XML documents, Electronic Data Interchange (EDI) documents, and other database systems/applications), you normally cannot wait until they are added to the Data Warehouse. For this reason, you must find other integration options.

Unstructured data In addition, increasingly more unstructured data (for example, documents on the file server, web logs, emails, Wikis, and so on) is excluded from a pure analysis of the data in the Data Warehouse. Furthermore, unstructured data will become even more significant in the future.

Goals of information integration How can you correctly, fully, and efficiently merge all required data from various heterogeneous sources into standardized, structured information that can be effectively interpreted by the user? Various approaches are possible here. However, an application scenario is the only way to assess a particular approach.

Data merging in BW is a very good basis for effective reporting. Before the data is used, it is physically integrated and immediately made available to reporting. You can use the data modeling techniques in this book to map high-performance data models that, as a result of the chosen architecture and despite their physical storage, provide the necessary adjustment flexibility.

At the core of modeling, however, is data reconciliation achieved through interpreting and representing data. For example, you must define key figure definitions that are generally applicable. However, the set of rules resulting from these considerations do not necessarily have to be applied to data that has been physically stored temporarily.

SAP BusinessObjects Data Federator gives you the opportunity to use a rules-based source to virtually integrate target mapping rules that are executed in real time when a query is executed. Various structured data sources (for example, Oracle, SAS, Teradata, Web services, and XML) can be connected this way. Shared metadata retention guarantees their integration into SAP BusinessObjects products.

SAP Business-
Objects Data
Federator

SAP BusinessObjects Integrator is a powerful data integration tool that supports all phases of an ETL process. In addition to structured information, it can be used to analyze and connect all text-based sources. Drag and drop can be used to gradually model the data flow from various predefined transformation functions (from source to target). The transformation result can be physically stored in the BW system, for example, but it does not have to be. You can also access the source system data in real time. In the data flow itself, you can directly establish the prerequisites for reporting. You can create or update an SAP BusinessObjects universe directly — the results are therefore immediately available to reporting. The user can always understand the transformation process for data retrieval because he can see when the data was updated, the source of the data, and how the data has changed. Misinterpretations are easily avoided and the user is better able to understand the results.

SAP Business-
Objects Integrator

The ETL functions of the Data Integrator are also particularly interesting if third-party systems are developed as data sources and connected to a BW system.

SAP BusinessObjects Integrator

Imagine that you want to add data from an external Customer Relationship Management (CRM) system to the customer data in your BW system. You can use SAP BusinessObjects Integrator to access both source systems, which stage the data in a logical data flow, and provide, as the result, objects from both data sources in one universe. You can then define evaluations that are based on this universe. Here, the data can be accessed in real time. If you ascertain that you have to repeatedly perform the evaluation and that physical data storage would therefore make sense, you can also store the data flow result in a data target (for example, in the BW system). The adjustment effort is low because neither the transformations nor reporting change significantly.

Virtual and materialized integration

The area of IT is also addressing the issue of information integration (see Naumann, 2006). An important differentiation criterion here is whether we are dealing with virtual systems or systems that have their own data retention. Table 5.4 shows the main differentiation criteria between materialized and virtual integration.

Criterion	Materialized Integration	Virtual Integration
Point in time	Integration occurs before the query	Integration occurs during the query
Centralization of query processing	Data is transformed and stored locally	Requests are divided into partial requests
Data storage	Centralized data basis	Decentralized data
Data processing	Centralized request processing	Decentralized request processing
Scope of data staging	Requests are made directly against the materialized data	Data is only transferred if required and only stored temporarily

Table 5.4 Comparison between Materialized and Virtual Integration

A typical example of a materialized system is a Data Warehouse such as BW. A system that uses virtual integration to combine several information sources is known as a mediator-based information system. In principle, this system is flexible when it comes to connecting new sources. However, the semantics of the data must also be known here to cleanse and merge data. Frequently, the query speed is a disadvantage here because the overall request cannot be answered until the last subquery has concluded. Furthermore, because processing occurs online, for the most part, and is new for each query, it is not possible to reduce the processing steps that need to be executed. Table 5.5 compares the fundamental advantages and disadvantages associated with materialized and virtual systems.

Criterion	Materialized System	Virtual System
Timeliness	–	+
Response time	+	–
Flexibility	–	+
Complexity	+	++
Autonomy	–	+
Request power	+	–
Read/write	+/+	+/–
Size	–	+
Data cleansing	+	–
Information quality	+	–

Table 5.5 Evaluation of Materialized and Virtual Data Integration

5.4   Conclusion

The requirements for data retrieval in a BW system have changed. Having individual data marts that operate side by side in a BW system does not satisfy the requirements for a central data hub that integrates and provides "easy-to-digest" data. With the LSA, we have introduced a reference architecture that gives you clues as to which services should be made available within a central BW instance and the basic considerations for designing the various layers of the layer model. Therefore, the layers assigned to the EDW, especially the DataPropagator, are extremely important. The DataPropagator is your data hub. If the quality and availability of data in this layer is good, this will also be the case for the Data Mart Layer. There are various different ways to design the Data Mart Layer. If you are using BWA, you do not necessarily have to implement time-consuming modeling that uses the resources of a relational database to optimize performance.

SAP has a powerful tool for staging and integrating data. This tool is known as SAP BusinessObjects Data Integrator. Its extensive transformation functions can be helpful in projects whose primary goal is to integrate non-SAP sources into the BW system. Standardized metadata retention facilitates gradual data integration (from source to target). The use of the Data Integrator (or another additional ETL tool) influences the layers to be modeled in BW. Because the processing logic here does not have to be implemented in the form of transformations within the BW system (possibly across several interim steps), temporary storage can be omitted here. In such cases, the Quality and Harmonization Layer and the Data Acquisition Layer, in particular, may become obsolete. However, the Corporate Memory and the Data Propagation Layer remain extremely important.

In this chapter, we will introduce you to the business side of SAP NetWeaver Business Warehouse (BW), at the heart of which lies SAP Business Content, which is a number of predefined solutions that you can use in your system with very little effort.

6 Business Content

Business Content in SAP NetWeaver BW comprises predefined extractors, data models, and reports. If you use Business Content effectively, you can considerably reduce the duration of your project. Simply by using objects supplied by SAP, you can implement developments much faster than you could ever implement pure custom developments. However, there is also a danger that your requirements will not be fully met if you adopt Business Content without making any changes. Furthermore, important modeling principles may not be upheld (see Chapter 5, Reference Architecture for Data Modeling). In this chapter, we will therefore not only describe Business Content, but we will also demonstrate some of its practical uses. However, due to the scope of Business Content, we cannot cover everything in this book. Instead, we will discuss those areas that have proven to be most important in real life, namely Financial Accounting (FI)/Controlling (CO), Sales and Distribution (SD), and Human Resources (HR). We will also discuss the most important master data in Business Content and explain how you can activate and enhance Business Content.

Terminology Used in this Book

SAP uses the terms Standard Content, Business Intelligence (BI) Content, and Business Content synonymously. In addition to Business Content, "Standard" Content also includes Demo Content and Technical Content. To avoid confusion, we will only use the term Business Content, even when we are not strictly discussing "business" content.

[«]

6.1 Basic Principles

Business Content is a set of predefined objects, ranging from extractors in various operational SAP systems to data models, queries, roles, and process chains in BW. Extractors, DataSources, and InfoObjects are particularly important in real life. This chapter will focus on Business Content DataSources. Because the data models and queries in Business Content only play a minor role in real life (as a sample or template), we will not discuss them in great detail here.

There are generally three ways to extract data from another SAP system (such as, SAP ERP, Advanced Planning and Optimization (APO) or Customer Relationship Management (CRM)):

- By using a Business Content DataSource
- By using an application-specific/customer-specific DataSource
- By using a generic DataSource

Standard DataSources   A Business Content DataSource is a DataSource that SAP supplies as a plug-in for you to adopt and use. This is only possible in areas with a very high degree of standardization (for example, FI) and for master data in general. However, you can also use a user exit to enhance Business Content DataSources. This will be discussed toward the end of the chapter. For the most part, enhancements to extraction structures are made in append structures, and not in the standard extraction structures themselves, so that the enhancements are not overwritten when you transfer a DataSource again. Often, it may be enough to add a new field to the append structure because the standard extractor will automatically fill this field if it is also contained in the source table of the extractor. Another particularly important object in this area is the Logistics extractor, which you set up in the Logistics Cockpit (Transaction LBWE). In Logistics, you not only maintain the extraction structures in this cockpit (that is, the list of fields available in BW), but you also initialize the process of updating values in SAP ERP Central Component (ECC).

Application-specific/ customer-specific DataSources   Because the data structures for many applications are so customer-specific that it would no longer be useful to implement a standardized DataSource, a second group of application-specific/customer-specific DataSources is available.

This group contains important DataSources for Profitability Analysis (CO-PA), the Special Purpose Ledger (FI-SL), and Classification. In SAP ERP, Transaction SBIW has a wizard for these applications, which you can use to generate DataSources for the relevant application.

If the first two groups do not yet have a DataSource that provides the data you need, you can create a generic DataSource.

Generic DataSources

You have three options here:

▶ **Table or view as a basis**
This is the simplest scenario: All of the data is in one table. Alternatively, several tables can easily be read together via one view. Ideally, the source table still has a change date that supports a generic delta. For technical reasons, however, or due to complex business logic, it is frequently not possible to use one view to make all of the required data available. Technical reasons are especially applicable if the source is a pool table or cluster table.

▶ **InfoSet query as a basis**
InfoSet queries are used in operational systems to create new reports. Only in exceptional situations does it make sense to create a generic InfoSet extractor, especially if an InfoSet query already exists with the required details.
Note: SAP object names are often very confusing. InfoSet queries exist in both the SAP Basis system and BW system at the application level, that is, for different functions. The InfoSet query in the Basis system is meant here.

▶ **Function module as a basis**
The most flexible way to create a new extractor is to use a function module to create a generic extractor. Here, the function module must have a particular structure. A sample structure is provided in the function group RSAX.

You can use the user exit RSAP0001 to enhance all types of extractors, not just standard extractors. In other words, it is possible, and may even make more sense, to create a generic extractor on a table basis and to use a user exit to program the logic for a field that does not exist in the table, instead of immediately writing a function module extractor.

User exit for a DataSource enhancement

Different namespaces apply to standard objects and customer-developed objects. Here, the intention is to prevent custom developments from

SAP namespace

being overwritten by Content objects. The namespaces are defined at the application level while the names at the ABAP Dictionary level are automatically generated when you create objects.

Standard SAP objects (that is, Business Content in the narrowest sense) always begin with the digits 0 to 9 (SAP namespace). Zero generally stands for Standard Content and any digit other than 0 indicates that the object is an application-specific object. One exception here is LO extractors, which begin with 2.

Customer namespace

Customer-specific objects can start with any letter. There is nothing to dictate that all customer-specific objects must start with Y or Z. However, such restrictions exist in SAP ERP, which is why you occasionally encounter these names in BW too, but they are neither useful nor necessary.

Names at ABAP Dictionary level

For the most part, the names generated in BW at the ABAP Dictionary level start with /BIO/ for standard objects or /BIC/ for customer-specific objects. Table 6.1 compares the names generated for Content objects with the names generated for custom developments.

Object	SAP Object	Customer Object
InfoObject	{0-9}xxxxxxxxx	{A-Z}xxxxxxxx
IO data element	/BIO/OIxxxxxxxxxx	/BIC/OI{A-Z}xxxxxxxx
IO domain	/BIO/Oxxxxxxxxxx	/BIC/O{A-Z}xxxxxxxx
SID tables	/BIO/Sxxxxxxxxxx	/BIC/S{A-Z}xxxxxxxx
Text tables	/BIO/Txxxxxxxxxx	/BIC/T{A-Z}xxxxxxxx
Master data (time-independent)	/BIO/Pxxxxxxxxxx	/BIC/P{A-Z}xxxxxxxx
Master data (time-dependent)	/BIO/Qxxxxxxxxxx	/BIC/Q{A-Z}xxxxxxxx
Master data SID (time-independent)	/BIO/Xxxxxxxxxx	/BIC/X{A-Z}xxxxxxxx
Master data SID (time-dependent)	/BIO/Yxxxxxxxxxx	/BIC/Y{A-Z}xxxxxxxx
Hierarchy tables	/BIO/Hxxxxxxxxxx	/BIC/H{A-Z}xxxxxxxx
DataStore Object (DSO)	0xxxxx	{A-Z}xxxxx

Table 6.1 Overview of Names Generated for Content and Custom Development

Object	SAP Object	Customer Object
DSO (active table)	/BIO/Axxxxx00	/BIC/A{A-Z}xxxxx00
InfoCube	0xxxxxxxx	{A-Z}xxxxxxxx
Normal fact table	/BIO/F0xxxxxxxx	/BIC/F{A-Z}xxxxxxxx
Compressed fact table	/BIO/E0xxxxxxxx	/BIC/E{A-Z}xxxxxxxx
Standard dimension tables	/BIO/D0xxxxxxxx{P,T,U}	/BIC/D0xxxxxxxx{P,T,U}
Free dimension tables	/BIO/D0xxxxxxxx{1-13}	/BIC/D0xxxxxxxx{1-13}

Table 6.1 Overview of Names Generated for Content and Custom Development (Cont.)

Enhancements to standard DataSources are common practice. In the case of a new installation, the custom development remains the same because you make the enhancement in a separate append that is not overwritten.

Using standard InfoObjects

This is not true for standard InfoObjects because a new installation would overwrite all changes made, sometimes with catastrophic results. It is quite possible that someone will unwittingly execute a new installation (for example, an inexperienced employee). We therefore recommend that you copy standard InfoObjects to the customer namespace before you make major changes to them. Unfortunately, the settings for standard InfoObjects are not always optimal, which is why you frequently make changes to standard InfoObjects. For example, texts are often preconfigured as language-dependent texts. In practice, however, this is rarely required.

Standard InfoCubes and DSOs (that is, 0 objects) are not used in real life. In FI/CO, you might use a model very close to standard InfoCubes (e.g., by copying and enhancing the 0 objects). For the most part, however, standard InfoCubes do not play a major role in other areas. In all cases, however, the dimension design must be checked from a customer-specific perspective. Standard queries, workbooks, roles, and so on, are, at best, examples. We are not yet aware of a situation where they are in productive use (one exception is the Technical Content). However, BW's strength lies in its ability to easily create queries and multidimensional data models.

Other standard objects

Summary BW Business Content contains preconfigured applications, ranging from DataSources to queries. In theory, you can use Business Content without modification. In practice, however, you will considerably enhance the standard extractors, application-specific extractors, and standard InfoObjects, which are very important in real life. There are various ways to make such enhancements (see Section 6.8, Activation and Enhancement).

6.2   Master Data in SAP NetWeaver BW

There is no doubt that Business Content is extremely beneficial to InfoObjects. In the case of master data, however, you have to ask yourself whether you want to use 0 objects directly or whether you want to work with copies, especially if you want to change some of the settings.

Using standard InfoObjects

Before you use master data Business Content objects, you should give the following points some consideration:

▸ **Attributes and navigation attributes**
Often, the attribute lists are very extensive and not relevant for every enterprise. Irrelevant attributes should be deleted, display attributes are rarely used in reporting, and time-dependent navigation attributes heavily influence reporting performance and should definitely be avoided. In most cases, time-dependent master data is only required for lookups in data import processes, and not in reporting. Here, you need to find other solutions. If, for example, you only need time dependency information for data import processes, you should create an extra load characteristic, that is, an InfoObject with master data that is only used for lookups in import processes. However, the navigation attribute of the "normal" characteristic should not be a time-dependent attribute.

[+] **Time-Dependent Navigation Attributes**

Navigation attributes are used to report the current view. Time-dependent navigation attributes can be used to evaluate an assignment at any time (but always only at one date for the entire query). However, it is not possible to evaluate the historically correct assignment (that is, the correct assignment for each month). To do this, the attributes must be added directly to the dimensions. It is also difficult to interpret "an assignment at any time." Furthermore, its content is not particularly relevant and it adversely affects performance, which is why you should avoid it, if possible.

▶ **Compounding according to technical viewpoints**
Generally, InfoObject compounding follows the foreign key relationship of the relevant table in the operational SAP system. These systems are highly flexible. In numerous customer projects, however, many of the foreign key relationships do not functionally exist as required for the flexibility in the standard system. Therefore, compounding is not necessary.

▶ **Document master data**
In Standard Content, documents, such as sales orders or accounting documents, are always modeled without master data and compounding. However, the absence of compounding may result in incorrect selections. If you need the current view at the document level, master data cannot be avoided here. Furthermore, most master data in the operational system is defined at the item level, that is, the document must be compounded with the item characteristic and the master data can only be stored uniquely in the item characteristic. However, a compound key, which comprises any compounding that takes place, the document number, and the item in a field, is very helpful in reporting. An accounting document could take the form of US01-2010-1234567890-010, that is, the company code, fiscal year, document number, and item. A compound key lets you drill down to the document level, so that you can perform a unique evaluation. Otherwise, you have to evaluate several characteristics. Compounding can be omitted here.

6.2.1 Customer

The table KNA1 is the central customer table in SAP ERP. The BW InfoObject for this table is 0CUSTOMER. Figure 6.1 contrasts SAP ERP tables with standard BW InfoObjects.

0CUSTOMER

The BW data model does not facilitate 1:n relationships with master data. Therefore, different contact persons (KNVK) or multiple addresses (which can be managed in SAP ECC) are not available in BW. Sales area–dependent master data (KNVV) is available in the InfoObject 0CUST_SALES, company code-dependent master data (KNB1) is found in the InfoObject 0CUST_COMPC and, if required, dunning area-dependent master data (KNB5) should be loaded into customer-specific InfoObjects with compounding. Partner roles are only supplied with transaction data, and not as master data. The Business Content contains the reference characteristics 0SOLD_TO, 0PAYER, 0SHIP_TO, and 0BILL_TO. Here, the referenced characteristic is 0CUSTOMER. The credit limit tables KNKA and KNKK are modeled as transaction data. However, this is not necessarily useful.

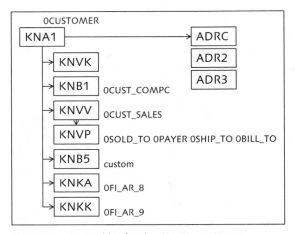

Figure 6.1 SAP Tables for the Customer Master

Other topics in customer reporting include customer hierarchies and customer groups. Standard Content for Dun & Bradstreet information is available here. However, customer-specific solutions are often necessary. Furthermore, the classification system is also frequently used for customer data. You can create application-specific DataSources for this purpose (see Section 6.7, Classification Data).

6.2.2 Material

0MATERIAL   MARA is the central material master table in the SAP system and corresponds to the InfoObject 0MATERIAL in BW (see Figure 6.2). BW also has the sales area–dependent and plant-dependent InfoObjects 0MAT_SALES and 0MAT_PLANT.

In the standard system, the characteristic 0MATERIAL contains a large number of attributes that are not used in most customer projects in the operational system. Therefore, the list of display attributes and navigation attributes should always be revised from a customer-specific perspective.

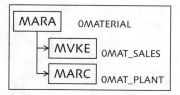

Figure 6.2 SAP Tables for the Material Master

Before you transfer 0MATERIAL from the Content, you must specify some material number conversion settings in Transaction OMSL.

6.2.3 Organizational Characteristics

In this section, we will briefly introduce the most important organizational characteristics in the SAP system and highlight some special features of BW.

The client is the highest organizational characteristic in the SAP system. A client is a closed technical unit in an SAP system. It has its own tables, master data, and user IDs. BW itself is not client-enabled, that is, there is just one client. In compounding, however, you can use the option MASTER DATA LOCALLY TO SOURCE SYSTEMS to create individual characteristics that obtain master data from multiple clients. This data is then automatically compounded with the source system ID to which the client also belongs.

Client

The absence of client capability is particularly unfavorable for test and training purposes. While numerous clients are usually created in SAP ERP for different purposes, a separate system must always be available for BW. Alternatively, you may have to use an existing system in lieu (for example, a test system for training purposes).

The controlling area is the organizational unit within a corporate group for which complete, self-contained cost accounting can be performed. The InfoObject 0CO_AREA is the controlling area in BW. It is also contained in the compounding of some other CO characteristics.

InfoObject 0CO_AREA

InfoObject 0COMP_CODE	The company code (InfoObject 0COMP_CODE) is the smallest organizational unit for which a self-contained set of accounts can be drawn up for external reporting (independent accounting unit) whereby several company codes can use the same chart of accounts (0CHRT_ACCTS). Accounts in BW are always compounded with the chart of accounts while company codes always have a unique assignment to a controlling area. However, a controlling area can contain several company codes. In general, the Content characteristics for a controlling area, company code, and chart of accounts are not changed at all or are only changed slightly. It is therefore common practice to work with 0 objects here. The controlling area and company code are often authorization-relevant in systems that are used in several countries.
Controlling	A cost center (InfoObject 0COSTCENTER) is the central organizational unit in Overhead Cost Controlling while the profit center (InfoObject 0PROFIT_CTR) is the central organizational unit in the component EC-PCA. Both cost centers and profit centers have standard extractors for hierarchies, which play an important role in real life.
Logistics	The most important organizational structure in Sales is the sales area, which comprises a sales organization (InfoObject 0SALES_ORG), distribution channel (0DISTR_CHAN), and division (0DIVISION). Here, the division is a classification according to material. In Logistics, the plant (0PLANT) is the most important organizational unit. Sales organizations and plants always have a unique assignment to a company code.
Human Resources	In HR, the organizational unit (InfoObject 0ORGUNIT) is the most important organizational structure. It also has a hierarchy extractor. The Content characteristic contains a range of attribute from purchasing and CRM. This can cause some confusion, especially in reporting. You may introduce additional reference characteristics here and, in all cases, review the attribute list and probably revise it, too.
Summary	The standard SAP model is very flexible. Customer projects generally do not fully benefit from its flexibility, for example, there is often a 1:1 relationship between the cost center and profit center or between the company code and sales organization. These restrictions may simplify the BW data models or, at the very least, make the data import process easier.

In the SAP ERP system, the master data for organizational characteristics is stored in configuration tables known as T tables.

6.2.4 Accounts

In FI, you work with general ledger (G/L) accounts (InfoObject 0GL_ACCOUNT), which are compounded with the chart of accounts. Key figure definitions created using external hierarchies play a central role for reports in FI. The financial statement versions defined in the source system are also available in BW without restrictions (via external hierarchies). However, BW cannot show or hide hierarchy nodes according to the balance result. However, you can invert the plus/minus sign for individual accounts. In the standard system, the InfoObject 0GL_ACCOUNT does not contain a group account. In most customer projects, however, the group account is enhanced to facilitate reporting via various local charts of accounts.

0GL_ACCOUNT

In Overhead Cost Controlling, you work with cost elements (0COSTELMNT) and, in Profit Center Accounting (PCA), you work with separate accounts (0ACCOUNT). Because these different accounts are almost identical, it may be useful to evaluate the FI data with the costs in CO. Often, you will also add, for example, 0COSTELMNT to FI Cubes, so that you can conveniently compare the data in one MultiProvider. Hierarchy extractors also exist for 0COSTELMNT and 0ACCOUNT.

0COSTELMNT, 0ACCOUNT

6.2.5 Employees

In SAP HR, master data is stored in infotypes (PA tables for master data and time data and HRP tables for personnel planning data). Personnel master data is stored in infotypes 0000 to 0999 (for example, personnel actions in the table PA0000, the organizational assignment in the table PA0001, and so on).

Infotypes

In addition to a four-digit infotype, each infotype contains a four-digit subtype for further subdivision.

Futhermore, every piece of information is always time-dependent (at the subtype level if subtypes are used). A special feature of extractors in HR is the breakdown of multiple infotypes into uniform time slices.

Most of the time, the otherwise rarely used ABAP command `PROVIDE` is used here.

0EMPLOYEE, 0PERSON A special curiosityof Business Content is that general information such as an employee's date of birth, language, gender, and nationality is not stored in the Employee InfoObject (0EMPLOYEE), but in the more general InfoObject 0PERSON. This is difficult for end users to comprehend even if it may be technically correct. We therefore recommend that you also save the necessary 0PERSON attributes in the 0EMPLOYEE InfoObject even though they are redundant there.

In general, however, the list of attributes in HR is more universally valid than those in the material or customer area, for example, so there is less need for revision here.

6.2.6   Time Characteristics

The time dimension is particularly important in BW. Time characteristics for which a separate dimension is provided in InfoCubes have special functions here. Time characteristics are very important for exception aggregation. For time, there are special conversion routines for the data import processes, and partitioning is only possible via time characteristics.

Only Business Content characteristics are real-time characteristics. Even though you can also define your own time characteristics, they will behave like normal characteristics, not time characteristics. For example, you cannot use your own characteristics in partitioning. You should therefore always use 0 objects for time characteristics. Only use your own objects in exceptional cases, and only then as additional objects.

Essentially, there are two types of time characteristics: calendar-based and fiscal. The design model for Business Content time characteristics is shown in Figure 6.3. Fiscal characteristics are always compounded with the fiscal year variant (0FISCVARNT). In Business Content, fiscal characteristics are mainly used in the FI/CO area while calendar-based characteristics are used in all other areas. Therefore, to evaluate FI/CO data with other data, you should also include the calendar-based characteristics in FI/CO InfoCubes. Table 6.2 lists all of the time characteristics in BW.

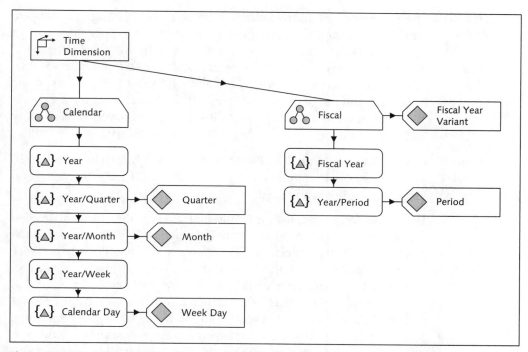

Figure 6.3 ADAPT Display for Business Content Time Characteristics

InfoObject	Name	Internal Format	
0CALDAY	Calendar day	YYYYMMDD	Calendar-based and fiscal
0CALMONTH	Calendar year/month	YYYYMM	
0CALMONTH2	Calendar month	MM	
0CALQUART1	Quarter	Q	
0CAL_QUARTER	Calendar year/quarter	YYYYQ	
0CALWEEK	Calendar year/week	YYYYWW	
0CALYEAR	Calendar year	YYYY	
0FISCPER	Fiscal year/period	YYYYPPP	
0FISCPER3	Posting period	PPP	
0FISCYEAR	Fiscal year	YYYY	
0HALFYEAR1	Half year	H	
0WEEKDAY1	Weekday	X	

Table 6.2 BW Time Characteristics

197

Special features
of fiscal periods There are only three fiscal characteristics. In Accounting, quarters are particularly common. In enterprises whose fiscal year does not start in January, it is very common to nevertheless start with the first quarter. Another special oddness of fiscal years that do not start in January is that, in the case of standard settings, the annual display corresponds to the fiscal year, and not to the calendar year. If, for example, a new fiscal year begins in July 2010 (that is, 2011), July 2010 is displayed in BW as July 2011. You can change this setting in Transaction RSRHIERARCHYVIRT.

External
hierarchies

0CALMONTH and 0FISCPER also have external hierarchies. However, you can also create your own external hierarchies. This is a very practical function, but it is rarely used.

When you design your own InfoCubes, please note that the most detailed characteristic always determines the granularity. Additional characteristics have little or no effect on the memory requirement or performance if they are not more detailed than the most detailed existing characteristic. Additional characteristics, however, are very helpful in reporting. If, for example, 0CALMONTH exists in an InfoCube, you should always add 0CALYEAR and 0CALMONTH2 to the InfoCube, too. In reporting, this facilitates simple period comparisons from various years. However, it would be rather cumbersome to add them retroactively.

Partitioning

You can only partition the fact table of an InfoCube into the characteristics 0CALMONTH or 0FISCPER. If you use 0FISCPER, you must also set the fiscal year variant as a constant, that is, so that only one fiscal year variant is possible. However, it is not totally unpossible that you will want to change the fiscal year variant because of a spin-off or transfer, for example. You should therefore also add 0CALMONTH to the InfoCube and use it in partitioning.

[+]   **Time Characteristics**

You should always include all useful calendar-based and fiscal (in the FI/CO environment) time characteristics up to the most detailed (required) level in all InfoCubes. This is for practical purposes. Besides, there are no known disadvantages.

6.2.7   Currencies

In BW, currency translations have extensive functions. Several currencies usually exist for data from individual applications. However, it is always better to use existing currencies because complex currency translations may be difficult to validate and the additional computational effort may impact negatively on performance.

Key figures in most standard DataSources in FI exist in two currencies (see Table 6.3).

Currencies in FI

Key Figure	Currency	Description
0DEB_CRE_LC	0LOC_CURRCY	Amount in local currency
0DEB_CRE_DC	0DOC_CURRCY	Amount in document currency

Table 6.3 Currencies in FI InfoCubes

In CO, however, there is usually only one value key figure, namely 0AMOUNT. All data is nevertheless available in multiple currency types (0CURTYPE). For the most part, this data is available in the company code currency, controlling area currency, and document currency. The currency unit is always 0CURRENCY. This design is extremely flexible. However, the fact table also contains three times as many entries if all three currencies are loaded. It goes without saying that this has a negative effect on performance and the memory requirement. In any case, the company code currency and controlling area currency are even identical. The Content design is not ideal here. If you need multiple currency types, you may have to create parallel InfoCubes (logical partitioning) or use additional key figures as is the case in FI.

Currencies in CO

Sales key figures are either in the statistics currency, which is provided in SD for reporting purposes, or in the document currency. These are always different key figures.

Currencies in Sales and Distribution

If the existing currencies are insufficient, you can perform a currency translation in BW (in the data import processes or in reporting). The translation is based on the same principles as those in SAP ECC, but it is not identical. To do this, you can use Transaction RSCUR to determine currency translation keys from the exchange rate type, source currency, target currency, and time base. For example, the exchange rate type can be the interbank exchange rate and the source currency can come from the data record. The target currency can be EUR (fixed currency) and the time base can occur for the month-end exchange rate (variable). You can use the COPY EXCHANGE RATES option in the context menu of the relevant source system to copy the exchange rates directly from the SAP ECC system.

Currency translation in BW

6.3   SAP NetWeaver BW in FI

Line item
extractors

The most important DataSources in FI are the delta extractors for line items in the G/L in Accounts Receivable Accounting and Accounts Payable Accounting. In BW Release 3.0A, the original line item extractors, which end with 3 (for example, 0FI_GL_3), were replaced with new extractors, which end with 4 (that is, 0FI_GL_4). These supply a time stamp–based delta and can be coupled. The data is extracted directly from the document tables, that is, from BKPF/BSEG for the G/L, BSID/BSAD for customers, and BSIK/BSAK for vendors.

The original line item extractors were delivered with Release 2.0B and use a delta queue. The migration process is described in SAP Note 410797.

New General
Ledger

One of the few important new features in Business Content is the new development of extractors for the New General Ledger (NewGL).

The content in FI is highly standardized. Pure FI reporting generally requires very few customer-specific enhancements. Often, however, the reports themselves are extremely complex. Here, you frequently work with hierarchies, both for account groups and organizational characteristics.

6.3.1   G/L Reporting

0FI_GL_4

The most important DataSource for G/L Reporting is 0FI_GL_4, which supplies line items in the delta process. The delta uses the time stamp field CPUDT in the document header table BKPF to supply all modified data records. The time stamps for the extraction are logged in the table BWOM2_TIMEST. Here, the data records are after-image records, which is why a direct update into an InfoCube is not possible, that is, a standard DSO is always required at the FI item level because values can be overwritten. Because the data is supplied directly from the document tables, you do not need to use a delta queue.

Coupling

Originally, the 0FI_GL_4 extractor could only be coupled with 0FI_AR_4, 0FI_AP_4, and 0FI_TAX_4 — 0FI_GL_4 was the leading extractor here. Coupling harmonizes the data in BW (in particular, the balances in the reconciliation accounts in the sub-ledgers correspond with the G/L data).

Another special feature of these DataSources is that CI include structures can be used to enhance all of the fields in the source tables without the need for any programming. The CI include for 0FI_GL_4 is CI_BSIS. If the source tables do not contain fields, you can fill them using a function module, which you must create in accordance with the SAMPLE_PRO-CESS_00005021 template. The exact process is described in SAP Note 410799.

An important new feature in SAP ECC is the introduction of the NewGL. NewGL facilitates parallel updates in multiple ledgers, for example, for several parallel accounting principles (for example, IFRS and US-GAAP). 0FI_GL_14 is the line item extractor of the leading ledger. In Transaction FAGLBW03, you can create generic extractors for other ledgers. Here, the line item extractors are called 3FI_GL_XX_SI. In each case, XX is the name of the relevant ledger.

NewGL

6.3.2 Accounts Receivable Reporting

Accounts Receivable Reporting is usually of great interest, even outside the finance area. In most cases, outgoing invoices are synonymous with sales while incoming payments are synonymous with liquidity. The two key performance indicators here are the actual payment history for cleared items and the Days Sales Outstanding (DSO) consideration for open items. Because financial customer accounts are also highly relevant for the sales area, the data is usually enriched with SD data.

The A/R extractor 0FI_AR_4 is similar to 0FI_GL_4. Therefore, the previous information regarding 0FI_GL_4 also applies here: The data is extracted from the tables BSID and BSAD, the fields for the due date for net payment are calculated using the function module DETERMINE_DUE_DATE, and the CI include for 0FI_AR_4 is CI_BSID.

0FI_AR_4

In addition to the line item extractors, there are also extractors for transaction figures (0FI_AR_6), payment history (0FI_AR_5), and credit management data (0FI_AR_9). Preferably, the payment history should be calculated in BW itself (on the basis of line items). 0FI_AR_5 is simply a copy of the table KNB4 from SAP ECC. In credit management, it is usually necessary to check a customer credit limit against open transactions.

Additional A/R extractors

The extractor captures all of the data in the SAP ECC table KNKK. However, more data is required for a dynamic credit line check. In SAP ECC, you can use the function module SD_CREDIT_EXPOSURE to retrieve this information.

Reporting requirements The purpose of analyzing open items is mainly to understand the ageing structure. An important key figure here is the DSO, which can be calculated using different methods. The Business Content method is the simplest method (balance/sales per period × 30), but it is only useful in very homogenous sales development. It may be very time-consuming to implement better methods (for example, the count-back) (see Chapter 9, Case Studies). The second type of open item analysis is the due date list analysis (ageing grids), that is, the consideration of open items from 0 to 30 days, from 31 to 60 days, and so on. This analysis is of particularly important because provisions have to be made as of a certain number of days.

You can perform a good payment history analysis on the basis of cleared items. Here, the Content provides a query on the basis of 0FI_AR_5. However, a custom development for line items provides better analysis options.

There are no Content examples for other topics such as dunning, incoming payments (cash reporting), and credit management.

Summary Business Content for Accounts Receivable Accounting essentially provides a good, easy-to-enhance line item extractor. The Content extractor is the basis for custom developments, but Content does not have any good solutions for individual issues concerning customer analysis.

6.3.3 Accounts Payable Reporting

When you analyze vendor data, you want to check to see if the maximum payment term is always exploited because this reduces the short-term capital requirement. Vendor reports are roughly analog to customer reports.

In the case of open items, you can calculate the Days of Payables Outstanding (DPO) in exactly the same way. A due date list report is also relevant here. Furthermore, the payment history analysis here based on cleared items does not differ much from the analysis in Accounts Receivable Reporting.

Because the source of vendor information is in Purchasing, it is common practice to enrich the data with purchasing information.

Here, the vendor extractor 0FI_AP_4 is identical to 0FI_GL_4. Once again, the previous information regarding 0FI_GL_4 and 0FI_AR_4 also applies here: The data is extracted from the tables BSIK and BSAK, and the CI include for 0FI_AP_4 is CI_BSIK.

Extractor 0FI_AP_4

In the case of vendors, there are also extractors for transaction figures (0FI_AP_6), but they are not very important here.

The previous statement in relation to Business Content for Accounts Payable Accounting also applies to Business Content for Accounts Receivable Accounting. The extractor is a good basis for custom developments, but Content does not have any good solutions for individual issues.

Summary

6.3.4 Asset Accounting Reporting

In Release 3.2, two new delta extractors were delivered for Asset Accounting, namely 0FI_AA_11 for transactions and 0FI_AA_12 for depreciations. To use these extractors, you must activate the Business Add-In (BAdI) FIAA_BW_DELTA_UPDATE. Therefore, the following change tables are updated when you update transactions and change master data: BWFIAA_AEDAT_TR (transactions), BWFIAA_AEDAT_AB (depreciation areas), and BWFIAA_AEDAT_AS (master data). During the next delta update, the system will only deliver the data contained in these change tables. Transaction data is extracted from the SAP ECC tables ANEP, ANEA, and ANLC while depreciations are extracted from the table ANLP.

Extractors 0FI_AA_11 and 0FI_AA_12

The delta transfer occurs in the same way as it does in other FI DataSources, that is, using after-image records. In other words, a standard DSO is absolutely necessary for these DataSources.

Figure 6.4 shows the data model for the two asset DataSources. The InfoCubes correspond to the DSOs. You should add your own special features to these data models, but still follow the proposed model in principle.

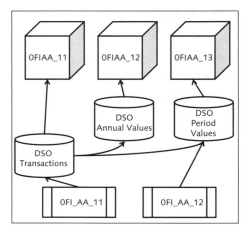

Figure 6.4 Data Model for Assets in Business Content

6.3.5 Special Purpose Ledger Reporting

Special purpose ledgers are generic ledgers that a customer can create for special purposes that are not handled in a sub-ledger. Often, a special purpose ledger is used, for example, for parallel accounting in a foreign GAAP or IFRS.

Generating DataSources for SL
Because the ledger itself is a generic application, a corresponding extractor can only be a DataSource that is generated for this generic application. In the SAP ECC system, Customizing takes place in Transaction ZBIW (or also directly in Transactions BW01 and BW03). You can also generate a totals record DataSource (3FI_SL_XX_TT) and a line item DataSource (3FI_SL_XX_SI). You require the totals record extractor for planning data and for the balance carried forward for balance sheet accounts because this information is not supplied by a line item extractor. The solution to this problem (balance carried forward and the missing 0BALANCE update) is described in SAP Note 577644. As is the case with most CO DataSources, the totals DataSource is necessary for the planning data in Full mode. The totals extractor also provides delta functions (via a delta queue) for actual data, but with some limitations (for example, you cannot use transactions that supports deletion). In teal life, however, the line item extractor is used for actual data, and the totals extractos for planning data.

In the delta process, the line item DataSource supplies data via a time stamp in the fields CPUDT and CPUTM, which are in the line item table in the special purpose ledger. The data is loaded with a safety interval of one hour.

Because this is a very customer-specific application, there is no Business Content outside of the DataSource.

6.3.6 Travel Expense Reporting

Travel Expense conrolling is an important topic in almost all enterprises. In the SAP ECC system, however, Travel Management is extremely flexible, especially in terms of cost distribution. Therefore, it is particularly difficult to denormalize data for reporting. The standard system contains two DataSources, namely 0FI_TV_01 for statistical data for travel expenses and 0FI_TV_02 for booking data. Neither DataSource is delta-capable. Because Business Content contains any amount of information about the individual trips, but not the cost assignment, the benefits of Travel Expense Reporting are weakened in most cases.

If you intend to use a more comprehensive solution here, you will have to implement a customer development for the extractor.

6.4 SAP NetWeaver BW in CO

CO is the most important area that deploys BW. SAP's front-end strategy allows for this, because even without programming knowledge, a proficient end user can define his own reports. As Excel is widely used in CO departments, BEx is clearly focused on these users. In this section, we will discuss the most important areas used in almost all customer projects: overhead costs, product costs, profitability analysis, and PCA.

For most if not all CO objects, you generally have to select the following fields to obtain a meaningful key figure: CURRENCY TYPE, VERSION, VALUE TYPE, and so on.

The following values are usually available for the currency types:

Currency type

▶ 00: Transaction currency
▶ 10: Company code currency (but, strictly speaking, the object currency of the CO object)
▶ 20: CO area currency

When the 0CO_OM* extractors were first delivered, there was still no currency type 70 (object currency). Instead, the object currency was mapped as currency type 10. However, you can change this in the table BWOM_SETTINGS (see SAP Notes 517909 and 367738).

During modeling, always bear in mind that this type of modeling is the most flexible method. However, it also has many disadvantages (memory requirement, performance) when you actually use all three currency types.

[+] **Currency Types**

In a customer project, you should always ask yourself which currency types you actually need. If multiple currency types are needed, you should change the data model (for example, key figure per currency type).

Value type — The value type in BW does not correspond to the value type in SAP ECC. Instead, the more technically oriented SAP ECC fields VALUE TYPE, ACTIVITY, and DEBIT TYPE are converted into the BW fields VALUE TYPE, KEY FIGURE TYPE, DETAILS OF VALUE TYPE, and STATISTICS INDICATOR. The conversion is made using some Customizing tables and function modules (see SAP Note 523742). In BW, the most important value type values are:

► 10: Actual values

► 20: Planning values

► 40: Commitment

► 50: Budget

You may need the "Details of Value Type" field to differentiate between the primary posting and a further allocation.

Version — Because several versions of planning data usually exist (for example, for several planning initiatives over the course of a year), you need the Version field here.

6.4.1 Cost Center Reporting and Overhead Cost Reporting

Cost center, internal order, WBS element — Overhead costs are general costs that cannot be assigned to any particular product or service. The opposite of overhead costs is direct costs, which are considered to be part of Product Cost CO. Overhead costs can generally be debited to a cost center, internal order, or work breakdown structure (WBS) element. In Business Content, these three objects originate from different DataSources. The following four DataSources exist respectively for cost centers, internal orders, and WBS elements:

▶ Costs and Allocations (Full) — In practice, these are required for planning data only because you cannot use a delta to extract planning data.

▶ Actual Cost Line Items (Delta)

▶ Commitment

▶ Statistical Key Figures

In Business Content, data from several DataSources is frequently loaded into one InfoCube. There is no reason for this, but it is associated with many disadvantages (for example, empty fields in dimension tables, in particular, result in poor performance and a greater disk space requirement). The explanation for this procedure is that there were no MultiProviders before Release 2.0A (or MultiCubes in Release 2.x) and, as a result, the only way to perform a cross-sectional evaluation of data was to load them into an InfoCube. This behavior was NOT changed for Business Content InfoCubes - the data should always be consolidated in a Multi-Provider initially. Table 6.4 lists the individual DataSources.

Type	CCA	OPA	WBS
Plan	0CO_OM_CCA_1	0CO_OM_OPA_1	0CO_OM_WBS_1
Actual	0CO_OM_CCA_9	0CO_OM_OPA_6	0CO_OM_WBS_6
Commitment	0CO_OM_CCA_10	0CO_OM_OPA_7	0CO_OM_WBS_7
SKF	0CO_OM_CCA_4	0CO_OM_OPA_4	0CO_OM_WBS_4

Table 6.4 DataSources in Overhead Cost CO

The original totals full extractors are only required for planning data (similar to FI-SL). A delta update into the InfoCube cannot be achieved here, even by using a DSO.

Totals full

The most important extractors for overhead costs are the actual line item delta extractors, which read data from the CO line item table (COEP). As is the case in FI, these extractors are extractors in the time stamp delta process, which is based on the field TIMEST in the table COEP. You can set individual safety intervals (default setting: two hours) for all

Actual line item delta

DataSources. It should be long enough to ensure that all documents are updated safely during this time. The time stamps for delta extraction are logged in the table BWOM2_TIMEST while the safety intervals are available in the view BWOM2_V_SAFETY. This update is an additive delta, that means, you could also perform a direct update into the InfoCube. Even though this would not be in accordance with the design principles of an Enterprise Data Warehouse (EDW), the data would at least be correct. However, data can also be loaded using an interim standard DSO and no safety interval, which would not be possible without a DSO (see SAP Note 553561). An additive delta is easily achieved here because a line item can no longer be changed once it has been posted in CO. The only exceptions here are changes to document text, which are ignored in the time stamp field and therefore not transferred by the delta logic.

Commitment delta Commitments are also loaded as delta. However, the line items here can change on an ongoing basis because commitments are usually reduced. Commitments are not actual costs but rather commitments that have already been received as a result of purchase orders or purchase requisitions. If the costs actually accrue, the commitment will be reduced again. The delta only provides the after image, that is, a standard DSO is required for a correct delta update. Because commitments are generally reduced again and this data would then no longer be extracted, the table COOI_PI (deleted commitment items) is built when the commitment DataSources are initialized.

SKF Statistical key figures (SKF) themselves are not costs but rather additional information that can be used in a further allocation, for example. Frequently, head count and Full Time Equivalent (FTE) are stored as SKFs. In SAP ECC, COSR is the table of origin. Furthermore, the DataSource does not support a delta extraction.

Statistical postings In the case of actual data, a CO object is always debited, that is, a cost center, internal order, or WBS element. However, other CO objects can be debited statistically. You can use the statistics indicator (0VTSTAT) to filter these data records. If you do not set a filter, statistical postings are displayed.

Partner objects The actual DataSource always contains one field for the partner object (0PIOVALUE) and one for the partner object type (0PIOBJSV). These are the CO objects that are usually credited by the same posting. The keys used for partner object types in BW differ from those used in SAP ECC. The keys for the partner objects are as follows:

▶ Cost center = 0CCT

▶ Internal order = 0COR

▶ WBS element = 0POS

For efficient reporting, it makes sense to distinguish between partner cost center, partner order, and partner WBS for these two fields.

Another important characteristic is the debit/credit indicator (0DB_CR_IND), which displays the debit and credit view in CO. It is based on the field BEKNZ (FI view), whereby the logic used in SAP ECC to determine the field BELKZ is also applied here, but without the more detailed breakdown into S (credit by settlement) and D (credit from delivery). BELKZ is a virtual characteristic in the Report Writer in SAP ECC. In other words, it is not physically available at the table level. The main difference between it and BEKNZ is that primary postings from FI and Logistics are always interpreted as debits, that is, transfer postings from these areas are always considered as corrections to incorrect primary postings, and not as credits from a CO perspective. You can also read about the differences between BELKZ and 0DB_CR_IND in SAP Note 65075.

0DB_CR_IND

6.4.2 Product Cost Reporting

Product Cost Reporting is not a pure controlling function. Rather, it involves close interaction between Materials Management (MM), Production, and CO. The production costs are those costs associated with material use and service performance. The data for both (for example, bills of material and task lists) must exist in SAP ECC. Product Cost Planning or the material cost estimate determines the expected costs associated with producing goods. The DataSources 0CO_PC_PCP_01 to 04 are available for cost estimates. The production costs that are actually accrued, and the comparison with planned costs, are in Cost Object CO. The DataSources 0CO_PC_01 and 0CO_PC_02 exist for this purpose.

None of the DataSources in Product Cost by Order or Period have delta functions. Because it is often not possible to load all of the data daily in real life, or it would, at the very least, be impractical, you must make do with always performing a very selective full load (pseudo delta). Usually,

Pseudo delta

only the current period is loaded. It may also be enough to load the data at month end.

6.4.3 Profitability Analysis Reporting

Profitability Analysis Reporting (CO-PA) lets you evaluate market segments, which can be classified according to product, customer, order, and any combination of these with respect to your company's profit or contribution margin. CO-PA is a particularly powerful reporting tool. However, it has the usual problems associated with such systems in an operational system (for example, system load, difficult to operate).

A number of fixed and free characteristics is define by operating concern in CO-PA. In CO-PA, key figures are called value fields and they are used to explain the contribution margin generated for a profitability segment. Data from various sources, especially SD (billing documents), FI, Overhead Cost CO, and Cost Object CO are transferred to these value fields.

CO-PA data model The CO-PA data model is shown in Figure 6.5. The table names always begin with CE[1–4][four characters for the controlling area]. For example, CE1US01 is the actual line item table for the controlling area US01.

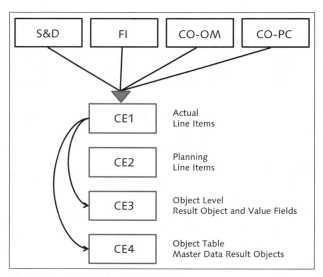

Figure 6.5 CO-PA Data Model

The line item table contains all of the data at the item level in the source transaction. CO-PA also assigns a document number. In the case of planning data, there is an additional line item table whereby the characteristics of the line items are coded as profitability segments. Individual characteristics (usually document fields) can be ignored here. The profitability segments (PAOBJNR) are stored in the CE4 tables while the value fields are stored in the CE3 tables. These roughly correspond to the dimension table and fact table in BW.

In addition to this costing-based profitability analysis, an account-based profitability analysis can occur in parallel.

Costing-based and account-based profitability analysis

For the costing-based profitability analysis, you can freely define costs and revenues according to value fields and characteristics (described previously). Account-based profitability analysis is profitability analysis in account form with an account-based valuation approach. It therefore can be validated with FI at any time. Differences may arise in the costing-based profitability analysis if goods are issued in one period and invoices created in another.

Similar to FI-SL, you must also generate the DataSource for CO-PA in Transaction SBIW in SAP ECC. Here, you must also distinguish between the two types of profitability analysis. The following is a suggested name for a new DataSource: 1_CO_PA_<%SY>_<%CL>_<%ERK> where SY denotes the system name, CL the client, and ERK the controlling area. 1_CO_PA_ cannot be changed.

Generating DataSources

Some fields are automatically converted into standard BW fields (for example, CURRENCY TYPE and VALUE TYPE). When you set up a DataSource, you must define the CO-PA characteristics that you also want to have as fields in the DataSource. The characteristics in the segment table (CE4) are selected as default characteristics. If you also select the fields in the line item table, all of the data import processes must always be loaded from this table. However, delta import processes are always based on this table. Account-based DataSources are generated in almost the same way. For Account-based, there are no characteristics from line item level. There is only an amount and quantity. COMPANY CODE and COST ELEMENT are mandatory fields here.

The extraction program generated here uses the same replication method as the method used internally in CO-PA for updating the totals tables. The standard safety interval for CO-PA is 30 minutes.

In the case of account-based profitability analysis, the initialization is loaded from CO totals tables (COSS, COSP) and the delta is loaded from CO single document tables (COEP, COBK). The initialization always occurs from the totals tables and the delta always occurs from the single document data.

In the case of the costing-based profitability analysis, data can only be loaded from the totals tables (that is, CE3 and CE4) if no characteristics have been selected at item level. In such cases, an initial load or full load may take place from the totals tables. Here, the delta is always based on single document data and the delta ID occurs via the time stamp.

6.4.4 Profit Center Reporting

PCA DataSources

While Overhead Cost Accounting (that is, the distribution of overhead costs to cost centers) is solely concerned with costs, revenues are compared against costs in PCA. This is achieved using transfer prices. The following four DataSources support PCA in BW:

▶ 0EC_PCA_1: Totals extractor

▶ 0EC_PCA_2: Statistical Key Figures

▶ 0EC_PCA_3: Line Items

▶ 0EC_PCA_4: Line Items for the Periodic Transfer of Balance Sheet Accounts

The restrictions that apply to totals extractors and line item extractors are similar to those for FI-SL extractors. Similar restrictions apply to the delta capability of the totals extractor (base table GLPCT). The line item extractor (base table GLPCA) does not supply any balance carried forward and the field 0BALANCE is not supplied by the DataSource (but can be filled in the transformation). Only 0EC_PCA_4 supplies the data for the periodic transfer of balance sheet accounts. Once again, the delta process here for all delta-capable DataSources is based on time stamp fields in the source tables.

6.5 SAP NetWeaver BW in SD

Extraction via
LIS structures

In Logistics, there are two ways to extract data, namely using Logistics Information System (LIS) structures and the Logistics Cockpit. The LIS structures method with Transaction LBW0 is the older method. The LIS is a reporting tool in SAP ERP that must be active for this type of extraction. LIS stores the data in information structures. For this type of data retrieval, these information structures are the basis for extracting data into BW, that is, the data is redundant in both systems. These methods only transfer aggregated data, which results in a lower volume of data. However, this means that data is not available at the document level in BW, which considerably limits its flexibility. LIS is no longer being developed by SAP. Furthermore, LIS has some functional shortcomings (for example, it does not report orders that have been delivered but not yet invoiced).

The second way to procure data is by using the Logistics Cockpit. You can access the Logistics Cockpit in Transaction SBIW or directly in Transaction LBWE (extraction structure Customizing), LBWF (log information), LBWG (deleting setup tables), and OLI*BW (initializing and filling setup tables). The LIS is for this method no longer required. In Customizing, you define the extraction structures, maintain and activate the DataSource, activate the delta update, and select the update mode.

Logistics Cockpit

The data is never updated directly from the source tables, but from setup tables in the case of full and initial loads and from a delta queue in the case of the delta process. In SAP ECC, update management (that is, initializing the structure, deleting the setup tables, and defining the update mode) does not occur individually for each DataSource, but always for a Logistics application.

The most important applications are:

Applications

- Application 02: Purchasing
- Application 03: Inventory CO
- Application 04: Shop Floor Control
- Application 05: Quality Management
- Application 06: Invoice Verification
- Application 08: Shipment
- Application 11: SD Sales
- Application 12: LE Shipping
- Application 13: SD Billing
- Application 17: Plant Maintenance

▶ Application 18: Customer Service

▶ Application 40, 43, 44, 45: SAP for Retail

We will now examine the SD DataSources in more detail. Their general operation and structure also apply to the remaining DataSources, that is, purchasing, change in inventory, production, and so on.

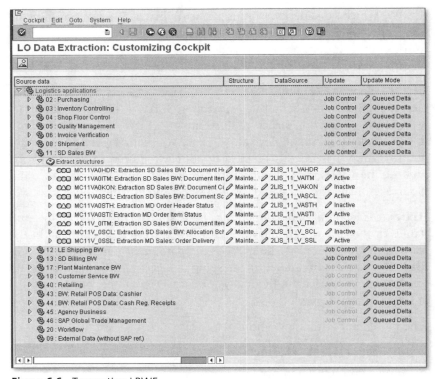

Figure 6.6 Transaction LBWE

In Transaction LBWE, you maintain the data structures for the DataSources and post-process the DataSources (post-processing is also available in Transaction RSA6 for all DataSources, that is, you show the field selection as a selection criterion, and so on, and then generate the DataSource). Furthermore, you activate the delta update and select the update mode.

Because the data is not loaded from operational tables into BW, but via a delta queue, you can use the update mode to define how or when you want to write the data to the queue. There are three options here:

V3 update

▶ Delta direct

▶ Delta queued

▶ Unserialized V3 update

Central delta management controls the update of operational data into delta queues, depending on the update option you choose. A job must also be scheduled for the V3 update. A direct update can impair the performance of the operational application.

For the initial load, you must use Transaction OLI*BW (* is not an application but a sequential number) or SBIW to create setup tables. Beforehand, you must maintain the extraction structure, maintain and activate the DataSource, and delete existing setup tables in the application.

Initialization

Following a successful initialization, you can load deltas.Bear in mind that you always need to initialize all DataSources of one application together. But, you do not have to retrieve the deltas in parallel. To start the delta mechanism, you must schedule a V3 job in LBWE and select an update mode. The delta mode is always ABR, that is, a before image is provided, which can be used to update data directly into an InfoCube. Please note the following difference: Only an after image delta is supplied for most FI DataSources, that is, a delta can only be created using a standard DSO. However, we do not recommend that you update data directly into an InfoCube. You can view the delta queue data in Transaction RSA7.

> **Note from the Experts: Emptying Delta Queues**
>
> In many cases, the delta queue must be empty (for example, for a re-initialization). Even though this is the case if you load a delta into BW, it is not yet recognized in SAP ECC. For this reason, you must re-start the same delta (InfoPackage) (0 records). Only then will SAP ECC recognize that the delta queue is empty.

[«]

There are numerous Logistics DataSources that can be easily maintained (enhanced) centrally in a Customizing transaction. BW loads data from the delta queue or setup tables, and an update job is used to update the delta queue from the operational tables.

Summary

Conditions
Another topic in SD is conditions. They are a very flexible tool for calculating prices, discounts, surcharges, and taxes.

Figure 6.7 shows how conditions are saved for orders, and so on.

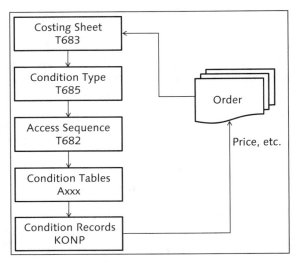

Figure 6.7 Overview of Conditions

Because Customizing is extremely complex in the T tables, it is difficult to interpret from a reporting perspective. A tables (condition tables always begin with A, followed by a three-digit number with leading zeros, for example, table A004) are the actual conditions tables. They contain a combination of characteristics, the validity duration, and a key for the condition record KNUMH. This record is available in the table KONP (for item records) and can be read using this key. Here, you also find the relevant value field (for example, PREIS).

However, what does all of this mean for BW? The individual subtotals in the costing sheet are not stored in physical tables in the operational system. Instead, they are calculated for display purposes. Many Logistics DataSources, however, have condition subtotals 1–6. These are also physically stored in SAP ECC. If the condition subtotals are insufficient, you can use special extractors to extract the current condition records. This data is supplied as a combination of condition types and condition values. Usually, this data is then converted into an easy-to-comprehend key figure (for example, using the transformation in Listing 6.1):

```
IF SOURCE_FIELDS-KNART EQ 'ABCD'.
  RESULT = SOURCE_FIELDS-KNVAL.
ELSE.
  CLEAR RESULT.
ENDIF.
```

Listing 6.1 Conversion of Condition Type and Value from a Specific Key Figure

However, because the system load may grow considerably when you extract condition records, you should use this option sparingly.

Often, you will also want to provide individual condition tables (for example, price lists) in BW (that is, an A table and, for example, KONP for the values). There is no standard extractor for this purpose and, due to technical restrictions, you must often use a function module as a source for the generic DataSource.

Logistics DataSources also supply a reversal indicator where X stands for reversed documents and R for deleted documents.

Reversal indicator

6.5.1 Quotation and Order Reporting (Application 11)

Business Content contains extensive DataSources for Quotation and Order Reporting, which we will describe in greater detail here.

The following DataSources extract sales orders, scheduling agreements, customer quotations, and contracts:

Sales documents

- ▶ 2LIS_11_VAOHDR Sales Document: Header Data
- ▶ 2LIS_11_VAOITM Sales Document: Item Data
- ▶ 2LIS_11_VAOKON Sales Document: Conditions
- ▶ 2LIS_11_VAOSCL Sales Document: Allocations

2LIS_11_VAOHDR supplies general header information about sales documents, especially the *Number of Orders* key figure, and 2LIS_11_VAOITM supplies information at the item level. This information is much more extensive than the header information. Here, you will also find the quantity, value, and condition subtotals 1–6. If you need additional conditions, you can use DataSource 2LIS_11_VAOKON. 2LIS_11_VAOSCL contains general allocation data (for example, the planned delivery date).

The following DataSources are updated by the sales order, scheduling agreement, and delivery:

▶ 2LIS_11_VASTH Sales Document Header: Status Data

▶ 2LIS_11_VASTI Sales Document Item: Status Data

▶ 2LIS_11_V_ITM Document Item: Allocation

▶ 2LIS_11_V_SCL Allocation: Schedule Line

▶ 2LIS_11_V_SSL Sales Document: Order Delivery

2LIS_11_VASTH and 2LIS_11_VASTI supply status information at the header and item level.

2LIS_11_V_ITM is used to extract open order values and 2LIS_11_V_SCL displays open quantities to be supplied. Both of these DataSources can only be enhanced to a limited extent and do not supply any deletion records.

You can use the DataSource 2LIS_11_V_SSL to extract all important delivery information from order schedule lines.

When modeling data models in accordance with the Layered, Scalable Architecture (LSA) concept, you can proceed as follows:

▶ **Data Acquisition Layer (and Corporate Memory)**
A 1:1 transfer of the necessary DataSources into write-optimized DSOs

▶ **Quality and Harmonization Layer**
Update into the standard DSO with a corresponding semantic key for each DataSource

▶ **Data Propagation Layer**
Consolidation of various DataSources, transformation of condition records into key figures, reading information from the Quality and Harmonization Layer (a corresponding example is shown in Section 6.8.4, Reading Information in the BW Back End), calculation of time differences

The Data Propagation Layer provides the data for the Reporting Layers in a very clear manner.

If, for example, you want a Data Propagation Layer DSO for order item data, you could perform the following updates (always using Quality and Harmonization Layer DSOs):

- 2LIS_11_VAITM: General Document Data
- 2LIS_11_VAHDR: Header Data to Be Added
- 2LIS_11_VAKON: Condition Data Converted into Descriptive Key Figures
- 2LIS_11_VASTI: Item Status Information Added
- 2LIS_11_VASTH: Header Status Information Is Added
- 2LIS_11_V_SSL: Order Deliveries Added Up for Each Item

The question then is which DSO key should you use and how should you use it. A header status field should be available, for example, in all items while the *Number of Orders* counter should be added only once. In the case of order deliveries, key figures must be added up in the transformation and they must not be overwritten (which is usually the case in the DSO).

Often, you will model sales documents (especially contracts) as characteristics with master data, thus making it possible to perform an evaluation with current master data.

6.5.2 Delivery Reporting (Application 12)

Deliveries are another area within SD. Business Content contains the following DataSources for this purpose:

Deliveries

- 2LIS_12_VCHDR Shipping: Header Data
- 2LIS_12_VCITM Shipping: Item Data
- 2LIS_12_VCSCL Schedule Line Delivery

2LIS_12_VCHDR and 2LIS_12_VCITM supply information about deliveries at the header and item level while 2LIS_12_VCSCL supplies the quantity delivered for each order schedule line.

For modeling, see Section 6.5.1, Quotation and Order Reporting.

6.5.3 Invoice Reporting (Application 13)

Billing documents are the last area within SD. The following DataSources are available here:

Billing documents

▸ 2LIS_13_VDHDR Billing: Header Data

▸ 2LIS_13_VDITM Billing: Item Data

▸ 2LIS_13_VDKON Billing: Document Conditions

2LIS_13_VCHDR and 2LIS_13_VCITM supply billing information at the header and item level. You can also use 2LIS_13_VDKON to extract individual conditions that do not exist in the subtotals in 2LIS_13_VCITM.

For modeling, see Section 6.5.1, Quotation and Order Reporting.

6.6 SAP NetWeaver BW in HR

Extensive Business Content is available for HR. Just like in the other areas, DataSources are particularly important here and the objects in BW should only be regarded as examples. In this section, we will introduce you to some DataSources from personnel administration, time recording, and payroll. We will also describe some common problems.

Full   Generally, many DataSources in SAP ERP HCM do not support any delta mechanism. However, this is not as problematic as it would be in the sales area, for example, because, for the most part, data does not have to be loaded from HCM on a daily basis (for example, payroll usually runs once a month), and because the volume of data here is generally considerably lower than it is in the sales area.

6.6.1 Personnel Administration Reporting (0HR_PA*)

Business Content contains extensive DataSources for the following areas:

▸ Compensation Management

▸ Benefits Administration

▸ Organizational Management (Staffing Assignment)

▸ Personnel Development (Qualifications and Appraisals)

▸ Number of Employees and Personnel Actions

▸ Recruitment

▸ Pension Fund

The Number of Employees and Personnel Actions (that is, hiring and terminations) are particularly important here. The Business Content Cube 0PA_C01 is filled by the two DataSources 0HR_PA_0 (Employees) and 0HR_PA_1 (Personnel Actions). Here, the Content can most likely be transferred with only minor changes. However, employees and actions should also be separated at the InfoCube level. In BW only, there is another DataSource for headcount, which is based on the BW master data for 0EMPLOYEE and 0PERSON. The DataSource is called 0HR_PA_PA_1. For more information, please see SAP Note 336229. The associated InfoCube 0PAPA_C02 models the headcount as a non-cumulative key figure.

Number of employees and personnel actions

Furthermore, please note that some DataSources exist to use the SAP ECC structural authorization check also in BW.

6.6.2 Time Management Reporting (0HR_PT*)

The following three DataSources exist for time management:

- 0HR_PT_1 Planned Working Times
- 0HR_PT_2 Actual Working Times
- 0HR_PT_3 Quota Transactions

All time management DataSources are delta-capable.

0HR_PT_1 specifies the individual planned working time from the personnel daily work schedule for each employee and day. Sources of actual data include info-types 2001 (Absences), 2002 (Attendances), 2010 (Employee Remuneration Information), and the time evaluation cluster PCL2 B2.

Times in HCM

Cross-Application Time Sheet (CATS) data is very closely related to time and labor data. Here, there are two DataSources, namely DataSource 0CA_TS_IS_1 for Approved CATS and 0CA_TS_IS_2 for CATS Released for Approval. 0CA_TS_IS_1 is delta-capable and 0CA_TS_IS_2 is not, nor is it necessary for CATS that are to be approved.

CATS (Cross-Application Time Sheet data)

Usually, 0HR_PT_1 is compared with 0HR_PT_2 or 0CA_TS_IS_1 to calculate employee utilization. Here, you should also model the target and actual data in separate InfoCubes and not load them together as done in the Business Content InfoCube 0PT_C01.

6.6.3 Payroll Reporting (0HR_PY*)

The old extractor 0HR_PY_1 contains very detailed payroll data. The problem, however, is that this DataSource cannot contain the in-period and for-period simultaneously — even though this is a frequent requirement. You must either read the data from the payroll cluster in the customer exit or make a copy of the standard extractor and configure one with in-period and for-period. Reading data in the customer exit is associated with a greater development effort while copying the extractor is associated with doubling the volume of data.

0HR_PY_1_CE Since SAP ERP Release 6.0 SPS 13, the DataSource 0HR_PY_1_CE (payroll data, concurrent employment-enabled) provides a new extractor that supplies both the payroll month and the payment month. Therefore, if you have this release in SAP ERP, you should use the new extractor.

Another DataSource is 0HR_PY_PP_2 for payroll posting documents. Payroll posting documents are created when you transfer payroll results to Accounting. 0HR_PY_PP_1 contains revision information for reconciling payroll posting documents with individual payroll results.

All DataSources are delta-capable and supply an additive delta.

6.7 Classification Data

Generating DataSources The classification system in SAP ERP is a very flexible tool for classifying objects (for example, products and customers). If classifications are used in SAP ERP, they should generally also be available in BW. In Business Content, you can create DataSources generically for all classifiable objects and you can create text DataSources for all characteristics used. You maintain and generate DataSources in Transaction SBIW via the menu path SETTINGS FOR APPLICATION-SPECIFIC COMPONENTS • CROSS-APPLICATION COMPONENTS • CLASSIFICATION SYSTEM. Classification DataSources always begin with 1CL_.

Figure 6.8 shows the data model for the classification system. The actual classification data is therefore available in table AUSP.

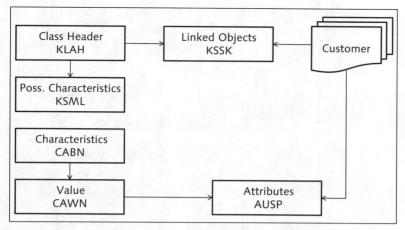

Figure 6.8 Data Model for the Classification System in SAP ECC

In SAP ECC, you can have multiple-value classifications (for example, a cell phone manufacturer could have a *Device type* product classification). For example, a product could be a business cell phone and smart phone simultaneously. Because there is no 1:n assignments to characteristics in BW, such a multiple-value classification is not possible in BW.

Multiple-value classifications

6.8 Activation and Enhancement

In this section, we will describe how you can activate Business Content in SAP ECC and BW, and how you can make necessary enhancements.

6.8.1 Activating Business Content in SAP ECC

Business Content in SAP ECC is part of a plug-in that contains Business Content DataSources. You must activate a DataSource before you can use it.

When you use new DataSources (BW Release 7) in BW, they are activated remotely in SAP ECC. However, you need to activate 3.x DataSources in SAP ECC. You do this in Transaction SBIW (see Figure 6.9). Before you transfer DataSources, you must transfer the entire application component hierarchy. DataSources, on the other hand, can be transferred indi-

Transaction SBIW

vidually. Once you have transferred the DataSources to SAP ECC, you still have to replicate them in BW (via the menu path RSA1 • Source System • Replicate Metadata). The DataSources will then be available in BW.

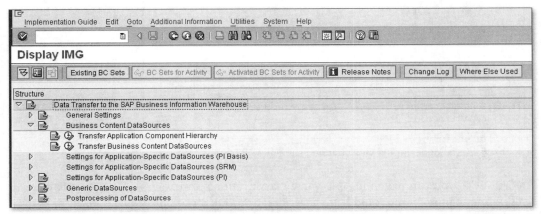

Figure 6.9 Transaction SBIW (Customizing Data Extraction in the Source System)

6.8.2 Activating Business Content in SAP NetWeaver BW

Versions of BW objects

All BW objects (for example, InfoObjects, InfoCubes, transformations, queries, and MultiProviders) can exist in several versions:

- ▶ A version: active version
- ▶ M version: changes not transferred to active version until they are activated
- ▶ D version: delivery version of Business Content

In BW, the entire Business Content exists in the D version, but the D version is not written until the Content is transferred to the A version. Because the D version is not deleted, you can always retroactively view changes to the Content. The Business Content is transferred using Transaction RSA1 (here it is called BI Content).

Figure 6.10 shows how to collect Content objects in the system and subsequently transfer them.

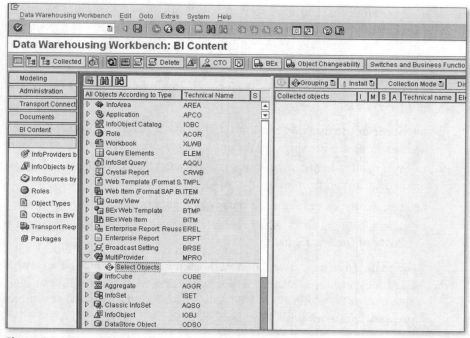

Figure 6.10 BI Content Transfer

During the transfer, an A version is created, which can be changed and overwritten as a result of a new transfer. Therefore, the Content object is often copied to the customer namespace.

Transferring Business Content objects

[+]

Recommendation for Transferring Content

You should avoid transferring the entire Content because it will impair performance during administration and the navigation will become very confusing. You should only copy what you need.

6.8.3 Enhancing a DataSource

In the case of fields that already exist in the source structure, you can often obtain the additional field by enhancing the extract structure. The Logistics Cockpit generally provides all of the fields in the source tables.

Customer exit Often, however, you have to read data from another area (for example, Logistics data in an FI DataSource). In such cases, you can use a customer exit to insert your own programming. If the data that needs to be read is also available in BW, you can also make the enhancement in BW.

The following are some reasons for such an implementation in an operational system:

- Some of the function modules, tables, etc., that you need for data calculations are missing in BW.
- You need to avoid import dependencies (an import dependency arises if data is read from other BW objects).
- Only some of the required data is available in BW.
- The additional field (which you want to enhance) changes the granularity of the DataSource.

The main advantage associated with such an implementation in BW is that the operational system is not burdened with the additional logic (system load). Furthermore, BW data is usually denormalized and therefore easier to work with.

An example of an enhancement to a standard DataSource is described in Chapter 9.

[+] **Should the DataSource Be Enhanced?**

For the most part, you can enhance the fields in the source tables of a standard DataSource by enhancing the extraction structure (append), without the need for source code in a user exit. Before you enhance a DataSource in an exit, you should check to see if this information can also be read into BW. It is technically easier to read information in BW. Furthermore, it relieves the burden on the operational system.

6.8.4 Reading Information in the BW Backend

Frequently, it is necessary to read information that is already available elsewhere in BW (for example, document information from a line item DSO or master data attributes from an InfoObject). You can generally also read this information in the DataSource. However, this is time-consuming because, in such cases, the new field must be added to all layers. This procedure also increases the runtime of the extractors in the operational system, which is generally more criticized as having an additional burden on the BW system. Lookups in the BW system are usually simpler to make because the data is stored in flat structures. Furthermore, in the BW system, you do not need any source code to read a field update concerning the attributes of a characteristic contained in the source structure. If you need source code, you can implement it in one of the following four places:

- **Start routine**

  As the start routine is executed before the single routines, you can access the data's input structure (SOURCE_PACKAGE) but not its target structure (RESULT_PACKAGE), which means that you cannot directly update fields that are not contained in the SOURCE_PACKAGE. However, because you can use InfoSources to add all of the target fields to the input structure, this means that you can also access the target fields in the start routine.

- **Single routine**

  In the transformation, you can define source code for each characteristic and key figure. Because this routine is called for every data record, you should not directly access the database from here.

- **End routine**

  The end routine is executed after the single routines. You now have no further access to the data's input structure (SOURCE_PACKAGE).

- **Expert routine**

  The advantage here is that you can see the data's input structure (SOURCE_PACKAGE) and target structure (RESULT_PACKAGE), but the system will no longer perform some standard tasks. Instead, you must take care of everything in your custom development. This is especially true for transformations in DSOs and for InfoObjects that require more than just additive updates. Only use the expert routine in exceptional cases.

A very good procedure here is to first load the (lean) data in the start routine into an internal table and then read the internal table in the single routines.

Proven procedure

Listing 6.2 is an example of reading the creation date for an SD billing document. First, you must define the structure and internal table in the declaration part of the start routine:

```
TYPES:
  BEGIN OF INVOICE_ITEM_STRUCTURE,
    BILL_NUM TYPE /BIO/OIBILL_NUM,
    BILL_ITEM TYPE /BIO/OIBILL_ITEM,
    CREATEDON TYPE /BIO/OICREATEDON,
  END OF INVOICE_ITEM_STRUCTURE.
DATA:
  INVOICE_ITEM_LINE TYPE INVOICE_ITEM_STRUCTURE,
  INVOICE_ITEM_ITAB TYPE
      HASHED TABLE OF INVOICE_ITEM_STRUCTURE
      WITH UNIQUE KEY BILL_NUM BILL_ITEM.
```

Listing 6.2 Declaration Part of the Start Routine for Reading from a DSO

Listing 6.3 shows how the internal table is then filled in the actual start routine:

```
DESCRIBE TABLE SOURCE_PACKAGE.
IF SY-TFILL > 0.
  SELECT BILL_NUM
         BILL_ITEM
         CREATEDON
      FROM /BIC/A{DSO Name}00
      INTO TABLE INVOICE_ITEM_ITAB
      FOR ALL ENTRIES IN SOURCE_PACKAGE
      WHERE  BILL_NUM = SOURCE_PACKAGE-BILL_NUM
      AND BILL_ITEM = SOURCE_PACKAGE-BILL_ITEM.
ENDIF.
```

Listing 6.3 Start Routine for Reading from a DSO

Finally, Listing 6.4 shows how the values in the single routine can be updated:

```
READ TABLE INVOICE_ITEM_ITAB
WITH TABLE KEY
  BILL_NUM = SOURCE_FIELDS-BILL_NUM
  BILL_ITEM = SOURCE_FIELDS-BILL_ITEM
    INTO INVOICE_ITEM_LINE.
IF SY-SUBRC = 0.
  RESULT = INVOICE_ITEM_LINE-CREATEDON.
ELSE.
  CLEAR RESULT.
ENDIF.
```

Listing 6.4 Reading from a DSO in a Single Routine

The single routines are always executed for each characteristic or key figure. If several characteristics need to be read from the same source, the "read" action is executed several times. If the logic is more complex, you can only execute it once and save the results. Unfortunately, you will not know which single routine is executed first, which is why you then always have to repeat the entire logic for each characteristic or key figure (preferably by using a function module). The start routine is executed before all of the records are transformed. Unfortunately, it is not possible to implement one type of start routine for every data record.

6.9   Miscellaneous

In addition to the areas described here, Business Content also exists for a number of rarely used applications, industry solutions, and non-SAP ECC systems such as SAP CRM, SAP APO, and SAP Business One. However, a detailed description of all of these areas would be far beyond the scope of this book.

There is also Demo Content and Technical Content. Demo Content pertains to examples that a program fills with sample data from flat files, so that the Content contains not only BW objects but also sample data. Technical Content, on the other hand, is used to evaluate statistics data concerning query runtime behavior and load performance.

Demo Content, Technical Content

6.10   Conclusion

In SAP ERP, standard reports are useful applications for every single customer. A similar strategy was also pursued early on in BW whereby countless queries and data models were created. However, they actually only play a minor role in practice. Instead, Business Content extractors (DataSources) and the associated InfoObjects for master data are particularly important here.

In summary, we can say that the real strength of Business Content lies in its ability to provide good delta-capable extractors in all of the main areas. This is also the biggest advantage that SAP NetWeaver BW has over other DWH vendors. This chapter also discussed the problem of individual extractors. Standard InfoObjects facilitate fast implementations even if you shouldn't copy them without first giving them some consideration. The DSO and Content data models for InfoCubes exist from a very early release and are rather outdated. Even though you can use Content data models as an initial template, you should not use them directly because they do not adhere to many of the principles associated with a good data model. In particular, Content does not pursue a layer model.

For almost all of the most important processes, line item extractors exist for actual data and they can be loaded using a delta process. Here, we introduced you to extractors for almost all processes in FI/CO, HR, and SD. At the document level, this data is usually stored at the DSO level. In InfoCubes, you should focus on high-performance reporting and avoid using the document level.

You can easily enhance the data from Business Content DataSources. Most of the time, enhancements are made directly in BW. If the data is not yet available in BW, you can also enhance the extraction in the source system. Fields from the same tables, which form the basis for the Business Content extractor, are usually filled automatically. If data procurement is more complex, you can use a customer exit to enhance Business Content extractors.

In the previous chapter, we introduced you to the Layered, Scalable Architecture (LSA), which differentiates between generally applicable Enterprise Data Warehouse (EDW) layers and application-specific layers. In this chapter, we will describe the key topics for creating EDW layers.

7 Modeling the EDW

This chapter will tell you what you need to know for modeling application-independent EDW layers. Here, we will describe how you can design a data flow and data storage (from sources to the Data Propagation Layer). This design will be based on the stepped layer arrangement that is used in the LSA and was introduced in Chapter 5, Reference Architecture for Data Modeling. Delta processes, modeling data storage in different layers, defining transformations, the history management concept, and the master data harmonization concept are fundamental to data modeling in SAP NetWeaver Business Warehouse (BW), and are also relevant if you do not strictly adhere to the LSA when creating layers.

When you create a data flow, you must define inbound interfaces (Section 7.2, Defining Inbound Interface). You can then select a delta process (Section 7.3, Delta Process), which will reduce the volume of data to be loaded. Because each layer fulfills a specific purpose, you must set up a suitable data store for each given purpose (Section 7.4, Modeling Data Storage). Transformations describe the processing rules for data in the data flow (Sections 7.5, Transformations, and 7.6, Domain Creation and Central Transformations). This data is automatically loaded during live operation. Process chains (Section 7.7, Process Chains) and possibly an additional load control (Section 7.8, Load Control) are used for this purpose. Special features associated with loading master data will be described in Sections 7.9.1, Special Features When Loading Master Data, and 7.9.2, Integrating Multiple Sources. Finally, Section 7.10, Data Timelines and History Management, will discuss how to map changes that are made to data over time.

First, let's take a look at a reference architecture for loading data into BW. We will outline some typical load paths in Section 7.1, Reference Architecture for Staging Scenarios.

7.1   Reference Architecture for Staging Scenarios

Figure 7.1 shows typical staging scenarios within the reference layers. The display has been simplified and only shows physical data stores, not InfoSources, as a means of designing a more flexible data flow.

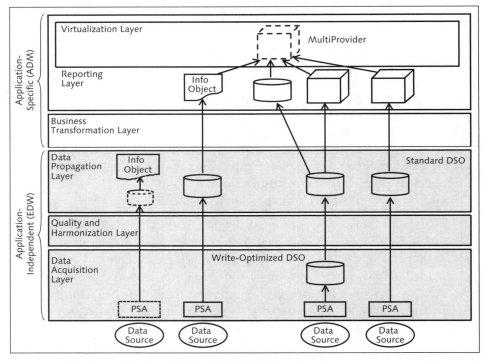

Figure 7.1   Reference Architecture with Staging Scenarios

The first two data flows relate to master data staging. In the first scenario, the master data tables of the InfoObject are updated directly. In the second scenario, however, the data is stored temporarily, which may be necessary if you need to harmonize keys. The right-hand side of the figure shows two update options for transaction data. The specific requirements of each application scenario will determine how often the data needs to be physically stored in the data flow. You must always make provisions for data storage in the Data Propagation Layer and Data Mart Layer. Furthermore, data is always accessed via the Virtual Layer.

7.2 Defining Inbound Interfaces

If you already have a specific requirement for the key figures and characteristics provided in BW, you must analyze the sources from which the data can be extracted. You can connect different sources to the BW system. Table 7.1 provides an overview of different transfer methods and sources for BW.

Data Source	Example	Transfer Method
Relational database	Teradata, IBM DB1	DB Connect, UD Connect
Multidimensional database	Hyperion	UD Connect
SAP source	SAP Customer Relationship Management (CRM), and so on	Business intelligence (BI) Service Application Programming Interface (API)
Flat file	–	File interface, SAP BusinessObjects Data Services
XML		Web service
Legacy applications	Oracle Financials	Extraction, Transformation, Load (ETL) tool via Business Application Programming Interface (BAPI), SAP BusinessObjects Data Services

Table 7.1 Data Sources and Transfer Methods

If you connect a third-party database or application, you should check to see how much data staging will be necessary. If required, we recommend that you use SAP BusinessObjects Data Services (for example, the Data Integrator) for data staging. In this section, we will only examine those options available in BW for data loading and data staging.

Connecting third-party tools

If you extract data from SAP ERP, you can often access preconfigured standard extractors. However, you also have the option of enhancing existing extractors or implementing your own extractors.

Extraction from SAP ERP

DataSource All transfer methods provide a DataSource for BW, which you can use as a basis for creating an intra-BW data flow.

A DataSource describes data that is extracted in one go. In BW, it corresponds to a flat structure, which combines a number of fields, and comprises related business fields that form a logical unit. There are two different types of DataSources:

▸ DataSources for master data (for texts, attributes, and hierarchies)
▸ DataSources for transaction data

By separating the data into master data and transaction data, you can keep the interfaces for loading transaction data small because, in the case of transaction data, only essential information (keys) that describes a business transaction must be transferred (keys and key figures).

The structure of the DataSource is also known to the source system. Furthermore, the DataSource in the source system is associated with tables, views, or programs that merge the data from SAP ERP in accordance with their structure.

Granularity The DataSource structure defines the granularity of the extracted data. In other words, the granularity is defined by key figure references to specific keys (and therefore to specific business objects such as customer, order, and so on). Because the granularity directly influences the evaluation options for loaded data, you should bear this in mind when defining the granularity, that is, the level of detail should be such that the data can provide answers to any analytical questions that relate to a particular context. For certain questions, aggregation does not make sense until the Data Mart level. Furthermore, disaggregation is associated with increased time and effort because you must either integrate a data merging program into a transformation or use InfoSets, for example, to connect several DataProviders. Due to their limited comprehensibility and performance, InfoSets are best suited for one-time analyses and, to a limited extent, for establishing Online Analytical Processing (OLAP) reporting or standard reporting (see Chapter 8, Section 8.4.2, InfoSets in the Virtual Layer).

Distinction between transaction data and master data The transaction data DataSource should not include all analysis-relevant fields. Only business objects that reference key figures are stored here. No other descriptive fields are transferred. Instead, such fields must be added to the attribute, text, or hierarchy DataSources of InfoObjects, which describe the central business objects. As a result of this separation, the data is only transferred to the BW system once during data loading. Let's consider, for example, transaction data that describes the sale of articles to customers. The *Number* key figure, article number, customer number, date, and time are all that you need to fully describe the business transaction. The customer's place of residence and the color of the article sold are completely irrelevant for the transaction data DataSource. This information is still available in BW (integrated for analysis purposes) if you load it as attributes for the *Customer* or *Business partner* objects or for the *Article* object.

You should commit the following maxim to memory: "extract once, deploy many" (see Haupt, 2003). In other words, extract data once, but deploy it in different analysis contexts. Here, the goal is to load data into the BW system only once, but to make it available there in a suitable format wherever necessary. By doing so, you shorten data loading times and reduce the volume of data to be stored in BW. This procedure is also a basic prerequisite for being able to work in BW with reconciled data that only describes "one truth." However, in addition to a suitable source system interface design, the structure of the EDW layers, especially the Data Propagation Layer, is relevant for achieving this goal.

Extract once, deploy many

In a BW implementation, you may have to organize numerous DataSources. For each master data–bearing InfoObject, there is one to three assigned DataSources (texts, attributes, hierarchies) and transaction data DataSources. To better manage DataSources, they are organized into an application component hierarchy, which is provided by the source system (SAP ERP, BW, and ETL tools) or must be maintained by the user.

Application component hierarchy

The volume of data to be transferred is determined not only by the quantity and scope of the data fields in an interface, but by the number of data records, which can be reduced by choosing a suitable delta process.

Reducing the volume of data

7.3 Delta Process

There are two ways to extract data from source systems, namely full data extraction (known as full extraction) and the use of a delta process (known as delta extraction). If the volume of data underlying the application is relatively small, you can, under certain circumstances, allow all data to be reloaded at all times. In this context, it is sufficient to only transfer new, changed, and deleted data. To do this, you can use a delta process to extract data, but this is generally deemed to be rather time-consuming if it has not already been delivered via Standard Content. On the other hand, you can easily determine a delta within the BW system because delta determination is one of the standard functions provided by standard DataStore Objects (DSOs).

Delta mode

Delta processes let you considerably reduce the volume of data to be processed. In principle, you can use delta processes for both master data and transaction data. If you use full extraction to load data, you must delete any data already available in BW. This is not necessary when you use delta extraction because the process causes the data in the data target to be changed and deleted.

Various delta modes exist. On the one hand, the delta modes are described by a special field in each data record that is loaded (the record mode, which is mapped via the InfoObject 0RECORDMODE) and, on the other hand, by the delta process used by the DataSource.

Record modes

Table 7.2 describes the different record modes available. Each delta data record must provide an "explanation" as to how the delta information should be transferred. This is the only way to suitably update the data record in the data target.

0RECORDMODE	Name	Description
N	New image	State after a new data record is created
X	Before image	State before changes are made to a data record
' ' (empty)	After image	State after changes are made to a data record
A	Additive image	State after a new data record is created or after changes are made to a data record, in the case of attributes that cannot be added up
		Description of the delta value in the case of attributes that can be added up
R	Reverse image	Identical to the before image, state before changes are made to a data record
		Further processing in the DSO causes a record with the same key to be deleted
D	Deletion	Deletion of a record with a corresponding key

Table 7.2 Record Modes (Mapping Delta Information to Data Records)

The delta process is determined by the DataSource and results in certain record modes that the relevant DataSource can supply. In BW, the table RODELTAM provides an overview of possible delta processes. This table also shows you which record modes can be created by which DataSource (in the ONLYFULL to UPD_RIM columns; see Figure 7.2).

Delta process for DataSources

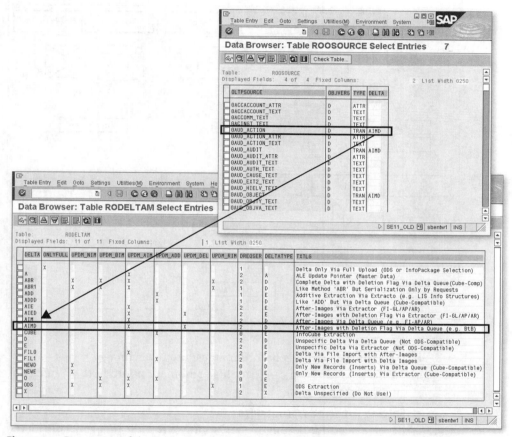

Figure 7.2 Description of the Properties of a DataSource in the Tables ROOSOURCE and RODELTAM

For data modeling, it is important that not every record mode can be updated into every data target. In principle, DSOs can process each record mode because they represent the central object, from modeling to the EDW layer. In the case of InfoCubes, however, only an additive

Record mode and permitted update methods

update is possible, which means that, in an InfoCube, data records with the same characteristic value are added up, but not overwritten. Figure 7.3 shows the relationship between the record mode and the option of updating data into data targets for transaction data. Please note the following dependencies:

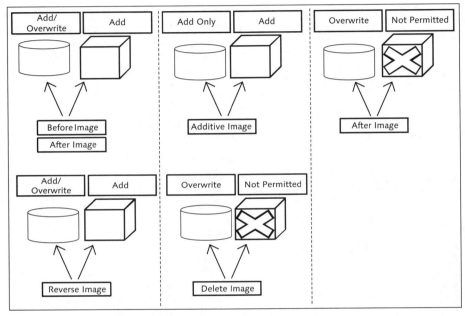

Figure 7.3 Update Options for Various Record Modes

▶ **DataSource supplies before images and after images**
  In this scenario, you can load this combination into both an InfoCube and DataStore object.

▶ **Setting for overwriting data**
  If you select this setting in DSOs, only the after image is considered during activation. If you configure the DSO in such a way that data is added, both the before image and after image are required to correctly load the data into the target.

▶ **Additive image**
  You can load an additive image into an InfoCube and DSO. In the case of the DSO, the update type for key figures must be ADDITION, not OVERWRITE.

▶ **After image only**
If the DataSource sends the after image only, it must be updated into a DSO that must be in OVERWRITE mode.

▶ **Reverse images**
All data targets can process reverse images.

▶ **Deletion of data in InfoCubes**
Delta processing cannot be used to delete data in InfoCubes.

It is therefore important that the Data Propagation Layer facilitates an additive update in the Reporting Layer (possibly based on various sources with different delta processing). Here, you can use a standard DSO to convert different inbound deltas into one additive delta (delta harmonization).

Delta harmonization

7.4 Modeling Data Storage

The LSA describes different layers, each of which has a specific purpose and therefore very different requirements in terms of data retention. In this section, we will provide you with an overview of the different Info-Providers to model the EDW layers.

Usually, the generally applicable LSA layers described in this chapter are not used directly for creating reports. Therefore, these layers are not optimized for query performance. Even though InfoCubes are generally not used at this level, you still have a certain degree of freedom in terms of data modeling. Since Release BW 7.0, you can choose between different DSO types (standard, write-optimized, or direct update), each of which is optimized for certain application scenarios. Because the different layers in our layer architecture have certain functions, a suitable means of storage can usually only be described for each layer. In addition to the general distribution of tasks among layers, you should always consider the application scenario to ensure that you obtain the best data modeling for you.

The Persistent Staging Area (PSA), the Data Acquisition Layer, and the Corporate Memory are used to store data in its raw form. Only the Corporate Memory needs to store the data permanently. The PSA and Data Acquisition Layer, on the other hand, are usually emptied before each new load run. The data stored in the aforementioned data stores is

Raw data

accessed during the staging process (usually not by reporting). Therefore, you can choose write-optimized data storage.

Persistent Staging Area The PSA is less suited to storing data over a longer period of time because the data stored here has not yet undergone a basic quality assurance process, which is exactly what the PSA does (that is, it detects and corrects errors). This mechanism is used for the quality assurance of downstream datasets in the staging process. However, the PSA is not always a good data store for creating new downstream layers. Depending on the interface's load history, it is possible that requests could be posted twice in the PSA, which may also contain incorrect data. If you wanted to reload the data in the PSA into data targets at a later time, you would first require an in-depth analysis of the load history of the PSA data.

Data Acquisition Layer and Corporate Memory The data in the Data Acquisition Layer and Corporate Memory is stored in its raw form. However, it can be useful to add a time stamp, check key figures for null values, or perform an enhanced technical quality check. It would therefore be wise to provide additional temporary data storage in the Data Acquisition Layer. Write-optimized DSOs are particularly suited for this purpose because they are high-performance objects that can be fully integrated into staging (read and write access). The sequence and granularity of the loaded data remains completely intact, which results in a large volume of data. Only the Corporate Memory provides for the permanent storage of raw data. On the other hand, the data in the Data Acquisition Layer must be deleted at regular intervals.

Write-optimized DSOs It is important that the storage of data in write-optimized DSOs does not conform with the importance of the data from a business perspective. There is no aggregation in accordance with a defined business key. Instead, a technical key prevents the data from being merged.

Data Propagation Layer For the Data Propagation Layer, however, the data must be stored according to business criteria. You should therefore use a suitable semantic key during data modeling (for example, a customer number, order number, or order item). Depending on which key value is loaded, new data records will be added or existing records updated, that is, you can update the key figures or characteristics. Furthermore, delta processing must be possible to populate downstream data targets. For this reason, standard DSOs are suitable for storing data in the Data Propagation Layer.

Quality and Harmonization Layer Both write-optimized DSOs and DSOs for direct update are unsuitable for the aforementioned requirements. DSOs for direct update cannot be integrated into the data flow and are only described via a program. They are frequently used if complex calculations are performed (for example, statistical calculations) and the results are stored directly from the calculation programs.

Both transaction data and master data can be stored in DSOs. When creating a multilayer architecture, it is common practice not to load the data directly into InfoObjects, but to stage it beforehand, if necessary, and then update it into the master data tables of the InfoObjects. InfoObjects can only be updated if the Data Propagation Layer (usually for objects that are valid globally) or Data Mart Layer (for objects that are valid locally) is updated.

If necessary, you can also temporarily store data in the Quality and Harmonization Layer. Various types of DSOs are used here.

You are now familiar with the storage options available for the different layers in the LSA. In the next section, you will learn how to use transformations to edit (that is, change) data.

Enhancement options

7.5 Transformations

A transformation describes a set of data processing rules. It defines how data is transferred from a source structure to a target structure. The source and target can be physical data stores such as Cubes and DSOs. They can also be InfoSources, which cannot store any data themselves, but describe a structure that can be used to link multiple processing steps. Figure 7.4 provides an overview of permitted links between sources and targets.

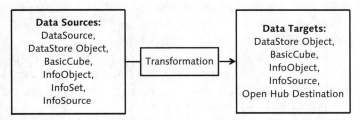

Figure 7.4 Permitted Data Sources and Data Targets in a Transformation

When it comes to enhancing transformations, numerous options are available (see Figure 7.5). On the one hand, you can derive characteristics and key figures at the single InfoObject level ❶. On the other hand, you can implement more complex transformation tasks by defining programs in the form of a start routine ❷, end routine ❸, and expert routine (via the menu path EDIT • EXPERT ROUTINE ❹).

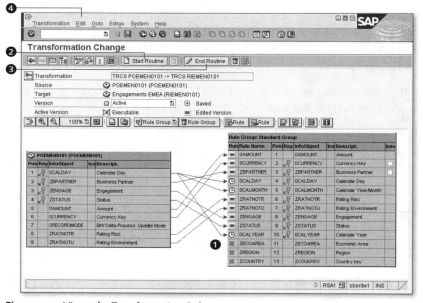

Figure 7.5 View of a Transformation Rule

Data granularity

Transformations are used at every level in a layer model. One characteristic of transformations up to the Data Propagation Layer is that they are usually modeled in such a way that the granularity of the data is retained. Transaction processing is therefore limited to processing data at the field level. Aggregations and, if necessary, disaggregations first become relevant in the context of a specific question concerning the Data Mart Layer. The granularity of the data supplied by the DataSource is usually retained when staging the data up to the Data Propagation Layer and is based on the business process described by the data.

Parallel staging

During staging, only compatible data is transformed into a data target, that is, data that describes the same business process or process step. In the Reporting Layer itself, such data is stored in separate physical stores, even if the data is to be evaluated together. Comprehensive views are only generated when you use MultiProviders or InfoSets. The approach to creating domains (see Section 7.6) allows for a more complex partitioning of the data flow during staging.

Transformations are created in the Data Warehousing Workbench. The context menu of the object that is working as a data target contains the entry CREATE TRANSFORMATION. If you create a new transformation, a transformation with a 1:1 assignment of all characteristics and key figures contained in the source and target is generated as the basis for your definition. You can enhance this initial transformation definition by defining your own rules and routines.

Creating transformations

Rules define the way in which the field values in the target structure are determined. In the simplest scenario, this is the direct assignment (DIRECT ASSIGNMENT) of a field from the source. The other rule types shown in Figure 7.6 are as follows:

Rule types

- Constant
- Formula
- Read Master Data
- Routine

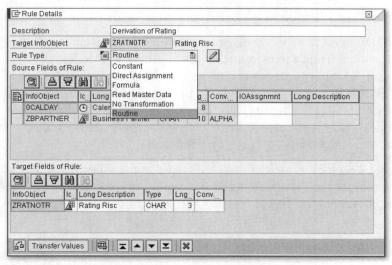

Figure 7.6 Selection of Rule Types in a Transformation

You also have the option of not updating a field (No Transformation).

The rules types Read Master Data, Formula, and Routine will be described in more detail in Section 7.5.1, Important Rule Types.

Rule groups You can also use rule groups to create multilevel target data records. For example, over the course of several runs, you can derive several target data records from one source data record. In the standard scenario, you work with just one standard rule group and only use additional rule groups if required. A new rule group gives you the option to specify other rules when deriving target fields. However, please note that you can only use rule groups if you first establish the exact number of records to be created. However, if this is dependent on the input data, you must access routines. In addition to "normal" rule groups, there is also a technical rule group, which you can use to determine the delta mode for the transformed data. This way, you can control how the updated data is updated in the data target. In Section 7.9.1, we will use the delta mode defined in a transformation to delete data records.

Start, end, and expert routines If you want to implement more complex transformations, you can use a start or end routine to insert an additional processing step at the start or end of a transformation, respectively. Alternatively, you can use an expert routine to fully implement your own transformation. We will describe each of these routines in greater detail in Section 7.5.2, Start, End, and Expert Routines.

Aggregation types In addition to deriving target data records from source data records, it is also important (from a transformation result perspective) to know which data records are already contained in the target and how the system deals with records that have the same key. You can control this behavior by configuring an aggregation type in the transformation for the relevant target field. Here, you can choose between Overwrite, Leave (no transformation), and Summation (for key figures).

We will take a look at each of these rule types in the following sections. Because simple field assignments do not require an explanation, we will not mention them here.

7.5.1 Important Rule Types

Formula When you use formulas, you can access predefined functions for character strings, mathematical calculations, and so on, thus enabling you to easily create rules without any knowledge of ABAP programming. For more complex rules, however, you soon reach the limits of the above functions, or the formulas are heavily nested and therefore difficult to read. You should therefore access routines instead.

By reading master data, you can access the attributes of an InfoObject directly and therefore fill a characteristic in the target structure with an attribute value. Attribute reading is frequently used when loading data into the Data Propagation Layer and Reporting Layer. If you want to read master data, you must map the object with the target object whose attributes you wish to read. In the example shown in Figure 7.7, the rating for a business partner (target object) is derived from the corresponding attribute of the business partner.

Reading master data

A system prerequisite here is that the corresponding target object is also modeled as an attribute and proposed accordingly. Please note that you have to make additional settings for time-dependent master data. Choose the clock symbol (highlighted in Figure 7.7) to access the relevant selection screen (see Figure 7.8).

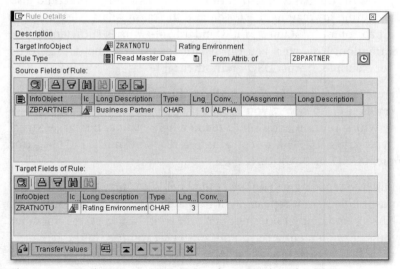

Figure 7.7 "Read Master Data" Rule Type for an Attribute for the InfoObject ZBPARTNER

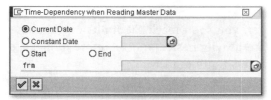

Figure 7.8 Defining the Time Base for Reading Master Data

Routine

You have the greatest flexibility when you program an ABAP routine. Because the system provides the relevant program framework, you only have to make your own individual enhancements and return the result by assigning the result value.

Deriving key figures

In the routine, you can access all of the fields that you have linked from the source structure via a field assignment (arrow in the transformation) to the target field to be derived (type: _ty_s_SC_1, SC = Source) and the actual field to be derived (type: _ty_s_TG_1, TG = Target). You therefore define which input information is necessary to derive characteristics (assigned source fields). In the routine itself, you can freely define how you want the data to be determined. For example, you could also use the routine for reading master data. If the master data is modeled as an attribute of an InfoObject, the standard rule type is sufficient in the transformation. However, you can no longer use it if the data is to be read, for example, from a DSO or another table.

Key figures and characteristics are derived in the same way. In the case of a key figure, however, you must make sure that you implement a routine with a unit. In addition to the key figure value, the target structure (type: _ty_s_TG_1) also contains the relevant unit InfoObject (for example, 0UNIT or 0CURRENCY).

If you use the same logic to derive several fields during a transformation, you must implement it repeatedly for each field, which may result in an unnecessary update that does not perform well. In this case, remember that you can implement a start, end, or expert routine. In the next section, we will describe how to use each routine.

7.5.2 Start, End, and Expert Routines

The transformation reads the data from the source and then writes it to the data target. The start routine is primarily intended for source-side staging of data in such a way that it takes the form expected by the data target. In the start routine, you could, for example, convert fields into internal formats. The start routine also lets you easily delete data that is no longer relevant for further processing. Here, the data is not deleted from the source itself, but from the internal table SOURCE_PACKAGE (statement: DELETE SOURCE_PACKAGE WHERE . . .) as part of the transformation. You could also perform this delete operation in a characteristic routine. However, we do not recommend this because you would first have to stage the characteristic calculation records that you want to delete and this would thwart the loading process unnecessarily.

In BW Release 7.0, the start routine was the only routine in which the entire data package was calculated. Therefore, it was used there for numerous additional calculations. Systematically, however, these calculations belong to the end routine, which was introduced with BW Release 7.0.

Start routine

Data can be postprocessed in the end routine. In contrast to the start routine, the target structure, and not the source structure, is available in the end routine. Any data fields contained solely in the data target are accessed in the end routine. You can therefore derive additional fields here (as an alternative to deriving characteristics or key figures at the field level). You can also validate data in the end routine. Regard the end routine as a mirror image of the start routine. The central internal table processed here is table RESULT_PACKAGE in the source code, not table SOURCE_PACKAGE.

End routine

You can use an expert routine to fully program your own transformation, including any necessary unit conversions, currency translations, or error handling. These are functions that a generated program implements in the case of a start and end routine. Therefore, programming expert routines is a more complex task. However, through skillful programming, you can boost performance and encapsulate all functions in a function module. A function module also has a change history, which is necessary for some applications (history management of the loading logic). You should therefore always use expert routines if you normally require start and end routines for the necessary derivations and if the derivation steps you need to execute are complex or for many characteristics. Changing the display from a key figure model to an account model is a typical example of using expert routines. One disadvantage associated with using expert routines is that they may complicate the data flow and

Expert routine

make it difficult to understand. For example, you will no longer know which fields in the transformation are possibly identical or are not transferred to the target and which fields are calculation results.

[+]

Data Flow When Using an Expert Routine

If you select an InfoSource as the target of a transformation using an expert routine, you can reduce its scope to those fields that are relevant for the transformation and thus design a more transparent data flow. You then need a second transformation that links the InfoSource with the actual data target.

7.6   Domain Creation and Central Transformations

In Chapter 5, we introduced you to the concept of vertical partitioning for a data flow. In the case of large BW implementations, it is useful to create domains that will partition the data flow into subareas, thus making data available in the Data Propagation Layer (and therefore also in the Reporting Layer) in a faster and more reliable manner.

Avoiding a redundant transformation logic

However, as a result of creating domains, you must map the data stores in conventional modeling and the processing logic to be implemented between each data store as redundant for each domain. You cannot avoid redundant data stores in this context because they are partitioned according to domain. With suitable modeling, however, you can achieve a transformation logic that can be used across all domains. To do this, you need to model central transformations.

Modeling InfoSources

InfoSources are used to implement central transformations. Before BW Release 7.0, InfoSources had to be used in every data flow. BW Release 7.0, however, contains a new InfoSource concept that only provides an InfoSource as an optional module that describes a transformation target, but does not store any data, thus facilitating the flexible creation of a data flow that does not have to store every processing result. Instead, another processing step can be connected to continue processing in the data flow. Figure 7.9 shows the structure of a central transformation between two layers in a layer model. The Outbound DataSources describe a structure that is identical to the corresponding DSO in the same layer. A 1:1 update to the Outbound DataSource occurs because there is usually no domain-specific transformation logic. The same applies to Inbound DataSources.

The central transformation (see Figure 7.9) links an Outbound InfoSource to an Inbound InfoSource, so that all of the data processing resources within a transformation are available (see Sections 7.5.1 and 7.5.2).

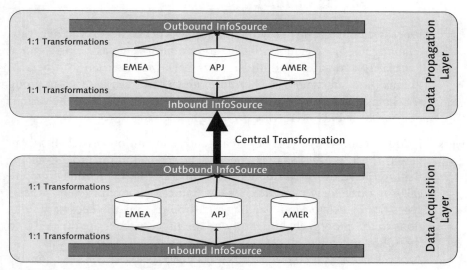

Figure 7.9 Central Transformation (Knapp, 2010)

Avoiding physical data storage

For this type of modeling, it does not matter whether the central transformation involves two layers in the layer model (one layer and the layer directly below it) or whether a layer is skipped. A central transformation can be used to map the processing logic of a layer (for example, the logic of the Quality and Transformation Layer or the logic of the Business Transformation Layer), thus avoiding any additional physical storage of the data. The actual data flow modeling must then be geared toward the requirements of the actual application scenario.

Even if you do not partition the data flow according to domain, Info-Sources are helpful for modeling flexible and lean data flows. You can work with InfoSources and use them to divide the data flow into logical steps wherever you do not need to physically store a transformation result.

Transformations and data transfer process (DTPs) merely describe steps within an overall process. If you want to automate data loading, you must combine these steps into one complete loading process. Process chains are used for this purpose (see Section 7.7).

7.7   Process Chains

Process chains group individual loading process steps together, thus enabling you to schedule, control, and monitor them as a single entity. For clarity and ease of administration, each process chain can be sub-divided into subchains. Furthermore, metachains can be used to group subchains into an entity. In this section, we will take a look at the various options available for creating process chains.

Process types

In Transaction RSPC, you can create and maintain process chains (plan view), check process chains (check view), and monitor process chains that you have executed (log view). A process chain is modeled graphically in a tree view or network view. You can choose different process types from a catalog and use drag and drop to copy the necessary functions to the process chain definition. The process types are divided into the following categories: GENERAL SERVICES, LOAD PROCESS AND POST-PROCESSING, DATA TARGET ADMINISTRATION, REPORTING AGENT, OTHER BW PROCESSES, and OTHER (see Figure 7.10).

Dependencies between process steps

The process sequence design depends on the status of the preceding process step (success, failure, always) and therefore gives rise to branches with different subsequent subprocesses (parallel or alternative sequences). Conversely, parallel sequences can be grouped together again using AND, OR, or XOR.

The process type does not yet describe all of the essential information. For example, in addition to the DATA TRANSFER PROCESS process type, you must specify which DTP you want to execute and, in the case of COMPRESS AN InfoCube, you must specify the InfoCube to be compressed.

Parameterization

This parameterization is described in a process type variant. You do not have to create a new variant for every process chain because, if the parameterization is suitable, it can be used to create any number of process chains, thus facilitating the central maintenance of process chain elements at the variant level.

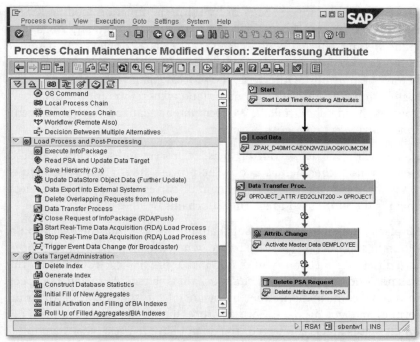

Figure 7.10 View of a Process Chain in the Data Warehousing Workbench

When you create the process chain, you define a logical sequence for the process steps. The event control system in the SAP Basis system is the technical basis for executing the process chain. It schedules batch jobs and starts jobs via events. An event is triggered by a preceding job and, in turn, starts subsequent jobs that are waiting for this event. When you choose ACTIVATE and SCHEDULE, the process chain that you have described graphically is converted into jobs and events.

Event control

The mechanism that starts the process steps of a process chain one below the other is also used to link multiple process chains. The start process is the connecting element here. Each process chain must have a start process. Two alternatives exist for this start process, namely a start process via direct scheduling in the form of a job or a start process via a meta-chain or API.

Start process

In the case of direct scheduling, you can automate the execution time at regular intervals by specifying a start time and time period. Alternatively, you can start execution via an event. You can trigger the event

Direct scheduling

manually in Transaction SM64 or by using the function module RSSM_ EVENT_RAISE. You can also call the process chain from any ABAP program. A third alternative is the immediate start. However, you should only use it for test purposes and then change the process chain again before the transport. Otherwise, the process chain will start in the target system immediately after the import (and is therefore, for the most part, unwanted and uncontrolled). We recommend that you work with events from the outset, even during testing.

Metachain/API

If you use the metachain or API, the start process and subsequent process steps are not scheduled as a job. The process steps are only scheduled when a call is made via the metachain or corresponding API. The metachain is therefore used to execute subchains.

Subchain

Similar to a main program, a subchain groups together the execution of different subprocess steps. Therefore, when dividing the loading process into different subchains, you should make sure that each subchain forms a standalone, usable unit. After a subchain is called, the metadata expects to receive confirmation either by means of the status *finished* or in the form of an error message. Further processing in the metachain depends on the status that is confirmed. You do not have to use a metachain to call a subchain. You can use the function module RSPC_API_CHAIN_START instead.

SAP Central Job Scheduling by Redwood

In this section, we introduced you to the components that form process chains and explained how to use them. The SAP Basis system is the technical basis for process chains. The technology shown here is wholly aimed at the ABAP stack, which is perfectly adequate for loading processes within BW. Growing from a need to provide a central job scheduling tool for the entire SAP NetWeaver system landscape, SAP established an Original Equipment Manufacturer (OEM) agreement with Redwood whereby the product Cronacle by Redwood is provided under the OEM name SAP Central Job Scheduling by Redwood. The SAP NetWeaver license covers the cross-system execution of ABAP programs, but no further integration of applications. Therefore, SAP Central Job Scheduling by Redwood represents an alternative for implementing BW loading processes. If you need an extensive job scheduling tool in the medium term, you already have the option of working toward standardization.

In the next section, we will show you how you can also use the resources in the BW system to implement a simple load control.

7.8   Load Control

Experience has shown that users frequently prefer to define data loading times themselves. We are aware of solutions within which a user
has developed his own interface for controlling process chains. Here,
the user doesn't come into contact with the process chains themselves
because it is enough to select an inbound interface (that is, a data source)
and a reference date (for example, which month is to be loaded). The
application schedules the process chain by using various Customizing
tables to enable an implementation from the interface to the process
chains to be executed.

If a process chain is started periodically, for example, to load the data of a
particular month, you also need to add this time base as a filter criterion
to the InfoPackage or DTP that will be used to load the data. This is easy
to do if you do not permanently define the filter in the DTP but instead
define it using a filter routine. The symbol circled in Figure 7.11 indicates
that a routine has been defined as a filter for the calendar day.

**Filter for the
time base**

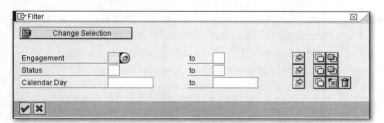

Figure 7.11   Filter Routine Defined in a DTP for a Calendar Day

This routine must procure the time base from the most central location.
In the simplest scenario, you could create a control table in which you
enter the load runs and filter value (that is, the time base for the load
run). A *Load run* InfoObject with a *Load month* attribute is also suitable
here. For the entry (load run) with the highest ID, the filter routine reads
the load month associated with the run from the master data table. Here,
the *Load run* InfoObject does not need to be added to the InfoProvider
because, in this model, it is used solely as a central data store.

We recommend that you enhance the model to include a more efficient
load control (see Figure 7.12).

**Concept of
load control**

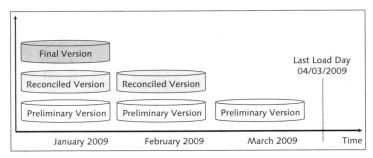

Figure 7.12 Data Versions

Here, the first step is to store not only the period or date of the current load run in the control table, but also the pending and completed load runs. The load control supplies a small log immediately. Please note the following prerequisite for defining a different status: Pending and completed load runs must also be recognizable as such. *Pending* means that all loading prerequisites have been fulfilled. *Loading* is a third status for active load runs. The loading control program sets this status in the status table as soon as a loading process starts. The control program or process chain end processing assumes responsibility for managing the control table and starts the required loading process if this is permitted by the status defined in the control table (*Pending* status). The loading process is defined by a normal process, which can include the usual further divisions according to master data, transaction data, and so on. At the end of the process chain, the status in the control table must change from *Loading* to *Completed*. Once a loading run is completed, you can check to see if other loading runs are pending. Process chain end processing should be stored externally in a separate program that is called by the process chain.

Versioning In addition to the time base, a characteristic for describing the data version for filtering data during staging is also provided, if required. You can easily enhance the load control to include version management. A release mechanism can also be enhanced. Version management is necessary if, for example, interfaces repeatedly supply data with the same time base but with varying importance because, for example, the data is loaded once in advance, once temporarily, and then once again after it undergoes a quality assurance check. Versioning makes it possible to retain different versions of data (see Figure 7.13). A conceivable application scenario here involves, for example, merging all reported financial data (highly aggregated data) in a corporate group. To manage the versions, you can create a *Version* InfoObject that is assigned the necessary attributes (for example, creation time/delivery time, check time/check user, release flag). Versioning can also be implemented whereby a counter that represents the data version is incremented for each period, thus creating a flexible solution that is not restricted to certain versions. For example, you can define a data version in the end routine of the relevant transformation.

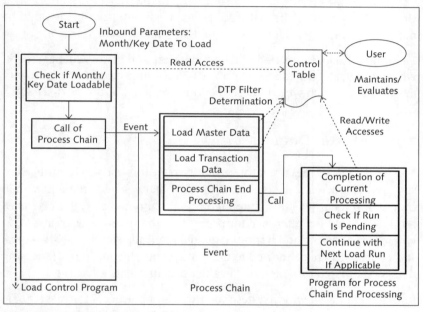

Figure 7.13 Load Control

When versioning is applied to the load control in subsequent layers, a specific period needs to be requested and a specific data version must be selected during data loading.

Load control and versioning

In addition to the attributes, the *Version* InfoObject should have suitable compounding for the application scenario. If you want to apply versioning to each period, compounding to 0CALMONTH, for example, is necessary. Compounding to the domain may also be necessary.

Compounding of the "Version" object

Data versioning increases the volume of data. The risk of misinterpretations rises if you work with incorrect versions or if you inadvertently work with different versions. Versioning is still useful in some scenarios, for example, if you want to perform complex calculations that are based on data from different inbound interfaces. The data versions differ in terms of the time when the data was delivered (if the time base is the same) or they could have been intentionally created for calculating different scenarios.

In principle, the statement that "the BW system should know only one truth" applies because this avoids any inconsistent evaluations. At the very least, however, the data transferred up to the Data Propagation Layer should be reconciled. In many scenarios, versioning can be avoided by providing temporary data only in the Operational Data Store.

Versioning is closely related to data timeliness and history management, which will be described in Section 7.10. Versioning can also be used with master data, which we will describe in more detail in the next section.

7.9   Master Data

Master data describes a relatively stable state. It is used to identify, classify, and characterize facts, and it usually changes less frequently than transaction data, which is generated on an ongoing basis. Because master data is used for reference purposes, it is the main focus of attention when consolidating and harmonizing data in Data Warehouse. If several source systems are connected to the BW system, the question of merging data to facilitate cross-sectional evaluations automatically rises.

In this section, we will first describe the loading process for master data within BW (see Section 7.9.1). In Section 7.9.2, we will outline scenarios in which master data from various sources can be merged in BW. Texts and hierarchies are usually loaded using special DataSources. Sections 7.9.3, Staging Texts, and 7.9.4, Staging Hierarchies, will describe how this works.

For many BW projects, the master data management options within BW are sufficient, especially if few source systems are used or if most of them already have a common master data basis. Auxiliary tools, however, can be particularly useful in heavily distributed, possibly service-oriented architectures. In Section 7.9.5, SAP NetWeaver MDM, we will briefly introduce you to the tool SAP NetWeaver Master Data Management (MDM).

7.9.1 Special Features When Loading Master Data

Before BW Release 3.0B, it was only possible to use the DataSources for attributes and texts to directly update the master data tables and text tables of an InfoObject. A major disadvantage here was that a DataSource could only be used to update a single InfoObject. Since then, flexible updates have made it possible to also use update rules or transformations to update data targets (attribute/text tables). Master data objects can therefore be flexibly integrated into staging. You must also consider the importance of the layer model in the LSA in terms of staging master data.

Flexible master data update

Frequently, it is enough to load attributes and, in particular, texts into the master data tables of the relevant InfoObjects without any additional temporary data storage. A prerequisite here is that no laborious processing is necessary and the data can simply be transferred from the source. If, for example, you use a standard DataSource to load a standard InfoObject, it generally does not make sense to implement additional staging. Possible signs that you should consider staging interim steps for attributes include:

Direct update for simple master data

▶ The InfoObject contains extensive master data that many other loading processes access.

▶ The master data of the InfoObject must initially be merged step by step.

▶ The master data must be harmonized and integrated (see Section 7.9.2).

The more central an attribute-bearing master data object is in the context of your enterprise's business activity, the more important it is to also make this master data available in a central location. It may make sense to store this data (in addition to the InfoObject) in a DSO in the Data Propagation Layer. This DSO can then populate one or, if required, more master-data-bearing InfoObjects (the Reporting Layer) with master data.

Central objects

Figure 7.14 shows a typical data flow for a central object (that is, for central master data). The data is initially loaded via a PSA into a DSO ❶. If required, the master data can be enriched with additional attributes or data integration steps can be performed (see Section 7.9.2). The central object data in the DSO is then loaded as the master data (attributes, and

Availability of master data and reference data

possibly texts) of a central InfoObject ❷. The central object can then be integrated into various area-specific data models in the Data Mart Layer ❸.

In exceptional cases, you can also create, if required, area-specific InfoObjects that are based on the central object. To do this, you create another InfoObject that, in an ideal scenario, is also populated with the central object data ❹. In this case, you must make the necessary transformations in the Business Transformation Layer.

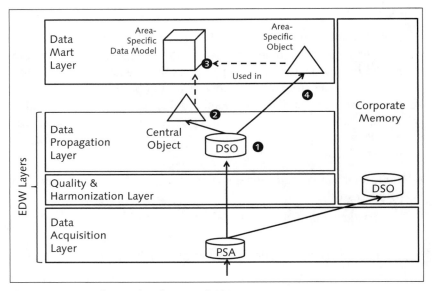

Figure 7.14 Typical Data Flow for Central Objects

Time dependency

When data is stored in the form of a DSO, you must make sure to separate time-dependent data from time-independent data. Otherwise, you will generate superfluous redundancies and therefore an unnecessary volume of data because the time-independent data will also be included in each data record. This process corresponds to the internal mapping of master data (attributes) to an InfoObject. Here, different tables are used for time-dependent and time-constant attributes and these tables are first merged when they are displayed in a table view.

Delete transformation

It is also important that the master data that is read when loading transaction data and added to transaction data as additional characteristics is always available. The fact that you load the master data into your process chains before you load the transaction data ensures that you always enrich the transaction data with the latest master data. However, if there are numerous dependent and parallel loading processes in a BW implementation, monitoring of the loading sequence will become increasingly laborious. At the very least, make sure that the master data DSOs are always populated with data. Many process chains are implemented in such a way that master data is loaded in full mode and the DSOs are initially deleted and then reloaded. However, this means that no reference data is available in the short term. If loading problems occur, this *No data* state can last a long time. Therefore, any scheduled loading processes that enrich data will not find any data. Furthermore, dependent datasets will be loaded with errors. If you select the OVERWRITE aggregation type for nonkey fields, the data in the DSO is updated when you load new data, but the values are not added up. This means that reference data is always available and there is no possibility of dependent transformations containing empty fields that would cause errors.

However, one possible disadvantage of this solution is that the data that the source no longer supplies (deletions) is retained in the DSO. If this is irritating, you can use a standard DSO object to make an alternative implementation that receives deleted data, which remains available as reference data. This solution is illustrated in Figure 7.15.

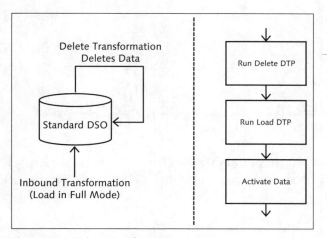

Figure 7.15 Delete Transformation

An additional delete transformation is executed before the actual loading process. This transformation reads all of the data records in the DSO, assigns a delete flag (0RECORDMODE = DEL) to them, and posts them to the DSO as a new request. If the request generated as a result of loading the new data and the delete request are activated at the same time, the changes caused by deleting and reloading data will also become active simultaneously. The DSO has valid records at any time and can therefore be used for reference purposes.

The implementation described previously is suitable for both master data and transaction data. You can also use this procedure in conjunction with data versions (see Section 7.10) to delete old data versions.

Figure 7.16 shows the implementation for a corresponding data flow in BW. The DSO HXXEAD01 (Economic Areas) is to be loaded here. This DSO has two inbound transformations, namely via the delete transformation itself and via the transformation of the "normal" data flow with the InfoSource HIXXEAD0101 as the data source. The FULL extraction mode is selected for the delete DTPs. For implementations in which only some DSO data is to be deleted, a corresponding filter routine must be assigned to the delete DTP.

▽ 🗂 Economic Areas		HXXEAD01
▽ 🔀 Delete ODSO HXXEAD01 -> ODSO HXXEAD01		09OTPOCNTTHZL6QMEGXV
🗂 Economic Areas		HXXEAD01
▽ 🔀 Load TRCS HIXXEA0101 -> ODSO HXXEAD01		0GGGBMVV516K05HYY4LMJ
▽ ⬢ HIXXEA0101		HIXXEA0101
▷ 🔀 TRCS AOXXEA0101 -> TRCS HIXXEA0101		0P0NOHLNG8CA9FNVCZYK
▽ 🗀 Data Transfer Processes		HXXEAD01
▽ 🔳 Delete HXXEAD01 -> HXXEAD01		DTP_D6WH02Q1XXHDQJ4C
▷ 🗂 Economic Areas		HXXEAD01
▽ 🔳 Load DATUP -> HXXEAD01		DTP_D6R7ZJDGC4H894830
▷ 🗺 Economic Areas		ZAA_LSA_KEY_ECOAREA

Figure 7.16 Delete Transformation and Delete DTP

In the delete transformation, 0RECORDMODE = D (delete flag) is set as a constant in the technical rule group for all data records (see Figure 7.17).

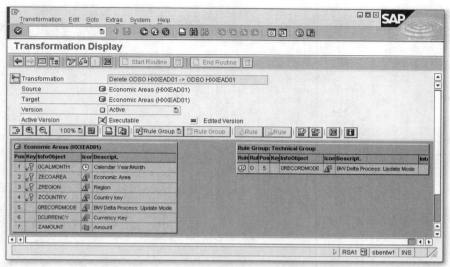

Figure 7.17 Rule for Setting the Delete Flag (0RECORDMODE=D)

To do this, use the CONSTANT rule type to assign the value D to the target field 0RECORDMODE (see Figure 7.18).

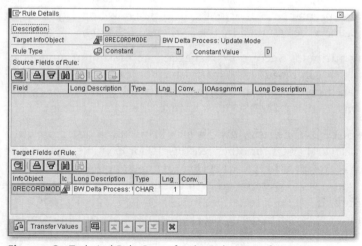

Figure 7.18 Technical Rule Group for the Delete Transformation

The standard rule group for this transformation describes a 1:1 transfer of all InfoObjects (see Figure 7.19).

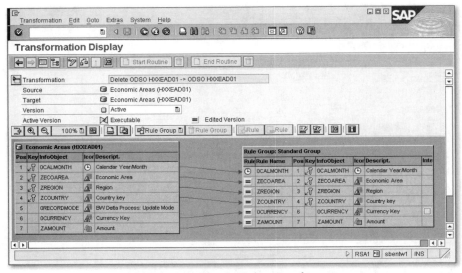

Figure 7.19 Standard Rule Group for the Delete Transformation

Interim steps If a more laborious staging of master data is required, it may also be useful to physically store the master data temporarily in the Quality and Harmonization Layer. As is the case with transaction data, you make no provisions for permanent data storage in the Acquisition Layer. Once again, this task can be assumed by the Corporate Memory.

Distribution across several DSOs If too many attributes need to be managed, the maximum number of InfoObjects that can be added to a DSO may be exceeded. If this happens, you can distribute the attributes across two DSOs. However, you must then ensure that both DSO keys have an identical structure.

In the case of DSOs for master data, it may be useful to distribute attributes across several DSOs for other reasons. If, for example, one part of the attributes is relevant for global evaluations and another part for local evaluations, it may make sense to divide the attributes into two datasets. Therefore, it is easier to differentiate between authorizations, for example, and it is easier to create user department–specific InfoObjects in the EDW layer.

7.9.2 Integrating Multiple Sources

If multiple source systems are connected to your BW system and you want to perform a cross-sectional evaluation of your data, some requirements will need to be met in terms of master data integration, because objects that share the same semantics but are from different source systems are usually qualified differently but still should be displayed uniformly in BW. This prompts the following questions: How can we detect and deal with collisions within a dataset? Which source system is the leading system for which data content? Which new data records can be imported from which system? How can we harmonize data in terms of its keys and attributes?

Such questions need to be answered in relation to the source system to be integrated. The following integration problems can arise between systems or objects (data records) and can be solved as follows:

▶ *Scenario 1*: Data records for which the source system is not the leading system and for which no additional attributes are available.

Procedure: Do not extract the data or filter it in staging.

▶ *Scenario 2*: Irrelevant data records for which the source system is the leading system. For example, this concerns data that is retained in the source system for internal or technical purposes, but is generally not relevant for evaluations.

Procedure: Do not extract the data or filter it in staging.

▶ *Scenario 3*: Data records (or key values) for which the source system is the leading system and the data are relevant for BW.

Procedure: The data must be updated with all available and relevant attributes from this source system up to the Data Propagation Layer.

▶ *Scenario 4*: Data records for which the source system is not the leading system, but for which additional attributes are available and have the source system as their leading system.

Procedure: For these data records, you must update the additional attributes up to the Data Propagation Layer without changing any other attributes.

Within the context of characteristics, the aforementioned integration questions relate not only to key values, but also to all of the attributes that need to be harmonized (for example, gender, which can be coded differently in different source system groups).

The scope of the processing steps to be performed during staging potentially rises with the number of source systems to be integrated. When designing transformation processes, the requirements must be considered accordingly (up to the EDW layer).

Globally Valid and Locally Valid Keys

When merging and integrating the data of a characteristic contained in various source system groups, the manner in which you deal with the keys plays an extremely important role here.

The following constellations may arise when you merge master data from different systems:

▶ **Local key**
The data always has a key that uniquely identifies it within a source system. If this key is only unique locally, you can call it a local key.

▶ **Global key**
If the master data from the different source systems is reconciled, each source system supplies a unique, globally valid key.

▶ **Qualified local key**
If the source systems are not reconciled with each other, the local keys are not necessarily compatible with each other. However, local keys can be enhanced to become globally valid keys. You can do this by adding the data origin to the key values when you load the data. However, the data is not yet fully integrated because overlaps remain whereby the same object is described by different qualified local key values.

You could use the source system ID to describe the data origin. However, this procedure is no longer adequate in larger system groups. Large enterprises usually have entire groups of systems that work with the same master data. Because it is not possible to accurately predict which data sources will be connected to a BW system in the future, you should identify an entire source system group together to describe the data origin.

For each characteristic, you must decide:

▶ Whether the characteristic must be integrated (if necessary, characteristics can only be used for operational reporting and are not updated into the Harmonization Layer)

▶ Whether to use global keys or qualified local keys in reporting

▶ How to map local keys to global keys (if necessary)

Master Data with Global Keys

In this implementation, the data is enriched with a global key. This is achieved by updating the data into the Data Propagation Layer (see Figure 7.20), but this can also take place earlier (in the Data Acquisition Layer). You should not dispense with storing the key tables in the Corporate Memory. It can also be useful to model the local key as an additional attribute. Then the global and local references are always available. At the very least, the global key is added to the data model wherever the object is relevant.

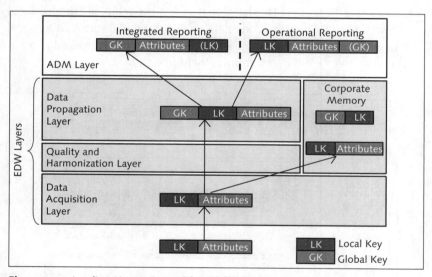

Figure 7.20   Loading Master Data with a Global Key

If you dispense with an additional local key, the advantage is that, during data loading, the data is aggregated with the same global key (thus reducing the volume of data). The greater the overlap between the data in the various (loaded) data sources, the greater the benefit.

Dispensing with a local key

If you want to use a global key, you must first implement a mechanism that maps the local keys from the various systems to the global key. This assignment must be continuously enhanced for new (source system–specific) data records. This procedure is prone to errors. During productive operation, the errors manifest themselves in such a way that loading processes have to be terminated if new keys are to be loaded for which a global key has not yet been defined. These disadvantages do not arise with qualified local keys.

Master Data with Qualified Local Keys

One disadvantage associated with the procedure involving global keys is that the data cannot be updated if a global key cannot be found. However, if you artificially make the local key unique, you can update the data even if a global key cannot be determined. You can determine the artificially unique key by adding the source system group ID (SSG) to the local key (see Figure 7.21). The global key is modeled as an additional nonkey attribute. Therefore, the data can always be updated. If a global key is missing, it only results in an empty attribute that is filled as soon as the global key can be determined (field update).

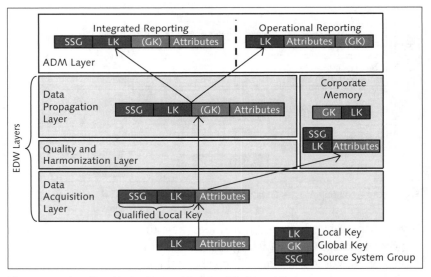

Figure 7.21 Loading Master Data with a Qualified Local Key

The advantage of this procedure is that the loading process is not as error-prone as the procedure in which only a global key is used. However, the disadvantage here (especially in the case of large volumes of data) is that you cannot merge data that describes the same object. The procedure in which only a global key is used has its advantages here. If the volume of data becomes too large, you can change the scenario retroactively.

Data Integration in the Staging Process

Let's assume that the master data in the (important) master data objects considered earlier is loaded via the various EDW layers. The data is therefore stored temporarily in DSOs before it is transferred downstream to the master data tables of the relevant InfoObjects.

All of the extracted master data that needs to be integrated is initially provided in DSOs in the Data Acquisition Layer. The data is then integrated when it is updated into the Data Propagation Layer. This integration comprises the following steps:

Master data management

▶ Determination of the global key and qualified local key (mapping). Alternatively, this key could also be enriched when the data is updated into the Data Propagation Layer.

▶ Filtering of data records for which the source system or source system group is not the leading source system or source system group and for which the source system does not supply any additional attributes. If possible, this type of filtering should already take place when the data is extracted or updated into the Data Propagation Layer.

▶ Filtering of attributes for which the source system or source system group is not the leading source system or source system group. For logical reasons, this is taken into account during extraction. Otherwise, this type of filtering takes place when the data is updated into the Data Propagation Layer.

▶ Mapping of attributes (characteristics) to integrated objects (global/qualified local keys).

The technical implementation of the data transformation into the Data Propagation Layer can require a great deal of time and effort because you must carefully differentiate between which attributes can be updated from which source during data loading. In the case of data records with additional attributes, only these additional attributes can be updated and, in the case of data records from a source system group that is the leading source system group, all attributes must be updated. If the attributes that are to be handled differently originate in different sources, the differentiation is easy to implement. However, if there is only one source, the differentiation must occur at the data record level. One solution is to use multiple InfoSources in the Data Acquisition Layer. An InfoSource is used to define a transformation in the Data Propagation Layer whereby all attributes are updated. A second InfoSource is used to only update some relevant attributes. Suitable data filtering occurs in the relevant DTPs.

7.9.3 Staging Texts

Text DataSources usually only have the key of the characteristic and possibly the language and text (whereby different lengths can be supplied).

Texts can be updated directly into the relevant InfoObject. Generally, there is no provision for additional staging. However, this requires that you find a source system that is the leading source system for texts (this is usually the case).

If you need to run through extensive integration operations for the relevant master data, it is useful to treat the texts as additional attributes and subject them to the normal integration process. When InfoObjects are updated in the DataPropagator or Data Mart Layer, the text fields can be loaded as texts for the corresponding InfoObjects.

You can initially load the texts into the PSA and, from there, transfer them via a transformation into one or more data targets. This scenario is shown in Figure 7.22.

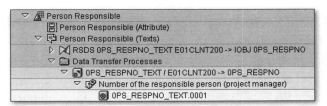

Figure 7.22 Sample Staging of Texts

You configure the InfoPackage that retrieves the data from the source system and updates it in the PSA in such a way that the data is not updated into the data targets. You use the ONLY PSA setting for this purpose (see Figure 7.23).

You also need a DTP that retrieves the data from the PSA and updates it into a data target. If you want to populate multiple data targets with texts (for example, an InfoObject and a DSO), you need several transformations and therefore several DTPs. In the DTP, make sure to set the extraction mode to DELTA (see Figure 7.24). This ensures that only requests that have not been posted yet are transferred from the PSA into the data target.

Data transfer process

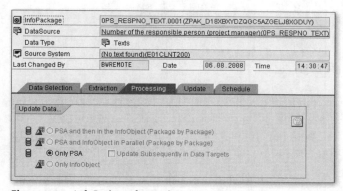

Figure 7.23 InfoPackage for Updating Texts in the PSA

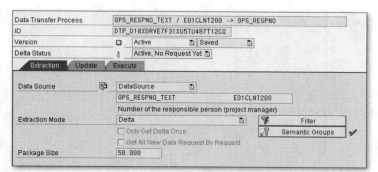

Figure 7.24 Extraction Setting in a DTP for Transferring Texts from the PSA into the Text Table of an InfoObject

7.9.4 Staging Hierarchies

In the source system, a special extractor extracts hierarchies and loads them directly into BW as an InfoObject hierarchy. Here, there is no provision for a flexible update via DSOs.

Figure 7.25 shows a typical scenario whereby the hierarchies (possibly extracted from various source systems) are loaded into an InfoObject (ACCOUNT NUMBER in our example). Each DataSource requires an InfoPackage for loading purposes.

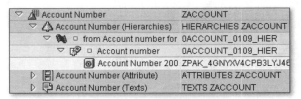

Figure 7.25 Sample Staging of Hierarchies

Alternatively, you can load hierarchy information into a DSO by creating an extractor (for example, via a master data DataSource). However, you cannot use a data update to create a hierarchy from the data stored in the DSO. Instead, you need to develop a function module here.

In the final section on "Master Data," we will introduce you to a specialized master data management tool known as SAP NetWeaver MDM.

7.9.5 SAP NetWeaver MDM

MDM is a master data management solution whose main functions are as follows:

Specialist requirements

- Master data consolidation
- Master data harmonization
- Central master data management
- Duplicate check
- History management of master data

MDM can be integrated with BW. For example, you can transfer master data to MDM, harmonize and consolidate it there, and then transfer the result back to BW. In other words, a bidirectional connection exists between BW and MDM.

However, MDM's strength lies in the fact that it not only makes the harmonized master data available to the BW system but decentrally to every process, thus automatically increasing the quality of the data loaded into the BW system and considerably reducing the time and effort associated with integrating and harmonizing master data.

A comprehensive description of MDM is available in Heilig et al. (2007).

MDM can accelerate the decentralized availability of master data changes, thus improving the quality of data in BW. Such changes are conserved during history management, which we will discuss in the next section, and sometimes do not permit any retroactive adjustments.

7.10   Data Timeliness and History Management

History management concerns every type of modeling that maps time, changes to data over time, and also conserves certain time bases in data.

Each enterprise and each process/application area to be supported places its own demands on the timeliness of the data provided in BW. Here, timeliness is not solely aimed at how soon the data is loaded (for example, at the end of the month) but whether, and if so to what extent, BW is to consider retroactive changes to a dataset.

For example, in Personnel Administration (evaluation of headcount and personnel actions), it is common practice to load headcount from SAP ERP HCM every month on the *Last day of the month* key date. This raises the question as to whether the month just closed should be loaded or whether this data is not yet representative enough because, for example, many changes have not been implemented yet. In Personnel Administration, however, retroactive adjustments occur not only for the previous month, but for other past periods. Therefore, a difference arises between the SAP ERP system and BW, and remains unless you reload past periods.

Full/delta upload To model requirements, BW provides different data loading settings. For example, when you load deltas, all changes are transferred. The problem of changes to past data does not arise here, but it does occur if the data is transferred monthly via full upload. You would be right to say that you can simply perform a delta upload and this problem could not occur. This is correct in principle, but you must decide whether the goal of data timeliness is your only goal because, in many application areas, figures that have already been published in reports (for example, as a result of you conveying this information to colleagues) should not change during the next load run. Users could lose faith in such reports and in BW itself if an involuntary change is made overnight to the results in a report.

Timeliness versus stability When you design the application that you want to implement in BW, you must consider the previous questions and your own requirements early on because the entire staging process design depends on your own assumptions. Frequently, a compromise must be found between data stability and data timeliness.

In our example from HR Management, the compromise could take the following form: You decide to transfer headcount monthly as a full upload. To make data available to reporting in the short term, you load the "last day of the month" data for the previous month at the start of each month. Because most of the changes made in SAP ERP relate to a retroactive period that, at most, concerns the past three months, you reload the "last day of the month" data for the past three months each month on a rolling basis. You communicate this fact within your enterprise so that everyone is aware of the provisional nature of any recent figures. In the case of data that is older than three months, however, you opt for stability and do not reload the data. This may result in some irregularities between SAP ERP and BW. However, you will suffer this for the greater good (stable reporting).

Modeling indicator The aforementioned relationships between the timeliness and stability of the data transferred to BW give rise to three alternative modeling scenarios, namely:

▶ Data timeliness (each change in the source system is transferred to the BW system during the next load run)

▶ Stability (once data has been loaded, it cannot be changed)

▶ A combination of data timeliness and stability

At the start of every project, you should clarify which goal you wish to pursue and which scenario best models your requirements.

The underlying modeling question is omnipresent in BW: Time-dependent master data attributes are added to transaction data to create a stable view. For example, the article is shown under the article group to which the article was assigned at the time the data was loaded. A regrouping performed at a later time is ignored as long as the transaction data is not reloaded and the derivation process is not repeated.

Other extensive scenarios exist for reporting because, in addition to the historically stable, mapped characteristic enrichments for transaction data, time-dependent master data (attributes, texts, hierarchies) is available, which (in the case of time-dependent modeling) also describes the current view and permits changes in past periods.

In this context, you generally have to differentiate between four report- Views in reporting
ing perspectives, namely:

▶ **Historical truth**
The user expects the validity of the data to refer to the key date of a business transaction. For example, this could be the material group to which a material was assigned at the time of sale.

▶ **Mapping the current status**
In this case, the user expects the system to display the current status. In our example concerning the material and material group, this would be the current assignment to the material group.

▶ **Flexible, time-dependent access**
Here, the user expects to choose the key date and the time base will then be selected accordingly. Depending on the selection, the view before or after the material is regrouped is selected.

▶ **Preservation of comparability**
If the user works with reports that compare two or more key dates with each other, he expects, in our example, to only use materials that applied to all comparison key dates. This way, irritating changes will be shown to detect trends.

When mapping the various views, both the (enriched) transaction data and the time-dependent master data (attributes, texts, hierarchies) in conjunction with the query key date are relevant. In this context, please note that the time base for the time-dependent hierarchy of an InfoObject can be defined separately regardless of the query key date. If you want to select a display in which the different assignments for a hierarchy node within a certain period of time are displayed together, you can use the temporal hierarchy join.

The literature frequently discusses adding attribute values as a characteristic to a transaction data record in the context of modeling InfoCubes in the Reporting Layer. Because we understand the Data Propagation Layer as a layer in which historical records are created and "easy-to-digest" data exists, we must examine the question of history management at this level. Because modeling of time-related aspects is particularly important, we will revisit this topic in Chapter 8, Data Modeling in the Reporting Layer.

Transaction data enrichment is always associated with an increase in the volume of data to be provided. In this case, additional characteristics must be added to the transaction data. You should therefore perform a proper analysis and only enrich as many attributes as necessary. This is especially true for the datasets in the Reporting Layer (because we wish to achieve the best possible performance here), but also for the datasets in the Data Propagation Layer. You can only properly answer the question of which data enrichments are necessary if you have an in-depth knowledge of the analysis applications. Because the Data Propagation Layer is the central basis for creating datasets that will be used later in reporting, you should already consider specific, known questions and also add those characteristics that, from your knowledge of the application area, must be mapped historically and correctly. When you create each individual Architected Data Mart (ADM), you must accurately check, at a later time, which characteristics must be transferred historically and correctly. The Data Propagation Layer provides the basis for dealing with different or new questions in a flexible manner.

7.11 Conclusion

LSA, introduced in Chapter 5, provides an ideal framework for discussing and categorizing different questions that arise when staging data within the EDW layers.

Designing the actual data flow is a task that must be completed as part of every project. Here, the LSA provides a framework that helps you to consider all of the necessary aspects of data modeling. You can seamlessly integrate generally applicable concepts such as the concept of master data harmonization into the architecture framework, thus enabling you to easily create a customer LSA that will take account of all modeling aspects that are relevant to your particular scenario.

The layer architecture is not only helpful for large projects. Its flexibility also lends itself to implementing exactly those layers and services that are relevant to a particular application scenario, thus also making it the ideal conceptual framework for data modeling in smaller solutions.

Layered, Scalable Architecture (LSA) clearly delimits the application-specific layers from the general, reusable layers. The Reporting Layer is the core of the application-specific layers. This chapter describes how you can structure a flexible, high-performance Reporting Layer.

8   Data Modeling in the Reporting Layer

The data propagation layer described in Chapter 7, Modeling the EDW, permanently saves the data in such a way that it can be used as flexibly as possible for various analysis purposes in another step. Reporting itself, however, usually doesn't take place in the Data Propagation Layer except for reconciliation and check reports. To provide the data optimized for queries to an organizational area or a specific application, you need an additional layer.

Datasets that are provided specifically for an organizational area are often referred to as data marts. In the case of LSA, this involves data marts that are supplied with data from the Data Propagation Layer. Ideally, they access the same master data.

It is essential for data marts that they format the data in such a way that reporting can take place based on this data. So the Reporting Layer is the central layer to consider in this chapter.

Section 8.1, Architecture of the Reporting Layer, describes the architecture of the Reporting Layer. The InfoCube is the central object for modeling the datasets. It provides data in a format optimized for queries. Besides the already-optimized basic structure, there are additional optimization options for InfoCubes. Sections 8.2, Modeling and Optimization of InfoCubes, and 8.3, Enhanced InfoCube Modeling, discuss the modeling and optimization of InfoCubes. The virtual layer described in Section 8.4, Virtual Layer, supplements the physical storage and serves as the basis for creating queries. You use the MultiProviders of the virtual layer to define an intermediate layer that is abstracted from the physical storage of data and whose presentation is based on the requirements of the user. The SAP BusinessObjects universes discussed in Section 8.5, Universes in SAP BusinessObjects, have a comparable task.

8.1   Architecture of the Reporting Layer

Figure 5.3 in Chapter 5, Section 5.1.2, Layer Model of the Reference Architecture, shows a schematic structure of the Reporting Layer. The following sections use this description to derive a sample data model.

Differentiation of data retention At the data retention level, the Reporting Layer differentiates data by different criteria, which results in physically separated datasets. The following criteria are possible:

▸ The affiliation of data to different domains, processes, and so on

▸ The separation of actual, planning, and forecast data

▸ The separation of data with different granularity (aggregated and detail data)

▸ The different time base of data, particularly:

  ▸ Archived data, for instance, of a Nearline Storage (NLS) system

  ▸ Integration of data from an operational data store

▸ Additional separation of data to increase query performance

Besides performance, better test and administration options are some advantages of dataset segmentation. Plus, there is no reason to merge data into one physical dataset because the Virtual Layer can use MultiProviders here and this variant is more flexible. But there's one exception: If the data records are supposed to be enlarged, that is, supplemented with additional characteristics, the characteristics must be enriched.

Typing of modeling The criteria mentioned previously are typical for many implementations. Therefore, the following sections present sample data models for various scenarios.

The basic type illustrated in Figure 8.1 is the starting point: Data is loaded from the Data Propagation Layer.

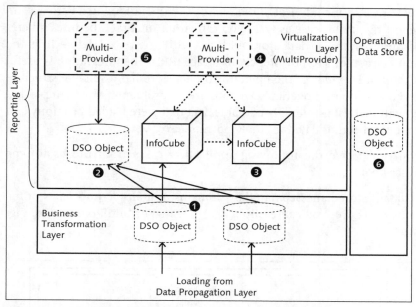

Figure 8.1 Architecture of the Reporting Layer

If it is necessary for the transformation, you can physically store data at the Business Transformation Layer ❶. Experience has shown, however, that this is not required in most cases, so the data can be written directly via a transformation to an InfoProvider in the Reporting Layer. In most cases, this involves storing data in an aggregated form in an InfoCube. The additional storage of data as a DataStore Object (DSO) ❷ is suitable if you want to enable analyses for detail data later on (for instance, via a query jump target). Queries are exclusively defined on the MultiProvider ❹, in which all relevant InfoCubes of an analysis context are integrated. There can be several reasons for separating data into multiple InfoCubes ❸ as described previously.

An ArchiveCube is used in this example, to which you outsource "old" data from the InfoCube that is mainly intended for reporting. You don't integrate the DSOs for the detail data with the MultiProvider directly, because there is a risk that the reports will provide duplicate results if you don't define an explicit filter on the object InfoProvider in the query. Therefore, it is better to use a jump target report that you can define on a separate MultiProvider ❺.

You can also include DataProviders of the operational data store ❻ in reporting. In this case as well, you can either integrate the InfoProvider of the operational data store with a MultiProvider or define it as the jump target for a Report-Report Interface (RRI). The integration is useful if the InfoProvider of the operational data store has a suitable structure and if data doesn't overlap. Overlaps are no problem if, for example, the operational data store only contains data that were loaded promptly and have not been updated to the Reporting Layer yet.

Modeling examples You can derive the following application cases from the basic type described:

If data is stored and separated by domains in multiple InfoCubes of the same structure, you can easily merge it using a MultiProvider (see Figure 8.2).

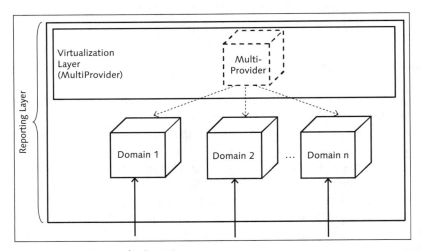

Figure 8.2 Separation by Domains

In contrast to a domain formation, in which each InfoCube has a separate update from the Business Transformation Layer, the data provision of the scenario shown in Figure 8.3 can be done from InfoCube to InfoCube. According to criteria to be determined, old data is outsourced to another InfoCube. Here, you can also use an NLS system.

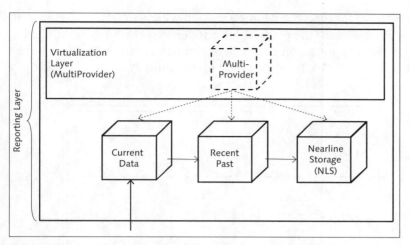

Figure 8.3 Separation by Time and Integration of the NLS System

Extrapolation is another application case (see Figure 8.4). Here, data from the actual data InfoCube is transferred to the extrapolation Info-Cube. You can design the transfer in such a way that the extrapolation data is derived from the actual data. Various implementations are possible with regard to content.

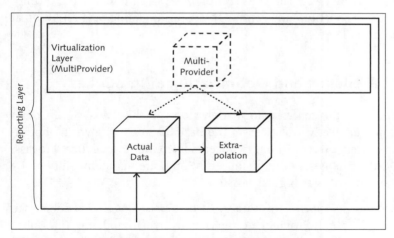

Figure 8.4 Separation by Value Type — Extrapolation

A similar application can be implemented with planning data. However, the data source for the planning data is not the actual data InfoCube but the planning application that is based on the MultiProvider (see Figure 8.5 and Chapter 10, Data Modeling for Planning Applications).

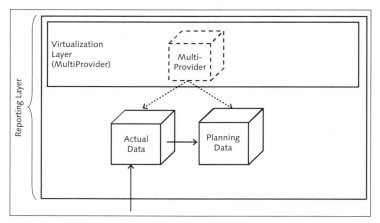

Figure 8.5 Separation by Value Type — Planning

So far, you've learned some basic structures for arranging DataProviders in the reporting level. The next section describes the modeling of Info-Cubes; these constitute the central object for modeling data retention at the reporting level.

8.2   Modeling and Optimization of InfoCubes

InfoCubes are the central information stores in the BW system from a reporting perspective. They form the basis for most analytical applications and are a prerequisite for concepts like Online Analytical Processing (OLAP). The goals of modeling InfoCubes are maintainability and a query speed that is as high as possible.

This section deals with InfoCubes. In contrast to MultiProviders (see Section 8.4.1, MultiProvider in the Virtual Layer), modeling InfoCubes depends on technical considerations. The scope of the characteristics summarized in an InfoCube is based on the implementation of a technical requirement (at least in parts), but the grouping of InfoObjects and the formation of dimensions is based on technical considerations.

First, we'll look at the modeling process of InfoCubes. Then you'll learn about the formation of aggregates, compression, and partitioning as ways of improving query performance. The last section of this chapter discusses Business Warehouse Accelerator (BWA). This not only increases the query speed of specific retroactively known query types, but it also promises to support unforeseeable navigation steps in OLAP analyses, too (see Section 8.2.6, BWA).

8.2.1   Modeling

If you take a look at a typical BW implementation, you'll note that it usually comprises numerous InfoCubes. Each InfoCube refers to a dataset that is self-contained from a reporting perspective; this dataset, in turn, refers to a specific business (sub)process. The key figures relevant to the respective processes are evaluated for each InfoCube according to different criteria described by InfoObjects.

Creating an InfoCube

Before considering the various aspects that must be taken into account for modeling InfoCubes, let's learn how to create an InfoCube. The underlying InfoObjects originate from SAP's demo content, so you can copy the scenario if Business Content has already been transferred to your system.

To create an InfoCube, start Transaction RSDCUBE (InfoCube Processing) or Transaction RSA1; IN THE INFOPROVIDER view in the MODELING area, navigate to the InfoArea for which you want to create the InfoCube. As an alternative to Transaction RSA1, YOU CAN also navigate to the InfoProvider view of Transaction RSA1 using Transaction RSA11. You create the InfoCube in the InfoProvider view by selecting CREATE INFOCUBE in the context menu (right-click). The system takes you to the dialog shown in Figure 8.6, where you can select a technical and a descriptive name for the InfoCube ❶.

Starting modeling

Using a template You can also create the InfoCube based on a template ❷, which may save you some of the modeling effort described in the following text. After you've entered a name for the InfoCube, click the button for creating the InfoCube ❸ to exit the dialog.

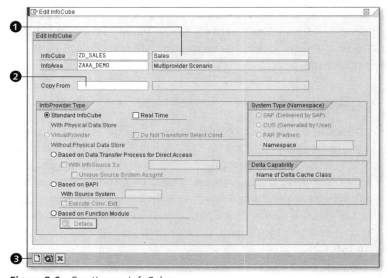

Figure 8.6 Creating an InfoCube

Empty InfoCube structure In the next dialog step (see Figure 8.7), the system provides a basic structure for the new InfoCube ❶. The basic structure already includes the standard dimensions of an InfoCube, such as the data package, time, unit, key figures, navigation attributes, and an initial empty dimension called DIMENSION 1. At this point, the categories are still empty. Your task is to add all of the InfoObjects (characteristics and key figures) that you need for the model. You can enter InfoObjects directly via the context menu or copy them from the TEMPLATE area ❷ via drag and drop.

Direct input To enter InfoObjects directly, right-click the dimension that you want to equip with InfoObjects. Figure 8.8 shows the procedure for the Time dimension. If you select the INFOOBJECT DIRECT INPUT menu item, the system opens a dialog where you can enter the InfoObjects, including their technical names. For the TIME dimension you can enter the InfoObjects OCALMONTH and OCALYEAR, for example.

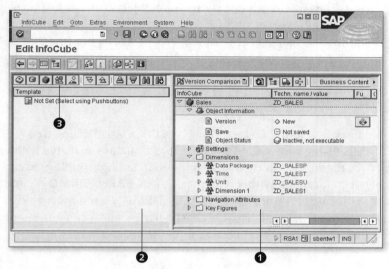

Figure 8.7 Initial View of a New InfoCube

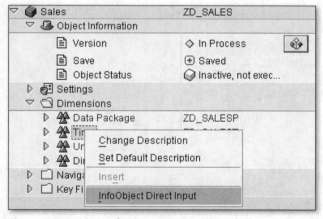

Figure 8.8 Adding InfoObjects via Direct Input

Selecting from the
"Template" area

As an alternative to direct input, you can select the InfoObjects from the TEMPLATE area and add them to a dimension in the InfoCube definition via drag and drop. You can determine the content of the Template area yourself. The system can display the InfoObjects from InfoSources, from various DataProviders, and from InfoObject catalogs. InfoObject catalogs summarize characteristic InfoObjects or key figure InfoObjects of a subject area and can be created in the INFOOBJECTS view of the Data Warehousing Workbench (using Transaction RSA1 or Transaction RSA14). In this example, select an InfoObject catalog by clicking the CREATE INFOOBJECT button (❸ in Figure 8.7).

Selecting the
InfoObject catalog

The system takes you to the SELECT INFOOBJECT CATALOG dialog (see Figure 8.9). This dialog shows all of the InfoObject catalogs available below the InfoArea for which you created an InfoCube. In this example, you can select between a catalog with key figures, ZAAA_SALES_DEMO_K, and a catalog with characteristics, ZAAA_SALES_DEMO_C. You must always use separate InfoObject catalogs for characteristics and key figures. For example, select the InfoObject catalog with the characteristics.

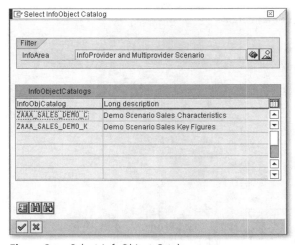

Figure 8.9 Select InfoObject Catalog

Renaming the
dimension

Before you add the InfoObjects to the InfoProvider definition, create the required dimensions. The system has already generated an empty dimension, DIMENSION 1, during the creation of the InfoCube. As shown in Figure 8.10, you can rename it via the context menu and the Properties menu item.

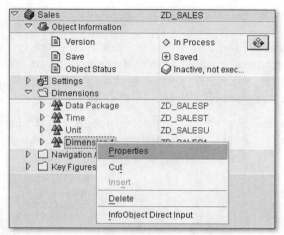

Figure 8.10 Changing the name of a Dimension

You can create additional dimensions via the context menu of the DIMEN- SIONS folder (see Figure 8.11).

Creating dimensions

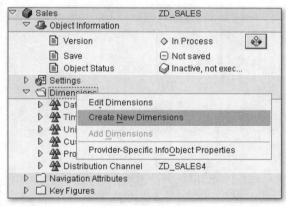

Figure 8.11 Create New Dimensions

After you've created a dimension, you can equip it with characteristics. You also need to add the required key figures in the KEY FIGURES area of the InfoProvider definition. The example in Figure 8.12 shows how you can copy key figures from the TEMPLATE area via drag and drop ❶. The system automatically copies the required unit or currency InfoObjects to the UNIT dimension together with the key figures.

Structure of the InfoCube

Activating the
InfoCube

Once you've copied all of the characteristics and key figures to the Info-Cube definition, it is complete and you can activate it ❷. The InfoCube definition is automatically saved upon activation. Additionally, the system generates all tables that are required for the data retention of the InfoCube. During generation, the system generates and displays a log so that you can detect any errors immediately.

The newly created InfoCube is placed in the corresponding InfoArea and can be provided with data via a transformation and a data transfer protocol (DTP).

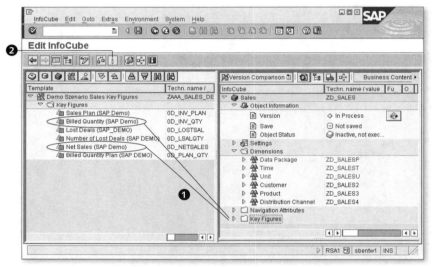

Figure 8.12 Defining and Activating the InfoCube

You now know how to create an InfoCube. With the definition of dimensions, you automatically influenced the physical implementation of the InfoCube. Because the execution speed of the queries defined on the InfoCube mainly depends on the implementation design, you must consider some modeling rules. The following section presents these rules.

Modeling Rules for InfoCubes

InfoCube scope

The more you can reduce the scope of an InfoCube for analysis purposes, the better it is for the analysis. The less granular the data is, the leaner and more powerful the InfoCube modeling is. Even if you have the option of creating aggregates and therefore precalculate frequently used aggregated views, the InfoCube should only contain those characteristics that are actually required for the analysis context. So you don't need to add all of the InfoObjects that describe the reporting requirements as a characteristic to the InfoCube. You only need to add them if master data can change and if you want to execute an evaluation using the status of the reference month. For datasets that are not too large, the modeling as a display or navigation attribute can be sufficient, but can lead to performance losses, however. You must pay attention to the user's requirements. If you're unaware of the requirements, it is unwise to simply add all available characteristics and key figures to the InfoCube — the system may not be accepted.

Scope of the InfoCube

Analyze the user's requirements precisely, and make sure that you only add InfoObjects to the InfoCube that are absolutely necessary.

[+]

In this context, this is frequently referred to as the aggregation of data during loading from the Data Propagation Layer to the Reporting Layer. The more data aggregates, that is, the more it can be compressed, the better it is for performance at the evaluation level. Note that the omission of an InfoObject when loading the data doesn't necessarily have the same consequences for the subsequent analysis: For example, you can still integrate dependent or weak InfoObjects as attributes with the reporting later on. But if you don't load a strong InfoObject, an essential data reference is lost. Consider, for example, the business partner InfoObject, and the customer class InfoObject which also exists in the transaction data. In this case it is also modeled as an attribute of the business partner, which results in a smaller information loss than if you leave out the business partner reference.

You don't implement the reporting requirement requested by the user department as a whole in the form of *one* InfoCube. You first analyze which processes and topics are relevant and which key figure and characteristics you need for each process. This requires one or more InfoCubes.

Breakdown of the reporting requirement

[+] **Recommendations for Classifying InfoCubes**

Data is only merged and modeled in a cube if this is required for implementing the reporting requirements. This is the case if the options of the MultiProviders to form a shared analysis view of data are no longer sufficient (see Section 8.4.1). Combining characteristics and key figures with different processes or topic references in a dataset results in abstract data models and should be avoided, if possible.

After you've determined which InfoObjects are supposed to be transferred to the InfoCube as characteristics and key figures, you can start with the actual modeling of the InfoCube. Chapter 4, Section 4.4.2, Modeling an InfoCube, describes how you create an InfoCube in the Data Warehousing Workbench. Some important aspects of modeling are further detailed in the following section.

Using dimensions

The first step in modeling an InfoCube is to consider how many dimensions are needed for the InfoObjects to be added. The InfoCube can comprise a total of 16 dimensions. The DATA PACKAGE, TIME, and UNIT dimensions are predefined by the system, and the DATA PACKAGE dimension contains technical characteristics. You must assign time characteristics to the Time dimension. Depending on the key figure transferred to the model, the system automatically assigns the corresponding unit InfoObjects to the Unit dimension. You can use the remaining 13 dimensions as needed.

[+] **Dimensioning of InfoCubes**

Use dimensions generously because it doesn't make sense to squeeze all of the InfoObjects into two or three dimensions. Use as many dimensions as you think are reasonable based on the modeling principles presented in the following text.

If you don't use up all 13 free dimensions and change the model later on, you have the option of creating a new dimension, if required. If you've created the BW according to LSA modeling principles, the Data Propagation Layer includes a data basis that lets you empty the InfoCube, remodel it, and reload the data without any losses within a short period of time. In this case, you can more easily afford to use up a lot of dimensions right from the beginning of modeling.

The main task in modeling the InfoCube is to distribute the InfoObjects to dimensions. The distribution to dimensions, and therefore the corresponding requirement, results from the InfoObjects' relations (cardinalities).

You must bear the following rules in mind:

▶ Two InfoObjects that have an n:m relationship should not be added to one dimension whenever possible.

▶ Two InfoObjects that have an n:1 relationship should be added to one dimension.

▶ An InfoObject with a large number of definitions should be added separately to a dimension, if possible. But by no means should you combine this InfoObject with other InfoObjects that have an n:m relationship.

Assignment to dimensions

Distributing InfoObjects to Dimensions

[+]

Nobody can immediately consider the dimensioning rules optimally and completely. So first make an initial dimensioning of the InfoCube based on your knowledge of the topic area, and check the result of your distribution by loading the data. The prerequisite here is that you have meaningful data at hand.

After you've loaded the data, you can check the result of your modeling using the SAP_INFOCUBE_DESIGNS program. You should run this report at regular intervals and redimension the InfoCubes, if necessary.

All of these rules have one goal: keep the dimension tables of the Info-Cube small; only then can the system quickly read the data of the Info-Cube. A rule of thumb says that the number of records in a dimension should ideally comprise not more than 20% of the number of records in the fact table. You will determine that this is frequently not possible. Because there are business processes for which this rule cannot be observed. If your model includes an InfoObject with the name, transaction ID, your dimension table may be as long as the fact table itself.

Record ratio in dimension and fact table

If you determine during modeling that you must model a dimension with a high cardinality, the system provides two setting options that result in an optimized data storage. If your dimension includes multiple InfoObjects, you can select the HIGH CARDINALITY setting (see Figure 8.13).

Line item and high cardinality

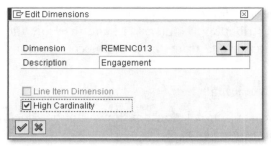

Figure 8.13 Dimension with the "High Cardinality" Setting

It is recommended to use this setting if the ratio between the dimension table and the fact table is 20% or more. With this setting, the system can use a suitable index. It is even better, however, if you can isolate an InfoObject with many definitions in a dimension. In such a case, you can use the LINE ITEM DIMENSION setting. This setting has the effect that no dimension table is created. The characteristic's SID table assumes the role of the dimension table. So one table is omitted resulting in fewer tables that must be merged during the query. But a line item dimension also has a disadvantage: It cannot be enhanced with further InfoObjects retroactively.

Order of InfoObjects in a dimension

The order of InfoObjects within a dimension can also influence the query speed of the InfoCube.

[+] **Order of InfoObjects in a Dimension**

Select the order of the InfoObjects so that the InfoObject with the least characteristic definitions is in the first position and so on. If you know that a hierarchical relation exists between the InfoObjects, you map it using the order of InfoObjects.

With an optimized InfoCube design, you've laid the foundation for high-performance reporting. However, the InfoCube modeling is not complete yet. For example, the modeling made so far is not sufficient if you must load detailed data and your reports query aggregated data. In this case you must create appropriate aggregates (see Section 8.2.2, Aggregates) or consider using BWA (see Section 8.2.6). In addition, there are other technologies for optimizing InfoCubes, that is, compression and partitioning (see Sections 8.2.3, Compression and 8.2.4, Partitioning).

8.2.2 Aggregates

An aggregate stores the dataset of a BasicCube in a compressed or prefiltered form. The aggregate results in redundancy, but the query performance is also considerably improved because the number of data records to be read is reduced in a query run if an appropriate aggregate exists. The OLAP processor decides whether and which aggregate is used in the query execution, and the user cannot control this decision directly.

In principle, all key figures of the BasicCube are added to the aggregate; it is your task to determine the characteristics to be added. By adding a characteristic, the navigation attributes that are not time-dependent are available to the aggregate. Instead of the characteristic, you can also add the navigation attribute itself to the aggregate. This can be beneficial if the number of possible definitions in the navigation attribute is less than in the characteristic itself.

Adding objects

You can create an aggregate via the context menu of the InfoCube or via Transaction RSDDV, Maintenance of Aggregates. Figure 8.14 shows the dialog in which you can add characteristics to the aggregation definition and activate the aggregate.

Creating aggregates

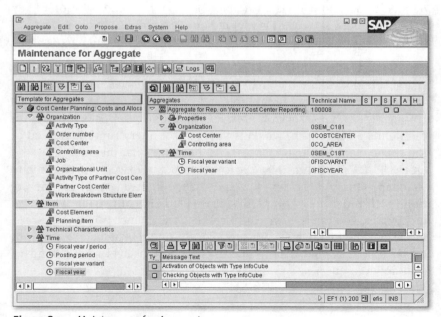

Figure 8.14 Maintenance for Aggregate

During the creation of an aggregate, the system creates two additional tables, the F and E fact table. The aggregate also includes request information (F fact table). By default, however, the aggregate is compressed directly after loading if you have not specified otherwise — only then can the aggregate become fully effective. The package information could strongly counteract the data compression, which is the purpose of an aggregate creation.

Dimensions of an aggregate

To determine an aggregate's dimensions, the system considers the dimensions of the InfoCube, that is, that the assignment of characteristics to dimensions is retained. But if the aggregate comprises no more than 13 characteristics, the system optimizes the aggregate to the effect that it creates a separate line item dimension for each of these characteristics. It is therefore recommended to ensure, for the definition of aggregates, that you create aggregates with a maximum of 13 characteristics (at least initially).

Aggregate on time-dependent navigation attributes

For the definition of aggregates on time-dependent navigation attributes, you must note that the system must create a separate aggregate for each relevant key date, that is, that an aggregate is only valid for the key date for which is was created. The specification of the key date can be predefined or determined via a variable. Because the administration of key date–dependent aggregates is very tedious, it is recommended to first utilize the optimization options on the basis of time-constant aggregates.

Aggregates for external hierarchies

You can also create aggregates for external hierarchies. Frequently, the chargeable nodes of a hierarchy are included as leaves in the hierarchy and must be aggregated in multiple steps at query runtime. With hierarchy aggregates, you can avoid this: For a specific level of a hierarchy you can define an aggregate, which is then read at query runtime instead of the single records. The prerequisite is, however, that the query uses the QUERY IS TO BE READ IN NAVIGATION/HIERARCHY EXPANSION read mode (standard setting). You can view and change the read mode in Transaction RSRT under query properties. Particularly in connection with large hierarchies, you can achieve considerable performance gains via the read mode and the hierarchy aggregates. For example, imagine a large profit center hierarchy that is only presented at a high level in the standard drill-down in queries.

The aggregates considered so far change the data's granularity to reduce the number of data records to be read. However, there is also a second form of aggregates: Aggregates that form data subsets. A constant value, referred to as fixed value in this context, defines which data records are added to the aggregate. It is also possible to select several fixed values for an aggregate. In this case, the definitions are logically linked with *and*. Aggregates that are based on subsets are useful if a specific subset is frequently accessed. This subset could be, for example, a particularly important material or customer group.

Fixed value aggregates

Aggregates can be used flexibly and are very effective. However, you must maintain and optimize them continuously. Because reporting is continuously further developed (both with regard to content and with regard to the frequency with which individual queries are used), you must continuously check and optimize the aggregate definitions. It can be useful if you use the technical content. Use the various statistics to identify frequently used queries, and search these queries for candidates with a relatively high proportion of database runtime compared to the overall runtime. Moreover, you can also have the system display the aggregate usage when you run queries in Transaction RSRT. This lets you draw conclusions about the aggregates' suitability for practical use.

Maintenance

An alternative to creating aggregates is the use of SAP NetWeaver BWA, which is outlined in Section 8.2.6. Compared to aggregates, BWA ensures a stable and high-performance response time behavior and the benefit that the indices, which replace the aggregates, don't need to be adjusted to changed usage conditions all of the time.

8.2.3 Compression

During the generation of an InfoCube, the system generates two fact tables for each InfoCube: One fact table to which the system writes the data during data loading (normal fact table or F table) and another fact table that stores the compressed data (compressed fact table or E table).

F and E fact tables

All of the data that is newly loaded into the BasicCube is initially stored in the normal fact table. Here data is filed separated by loading processes. A loading process can be identified based on the request ID. The fact that the loading process of the respective data can be easily identified facilitates the administration and quality assurance.

When you load data in a BasicCube, the key figures of incoming data are aggregated with the existing fact records if the incoming data has a characteristic combination that already occurs in the fact table. In the normal fact table, however, the aggregation can only take place within a request. But because reporting doesn't usually differentiate by requests, the aggregation unnecessarily occurs during the query execution, which results in performance losses — from a technical perspective another aggregation of data would have been possible during loading. Therefore, the level of detail of the normal fact table depends on its technical implementation and it is not determined based on purely technical criteria.

Implementing compression

For reasons of query performance you should compress InfoCubes regularly. This is possible as soon as the quality assurance processes are complete. In compression, the BW system moves the data from the normal fact table to the compressed fact table. There is no difference from an analysis perspective, because the data is considered without user intervention within the scope of query execution, regardless of whether data is in the normal fact table or already in the compressed fact table. Note that you cannot execute any queries during compression (an exception is, for example, if you use an Oracle database). In principle, you should use the option to schedule compression via the process chain at an appropriate time. But it is also possible to start the process chain immediately.

Deleting zero values

Due to the merging of data from several requests the compression can result in zero records. Imagine, for example, a posting that is reversed again in a subsequent request; you can delete the zero records that are created by implementing zero elimination in parallel to the compression. The zero elimination is only possible for InfoCubes in which only key figures with the SUM aggregation behavior can be found.

You implement the compression of an InfoCube in the COLLAPSE tab in the administration view of the InfoProvider (see Figure 8.15).

Compression for noncumulative InfoCubes

Compression has a slightly different meaning within the scope of noncumulative InfoCubes: The marker for noncumulative is updated here. As a result, less data needs to be read in the query execution to determine the current noncumulative. This leads to a better query performance. Note that you mustn't run a zero elimination for noncumulative key figures.

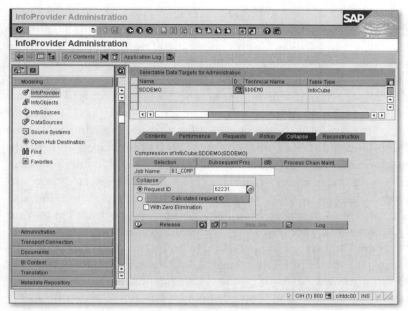

Figure 8.15 Compression of an InfoCube

8.2.4 Partitioning

Database operations in very large database tables with several millions of entries can be very time-consuming. Therefore, it is helpful to split the database table into several smaller units. The benefit of this is that read and write operations can be in parallel without impeding one another. The splitting into smaller units is referred to as *partitioning*. If you perform a partitioning based on the value ranges of a characteristic, this is referred to as *range partitioning*. In principle, you can implement a partitioning both at the database level and in BW. The range partitioning provided by BW is database-dependent and is not available for all databases. Familiarize yourself with the options available in your database system.

The range partitioning is used for both partitioning of the uncompressed fact table and for partitioning of the compressed fact table (of InfoCubes and aggregates, respectively).

The system automatically executes the partitioning of the uncompressed fact table based on the request ID. This results in a simpler administration of requests because data of individual requests can be deleted and easily moved this way.

Uncompressed fact table of the InfoCube

297

Compressed
fact table of
the InfoCube

The partitioning of the compressed fact table is not automatic and must therefore be set when you create the InfoCube. All partitions are already created when you activate an InfoCube. Therefore, you must determine the partitioning during the design time. For the partitioning of the compressed fact table, you can only use the standard InfoObjects, 0FISCPER and 0CALMONTH. The dialog for setting the partitioning of the compressed fact table of an InfoCube is available under EXTRAS DB PERFORMANCE PARTITIONING. There you select the partitioning criterion (either the 0FISCPER InfoObject or the 0CALMONTH InfoObject) and specify the value range. A separate partition is created for each definition of the partitioning characteristic. Values that are outside the selected range are posted to the first or to a separate n+1th "top-level" partition. Because the partitioning criteria are time characteristics, the partitioning may no longer be optimal after a while, for example, because too much data has accumulated in the top-level partition. In such cases, you must perform a repartitioning of the InfoCube. You can find the corresponding function in the context menu of an InfoCube via the menu path OTHER FUNCTIONS • REPARTITIONING. To avoid repartitioning, you can create partitions for later use. But because creating an empty partition consumes disk space, this is only possible to a limited extent.

Aggregates

Aggregates are partitioned automatically, in accordance with the underlying InfoCube. The partitioning schema on the basis of time characteristics is not adopted for compressed aggregates, however. For these aggregates as well, the compression depends on the uncompressed fact table of the InfoCube. Because this type of partitioning can be inappropriate, particularly for small aggregates, you can exclude aggregates from partitioning. You can make the corresponding setting in the context menu of the aggregate maintenance.

8.2.5   OLAP Cache

The OLAP-BW server includes a cache memory. Query results are stored in the cache memory according to specific strategies. If additional queries are executed, and if the relevant data can be read from the cache memory completely or in parts, this increases the performance of the query execution, because the access to the cache memory is much faster than a new access to the database. Besides the data modeling procedures described here (dimensioning, aggregates), an appropriate configuration of the cache memory can considerably contribute to the decrease of query runtimes. For more information on the configuration options of the cache memory, refer to Schröder, 2009, p. 431.

8.2.6   SAP NetWeaver BWA

The technologies discussed so far for improving the query performance are based on the technological and functional options of the BW system. They are basically the options of an optimized data modeling and data retention in a relational environment.

Besides these options for query optimization, as of BW 7.0 you are provided with a supplementary new technology, SAP NetWeaver BWA. It comprises a combined hardware and software solution that is based on a "massive-parallel" computer technology. One part of this technology is that the query-relevant data (the BWA index) in the main memory can be retained by several processing units that are switched in parallel. This architecture leads to considerably better query performance.

The BWA index doesn't consist of a database index as you know it from relational databases, but the BWA index is a special form of storage of InfoCube data from the BW system. The BWA index contains all of an InfoCube's data in a special compressed form. In contrast to an aggregate, the index not only comprises the entire dataset of an InfoCube, but also any additional information on all index names, join conditions, and join paths between the indices.

The data of the BWA index is stored in a special nonrelational form of storage. Instead of a row-tuple, data is stored by columns according to attribute values. So the memory is used very efficiently, because in comparison to the storage by rows you only need to load the data of the relevant attributes or characteristics into the memory (and not the entire table). Using the read access of an attribute value, you can select all of the relevant data records; the indices of BWA are stored as a flat file. You can further split (partition) an index according to different criteria. These additional units are distributed to various computers and storage units at system runtime.

BWA index

The distribution of the index provides the option to split a query into multiple parallel steps. This way, you can perform all of the processing steps of the query independently through separate physical processing units. This results in a shorter query execution time. This is supported by

Parallel processing

the fact that the indices are highly compressed and can be retained completely in the main memory of the processing units. Read accesses to the main memory are 10 to 100 times faster than database read accesses.

In addition to SAP NetWeaver BWA or SAP Business Explorer (BEx), the SAP in-memory procedures are already used today in the LiveCache of the SAP Supple Chain Management (SCM) component, Advanced Planning and Optimization (APO).

8.3 Enhanced InfoCube Modeling

The goal of the data modeling of an InfoCube is to store the loaded data in a form that optimally supports the query of data. Through enhancements of the data model, you can also enhance the available contents. Virtual characteristics and key figures (see Section 8.3.1, Virtual Key Figures and Characteristics) enable you to determine additional characteristics and key figures while the query is executed. Restricted and calculated key figures are based on the already-available key figures and allow for further calculations (see Section 8.3.3, Restricted and Calculated Key Figures).

8.3.1 Virtual Key Figures and Characteristics

Key figures and characteristics in the InfoCube are usually provided with values when data is loaded. This data is read and displayed when you run a report. However, there are situations in which you want to add InfoObjects (characteristics or key figures) to a report whose values cannot be determined at the time the data is loaded. Therefore, simply spare the mapping of the corresponding InfoObjects in the incoming transformation. Also, in the BW system you store a program that determines the values of the key figures or characteristics when the query is run. Such InfoObjects, which are contained in the InfoProvider but whose values are not read from the InfoProvider but are determined at the time the query is run, are referred to as virtual characteristics or virtual key figures. In BW, the logic for deriving the values is implemented in an exit for this purpose.

Usage options | You need to use virtual characteristics and key figures in the following cases:

▶ **Values are only supposed to be considered temporarily**
A report is supposed to include specific contents only for specific times. Depending on the system date, the exit can provide values or not.

▶ **User input required for calculation**
If you need user input for deriving a calculation result, you don't have all of the input values until the query's runtime. But you should only use the solution option of virtual key figures if the calculation is too complex for an implementation via a calculated key figure in combination with a formula variable.

▶ **Availability of information**
It doesn't necessarily have to be a user input for which a dependency exists. For calculations, you may need to access other external information that is not yet known at the time of loading.

▶ **Different aggregation level of data**
If the calculation occurs at a more detailed aggregation level of data than is specified in the modeling of the InfoCube, the calculation can still be done via virtual key figures.

▶ **Adaptability of the data model**
You may considerably (also temporarily) extend the reporting options for an existing data model if you supplement essential missing characteristics or key figures with virtual InfoObjects. But for performance reasons, you should first check to see if you can also derive the characteristic values by enhancing the transformation and reloading the data. Only in cases in which this would involve too much effort, you should use virtual characteristics.

Since BW 7.0, you can implement virtual characteristics and key figures using the RSR_OLAP_BADI Business Add-In (BAdI); previously, Exit RSR00002 was used. The new method results in a clearer and more flexible implementation. The implementation steps can roughly be described as follows (see Herzog, 2009):

Implementation

▶ **Creating the BAdI implementation**
You create a classic BAdI implementation using Transaction SE19. Select RSR_OLAP_BADI as the implementation. After saving, follow the GOTO • COPY SAMPLE CODING menu path to copy the sample coding provided by SAP. You can now see that the implementation com-

prises the three methods, DEFINE, INITIALIZATION, and COMPUTE.

▶ **Implementation of the Define method**
The DEFINE method is called at the time the query is generated, and it tells the system which characteristics and key figures are virtual (table C_T_CHAMN or table C_T_KYFNM) and which characteristics may be used for calculating these (table I_TH_CHANM_USED or table I_TH_KYFNM_USED).

▶ **Creating instance attributes**
For all InfoObjects that you've previously added to the C_T_CHAMN and C_T_KYFNM tables, you must create instance attributes (comparable to global variables) in the class definition.

▶ **Implementation of the Compute method**
You use the COMPUTE method for the actual calculation of virtual key figures and characteristics. Here, it is important that you implement the derivation logic whose performance is as high as possible. This includes the use of hashed tables and a reduction of database accesses to a minimum.

▶ **Implementation of a variable transfer, if required**
In the implementing class, you can create a static public attribute for each variable that is supposed to be transferred. The value transfer is done in processing step 3 of the reporting's variable exit (EXIT_SAPL-RRS0_001) by assigning the value to the static public attribute of a class.

Performance A high-performance implementation of the logic for deriving the virtual characteristics and key figures is extremely important. Note that the coding is also called during the query run if the corresponding characteristic or the respective key figure is not in the query's drill-down.

The virtual key figures and characteristics represent a very flexible way to extend reporting. The following section provides a concrete example for the use of virtual characteristics, which is based on the case study presented in Chapter 9, Case Studies. The following example involves an enterprise that finances projects on a global scale and that needs to regularly check the credit standing of its business partners.

Application example The business partners' ratings are provided every month as a full upload in the Reporting Layer. For the implementation of the reports it was determined that the user is supposed to select a reference and a comparison month when he opens the report; the report is supposed to display the capital-at-risk key figure. This key figure is to be analyzed by risk categories. Because the system compares the two different months with one another, the rating may have changed in the meantime. The old and the new rating are supposed to be modeled as separate objects so that a transformation matrix can be created; in addition, a classification of the rating change should be possible based on the additional characteristic, rating classification (downgrade, upgrade, no rating).

The rating classification and the comparison rating cannot be determined until the runtime of the query because it is not known until then which months are supposed to be compared. The InfoObjects for mapping the rating classifications are implemented as virtual characteristics.

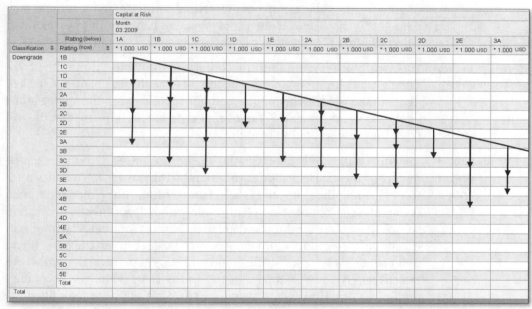

Figure 8.16 Rating Migration Matrix (Shown for Downgrades) with Virtual Characteristics

Figure 8.16 shows the result of a query for presenting a rating migration matrix that is based on the virtual characteristics described. Only rating downgrades are shown (downgrade *rating classification*). For this reason, values are displayed only in the cells below the diagonal for the capital-at-risk key figure. For each before rating in the columns, the system displays how much capital has a worse rating now (total row) and also which new risk valuation (current rating in the rows) is linked to the capital.

Also, for virtual key figures you can use the aggregation behavior, which you set in the key figure, to determine the calculation rule for adding the key figure values. The following section discusses the exception aggregation.

8.3.2 Exception Aggregation

The exception aggregation lets you influence the aggregation behavior of a key figure; you can make this setting in the InfoObject (here: key figure). You can also override the aggregation behavior of a key figure in Query Designer by creating calculated key figures.

Setting in the key figure InfoObject

You usually make settings in the key figure InfoObject during the Info-Cube's design time. You must transfer the (technical) semantic of the key figure to the model. The requirement for specific exception aggregations arises from the context of the overall data model implementation and from the method used to load the data.

Headcount example

Imagine a data model for evaluating the headcount: Each month, the system loads the dataset valid for this month. The time characteristics refer to the loading date, and the other characteristics of the model describe the employees in more detail (employee group, department, gender, and so on). If you create the number of employees key figure without an exception aggregation, it provides incorrect values in certain areas: If you don't set the limit to a specific month, but aggregate several months, the system falsely shows a total — one and the same employee is counted multiple times. However, it would be correct if the system didn't show the total, but displayed the data of the month that was loaded last. You can do this if you create a last value exception aggregation for the key figure with the reference characteristic, 0CALMONTH (calendar month). You can also select the average exception aggregation, for example. Both alternatives are useful in principle. It must be decided functionally which alternative is supposed to be selected.

Figure 8.17 shows the key figure, 0HDCNT_LAST (headcount), from Business Content. This key figure has a cumulative value with the last value exception aggregation set to 0CALDAY (calendar day), and it implements the requirement from the example described.

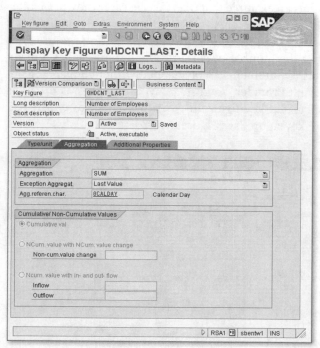

Figure 8.17 Exception Aggregation in the "Number of Employees" InfoObject

Experience has shown that the settings for the exception aggregation in the actual key figure InfoObject hardly change once the data model is used in live operation. This is understandable because you can assume that the functional requirements with regard to aggregation behavior were mapped correctly in the initial implementation — and a change to the settings would concern all reports already implemented.

Determining the aggregation behavior in reporting

Frequently, there are requirements for new key figures that can only be defined based on an existing key figure by changing the aggregation behavior. In cases like these it is not necessary to enhance the physical model. Here, it is sufficient to create a calculated key figure with the corresponding exception aggregation in reporting. Calculated and restricted key figures (see Section 8.3.3) also have disadvantages that have no effect in many cases, so this solution is acceptable and brings results quickly and with little effort.

The following presents an example that refers to the case study in Chapter 9 again. The sample enterprise already uses a MultiProvider and has set up a reporting to analyze an investment. A new reporting requirement is supposed to count the number of counties the enterprise has already invested capital. This requirement can be mapped without enhancing the InfoCube and the MultiProvider. You use the MultiProvider as the basis to create a new calculated key figure in Query Designer, to which you add the 0AMOUNT key figure (see Figure 8.18).

Figure 8.18 Query Designer — Dialog for Creating a Calculated Key Figure

In addition, you specify the following exception aggregation rule in the AGGREGATION tab: Counter for all detailed values that are not zero, null, or error. Select the 0COUNTRY InfoObject as the reference characteristic (see Figure 8.19).

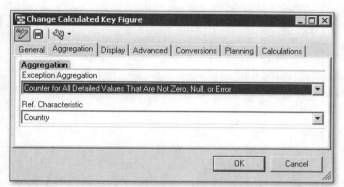

Figure 8.19 Query Designer — Dialog for Specifying the Exception Aggregation

The result, except for the necessity of the transport for the production environment, is immediately available and can be added to all reports that are defined based on the MultiProvider.

Unfortunately, the preceding procedure has some disadvantages: If the key figure is only defined in reporting and is supposed to be available on multiple InfoProviders, you must create them several times with different technical names. Alternatively, you can copy the restricted key figure, which also generates a new object, however. In both cases both the maintenance and service of the system is more complicated.

Restrictions

The next section discusses the handling of restricted and calculated key figures in more detail.

8.3.3 Restricted and Calculated Key Figures

In reporting, you can create restricted and calculated key figures. They are available in the context of the DataProvider on which they are defined and can be added to queries, if required.

Note that restricted and calculated key figures can't be transferred to a MultiProvider definition if, for example, they were defined on an Info-Cube. The restricted and calculated key figures are not part of the data model and are permanently linked with the InfoProvider on which they are defined. You'll encounter this problem when you create reporting (and therefore the restricted and calculated key figures) on the basis of MultiProviders.

Definition for only
one InfoProvider

The biggest restriction for restricted and calculated key figures is that their validity is restricted to only one DataProvider. You should use key figure InfoObjects to ensure that important central key figures are subjected to an enterprise-wide coordination process in which they can be defined once at a central location and then used at different locations of the data model. The result is that adaptations must be made centrally, which minimizes the effort.

Increased flexibility

As you've learned in Section 8.3.2, Exception Aggregation, restricted and calculated key figures increase flexibility in reporting and enable a standardization of key figures in the context of the MultiProvider (in contrast to the structure elements, which are only valid within a query if they were not saved as part of the overall structure). At the level of a user department reporting for which globally defined objects may be enhanced with their own requirements, the restricted and calculated key figures are a useful means to structure flexible reporting.

Copying key
figures and queries

You can copy restricted and calculated key figures (and queries) from one DataProvider to another. This is only possible, however, if the target InfoProvider includes all of the characteristics of the source InfoProvider — regardless of whether the respective characteristic is required for defining the query or the key figure. Moreover, the copied key figure receives a new technical name. Due to these restrictions, using a key figure InfoObject at the data model level is the better choice. The key figure InfoObject can be added to different contexts, has the same identity in all locations, and can be maintained centrally.

[+] **Implementing New Key Figure Requirements**

It is recommended to carefully check the requirements for new key figures. You should scrutinize whether it is identifiable from the outset that the key figure is relevant for several InfoProviders. Or is it only a local calculation that only makes sense in the context of a specific InfoProvider? Perhaps you don't need to create a new key figure InfoObject in these cases. If the requirement only refers to one report, the supplementation of a structure element in the report is sufficient (initially).

This way, reporting is still clear and relatively easy to maintain. If you use the flexible options for deriving calculated and restricted key figures (particularly the ones of the exception aggregation), you can possibly convince the user department with short implementation times.

8.4   Virtual Layer

The Virtual Layer itself doesn't store any data. Nevertheless it has a special role: Users usually come into contact with the data models implemented in BW via the Virtual Layer. The DataProviders of the Virtual Layer include InfoSets and MultiProviders, whereas the MultiProvider is the object most often used. InfoSets, however, are critical for the implementation of special requirements.

8.4.1   MultiProvider in the Virtual Layer

SAP has recommended for a long time to create queries exclusively on MultiProviders, even if the MultiProvider itself is trivial and only describes an individual InfoCube. There are two main reasons for this approach: the separation of the physical and functional levels and the higher flexibility of changing requirements.

Before discussing the various aspects of modeling MultiProviders, let's first see how you can create MultiProviders on the basis of existing InfoProviders.

Creating MultiProviders

Just like an InfoCube, you create a MultiProvider in the InfoArea's context menu in the INFOPROVIDER view of the MODELING area of the Data Warehousing Workbench (Transaction RSA1 or Transaction RSA11). Alternatively, you can also use Transaction RSDMPRO (Edit MultiProvider). First select the EDIT MULTIPROVIDER menu item. The system takes you to the EDIT MULTIPROVIDER dialog, where you can enter a technical and a descriptive name ❶ (see Figure 8.20). Then click the button to create the MultiProviders ❷.

Create
MultiProvider

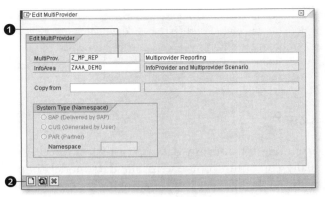

Figure 8.20 Entering the Name for the MultiProvider

Select relevant
InfoProviders

To select the relevant InfoProviders, the system takes you to the MULTI-PROVIDER: RELEVANT INFOPROVIDERS dialog (see Figure 8.21). Besides the InfoProviders that store data physically, you can also select InfoSets and aggregation levels. Choose the InfoProviders ❶ and then close the dialog by clicking the OK button (the button with a checkmark) ❷.

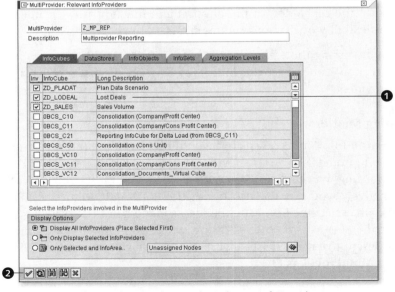

Figure 8.21 MultiProvider — Selecting the Relevant InfoProviders

The system now takes you to a user interface that is very similar to the one for processing InfoCubes (see Figure 8.22). In the INVOLVED INFO-PROVIDERS area, you can view the dimensions and InfoObjects of the InfoProviders that form the basis of the MultiProvider. To define the MultiProvider, select from these elements. Drag and drop all of the elements required (that is, characteristics ❶ and key figures ❷) to the MULTI-PROVIDER area on the right. In doing so, you can copy entire dimensions or individual characteristics. All of the InfoProviders involved are available as the basis of the MultiProvider.

Add InfoObjects

You must also identify all objects copied (characteristics and key figures), that is, you must determine from which InfoProvider they are supposed to be transferred ❸. This is also required if an InfoObject only occurs in one InfoProvider. Once you've completed the definition of the MultiProvider, you must activate it ❹.

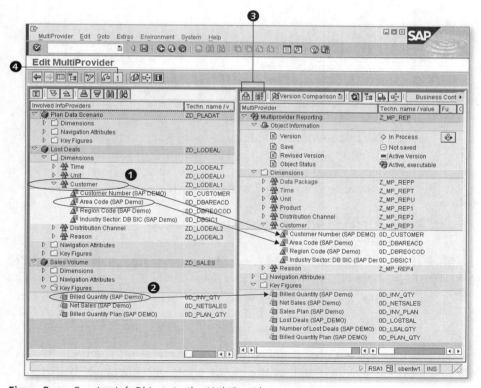

Figure 8.22 Copying InfoObjects to the MultiProvider

311

Identifying
InfoObjects

In the IDENTIFICATION of PARTICIPATING CHARACTERISTICS/NAVIGATION ATTRIBUTES dialog (see Figure 8.23), you have the option of assigning objects ❶ manually or automatically ❷. An automatic assignment is helpful if the definition is trivial. This is the case, for example, if the underlying InfoProviders have the same structure or if the MultiProvider is only based on one InfoProvider. Click the OK button to close the identification dialog ❸. Handle the dialog for identifying key figures accordingly.

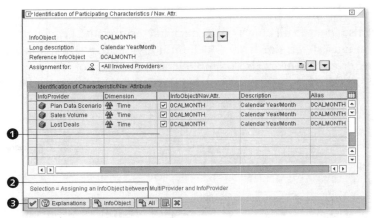

Figure 8.23 Identification of Participating Characteristics/Navigation Attributes

When you define MultiProviders, you access the structure of the participating InfoProviders and define a partial view of the objects involved. The grouping and identification of InfoObjects offers some design options, which are presented in the following section.

Design Options and Specific Features of MultiProviders

Separating the
physical from the
functional level

The design options with regard to MultiProviders enable you to "hide" the structure of the InfoCube and develop a view of the data in which users have a better orientation. This particularly concerns the dimensioning of DataProviders, but you can also change the name of the InfoObjects.

Modeling InfoCubes should only be based on technical criteria (see Section 8.2.1, Modeling); at this point, the requirements of the user for grouping objects may or may not play a role. You don't consider these until the modeling of the MultiProvider. Here, you can add dimensions and InfoObjects from the InfoCube definition to the MultiProvider structure, you can regroup them, create new dimensions, and rename existing dimensions — you can also change the description InfoObjects of the respective MultiProvider are shown under in reporting. These structure-specific settings also include those that refer to the display of characteristic values and selection and filter parameters.

If requirements should change or additional requirements should arise, you have an advantage in that you've already developed the reports on a MultiProvider. You can easily add more DataProviders to the MultiProvider and make them available in reporting. It is also possible to develop, test, and go live with a new version of the BasicCube. Only when everything is completed do you adapt the MultiProvider and transport it. This way, you enable a relatively safe and quick transfer to a new data model version. The following are some examples of requirements that can be easily integrated later on if a MultiProvider is already used as the basis (see Section 8.1):

Flexibility in modeling

▸ Supplementation of planning or extrapolation data

▸ Supplementation of an NLS solution

▸ Retroactive splitting into various domains or into partitions that are formed based on other criteria

It is often the case, for example, that the data volume of an InfoCube continuously grows over the years and is then supposed to be distributed to multiple InfoCubes. Where appropriate, an NLS system should be used. It also helps if you've developed reports only on the basis of MultiProviders from the outset.

Copying Queries and Query Elements

If you've already developed queries on InfoCubes in an application area, you can copy them to a MultiProvider (Transaction RSZC). To do this, you should first model the MultiProvider as a 1:1 copy of the InfoCube.

You can only copy queries and query objects if the target includes all of the objects of the source. The process itself is simple, but it can entail considerable postprocessing work. Queries and query objects (restricted and calculated key figures and structures) obtain a new technical name during the copy process and therefore a new identity. So you must expect postprocessing in (web) reporting, for the connection of SAP BusinessObjects, and for the authorization assignment.

The separation of the physical and functional level and flexibility are not the only reasons for using MultiProviders.

Design options in mapping InfoObjects By mapping characteristics and key figures, which is performed within the scope of the MultiProvider definition, you don't generate a simple 1:1 copy of the underlying InfoCubes. When you define MultiProviders, you select InfoObjects and decide from which InfoCube they are supposed to be copied into the MultiProvider.

You can imagine the total amount of data provided by the MultiProvider as a large union of data records of all underlying DataProviders. In this process, InfoObjects that are merged via mapping are included in one column. If an object doesn't exist in a specific InfoProvider, or was not added to the MultiProvider definition, the corresponding column is empty for all data records of this data source (see the example in Table 8.5).

Because all of the referencing InfoObjects can be mapped on one another (this applies to characteristic InfoObjects and to attributes), you can generate a completely new semantic using the MultiProvider definition. You can then use the semantic for modeling, but it involves a certain potential for errors.

The following example illustrates this: Assume that you merge two InfoCubes into one MultiProvider, which comprises the characteristics and navigation attributes shown in Table 8.1.

Category	InfoCube 1	InfoCube 2
Characteristics	0COSTCENTER cost center 0PROFIT_CTR profit center	0COSTCENTER cost center
Navigation attributes		0COSTCENTER_0PROFIT_CTR profit center

Table 8.1 Structure of Two InfoCubes for the MultiProvider Example

Now assume that you add the 0PROFIT_CTR InfoCube to the MultiProvider definition — then you must determine in the characteristic identification how the 0PROFIT_CTR InfoObject is supposed to be identified (see Figure 8.24).

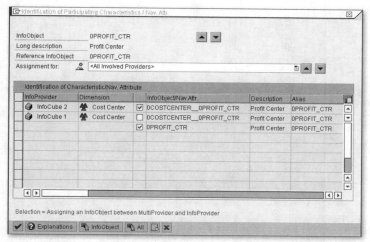

Figure 8.24 Mapping of the 0PROFT_CTR InfoObject in the MultiProvider Example

In the dialog for mapping the object of the InfoProviders involved, you can now merge a navigation attribute from one InfoCube with the characteristic of the other InfoCube. Bear in mind that the navigation attribute can have a totally different time base than the characteristic InfoObject, giving you a mixed InfoObject in the MultiProvider. However, the user cannot see this, because in the reporting on the MultiProvider he only sees a characteristic InfoObject with the technical name, 0PROFIT_CTR. Nothing indicates that he (partially) accessed master data tables and therefore another time base. And he can't anticipate the possibly related deviating runtime behavior during access. A better solution at this point would be if you first added 0PROFIT_CTR as an additional characteristic to the InfoCube.

But contents can also be mixed without navigation attributes. Another example, which is illustrated in Figure 8.25, shows that you can also merge InfoObjects with different meaning if these involve referencing InfoObjects. The partner cost center (origin) has a different semantic than the original cost center.

You can see that you have versatile options in defining a MultiProvider. Therefore, you should proceed carefully in mapping because error sources in the interpretation of data could easily arise.

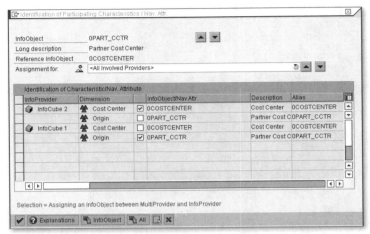

Figure 8.25 Mapping of the 0PART_CCTR InfoObject in the MultiProvider Example

Flexible assignment of authorizations

Using a MultiProvider facilitates a differentiated assignment of authorizations. You can create several MultiProviders for one and the same underlying InfoCube. You can then authorize these MultiProviders individually. Each MultiProvider can provide a different scope of characteristics and key figures.

Performance

In principle, you can use MultiProviders as a means for optimizing performance. You must remerge the data read by the individual InfoProviders in a second processing step, but if the queries can run in parallel, that is, at the same time on the InfoProviders, this results in a considerable speed benefit (compared to reading in a single large dataset). If you define queries that you know are only supposed to be executed on a specific InfoCube of a MultiProvider, you can use the 0INFOPROV characteristic (InfoProvider), which is available on each MultiProvider to limit the query accordingly from the outset. This saves unnecessary overhead and accelerates processing.

Functional restrictions of the MultiProvider

Even if MultiProviders merge data from several InfoProviders and therefore combine all participating characteristics and key figures into one view, you must accept some restrictions that you must consider for the definition of requirements. However, it is often difficult for the user department, which is not familiar with the concept of MultiProviders, to accept these restrictions. In a nutshell: this restriction means that no key figure can be evaluated by characteristics for which no relation exists. In other words, this is the case if no data record exists in which the corresponding key figure and the corresponding characteristic both occur. This is easy to understand — but why does this restriction for MultiProviders play a role?

Consider the following example:

► InfoCube 1 includes quantity {C1} of characteristics and {K1} of key figures.

► InfoCube 2 includes quantity {C2} of characteristics and {K2} of key figures.

The MultiProvider consists of the total quantity of characteristics and key figures, that is, for characteristics {C1, C2} and for key figures {K1, K2}.

Now image the MultiProvider as a union of all data records of the two InfoProviders, for which you map the same characteristics on the same characteristics and the same key figures on the same key figures. Then the following statements apply:

1. If {C1} and {C2} have no intersection, you cannot analyze any key figure from {K2} according to characteristics from {C1} and no key figure from {K1} according to characteristics from {C2}.

2. If {C1} and {C2} have an intersection, this involves those characteristics according to which you can analyze all key figures {K1, K2}. For all others, one of the statements in 1 applies.

3. If {C1} = {C2}, you can analyze all key figures {K1, K2} according to all characteristics {C1, C2}.

These restrictions exist because the MultiProvider doesn't effect a merging of the participating InfoCubes. So there is no data record that merges all characteristics and key figures; the InfoCubes only describe the structure of available data records.

However, case 1 usually doesn't occur in real life. If you link InfoCubes of the same structure, which emerged due to a division by domains, for example, this involves case 3. If you merge two different views that still have similarities, this results in case 2. This often causes discussions between user and development departments, if a full flexibility in evaluation is expected. Instead, the following restrictions exist:

► Filters that are not defined based on the intersection of {C1} and {C2} only provide results with values for key figures from {K1} or from

{K2}. A possibly existing, calculated key figure that operates with key figures from {K1} and {K2} doesn't provide the expected result.

▶ A key figure can only be evaluated by a characteristic in the report (that is, it delivers characteristic values in the characteristic drill-down other than "not assigned") if the characteristic and key figure originate from an underlying InfoProvider. This means that a characteristic drill-down by a characteristic that is not in the intersection only delivers values for a key figure from {K1} if the characteristic originates from {C1}. This applies accordingly to the combination of characteristics from {C2} and key figures from {K2}. In other words: A MultiProvider doesn't change the aggregation level of data. Each key figure can only be evaluated by those characteristics that are available in the data record.

Example from the HR area

Let's look at an example that outlines the effects that the formally described properties can have on the functioning of MultiProviders: In Human Resources (HR), you differentiate between two topics that are mapped through their own InfoProviders in the BW system: personnel administration and organizational management.

In personnel administration, you evaluate the headcount. You evaluate the employee by all of the characteristics that describe the employee, for example, gender, employee group, employee subgroup, and so on.

Staff assignments is a typical report for organizational management, for example. This report displays the relevant staff assignments (positions and people) for one or more organizational units. A position describes a concrete position occupied by an employee within the enterprise. Moreover, the job object exists in this context. This object describes the general functions (for instance, area manager) within an enterprise.

The InfoCubes from personnel administration and organizational management are often used to create MultiProviders to enable a shared evaluation. This is possible at the level of common characteristics, for instance, if you present the headcount key figure together with a number of positions KEY FIGURE, WHICH IS drilled down according to the hierarchically presented organizational structure, in one report.

In this context, consider the following question: How many positions with a specific activity profile (underlying job) are occupied by women?

If the gender characteristic is only available in the dataset of personnel administration, there is a problem in that you cannot implement the corresponding report on the MultiProvider because you cannot filter the number of positions key figure by gender.

You have the following options for solving this problem:

► **Characteristic derivation**
You add the gender characteristic to the organizational management data. This hurts with regard to content, but achieves the anticipated result thanks to the MultiProvider.

► **Jump target**
You utilize jump targets in reporting. In personnel administration, you implement an initial report in which you filter all of the female employees using the gender characteristic. With this list, you then navigate to organizational management and have the system display the number of positions with the corresponding criteria. This way, you obtain the correct result, but, unfortunately, you cannot implement this process as an individual standard report.

► **InfoSet**
You use an InfoSet to merge the two InfoCubes. As a result, you execute a join operation that cancels the restrictions of the MultiProvider. You can implement your report as desired.

Besides MultiProviders, InfoSets are the second essential InfoProvider type for modeling the Virtual Layer. The next section discusses InfoSets.

8.4.2 InfoSets in the Virtual Layer

Through the join operation of InfoSets, you merge all of the characteristics and key figures of the relevant InfoProviders on the basis of a join condition (inner join, left outer join). On the overall structure, you can develop reports as if all of the information was posted in a data record. Here, the InfoSets are not restricted to InfoCube data. You can also integrate DSOs and master data tables. This increases the flexibility for defining queries. Due to the performance restrictions and due to the fact that InfoObjects work with separate field definitions, the usage area of InfoSets is restricted to special issues.

Before discussing the functioning of InfoSets in detail, let's learn how to create an InfoSet.

Process for Creating InfoSets

Create InfoSet Just like for other InfoProviders, you create the InfoSet in the InfoArea's context menu in the INFOPROVIDER view of the MODELING area of the Data Warehousing Workbench (Transaction RSA1 or Transaction RSA11). Alternatively, you can use Transaction RSISET (Edit InfoSet). Select the CREATE INFOSET menu item. The system opens the CREATE INFOSET dialog, where you need to enter a technical and a descriptive name ❶ (see Figure 8.26). In addition, select the first InfoProvider that you want to add to the InfoSet. In this example, choose InfoCube, ZD_SALES ❷. Click the OK button ❸ to close the dialog.

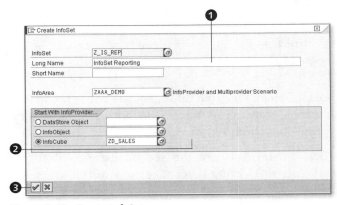

Figure 8.26 Create InfoSet

The system opens the user interface for processing the definition of Info-Sets. There you can choose between a network and a tree structure. The following sections describe a network structure (similar to the Entity Relationship (ER)).

Add InfoProviders The previously selected InfoProvider, an InfoCube here, is already included in the definition (see Figure 8.27). You can add more Info-Providers to the definition. To do this, drag and drop another InfoProvider to any point in the work area ❶. In this example, add InfoCube ZD_LODEAL (lost deals).

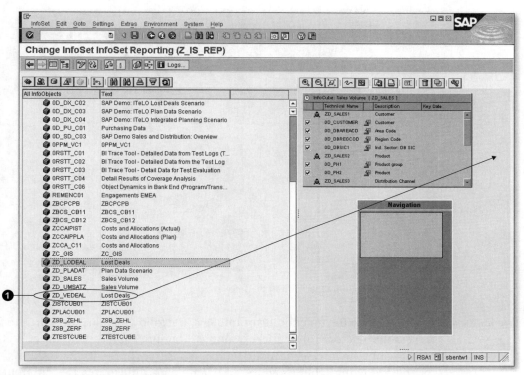

Figure 8.27 Expanding the InfoSets

The second InfoCube is inserted in the InfoSet definition. Initially, the two InfoProviders are not linked. So you must define a join operation that describes how their information must be linked. To do this you need an InfoObject that is contained in the two InfoCubes. Click the corresponding InfoObject in one of the InfoCubes, hold down the mouse button, and drag it to the appropriate field in the second InfoCube. The join condition is displayed graphically as a line that links the two fields (see ❶ in Figure 8.28). In this example, you use the 0D_CUSTOMER field (customer) for linking. You can reduce the scope of the fields in the Info-Set by deactivating the checkbox in front of the respective field. Before you can use the InfoSet, you must activate it.

Defining join operations

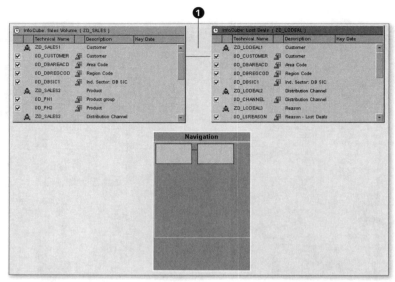

Figure 8.28 Join Operation in the InfoSet

Numerical example

To illustrate the functioning of InfoSets, the following illustrates the processing base on a numerical example. The inner join operation effects that only the intersection of data records is transferred to the result set. The following table provides an example and illustrates the different functioning of the InfoSet and the MultiProvider. The MultiProvider generates a union. For the inner join, profit center 1000000002 is not included in the result set because it doesn't exist in the second table.

Tables 8.2 and 8.3 show the data of the two sample InfoCubes.

Profit Center	Number of Employees
1000000000	150
1000000001	40
1000000002	200

Table 8.2 Data of the First InfoProvider

Profit Center	Telephone Costs
1000000000	$ 10,500
1000000001	$ 5,300

Table 8.3 Data of the Second InfoProvider

Table 8.4 shows the result delivered by the MultiProvider.

Profit Center	Number of Employees	Telephone Costs
1000000000	150	
1000000001	40	
1000000002	200	
1000000000		$ 10,500
1000000001		$ 5,300

Table 8.4 MultiProvider Result

Table 8.5 shows the result provided by the InfoSet.

Profit Center	Number of Employees	Telephone Costs
1000000000	150	$ 10,500
1000000001	40	$ 5,300

Table 8.5 InfoSet Result

The InfoSet has the option to define a temporal join as another operation, which is useful for processing master data. A temporal join can
map a time. In reporting other InfoProviders you must always specify a
specific key date that describes the time base of the master data. In this
regard, an InfoSet is more flexible because you can use temporal oper-
ands to import master data that corresponds to the time of transaction
data. This means that the transaction date from the transaction data is
used as the time base for the master data.

Temporal join

To define a temporal join, in the InfoSet maintenance you must select an
available time characteristic as the key date for the temporal join. Time
characteristics that refer to a specific day (0CALDAY) can be selected
directly; for characteristics that describe a time interval (0CALWEEK,
0CALMONTH, 0CALQUARTER, 0CALYEAR, 0FISCPER, and 0FISCYEAR)
you must define additional rules. In reporting, you are then provided
with a separate dimension for the valid time interval (VALIDTIMEINTER-
VAL), which is used for the time selection.

The following restrictions for using InfoSets illustrate that you should
only use them for special issues:

InfoSets
restrictions

- ▸ You can integrate a maximum of two InfoCubes.
- ▸ When you process a data query that is based on an InfoSet, parallel processing (like for MultiProviders) cannot take place. This and the fact that data is merged via a join operation impair performance.
- ▸ It is not possible to integrate SAP NetWeaver BWA. An InfoSet is executed as an operation in the relational database; Therefore, BWA is not supported.

Because, in principle, an InfoObject can emerge in multiple roles within an InfoSet and you must ensure that each field of the InfoSet is uniquely identified, the system assigns technical IDs for the individual fields. These IDs and the texts are also available in reporting. Because texts are often not unique, you usually use the technical names of the InfoObjects for defining reports. However, this option is not available for InfoSets, so creating reports is considerably more difficult.

Using InfoSets   Due to the reasons mentioned earlier, InfoSets are used to cover special reporting requirements. This is particularly the case if data from different InfoProviders is supposed to be merged and the restrictions of the MultiProviders have the result that the requirements cannot be met. InfoSets are often used in master data reporting and in the evaluation of transactional DSOs.

[+] **Queries on the Basis of MultiProviders**

It is recommended that you not create queries based directly on InfoSets. You should use a MultiProvider to increase flexibility and to decouple reporting components from the data model. If you add the InfoProviders, which are merged in the InfoSet to the MultiProvider definition in addition to the InfoSet, you also have the option of building the InfoSet on the basis of InfoObjects (instead of fields of the InfoSets). Then, the InfoObjects of the MultiProvider are only identified with the fields of the InfoSet. This increases the clarity of the data model, reduces the effort for query creation, and it is very flexible in case of changes.

8.5   Universes in SAP BusinessObjects

The MultiProvider in BW already abstracts from the technical implementation of an InfoCube. The presentation of dimensions and objects can be selected in such a way that the grouping and the name of the objects is based on the user's requirements (see Section 8.4).

SAP BusinessObjects also provide a similar description level as the MultiProvider, the universe. A universe also describes a set of objects, which are grouped by specific criteria in a tree structure. These groups are referred to as a class in the SAP BusinessObjects universe. A universe describes a metadata layer that is between the backend system (relational database, OLAP system, and BW) and the query tools. Via this metadata layer, the user can access a variety of systems. Besides the objects and classes (as the actual content structures), the universe also describes specific parameters that are required for accessing the backend system. Various SAP BusinessObjects front-end components use the universe as the basis for defining reports and analyses.

8.5.1 SAP BusinessObjects Universes on the Basis of SAP NetWeaver BW

You have two options to define a universe on the basis of BW: You either create a universe on the basis of a DataProvider ❶, or you use a query as an interface ❷. Figure 8.29 illustrates these access paths.

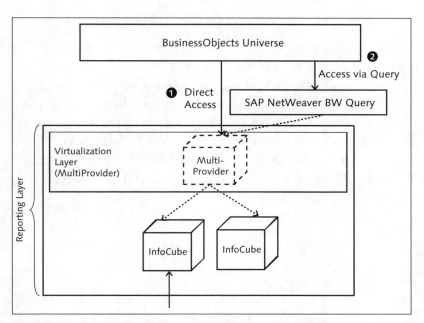

Figure 8.29 The SAP BusinessObjects Universe as a Metadata Layer on the Basis of SAP NetWeaver BW

The figure only shows the direct or the indirect access via a MultiProvider. It is highly recommended to also use a MultiProvider in case of direct access (see the discussion in Section 8.4). Moreover, from a technical perspective, you can also define the universe directly on an InfoCube or based on a query that is defined on an InfoCube.

Access to the BW system is based on the OLAP–Business Application Programming Interface (BAPI). Therefore, access via the SAP BusinessObjects universe doesn't require any other installations or ABAP transports. However, these are required for the implementation of a single sign-on (SSO) functionality.

8.5.2 Defining the Universe on a DataProvider or Query

You start the designer via the WINDOWS • START • PROGRAMS • BUSINESS OBJECTS XI 3.1 • BUSINESS OBJECTS ENTERPRISE CLIENT TOOLS DESIGNER menu path in an SAP BusinessObjects XI 3.1 Enterprise installation to create an SAP BusinessObjects universe. After you've called the designer, you must log on to the BusinessObjects server.

To create a universe, you must carry out the following steps:

1. Within the designer, start the UNIVERSE PARAMETERS dialog via the FILE • NEW menu path (see Figure 8.30).

2. In the UNIVERSE PARAMETERS dialog, choose NEW... to create a new connection. Depending on the settings you've selected, it is possible that the Connection Wizard, which the system would now open, has already been opened automatically together with the Designer. In this case, you can continue with the following dialog steps.

3. In the first dialog, DEFINE A NEW CONNECTION, of the Connection Wizard, click NEXT > (see Figure 8.31).

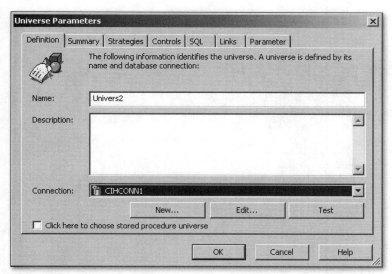

Figure 8.30 "Universe Parameters" Dialog

Figure 8.31 Wizard for Creating a Connection

4. Select SAP CLIENT as the connection type, and enter a name for the connection. Then click NEXT > (see Figure 8.32).

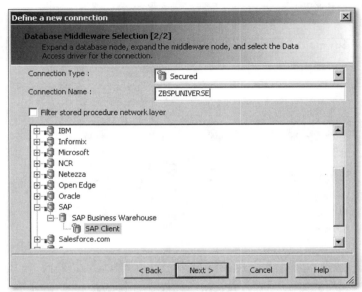

Figure 8.32 Selecting the Database Middleware

5. In the next step of the DEFINE A NEW CONNECTION dialog, you must enter the connection parameters, that is, the user in the BW system, the password, and the connection information about the system. Then click NEXT > (see Figure 8.33).

6. In the next step, CATALOG/DATABASE PARAMETERS, of the DEFINE A NEW CONNECTION DIALOG, select an InfoCube or a MultiProvider (see Figure 8.34). Alternatively, select a query. Note that the only queries available for selection are those released for OLE DB for OLAP. In the upper area of the selection list, you can view the InfoProviders with the queries assigned. In this area, you can select the queries. The list of queries is followed by an InfoProvider list; here you can select the InfoProviders. In this dialog you can browse for an InfoProvider, for example. Then click NEXT >.

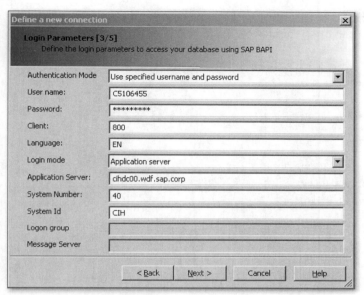

Figure 8.33 Logon Parameters

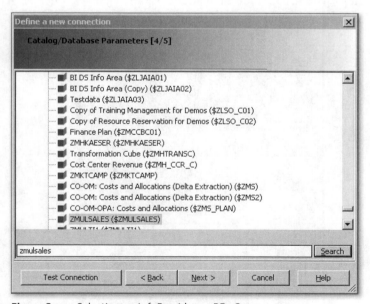

Figure 8.34 Selecting an InfoProvider or BEx Query

Figure 8.35 shows how to set the release for the OLE DB for OLAP access in the query definition.

Figure 8.35　Release of a Query for OLE DB for OLAP

7. In step 5, you can specify further configuration parameters. During the first steps, you usually don't have to make any changes. Click FIN-ISH to close the wizard (see Figure 8.36).

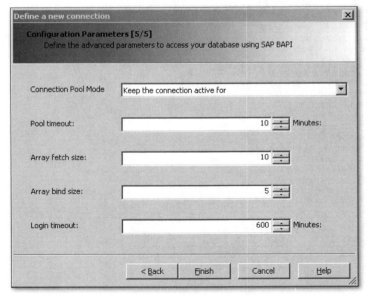

Figure 8.36　Configuration Parameters for the Universe

The system now automatically generates a universe that is based on the information found about the InfoProvider or the query (*see* Figure 8.37).

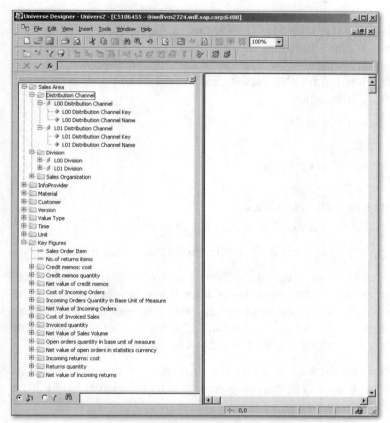

Figure 8.37 "Rough" Universe that was Generated Automatically

Save the universe by selecting FILE • SAVE. The file contains all of the metadata of the universe. Before you or another user can use the universe in reporting, you must export it first (via FILE • EXPORT).

Prior to exporting, you should revise the universe. The universe comprises all of the characteristics, key figures, attributes, and hierarchies; the name and arrangement of objects may be confusing, however. The following section describes which adaptations you should make to the automatically generated universe.

8.5.3   Revising the Universe

The automatically created universe presents all of the objects of the InfoProvider or the query. In most cases, however, you must revise the universe.

Postprocessing
the universe

You can make the following adaptations to the universe; you can find the corresponding functions in the context menu, which opens if you right-click an element of the universe in the Universe Designer. The drag-and-drop function for elements is also available. The possible functions include the following:

▶ Renaming of elements

▶ Moving elements

▶ Cutting/deleting elements

▶ Hiding elements

▶ Creating new classes/subclasses

▶ Summarizing and splitting of classes and subclasses

In principle, you can revise the entire appearance of the universe.

Properties of the
automatically
generated universe

InfoProviders, as the basis of a universe, deliver similar results as queries. But the query also provides additional key figures (restricted and calculated) and other query-specific objects (like input-ready variables), if applicable. Moreover, the selection of hierarchies for a characteristic is restricted to the information stored in the query.

The following sections describe the properties of the universe in its rough state as it was automatically generated by the system based on an InfoProvider or a query.

Description of the Universe in Its Rough State

Characteristics,
attributes,
variables

Each characteristic is described by four entries, and it appears twice with the respective characteristic name, that is, once with the prefix L0 and once with the prefix L1. This involves a differentiation of aggregation levels. L1 stands for the individual characteristic values and L0 for all values. In addition to the characteristic text, you are also provided with the corresponding key. For users, these four entries may be confusing. Therefore, you should make a preselection of the relevant elements in the universe.

Note that all attributes are imported. Normally, you will reduce their scope during postprocessing.

Input-ready variables are copied as predefined filters to the universe.

The hierarchies for the characteristics also have the level names, L0 to LN (depending on the number of hierarchy levels). When you create the universe, you are provided with all of the hierarchies of a characteristic; if a query is the basis, only the currently set hierarchy is available. All attributes of a characteristic are displayed repeatedly in every hierarchy level, which leads to an unclear presentation.

Hierarchies

Some key figures are shown three times. Provided that they have a unit, they are made available with and without the unit. In addition, the unit is available as a separate element. Here again, you can simplify the display through reduction and restructuring.

Key figures

Calculated and restricted key figures in a query are handled like normal key figures.

The InfoProvider's dimensions are copied to the universe as classes. If the dimension has the same name as the characteristic below, the system creates uniqueness through numbering. To improve the clarity of the universe, you should revise the names.

Dimensions/ classes

L00 Distribution Channel	L01 Distribution Channel	Net Value of Incoming Orders	Net Value of Incoming Orders Unit	Net Value of Incoming Orders Formatted Value
All Distribution Channel	Direct Sales	725,774.01	*	725.774,01 MIX
All Distribution Channel	Direct Sales	314.33	USD	$ 314,33
All Distribution Channel	Factory sales	0	EUR	0,00 EUR
All Distribution Channel	Final customer sales	251,671,543.28	*	251.671.543,28 MIX
All Distribution Channel	GM store	0	USD	$ 0,00
All Distribution Channel	Internet Sales	3,960,238.6	USD	$ 3.960.238,60
All Distribution Channel	Service	2,764,428.16	*	2.764.428,16 MIX
All Distribution Channel	Services	1,820,000	USD	$ 1.820.000,00
All Distribution Channel	Sold for resale	278,434,172.01	*	278.434.172,01 MIX
All Distribution Channel	Store chain	75,464	USD	$ 75.464,00

Figure 8.38 Comparison of Various Objects of the Universe That Are Provided By Default

The following shows the contents of the universe based on a sample report that was created on the basis of the universe. Figure 8.38 shows which contents the fields L00 and L01 of the distribution channel characteristic contain. You presumably only need field L01 because it contains the characteristic values. You can also view which contents are mapped

Report contents

via the various versions of the key figure. Depending on how you want to work with the key figures, it could absolutely be sufficient to only copy the combined key figure of value and unit when you revise the universe.

All in all, it is better to not publish the universe in its "rough" form, but to optimize the contents and names first. Figure 8.39 shows a revised universe.

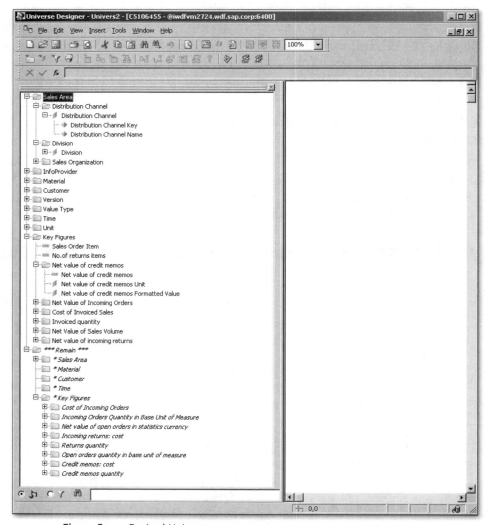

Figure 8.39 Revised Universe

The following adaptations were made:

▶ **Moving of all elements not required to a hidden area called *** Remain *****
For this structure, the same substructure was selected as for the total universe (class structure). This enables you to easily recognize the affiliation of objects. This is very important for subsequent maintenance of the universe. Alternatively, you can omit the moving of objects and hide them directly. In this case, however, the result may be less clear.

▶ **Removing the subdivision of the characteristic presentation by level**
This requires that the information to be removed is not necessary.

▶ **Hiding of key figures by moving them to the remaining class**
This reduces the scope of the universe and increases the clarity.

▶ **Restriction to key figure presentations that are useful in the context**
Moreover, it may be helpful to make a selection of key figure objects that contain a unit or currency and that are summarized as folders (for example, by preselecting the key figure with a unit) so that all key figures can be made available for selection at one level.

▶ **Removing irrelevant hierarchies**
Particularly if the universe is based on an InfoProvider, the number of available hierarchies may be high. If you remove superfluous hierarchies, you simplify the selection for the universe user.

The sample universe illustrated that, in principle, all of the elements of the DataProvider and the BEx query can be found in the universe. The question therefore arises whether the mapping in the universe is really complete.

Restrictions

According to Hilgefort (2009), for Release XI 3.1 the following restrictions are known for integrating the BW function:

▶ Conditions and exceptions of a query are not copied.

▶ The data types, date field (DATS) for characteristics, and time for key figures are not supported.

▶ A variable personalization, like in BW, is not available.

▶ Text and hierarchy variables are not supported.

8.6 Conclusion

The acceptance of a reporting solution basically depends on the performance and the contents of the reports or the analysis areas provided. There are various technologies to structure a high-performance Reporting Layer:

- ▶ Separation of the dataset into multiple InfoCubes
- ▶ Suitable dimensioning of InfoCubes
- ▶ Use of segmentation and compression
- ▶ Use of aggregates
- ▶ Use of jump target reports to navigate in the details
- ▶ Use of current technologies, for instance, BWA

Here, the consistent use of MultiProviders and the structure of a comprehensive Data Propagation Layer provide the flexibility to reorganize the physical data storage of the Reporting Layer, make model changes for mapping new requirements, and implement new technologies, such as BWA and NLS.

The MultiProviders' organization is based on the functional requirements, which should be documented well. This particularly applies to the details of the mapping on underlying InfoCubes.

SAP BusinessObjects universes are another metadata layer. Universes can be built automatically based on a query or an InfoProvider. However, this requires postprocessing to achieve a user-friendly presentation.

Due to the high number of dependent reporting objects, which are defined on a universe, the interface — the universe — should be as stable as possible. Therefore, it is recommended to create universes either only on MultiProviders or on the basis of queries which, in turn, are based on MultiProviders.

This chapter uses two case studies to explain how you can apply the principles introduced in the previous chapters. The first case study discusses a layer and domain formation based on Layered, Scalable Architecture (LSA) principles. The second case study describes how you use a Business Content model as the basis for developing a model that implements your requirements and that can be enhanced.

9   Case Studies

This chapter uses examples to demonstrate real-life problems that have to be solved during the data modeling process and how you can deal with them.

The first example discusses the creation of a completely new data model for data from a non-SAP system. It focuses on LSA aspects in particular.

The second example describes how to enhance Business Content for customer analyses. Based on examples of various problems that occur in this area, innovative solution approaches are discussed.

9.1   Modeling According to LSA Principles

The LSA describes basic modeling principles, which you won't apply directly to your project but from which you will develop your own standards (as a customer LSA) to include your preferences and project situation. In this context, you can consider the naming conventions listed in Chapter 4, Structure of a BW Data Model, as part of a guideline for implementing a customer LSA. However, your specific specifications are usually much more complex and include all essential LSA aspects.

This section does not develop additional individual specifications in the sense of a customer LSA. Instead, it describes a step-by-step development of an application and a modeling process that is based on the LSA. However, the example also includes some general modeling aspects so that, even if your project is not strictly developed according to LSA principles, you will still find some useful information. This section first describes the application area and then the application itself. Sections 9.1.2 through 9.1.4 define the architecture of the application, and the following sections deal with implementing the application.

9.1.1 Introduction of the Application Case

The sample enterprise is an enterprise from the financial sector, which is committed to the financing of enterprises and projects. The commitment can vary, for example, by awarding loans or investing.

The enterprise's business partners are rated on a regular basis. Ratings are assigned, in particular, for credit standing, but other aspects also play a role when decisions about commitments have to be made, for example, environmental awareness. The award process, which ends with the acceptance or rejection of a commitment, comprises several stages, and the state of the investment decision is described by a status.

Management requests evaluations that are supposed to provide an overview of the risk development of the commitments and the investment decision process. In this context, the current risk profile is just as important as historical changes. It is also critical that the various foreign subsidiaries can use the system at a later stage. In the first step, however, the system is supposed to provide reports for management. The evaluations at this level are made for every single economic area and across all economic areas. Data that is provided as quickly as possible and a high system performance were identified as key factors for successful acceptance within management.

Your task now is to provide the required data in the Business Warehouse (BW) system. The user department is supposed to implement the reporting solution at a later stage. Only one concrete reporting requirement was mentioned for the immediate implementation: The system is supposed to create a report that maps the average investment volume per country, sorted by economic areas.

9.1.2 Interface Description for the Source System

In this case study, you load the data as CSV files, because no SAP ERP system is available as the source. You have to load master and transaction data.

You have to load master data that is related to the business partner. Business partners are described by a name, the country in which the headquarters are located, and two ratings (risk and environment).

Attributes/texts

Table 9.1 describes the structure of the business partner data. Usually, BW distinguishes between attributes and texts. Therefore, you should load the InfoObject texts as texts and not as attributes to the InfoObject, because this is the only way you can ensure that the presentation (mapping as key or text) in the reporting can be selected using standard tools. A separation of texts and attributes can be implemented in the data flow later on. Therefore, you don't have to create a dedicated text DataSource. If you want to split an interface for master data, you should use the criteria "time-dependent/not time-dependent" for differentiation. This way, you avoid that constant characteristics need to be loaded unnecessarily.

Description	InfoObject	Sample Data
Business partner	ZBPRTNER (CHAR(10))	1000000005
Language	CHAR(2)	EN
Text	CHAR(40)	Sweet Sugar South
Rating risk	ZRATNOTR (CHAR(3))	2A
Rating environment	ZRATNOTU (CHAR(3))	2
Country	ZCOUNTRY (CHAR(3))	BR

Table 9.1 Master Data Interface — Business Partner

It makes sense to also describe the corresponding data types in this kind of interface description. As soon as you know the InfoObjects, you should list them as well.

You then have to load the respective texts for the commitments (see Table 9.2) and for the status (see Table 9.3). You could have also defined a specific text interface for the business partner. Another option is to separate attributes and texts at a later stage and then post them as texts and attributes with two separate transformations.

Texts

Description	InfoObject	Sample Data
Commitment	ZENGAGE (CHAR (2))	10
Language	CHAR(2)	DE
Text	CHAR(40)	Short-term loan

Table 9.2 Text Interface — Commitment

The status is also described by a key and a text (see Table 9.3).

Description	InfoObject	Sample Data
Status	ZSTATUS (CHAR (2))	10
Language	CHAR(2)	DE
Text	CHAR(40)	Invested

Table 9.3 Text Interface — Status

Transaction data

You've decided that it is sufficient to load transaction data on a monthly basis. The data is supposed to be transferred to the BW system in Full mode, that is, the extraction includes all data records that are required to provide all relevant commitments for the analysis.

A transaction data record is structured as shown in Table 9.4: A month field describes the data's reference month. The commitment and the status are the main descriptive characteristics. A currency is also transferred for the key figure. To keep the data volume to a minimum, content is only described by its key, and text and attribute information is provided via master data. The BW data model then merges the information in such a way that you can include and use it collectively in reports.

Description	InfoObject	Sample Data
Calendar month	0CALMONTH (NUMC (6))	200910
Business partner	ZBPARTNER (CHAR(10))	1000000001
Commitment	ZENGAGE (CHAR (2))	10
Status	ZSTATUS (CHAR (2))	20
Currency	0CURRENCY	EUR
Key figure	0AMOUNT	100000

Table 9.4 Structure of the Transaction Data Record

9.1.3 Formation of Layers and Data Storage

Our goal is to load the data up to the Data Propagation Layer and perform all of the necessary transformations during this process. For every single LSA application case, you have to check which layers will be provided with specific InfoProviders and which layers won't be mapped at all or only virtually, e.g. through InfoSources. The characteristics of the layers are based on the scope of the respectively required services and on organizational requirements. The scope and the complexity of the transformations that are supposed to be performed affect the number of intermediate steps that are supposed to be performed and especially the implementation of the Data Propagation Layer.

Because you load flat files, you have to make sure that for every single load operation the appropriate data format is provided for each of the InfoObjects. Therefore, you need to temporarily store the data in the Persistent Staging Area (PSA) in the Data Acquisition Layer first and then transform the data. Because the data is already stored in the inbound layer, you don't have to store it in the Data Acquisition Layer again.

Staging transaction data

In addition, the data is supposed to be stored in the corporate memory. However, because no irreversible changes are made during the staging of the data up to the Data Propagation Layer (as you'll see later on), you can skip this step because the Data Propagation Layer has the same data basis as the corporate memory. Please note that this is only the case because this is a simple example. A corporate memory is often required to set up datasets in the Data Propagation Layer, which can also retroactively map a new set of business rules (of the Quality and Transformation Layer).

In this application case, no conversions of master data or calculations need to be performed, because only characteristics for transaction data records are supposed to be enriched. You don't have to additionally store the data in the Quality and Harmonization Layer, because one transformation is usually sufficient for reading characteristics.

When taking a look at the transaction data record (commitment) of this example, you notice that some of the characteristics that are frequently used in reports are not included, for example, the risk rating and environment rating. These two pieces of information are modeled as time-dependent attributes of the business partner. The task of the Data Propagation Layer is to provide data in such a way that the reporting requirements can be flexibly implemented based on the data. Therefore, the ratings are supposed to already be enriched in the transaction data records in this layer. This ensures that, within a one month data slice, the rating information in the Data Propagation Layer corresponds to the status of the master data at the time of the data loading. If, at a later stage, several analysis datasets are supposed to be created in the Data Mart Layer using the Data Propagation Layer as the basis, the master data does not have to be read for every single transformation. Furthermore, the comparability of the data is ensured across all levels, because all targets were enriched simultaneously.

Because you want to categorize the transaction data flow by domains, you have to provide inbound and outbound InfoSources for the individual layers. This lets you define central transformations.

The data flow shown in Figure 9.1 takes these considerations into account: The enrichment with risk information is implemented in the transformation between the Data Acquisition Layer and the Data Propagation Layer ❷. Transformations ❶ and ❸ always map the data on a one-to-one basis.

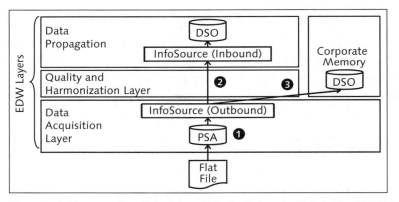

Figure 9.1 Diagram of the Data Flow within the Enterprise Data Layers (EDW) Layers

At the Data Acquisition Layer and Corporate Memory level, you can use the write-optimized DataStore Object (DSO) to store data. The DSO in the Data Propagation Layer is implemented as a standard DSO.

Staging
master data

Figure 9.2 shows a diagram of the data flow for the master data in this example. The texts are supposed to be loaded directly to the InfoObjects ❶. The attributes for the business partner are stored as a DSO in the Data Propagation Layer first ❷. There, the system then updates them to the master data of the business partner InfoObject ❸. You could also store the business partner data in the corporate memory ❹.

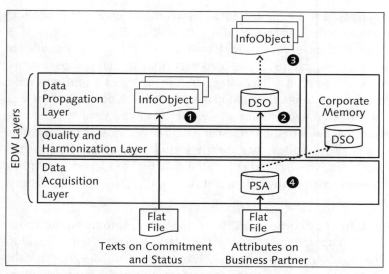

Figure 9.2 Diagram of the Data Flow for Texts and Attributes

Besides transaction and master data, you must also load a file with country/economic area assignments. These are supposed to be stored in the Quality and Harmonization Layer. The data is used as a reference to provide additional characteristics (country assignments to regions and economic areas) for reporting. For performance reasons, you enrich the characteristics in the reporting. Historical views are not required here. However, it usually makes sense to also archive reference data in the corporate memory. This ensures that previous data load processes can be repeated in a historically correct way.

Staging reference data

9.1.4 Domain Formation

In this application case, reporting by economic area is supposed to be supported efficiently. Efficiently means, for example, that the failure of a load process shouldn't have unnecessary negative effects on other load processes. For example, if a problem occurs during the loading of APJ data, the reporting of the EMEA economic area shouldn't be affected. You should also fully utilize all parallel processing options for data load processes to reduce the loading times to a minimum. Therefore, you should load the data in multiple parallel data streams. The categorization is supposed to be implemented by economic areas. You therefore define three economic areas: EMEA, APJ, and AMER. They are used as criteria for the domain formation. Ideally, the data should be provided in the appropriate segments. If you load data from several source systems, the data is often automatically categorized by domains. In this example, where flat files are used, it would make sense if each of the flat files supplied the data of one economic area. Otherwise, you have to categorize the data retroactively in the Data Acquisition Layer. However, this would require that the provided data already includes the *economic area* characteristic. If not, you have to enrich the data first to further post it in a differentiated manner (by filtering it during the Data Transfer Process (DTP)).

Avoiding unnecessary redundancies A categorization by domains is usually only relevant to transaction data, because the data volume of transaction data is larger. Figure 9.3 illustrates the disadvantage of this modeling type: redundancies. Both the structure of the various DSOs and the update logic of the transformations exist redundantly. You therefore create central transformations between the layers. The central transformation is set up between the inbound and outbound InfoSources, as shown in Figure 9.3.

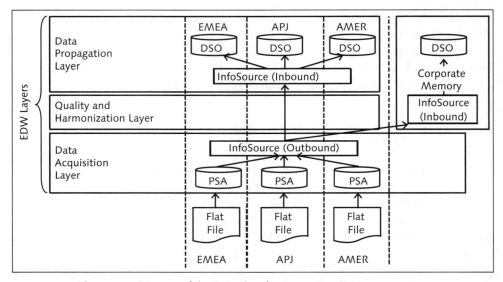

Figure 9.3   Diagram of the Data Flow for Transaction Data

9.1.5 Creating Application Components

In a first implementation step, you have to implement the application components for the layer mapping (see Figure 9.4).

▷ ◈ BW integrated planning application	ZAAA_IMP_PLANUNG	Change
▽ ◈ LSA sample application	ZAAA_LSA	Change
▽ ◈ Data Acquisition Layer	LSA10_A	Change
▷ ◈ Domain EMEA	LSA10_AEM	Change
◈ Domain APJ	LSA10_AAP	Change
◈ Domain AMER	LSA10_AAM	Change
▷ ◈ Overall Trans. Data	LSA10_AXXT	Change
◈ Overall Master Data	LSA10_AXXM	Change
◈ Operational Data Store	LSA11_O	Change
▷ ◈ Quality & Harmonization Layer	LSA20_H	Change
▷ ◈ Data Propagation Layer	LSA30_P	Change
▷ ◈ Business Transformation Layer	LSA40_B	Change
▽ ◈ Reporting Layer	LSA50_R	Change
▷ ◈ Domain EMEA	LSA50_REM	Change
◈ Domain APJ	LSA50_RAP	Change
◈ Domain AMER	LSA50_RAM	Change
◈ Overall Master Data	LSA30_RXXM	Change
▷ ◈ InfoObjects	LSA50_RXXIO	Change
▷ ◈ Virtualization Layer	LSA60_V	Change
◈ InfoObjects	LSAIO	Change

Figure 9.4 Application Components, Sorted by LSA Layers

At this point, it is obvious how important appropriate naming conventions are. Don't interpret the names used in this example (see Chapter 5, Section 5.3, Information Integration as a Prerequisite for Cross-Sectional Evaluations) as a direct requirement for your project; they need to be adapted to your individual needs.

Relevance of the naming conventions

An appropriate structure of the DataSource tree (see Figure 9.5) and InfoSource tree (see Figure 9.6) is just as important as the application components for the DataProvider.

DataSource and InfoSource tree

We recommend *inbound* and *outbound categories* for every level. There are no inbound InfoSources at the Data Acquisition Layer level. Here, you have to include DataSources, respectively.

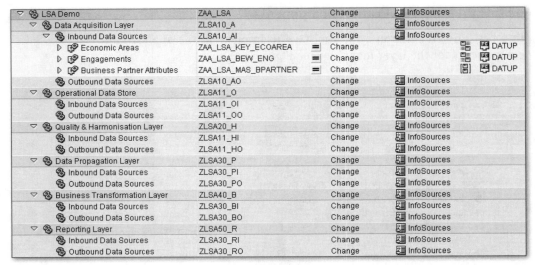

Figure 9.5 DataSource Tree, Sorted by LSA Layers

▽ 🐾 LSA Demo	ZAA_LSA	Andern	
▽ 🐾 Data Acquisition Layer	ZLSA10_A	Ändern	
▽ 🐾 Inbound Data Sources	ZLSA10_AI	Ändern	
▽ 🔵 Data Acu. In GP Attributes	AIXXBP0101	≡ Ändern	
▷ 🔀 RSDS ZAA_LSA_MAS_BPARTNER DATUP -> TRCS AI 08FUW5Y2JWPWRB3KDISF...	≡ Ändern		
▷ 🔵 Data Acu. In Keys Econ Area DS 01 IS 01	AIXXEA0101	≡ Ändern	
▽ 🐾 Outbound InfoSources	ZLSA10_AO	Ändern	
▷ 🔵 Data Acqu. Business Partner Attribute 01 01	AOXXBP0101	≡ Ändern	
▷ 🔵 Data Acqu. Out Economic Areas PROV 01 IS 01	AOXXEA0101	≡ Ändern	
▷ 🔵 Data Acqu. Out Engagem. PROV 01 IS 01	AOXXEN0101	≡ Ändern	
▷ 🐾 Operational Data Store	ZLSA11_O	Ändern	
▷ 🐾 Quality & Harmonization Layer	ZLSA20_H	Ändern	
▽ 🐾 Data Propagation Layer	ZLSA30_P	Ändern	
▽ 🐾 Inbound InfoSources	ZLSA30_PI	Ändern	
▷ 🔵 Data Prop. In Business Partner Attr 01 IS 01	PIXXBP0101	≡ Ändern	
▷ 🔵 Data Prop. In Engagements Prov 01 IS 01	PIEMEN0101	≡ Ändern	
▽ 🐾 Outbound InfoSources	ZLSA30_PO	Ändern	
▷ 🔵 Data Prop. Out Business Partner Attributes	POXXBP0101	≡ Ändern	
▷ 🔵 Engagements EMEA	POEMEN0101	≡ Ändern	
▷ 🐾 Business Transformation Layer	ZLSA40_B	Ändern	
▷ 🐾 Reporting Layer	ZLSA50_R	Ändern	

Figure 9.6 InfoSource Tree, Sorted by LSA Layers

9.1.6   Implementing Flat File DataSources

When creating flat file DataSources, you have to select the storage location, the file name, and the file format. Try not to store the files locally but instead copy them to the application server of the BW system prior to the load process. To do this, you can use the programs ARCHIVFILE_CLIENT_TO_SERVER and ARCHIVFILE_SERVER_TO_CLIENT. Figure 9.7 shows a variant for loading data from the workstation.

DataSource	ZAA_LSA_BEW_ENG	Engagements
Source System	DATUP	<No Text Available in this Language>
Version	Active	Compare with...
Active Version	Executable	Edited Version

General Info. | Extraction | Proposal | Fields | Preview

Delta Process	Full Upload (Delta from InfoPackage Selection Only)
Direct Access	NO DTP Allowed for Direct Access
Real Time	Real-Time Data Acquisition Is Not Supported

Adapter	Load Text-Type File from Local Workstation	Properties
File Name	C:\Users\Frank Wolf\Documents\01 Projekte\98 Buch\Fall
Header Rows to be Ignored	1
Character Set Settings	Default Setting
System Codepage	4103 UTF-16LE Unicode / ISO/IEC 10646

Data Format	Separated with Separator (for Example, CSV)
Data Separator	; □ Hex
Escape Sign	" □ Hex

| Convers. Lang. | User Master Record |
| Number format | User Master Record |

Figure 9.7   Source File Assignment and Selection of the File Format

You can have the system generate the format of the fields based on the data that the system finds in the flat file (PROPOSAL tab) or specify the format yourself (FIELDS TAB), see Figure 9.8. If you already know the target InfoObjects, the easiest thing to do is to enter them as template InfoObjects (Template InfoObject) in the flat file in the order of the columns to be assigned.

Defining the field format

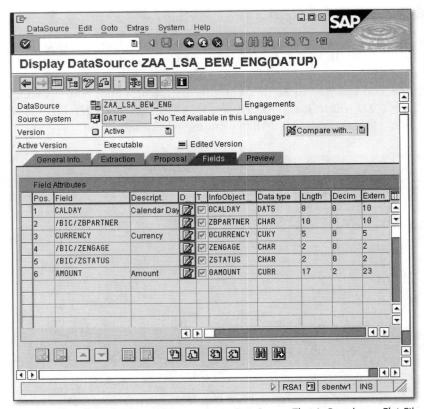

Figure 9.8 Field/InfoObject Assignment in a DataSource That Is Based on a Flat File

9.1.7 Defining Data Storage and InfoSources

First, you should create the DSOs of the various layers. You can then easily define the outbound and inbound InfoSources using the respective DSO as a template (see Figure 9.9). If required, you can also add individual InfoObjects to the InfoSource definition at a later stage. However, if you follow the approach described here, you shouldn't do this, because differences in the structure usually only emerge between the outbound and inbound InfoSources.

Inbound and outbound InfoSources

Categorizing the InfoSources by layers and *inbound* and *outbound* lets you easily access all of the InfoSources and create new InfoSources at the appropriate place.

You can use the originally created DSO as a template to create various DSOs for the different domains.

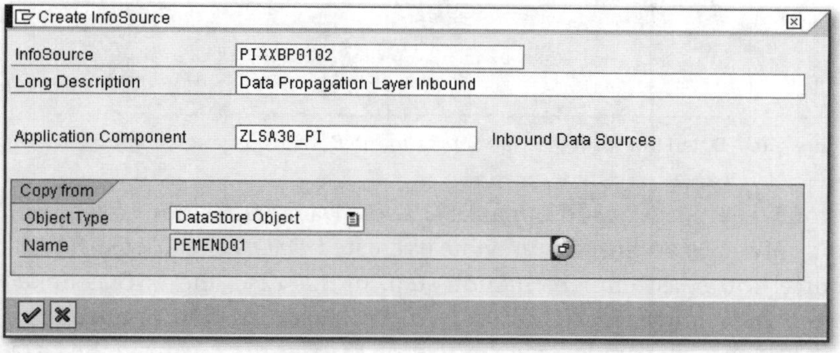

Figure 9.9 Creating an InfoSource Using a DSO as a Template

9.1.8 Setting Up the Data Flow

If you have already defined the DSOs and InfoSources, the initial set up of the data flow is quite easy. You can develop from either the source to the target or from the target to the source.

For example, begin with the target DSO at the Data Propagation Layer level (PEMEND01, see Figure 9.10) for the transaction data. Select CREATE TRANSFORMATION in the context menu and then the corresponding inbound InfoSource as the data source. The system now automatically links all of the InfoObjects. Usually, there is no structural difference between the data target and the inbound InfoSource. Now you can create the data flow. To do this, select the CREATE TRANSFORMATION ITEM again IN THE CONTEXT MENU OF THE PREVIOUSLY LINKED InfoSource. Next, you define the central transformation between the InfoSources; that means you have to choose an InfoSource again, namely, the outbound DataSource of the Data Acquisition Layer. Routines and characteristic derivations can be considered at a later stage. Where an assignment is possible, you link all of the fields on a one-to-one basis. The last thing you now need to do is to create a last transformation for linking the DataSource (ZAA_LSA_BEW_ENG) that is based on the flat file. Figure 9.10 shows the result of this definition process.

Linking the objects for a data flow

349

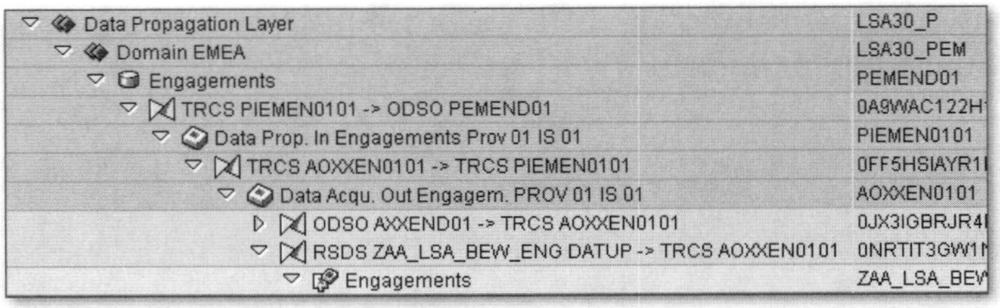

Figure 9.10 Data Flow from the DataSource to the Data Propagation Layer

Alternative
loading routes

If you want to use an additional DSO at the Data Acquisition Layer level, you only have to link the previously created DSO instead of the Data-Source in the last implementation step. In this case, the DSO is linked to the DataSource. In Figure 9.11, you can see that both implementations can exist in parallel: Transformation ❶ loads directly from the Data-Source, whereas the data flow ❷ includes the additional DSO.

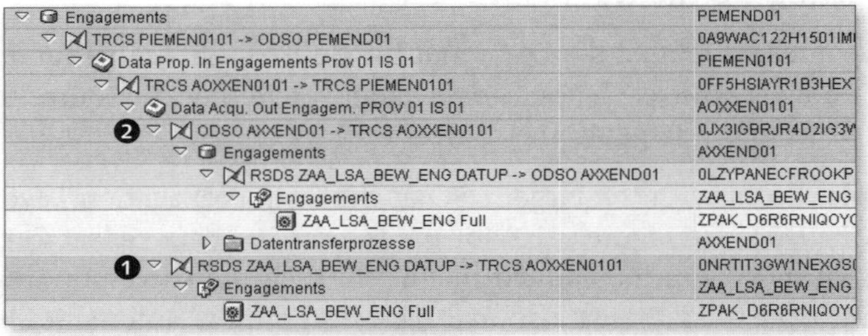

Figure 9.11 Alternative Data Flows in the Data Acquisition Layer

Flexibility gained
by copying
transformations

This example uses variant ❶, therefore, you don't have to create ❷. If you realize at a later stage that you need an additional storage option in the Data Acquisition Layer, you can easily change the loading route. To change the loading route as shown for variant ❷, copy the transformation using the COPY... function in the context menu of transformation ❶ and link the newly created DSO as the data source. In the COPY dialog, simply enter the previously created DSO as the new data source (see Figure 9.12).

The two loading routes can exist in parallel in a system. However, if you no longer need one of the routes, you should remove it by deleting the corresponding transformation. The leaner the system, the easier you can understand and maintain it.

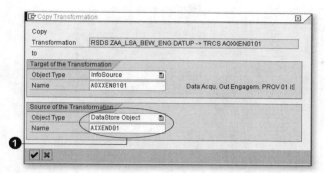

Figure 9.12   Copying the Transformation to the New Data Source

9.1.9   Implementing Central Transformations with Characteristic Routines

Figure 9.13 shows the central transformation between the Data Acquisition Layer and the Data Propagation Layer.

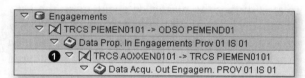

Figure 9.13   Central Transformation between the Data Acquisition Layer and the Reporting Layer

In this transformation you define the derivations of the rating classes. To do this, create derivation rules of the ROUTINE rule type for the InfoObjects ZRATNOTR, and ZRATNOTU (see Figures 9.14 and 9.15).

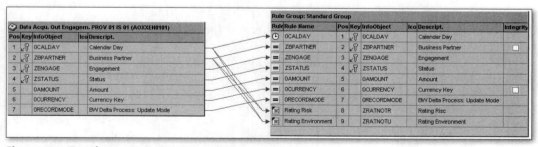

Figure 9.14   Transformation to the Data Propagation Layer

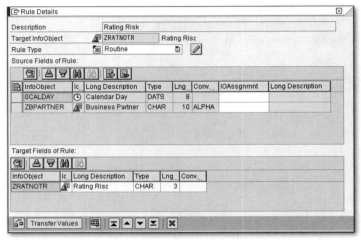

Figure 9.15 "Routine" Rule Type for Deriving Characteristics

The rules read the rating from the business partner data considering the validity period. The source here is the DSO with the business partner data, which was created during the master data staging in the Data Propagation Layer. Alternatively, you can also read the data in the master data table of the characteristic. Due to this dependency, you have to load the master data before the transaction data. This must also be considered when creating the process chain (see Listing 9.1).

```
CLASS lcl_transform IMPLEMENTATION.

  METHOD compute_ZRATNOTR.

*    IMPORTING
*       request      type rsrequest
*       datapackid   type rsdatapid
*       SOURCE_FIELDS-CALDAY TYPE /BI0/OICALDAY
*       SOURCE_FIELDS-/BIC/ZBPARTNER TYPE /BIC/OIZBPARTNER
*    EXPORTING
*       RESULT type _ty_s_TG_1-/BIC/ZRATNOTR

    DATA:
      MONITOR_REC    TYPE rsmonitor.

*$*$ begin of routine - insert your code only below this
      line        *-*
```

```
* Define local variables

    DATA: l_zratnotr TYPE /bic/oizratnotr.
    DATA: l_n_datum TYPE n LENGTH 8.

* Determine last day of previous month
    l_n_datum = sy-datum.
    l_n_datum+6(2) = '01'.
    l_n_datum = l_n_datum - 1.

* Read rating grades from the DSO
* PXXBPD01 business partner attribute.
* Consider the time dependency
* of the data.

    SELECT SINGLE /bic/zratnotr
      FROM /bic/apxxbpd0100
      INTO l_zratnotr
      WHERE
      dateto GE  l_n_datum AND
      datefrom LE l_n_datum AND
      /bic/zbpartner = SOURCE_FIELDS-/bic/zbpartner.

    RESULT = l_zratnotr.

*$*$ end of routine - insert your code only before this
    line         *-*
  ENDMETHOD.                    "compute_ZRATNOTR
```

Listing 9.1 Characteristic Routine for Deriving the Rating of a Business Partner

9.1.10 Creating the Process Chain

You have to load the master data for the business partner, the texts of the objects, and the assignments of the countries to the economic areas before loading the transaction data. After having loaded all of the master data, you must run an attribute change run. Afterward, you can load the transaction data (commitments) for the domains in parallel.

Try to include as much parallel processing in your process chains as possible. Parallel processes should have similar runtimes (if this is useful). The process chain shown in Figure 9.16 combines the (simple) loading of the texts of the different InfoObjects in one loading route.

Parallel processing

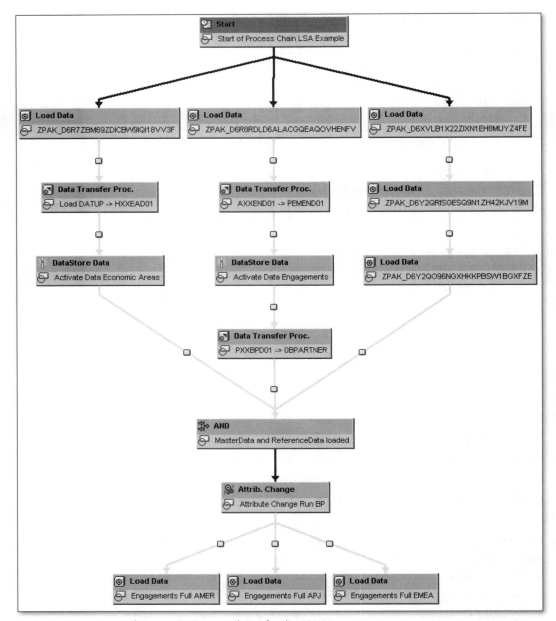

Figure 9.16 Process Chains for the EDW Layers

The sample process chain includes loading the master data and the transaction data. Considering that you probably want to enhance the process chain, you should load the master data and transaction data in separate process chains and include them as subchains in a metachain.

Do not set the start process to Start Immediately. This may be very comfortable for testing, but if you want to transport the process chain, this setting starts the chain on the target system immediately after the import. In production environments, this can lead to serious data inconsistencies. You should therefore use events to start process chains. You can then start the process chain using the RSPC_API_CHAIN_START program, for example.

9.1.11 Setting Up the Reporting and Virtual Layer

You first set up the InfoCube in the Reporting Layer. Use the scope of the DSOs for the commitments in the Data Propagation Layer for orientation. Optimize the model of the InfoCube by following the modeling rules from Chapter 8, Section 8.2.1, Modeling.

You also have to enrich the characteristics that are required for reporting. Because a lot of reports that provide a hierarchical summary of the economic areas are supposed to be created in this example, enrich the *economic area*, *region*, and *country* characteristics for the transaction data. Compared to the navigation attribute, this solution has a much higher performance. You can also create a characteristic hierarchy for the Country InfoObject.

Between the Data Propagation Layer and Reporting Layer, a central transformation is set up as well. The required InfoSources are based on the structure of the InfoCube or DSO. After having created the InfoSources, you define the transformation (see Figure 9.17).

Because the transaction data itself does not supply the Country InfoObject, you first have to determine the country of the business partner to determine in the DSO the economic area and region assigned to the country using the assignments of the economic areas. Because the data is accessed in two steps, you implement an end routine instead of using the characteristic derivations (Note: you could avoid this coding, by having the first characteristic derivation in the transformation to the inbound InfoSource and the second in the central transformation, but this would violate the rule that all logic should be implemented in the central transformation). Listing 9.2 illustrates the program code of the end routine of the central transformation between the Data Propagation Layer and Reporting Layer.

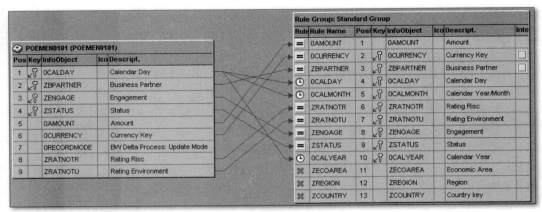

Figure 9.17 Transformation to the Reporting Layer

```
PROGRAM trans_routine.

*-------------------------------------------------------------------*
*          CLASS routine DEFINITION
*-------------------------------------------------------------------*
*
*-------------------------------------------------------------------*
CLASS lcl_transform DEFINITION.
  PUBLIC SECTION.

*    Attributes
      DATA:
        p_check_master_data_exist
              TYPE RSODSOCHECKONLY READ-ONLY,
*-      Instance for getting request runtime attributes;
*       Available information: Refer to methods of
*       interface 'if_rsbk_request_admintab_view'
        p_r_request
              TYPE REF TO if_rsbk_request_admintab_view READ-
ONLY.

    PRIVATE SECTION.
```

```
    TYPE-POOLS: rsd, rstr.

*   Rule specific types
    TYPES:
      BEGIN OF _ty_s_TG_1,
*       InfoObject: 0AMOUNT Betrag.
        AMOUNT              TYPE /BI0/OIAMOUNT,
*       InfoObject: 0CURRENCY Currency Key.
        CURRENCY            TYPE /BI0/OICURRENCY,
*       InfoObject: ZBPARTNER Business Partner.
        /BIC/ZBPARTNER          TYPE /BIC/OIZBPARTNER,
*       InfoObject: 0CALDAY Calendar Day.
        CALDAY              TYPE /BI0/OICALDAY,
*       InfoObject: 0CALMONTH Calendar Year / Month.
        CALMONTH            TYPE /BI0/OICALMONTH,
*       InfoObject: ZRATNOTR Rating Risk.
        /BIC/ZRATNOTR          TYPE /BIC/OIZRATNOTR,
*       InfoObject: ZRATNOTU Rating Environment.
        /BIC/ZRATNOTU          TYPE /BIC/OIZRATNOTU,
*       InfoObject: ZENGAGE Commitment.
        /BIC/ZENGAGE          TYPE /BIC/OIZENGAGE,
*       InfoObject: ZSTATUS Status.
        /BIC/ZSTATUS          TYPE /BIC/OIZSTATUS,
*       InfoObject: 0CALYEAR Calendar Year.
        CALYEAR            TYPE /BI0/OICALYEAR,
*       InfoObject: ZECOAREA Economic Area.
        /BIC/ZECOAREA          TYPE /BIC/OIZECOAREA,
*       InfoObject: ZREGION Region.
        /BIC/ZREGION          TYPE /BIC/OIZREGION,
*       InfoObject: ZCOUNTRY Country Key.
        /BIC/ZCOUNTRY          TYPE /BIC/OIZCOUNTRY,
*       Field: RECORD.
        RECORD              TYPE RSARECORD,
      END   OF _ty_s_TG_1.
    TYPES:
      _ty_t_TG_1          TYPE STANDARD TABLE OF _ty_s_TG_1
                          WITH NON-UNIQUE DEFAULT KEY.

*$*$ begin of global - insert your declaration only be-
low this line   *-*
    ... "insert your code here
*$*$ end of global - insert your declaration only be-
fore this line   *-*
```

```
      METHODS
        new_record__end_routine
          IMPORTING
            source_segid              type rstran_segid
            source_record             type sytabix
          EXPORTING
            record_new                type sytabix.


      METHODS
        end_routine
          IMPORTING
            request                   type rsrequest
            datapackid                type rsdatapid
          EXPORTING
            monitor                   type rstr_ty_t_monitors
          CHANGING
            RESULT_PACKAGE               type _ty_t_TG_1
          RAISING
            cx_rsrout_abort.
      METHODS
        inverse_end_routine
          IMPORTING
            i_th_fields_outbound        TYPE rstran_t_field_inv
            i_r_selset_outbound         TYPE REF TO cl_rsmds_set
            i_is_main_selection         TYPE rs_bool
            i_r_selset_outbound_complete TYPE REF TO cl_rsmds_set
            i_r_universe_inbound        TYPE REF TO cl_rsmds_
universe
          CHANGING
            c_th_fields_inbound         TYPE rstran_t_field_inv
            c_r_selset_inbound          TYPE REF TO cl_rsmds_set
            c_exact                     TYPE rs_bool.
ENDCLASS.                      "routine DEFINITION

*$*$ begin of 2nd part global - insert your code only be-
low this line   *

DATA: BEGIN OF s_tab_region,
  bpartner TYPE /bic/oizbpartner,
  /bic/zcountry TYPE /bic/oizcountry,
  /bic/zregion TYPE /bic/oizregion,
  /bic/zecoarea TYPE /bic/oizecoarea,
  END OF s_tab_region.
```

```
DATA: t_tab_region LIKE TABLE OF s_tab_region.

DATA: BEGIN OF s_tab_area,
  /bic/zcountry TYPE /bic/oizcountry,
  /bic/zregion TYPE /bic/oizregion,
  /bic/zecoarea TYPE /bic/oizecoarea,
  END OF s_tab_area.

DATA: t_tab_area LIKE TABLE OF s_tab_area.

DATA: l_region TYPE /bic/oizregion.
DATA: l_ecoarea TYPE /bic/oizecoarea.
DATA: l_n_date TYPE n LENGTH 8.



*$*$ end of 2nd part global - insert your code only be-
fore this line    *

*---------------------------------------------------------------*
*        CLASS routine IMPLEMENTATION
*---------------------------------------------------------------*
*
*---------------------------------------------------------------*
CLASS lcl_transform IMPLEMENTATION.

*---------------------------------------------------------------*
*        Method end_routine
*---------------------------------------------------------------*
*        Calculation of result package via end routine
*        Note: Update of target fields depends on rule assign-
ment in
*        transformation editor. Only fields that have a rule as-
signed,
*        are updated to the data target.
*---------------------------------------------------------------*
*    <-> result package
*---------------------------------------------------------------*
  METHOD end_routine.
*=== Segments ===

    FIELD-SYMBOLS:
```

```
          <RESULT_FIELDS>      TYPE _ty_s_TG_1.

      DATA:
        MONITOR_REC       TYPE rstmonitor.

*$*$ begin of routine - insert your code only be-
low this line        *-*


      DATA: e_s_result TYPE _ty_s_tg_1.

      l_n_date = sy-datum.
      l_n_date+6(2) = '01'.
      l_n_date = l_n_datum - 1.

* 1. Select
      SELECT bpartner /bic/zcountry
             FROM /bi0/mbpartner
             INTO TABLE t_tab_region
             WHERE objvers = 'A'
             AND   datefrom LE l_n_date
             AND   dateto   GE l_n_date.


* 2. Select
      SELECT /bic/zcountry /bic/zregion /bic/zecoarea
             FROM /bic/ahxxead0100
             INTO TABLE t_tab_area
             WHERE calmonth = '200910'.

* Sort by keys
      SORT t_tab_region BY bpartner.
      SORT t_tab_area   BY /bic/zcountry.

* Delete duplicats
      DELETE ADJACENT DUPLICATES FROM t_tab_region.
      DELETE ADJACENT DUPLICATES FROM t_tab_area.

* Collect data
      LOOP AT RESULT_PACKAGE INTO e_s_result.

        READ TABLE t_tab_region
        INTO s_tab_region
```

```
      WITH KEY bpartner = e_s_result-/bic/zbpartner.

   IF sy-subrc = 0.
     READ TABLE t_tab_area
     INTO s_tab_area
     WITH KEY /bic/zcountry = s_tab_region-/bic/zcountry.

     IF sy-subrc = 0.
       MOVE s_tab_area-/bic/zcountry TO e_s_result-/bic/
zcountry.
       MOVE s_tab_area-/bic/zregion  TO e_s_result-/bic/zre-
gion.
       MOVE s_tab_area-/bic/zecoarea TO e_s_result-/bic/ze-
coarea.

       MODIFY RESULT_PACKAGE FROM e_s_result.
     ENDIF.
   ENDIF.

  ENDLOOP.


*$*$ end of routine - insert your code only be-
fore this line         *-*
  ENDMETHOD.                    "end_routine
*----------------------------------------------------------------*
*        Method inverse_end_routine
*----------------------------------------------------------------*
*
*        This subroutine needs to be implemented only for di-
rect access
*        (for better performance) and for the Report/
Report Interface
*        (drill through).
*        The inverse routine should transform a projection and
*        a selection for the target to a projection and a selec-
tion
*        for the source, respectively.
*        If the implementation remains emp-
ty all fields are filled and
*        all values are selected.
*
*----------------------------------------------------------------*
```

```
*
*---------------------------------------------------------------*
   METHOD inverse_end_routine.

*$*$ begin of inverse routine - insert your code only be-
low this line*-*
   ... "insert your code here
*$*$ end of inverse routine - insert your code only be-
fore this line *-*

   ENDMETHOD.                    "inverse_end_routine

   METHOD new_record__end_routine.

***** IMPLEMENTATION  is only visible in generated pro-
gram *****

   ENDMETHOD.
ENDCLASS.                      "routine IMPLEMENTATION
```

Listing 9.2 End Routine for Determining the Region and Economic Area of the Country of the Business Partner

After having completed the data flow, create a DTP and include it in the process chain. Figure 9.18 illustrates the staging from the Data Propagation Layer to the InfoCube using the EMEA domain as an example.

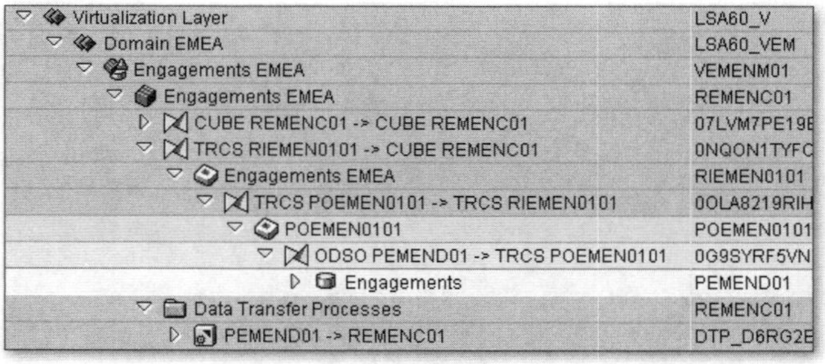

Figure 9.18 Data Flow to the Reporting Layer

Creating an InfoCube with a template

Because the InfoCube data model is the same for all domains, you can create the other InfoCubes using the CREATE WITH TEMPLATE function. All three InfoProviders are combined in one MultiProvider. Copy all of the characteristics and key figures of any of the three InfoCubes. You can easily identify the characteristics and key figures because all underlying InfoCubes have the same structure. Then, sort the characteristics in the MultiProvider definition according to functional aspects. You can rename, newly create, or combine objects and dimensions.

To compare ratings from different periods and map a migration matrix, implement the required virtual characteristics for the risk rating (old and new) and the classification into upgrades and downgrades of the rating (see Chapter 8, Section 8.3.1, Virtual Key Figures and Characteristics).

Virtual characteristics

You should also create aggregates. Because no specifications have been made for certain reports, you have to define the aggregates using your knowledge of the application area. Because user behavior can deviate from your specifications later on, you should check the definition after some time, delete superfluous definitions, and create new definitions. You should also check the InfoCube design (dimensioning) after some time (see Chapter 8, Section 8.2.1).

Optimization by aggregation

When you have completed your work with the data model, load the data. You can fulfill the requirement for counting the countries in which the company has commitments by creating a newly determined key figure with an exception aggregation (see Chapter 8, Section 8.3.2). Now create the first report to have the user department accept the figures (see Figure 9.19).

Exception aggregation

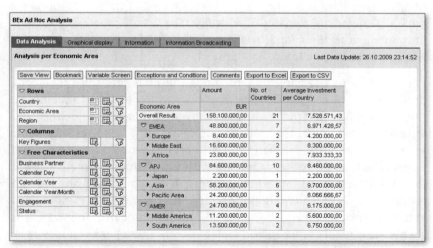

Figure 9.19 Sample Report with Determined Key Figure, "Number of Countries" (Exception Aggregation)

The user department is responsible for creating further reports, which means that you can, after having tested the data and data load processes, hand the application over to the user department or forward it for normal operation.

9.1.12 Conclusion

The application example illustrated that you can use LSA criteria for modeling very simple application cases. The layers described in theory are only proposals, because you don't have to implement all of them. Virtually every data model includes a Data Acquisition Layer, a Data Propagation Layer, and a Reporting Layer and Virtual Layer. You shouldn't reduce this selection of layers, because this would violate basic modeling principles and thus result in a model that you can hardly enhance. You can reduce the mapping of the Data Acquisition Layer to the PSA to avoid redundant data retention. You have to work with inbound and outbound InfoSources, when using domains or generally when using transformations from n sources to m targets with centralized transformations. You don't necessarily have to model InfoSources in a model without data flow segmentation. Because load processes are often parallelized retroactively to increase loading performance, you should follow a modeling guideline referring to the general use of inbound and outbound InfoSources in combination with central transformations. One possible disadvantage here is the relatively large number of transformations for which all fields are updated identically. The actual processing logic is only mapped in the central transformation. In this case, an option for hiding trivial objects in the data flow view would be useful.

Because of the large number of modeling elements (due to layers, domains, and InfoSources), you can only provide a smooth implementation in the long run if proper naming conventions have been defined and are always used — like the modeling principles. This requires reasonable instructions and a coordination of all parties involved (internally and externally). The decision for implementing an LSA is doomed to fail if the idea behind it cannot be communicated. But you can ensure smooth modeling and implementation processes if the modeling is standardized and all parties involved have internalized this standard. This way, it is always clear where you can find which objects and where you may have to create new objects.

9.2   Case Study Using Business Content

This section uses an example of Accounts Receivable Accounting to illustrate which issues can emerge in real life and how you can create data models to enhance Business Content. It is less about specific business aspects and more about individual solution approaches, which you can similarly transfer to other areas.

This area is an excellent example for illustrating typical problems, because it involves very different requirements. The overview shown in Table 9.5 lists the individual solutions of this case study and the general problem that is addressed by the respective solution.

Solution	Problems
Period pattern analysis	Optimized data model, updated view on key date, control characteristic
Payment history	Interval key figures and storage of complex key figures
DSO determination	Complex key figure determination
Dynamic credit review	Enhancement of a Business Content DataSource in the user exit
Dunning history	Generic DataSource and number key figures
"Cash"	Updates from the change log (here: of cleared items)
Enhancement with revenue side	Generation of multiple entries in the start routine

Table 9.5 Overview of the General Problems for the Solutions Introduced in the Case Study

The 0FI_AR_4 line item extractor is the source for accounts receivable reporting. This extractor and the 0FI_**_4 extractors in general were already detailed in Chapter 6, Business Content. The content DSO for the line items is 0FIAR_O03. It does not matter whether the content DSO is used or not. However, what does matter is that a standard DSO is used and that data fields need to be overwritten. 0FI_AR_4 provides a pure after-image delta; therefore, a DSO is required, because you can only generate a delta for the InfoCube update with a DSO.

9.2.1 Processes in Accounts Receivable Accounting

In the context of Financial Accounting/Controlling (FI/CO) data, a lot of sometimes very different processes usually need to be considered. Ideally, you get an overview of all of the relevant processes and analyze if the individual logics in the BW system (for example, reading the Sales and Distribution (SD) billing number using reference field 3) can also be implemented in all other documents.

The following section introduces some critical processes in Accounts Receivable Accounting and shows how the DSO receives these documents.

Outgoing invoice   The posting of an outgoing invoice is the most important process in this area. The corresponding posting record usually looks like the one shown in Figure 9.20.

Debit		Credit	
Customer	$ 12,000	Sales Revenues	$ 10,000
		VAT	$ 2,000

Figure 9.20 Posting Record — Outgoing Invoice

The DSO only contains the customer side; the item in the DSO then looks like the one shown in Table 9.6.

Document	Item	CoCd	Period	Posting Date	Status	Taxes	Amount
123	1	US01	007.2010	07/15/2010	Open	2,000	12,000

Table 9.6 DSO Record — Outgoing Invoice

The illustration has been simplified to a large extent. For example, besides local currency, the key figures are also listed in foreign currency (transaction currency), cash discount amounts and, in addition to the total amount, key figures for the debit amount and credit amount are given.

The sales side is not available in the DSO but can be imported. This is illustrated at the end of this case study.

Now, if a document changes (for example, if it is cleared), the system generates a new after-image record with information on these changes.

The new record overwrites the existing record in the DSO's active table and generates the following entries in the change log table, for example, for the clearing process (see Table 9.7).

Document	Item	CoCd	Period	Posting Date	C Date	Status	Taxes	Amount
123	1	US01	007.2010	07/15/2010		Open	−2,000	−12,000
123	1	US01	007.2010	07/15/2010	08/15/2010	Cleared	2,000	12,000

Table 9.7 DSO Change Log for Clearing

The change log is the basis for the delta update to the InfoCube.

Another process involves the credit memo. Figure 9.21 shows the corresponding posting record.

Credit memo

Debit		Credit	
Sales Revenues	$ 10,000	Customer	$ 12,000
VAT	$ 2,000		

Figure 9.21 Posting Record — Credit Memo

Simplified, the posting in the DSO looks like the one shown in Table 9.8.

Document	Item	CoCd	Period	Posting Date	Status	Taxes	Amount
234	1	US01	008.2010	08/15/2010	Cleared	−2,000	−12,000

Table 9.8 DSO Record—Credit Memo

If the credit memo refers to invoice 123, the credit memo in the BW system should be evaluated together with the invoice. To do this, the default DataSource contains fields that make the invoice available for follow-up documents. These are the 0INV_YEAR, 0INV_DOC_NO, and 0INV_ITEM fields. These fields present the FI document number of the invoice posting. If you don't use the default fields in SAP ERP Central Component (ECC) for the invoice number, you won't find any reference to the invoice. If this is the case, you can also establish a relationship via documents with the same clearing document, for example. Often, however, business prefers to display the SD invoice number instead of the FI document number of the invoice. The invoice number is at least specified for the invoice document in the 0REF_DOC_NO field but not necessarily for all follow-up documents. Reversal postings follow the same logic as credit memos.

Incoming payment

Incoming payments can be very complex from a reporting perspective. For example, customers can clear multiple invoices with one payment or allocate their own receivables as partial amounts. And when the original clearing entry is retroactively corrected, everything becomes even more complex. From a business point of view, it is more about which invoices have been paid and less about how they have been paid. Because the incoming payment for the clearing process also changes the status of the invoice posting, you get more reliable data when you evaluate the clearing of the invoice instead of the payment document itself if reporting on incoming payments is desired (cash reporting).

Postings for incoming payments usually look like the one shown in Figure 9.22.

Debit		Credit	
Bank	$ 12,000	Customer	$ 12,000

Figure 9.22 Posting Record — Incoming Payment

Simplified, the posting in the DSO looks like the one shown in Table 9.9.

Document	Item	CoCd	Period	Posting Date	Status	Taxes	Amount
999	1	US01	008.2010	08/15/2010	Cleared	–2,000	–12,000

Table 9.9 DSO Record — Incoming Payment

Down payments

Down payments are special processes. They are recorded with special G/L indicators (SG/L I). Special G/L transactions are postings that have to be specified separately in the financial statement, that is, the G/L account and the reconciliation account mustn't be the same for these postings. First, a down payment request is posted. This is done via a document that is not relevant to FI (noted item) using the special G/L indicator F. The incoming down payment is posted using the special G/L indicator A. Because down payments are made before the invoice is created, they cannot contain a reference to the invoice document. Down payments are usually allocated to an invoice (see Table 9.10).

Document	Item	CoCd	Period	Posting Date	SG/L I	Status	Taxes	Amount
456	1	US01	006.2010	06/15/2010	F	Cleared		−6,000
567	1	US01	006.2010	06/25/2010	A	Cleared		6,000
678	1	US01	007.2010	07/15/2010		Cleared		−6,000

Table 9.10 DSO Records — Down Payments

The last item presents the allocation of the down payment and invoice. This item is posted together with the invoice. The last item normally contains the invoice information, the first two items don't. Table 9.11 shows the invoice once more.

Document	Item	CoCd	Period	Posting Date	Status	Taxes	Amount
123	1	US01	007.2010	07/15/2010	Open	2,000	12,000

Table 9.11 DSO Record of the Outgoing Invoice

The invoice states the following: invoiced amount = $ 12,000 minus the down payment of $ 6,000, which results in a payment amount of $ 6,000.

In real life this means that the special G/L transactions for down payments are supposed to be hidden unless the down payments are supposed to be evaluated. Another special G/L transaction is the allocation of interests on arrears, for example, which is similar to the allocation of down payments.

If the payment amount does not correspond to the invoiced amount and if this amount is too small to claim residual items, this results in payment differences. Payments in foreign currencies can also involve differences. These differences are normally part of the clearing entry. Here as well, most of the transactions are not displayed in reports unless payment and currency differences are supposed to be analyzed, in particular.

Payment differences

If an invoice is not paid over a longer period of time, provisions need to be posted. However, not all provisions can be implemented via the 0FI_AR_4 DataSource. Some of them are exclusively available in the 0FI_GL_4 DataSource.

Provisions and write-offs

Irrecoverable debts must eventually be written off. The posting is implemented as shown in Figure 9.23.

Debit		Credit	
Depreciation Recs.	$ 10,000	Customer	$ 12,000
VAT	$ 2,000		

Figure 9.23 Posting Record — Bad Debts Written Off

The depreciation is used to clear an invoice; the same principles apply as to other clearing entries.

You can identify the various posting procedures through the posting key. Table 9.12 lists the most important procedures.

Posting Key	Reversal	Sales	Payment	Debit/Credit	Procedure
01	12	X		Debit	Invoice
02	11	X		Debit	Reversal credit memo
03	13			Debit	Expenses
04	14			Debit	Other receivable
05	15		X	Debit	Outgoing Payment
06	16		X	Debit	Payment difference
07	17			Debit	Other allocation
08	18		X	Debit	Payment clearing
09	19			Debit	Special G/L transaction
11	02	X		Credit	Credit memo
12	01	X		Credit	Reversal invoice
13	03			Credit	Reversal expenses
14	04			Credit	Other payable
15	05		X	Credit	Incoming payment
16	06		X	Credit	Payment difference
17	07			Credit	Other allocation
18	08		X	Credit	Payment clearing
19	09			Credit	Special G/L transaction

Table 9.12 Posting Keys in FI-AR

Posting Keys in SAP NetWeaver BW   **[«]**

BW expresses posting keys using the 0POST_KEY characteristic, which doesn't
have any text content. Because not all users know all of the posting keys by
heart, missing text is often regarded as disruptive. The text table in SAP ECC
is table TBSLT, a pool table. Therefore, no direct generic extractor is possible,
that is, a function module needs to be written. You can also find an overview
of all posting keys in the appendix.

9.2.2 Aging Grid Analyses

Aging grid analyses are frequently used in customer reporting. Aging
grid analyses involve the evaluation of open items on a key date in due
date columns. The determination either refers to the due date or to the
posting date. A distinction is therefore made here between overdue analysis and aging structure analysis. These analysis reports not only support
employees in the enterprise in day-to-day business operations, they are
also useful for analyzing the entire enterprise.

The default method for the implementation of this kind of analysis
report uses individual restricted key figures on a detail InfoCube (Info-
Cube with document level). The following key figures are defined here,
for example:

▶ **Not yet due**
  Posting date <= key date
  due date for net payment <= key date
  clearing date > key date

▶ **Due within 1–15 days**
  Posting date <= key date
  key date < due date for net payment <= key date + 15
  clearing date > key date

▶ **Due within 16–30 days**
  Posting date <= key date
  key date + 15 < due date for net payment <= key date + 30
  clearing date > key date

The problem with the procedure introduced previously is that numerous restrictions are necessary and that the calculation is made at the
document level. For operational reporting, this procedure is well suited,
because the evaluation is only supposed to be made for a limited cus-

tomer group. If large data volumes are accessed, performance problems are likely to occur. Usually, for the selection of the key date, restricted flexibility is sufficient, as only the current data or the last day of a month is supposed to be evaluated in most cases.

Current view for the key date

Let's assume that time comparisons of the individual months (that is, always with reference to the last day of a month) are supposed to be implemented and that the relevant characteristic is a navigation characteristic, that is, you're interested in the current view. For example, the key account manager is an attribute for a customer and you want to analyze how the portfolio of the outstanding invoices has developed for this customer during the last year. The assignment to the respective key date plays a major role. From a technical perspective, this time-based assignment would only be provided via time-dependent master data (that is, time-dependent navigation attributes), which would lead to two problems: First, the master data key date would always apply to the entire query, that is, the user would have to run the query for each month of the time comparison and save the data separately in Excel. Second, time-dependent master data would impair performance significantly.

Figure 9.24 illustrates a solution approach for these problems.

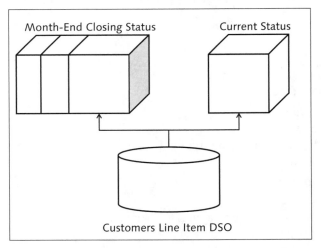

Figure 9.24 Data Flow for Optimized Time Pattern Analyses

The solution approach includes the following InfoCubes:

▸ **InfoCube — Month-End Closing Status**
This InfoCube needs to be updated for the respective month-end closing statuses as a snapshot of the open items with the corresponding aging grid key figures; the characteristics (here: current view for the key date) have to be read from the master data time-dependently. The InfoCube is partitioned by calendar month.

▸ **InfoCube — Current View**
The InfoCube for the current view is loaded for all open items in Full mode on a daily basis. To reduce the loading time, navigation attributes are used and no additional data is imported.

The first InfoCube must be loaded once per month, which is usually done after the month-end closing. However, the question is how the transformation knows the key date that is supposed to be used. If the key date is always supposed to be the previous month, this can be easily derived from the system date. But what do you do if a year is supposed to be reproduced retroactively or if everything needs to be reproduced in support cases?

Control
characteristic

It'd be ideal if you could define parameters in a DTP in addition to selections. Unfortunately, this is not possible. A tried and tested workaround is to store loading settings in a table or InfoObject and read the information from there. This kind of InfoObject is also referred to as a control characteristic. Master data maintenance for InfoObjects in BW is quite simple, and the effort required is kept to a minimum. You only have to create a new characteristic (technical name: KEY_DATE; key, for example Char 1) with a master data attribute, 0DATE. When maintaining the desired key date in a record with key A, you avoid having any kind of key date loaded if the control characteristic accidentally contains several records. You also need to activate the master data after the manual master data maintenance. To be on the safe side, you should integrate an attribute change run for the respective control characteristic in the process chain before the system is supposed to read the data.

The system can now read the information in the start routine and in the DTP.

Listing 9.3 shows the declaration in the start routine.

```
DATA:
KEY_DATE_RECORD TYPE /BIC/PKEY_DATE.
```

Listing 9.3   Declaration in the Start Routine (Key Date)

In the start routine itself, the information is read from the KEY_DATE InfoObject (see Listing 9.4).

```
SELECT SINGLE DATE FROM /BIC/PKEY_DATE
  INTO CORRESPONDING FIELDS OF KEY_DATE_RECORD
  WHERE OBVERS EQ 'A' AND
    /BIC/KEY_DATE = 'A'.
```

Listing 9.4   Reading the Key Date from the InfoObject

You can determine the individual time pattern key figures in the update process of the individual key figures as shown in Listing 9.5 (example: 0–15 days, considering the posting date).

```
DAYS = KEY_DATE_RECORD-DATE - SOURCE_FIELDS-PSTNG_DATE.
IF DAYS GE 0 AND DAYS LT 16.
  RESULT = SOURCE_FIELD-DEB_CRE_LC.
ELSE.
  CLEAR RESULT.
ENDIF.
```

Listing 9.5   Updating the Key Figure — 0–15 Days

The data model's granularity was considerably reduced without having to neglect information that is critical for fulfilling the reporting requirements. All of the date fields and all of the information at the document level are no longer necessary.

[+]   **Optimized Data Model**

If you accept justifiable restrictions regarding the flexibility, you can set up data models with a very high performance. The solution introduced here includes some more interesting aspects, particularly the "current assignment to key date" view.

9.2.3   Payment History

To analyze the payment history retroactively, you should determine the period from the invoicing date (payment history) or from the due date (delay in payment) up to the clearing date. You must also consider if cash discounts are used.

When performing calculations with time intervals, the problem is that the respective key figures cannot be added up. The best way is to calculate a weighted average on the basis of 0DEBIT_LC.

However, you have to calculate the weighted average prior to reporting, because the multiplication of payment history/delay in payment and 0DEBIT_LC must already be made at the document level. Up to BW Release 3.5, the reporting did include a function to perform calculations before the aggregation process; however, this was implemented directly at the database level and not at the semantic document level, that is, this function worked exclusively for compressed InfoCubes. Because this function is no longer available, you have to store the interim results, which must be determined at the document level, in the physical model.

Determination at details level

This example uses the following key figures:

▸ **Payment history**
Difference between document date and clearing date

▸ **Delay in payment**
Difference between due date and clearing date

▸ **Delay in payment with cash discount**
Difference between due date for the cash discount used and clearing date

▸ **Weighted payment history**
Days multiplied by 0DEBIT_LC

▸ **Weighted delay in payment without cash discount**
Days multiplied by 0DEBIT_LC

▸ **Weighted delay in payment with cash discount**
Days multiplied by 0DEBIT_LC

The most important key figures in reporting here are the weighted average for the payment history and for the delay in payment. To calculate them, you can divide the weighted payment history/weighted delay in payment at any level.

Aggregation Behavior of Calculated Key Figures

Usually, calculated key figures cannot be aggregated. It is critical to design the data model in such a way that aggregateable components do exist in the physical model, which contains subsets of calculations that you may not be able to perform in the reporting. Particularly in reporting, you cannot force a determination at the details level.

9.2.4 DSO Determination

The analysis of the payment history solely refers to items that are already cleared. Because the clearing date for open items is not known, you cannot determine the delay in payment or the days between the invoicing date and the date for the clearing of the invoice. Instead, you determine how long an item has already been open. This cannot be determined at the document level. Instead, the average needs to be considered, comparing the issuing processes of invoices of previous periods (*open* and *cleared*) with the current balance or with an average balance.

The open items/gross sales ratio is called Days Sales Outstanding (DSO) and is expressed in days. The DSO is a critical indicator for the good functioning of an enterprise's receivables management. But a high DSO can also indicate that the SD department handles risks without due consideration and doesn't carry out sufficient credit reviews.

The easiest way to determine the DSO

The easiest way to determine the DSO is the following (p refers to the evaluation period):

$$30 \times \frac{A/R}{Sales_p}$$

This formula is also used in a Business Content query. The calculation of this formula should be no problem; this type of calculation, however, is very prone to fluctuations. Let's assume that an enterprise sells Christmas trees by invoice. In December, the sales will increase to such an extent that the calculation will be falsified. In January, the sales will suddenly minimize to almost zero and have the calculation increase to incredible volumes although hardly any invoice will probably be older than 30 days. Seasonal fluctuations are common in nearly all economic areas.

A better method is to also consider the average of a year in addition to the current status:

Average method

$$365 \times \frac{\sum\limits_{i=p-11}^{p} A/R_i}{12} \times \frac{1}{\sum\limits_{i=p-11}^{p} Sales_i}$$

Reducing this fraction leads to the following formula:

$$30{,}416 \times \frac{\sum\limits_{i=p-11}^{p} A/R_i}{\sum\limits_{i=p-11}^{p} Sales_i}$$

The gross sales for one year can be directly determined. Sales-relevant postings are normally identified by posting keys 1, 2, 11, and 12 and a time selection by period (interval of variable with an offset −11 to 0) for the 0DEB_CRE_LC key figure. To determine the average of the open items, you first need individual calculations (restricted key figures) for the open items of the last 12 months (AR/M-0 to AR/M-11). The open items for a key date are always determined in such a way that the clearing date is always greater than the last day of a month and the posting date less than or equal to the last day of a month. In BW, you can use a variable for only one characteristic, that is, you need 24 variables. You can use the following variable exit for all variables; the offset is derived from the variable name here (see Listing 9.6).

```
IF I_STEP = 2.
DATA: L_S_RANGE TYPE RSR_S_RANGESID.
DATA: BEGIN OF I_VAR_RANGE OCCURS 0.
INCLUDE STRUCTURE RRRANGEEXIT.
DATA: END OF I_VAR_RANGE.
DATA: L_PERIODE(7),
L_CALMONTH(6),
L_PERIODE3(3),
L_YEAR(4),
L_DATE LIKE SY-DATUM,
```

```
L_OFFSET TYPE I. " From variable name

* The 'VAR_FISCALYEARPERIOD' variable contains the month
* specified by the user
LOOP AT I_T_VAR_RANGE INTO I_VAR_RANGE.
  IF I_VAR_RANGE-VNAM = 'VAR_FISCALYEARPERIOD'.
    L_PERIODE = I_VAR_RANGE-LOW.
  ENDIF.
ENDLOOP.

* Convert into calendar format
L_CALMONTH(4) = L_PERIODE(4).
L_CALMONTH+4(2) = L_PERIODE+5(2).

* The desired offset is specified at position7 and 8
* of the variable name, e.  g., CLEAR_04 is the variable for
* the clearing date, and the last date of
* the month specified up to 4 is supposed to be provided.
L_OFFSET = I_VNAM+6(2).

L_DATE(6) = L_CALMONTH.
L_DATE+6(2) = '15'.
L_DATE = L_DATE - L_OFFSET * 30.
L_PERIODE3(1) = '0'.
L_PERIODE3+1(2) = L_DATE+4(2).
L_YEAR = L_DATE(4).

CALL FUNCTION 'LAST_DAY_IN_PERIOD_GET'
EXPORTING
  I_GJAHR = L_YEAR
  I_MONMIT = '00'
  I_PERIV = 'K4'
  I_POPER = L_PERIODE3
IMPORTING
  E_DATE = L_DATE
EXCEPTIONS
  INPUT_FALSE
  T009_NOTFOUND
  T009B_NOTFOUND.
CLEAR L_S_RANGE.
L_S_RANGE-LOW = L_DATE.
L_S_RANGE-SIGN = 'I'.
L_S_RANGE-OPT = 'EQ'.
```

```
APPEND L_S_RANGE TO E_T_RANGE.
ENDIF.
```

Listing 9.6 Variable Exit, Which Can Be Used for Several Variables

It is possible that the data for 12 periods are not available yet, which can be corrected. Instead of considering 12 months, you should use the following formula for calculation:

$$\sum_{i=0}^{11} 1 \ldots \text{if} \sum_{j=p-11}^{p-i} |A/R_j| \neq 0$$

The total of the absolute amount of the last month's open items to the xth month needs to be 0 if a month is no longer supposed to be considered. Once an open item has existed for the last 12 months, every month counts, that is, months in which the amount was zero at the end of the month are also considered.

The following auxiliary calculation, A09, is an example of a calculation in BW:

(ABS('AR/M-9') +
ABS('AR /M-10') +
ABS('AR /M-11')) <> 0

The number of months for the average determination is then as follows:

'A00' + 'A01' + 'A02' + 'A03' + 'A04' + 'A05' + 'A06' + 'A07' + 'A08' + 'A09' + 'A10' + 'A11'

BW determines the DSO as follows:

NDIV0(NODIM(' AR /M-0' +
'AR /M-1' +
...
'AR /M-11') /
NODIM('SALES') /
*NODIM('NUMBER_OF_MONTHS')) * 365*

This calculation type is smoothened for one year; however, you'll receive better results by counting back the individual months, namely, with the

Countback method

monthly gross sales up to this month in which the gross sales are higher than the remaining balance.

The following example is supposed to illustrate this:

Balance: $ 800
Sales of the last 30 days: $ 350
Remaining: $ 450
Sales for the next 30 days: $ 500
Corresponds to: 27 days (450/500 × 30)
Total: 57 days

The example illustrates the calculation once more. You need the gross sales of the individual months for this calculation (the two simpler calculations merely require a sales key figure).

In general, this can be defined as follows:

$$30 \times \frac{A/R_p - \sum_{i=1-m}^{p} Sales_i}{Sales_{-m}} + 30 \times m$$

m refers to a specific month in which the remaining balance is less than the sales of the next period, that is:

$$\sum_{i=p-m+1}^{p} Sales_i < A/R_p \leq \sum_{i=p-m}^{p} Sales_i$$

However, the calculation must have a definite end at some point, for example, after 12 periods, the following applies for $m = 12$:

$$\sum_{i=p-1"}^{p} Sales_i < A/R_p$$

To simplify the calculation, the cumulated sales can be illustrated as follows:

$$S(m) = \sum_{i=p-m}^{p} Sales_i$$

This results in the following formula:

$$30 \cdot \frac{A/R_p - S(m)}{S(m+1) - S(m)} + 30 \cdot m$$

$S(m)$ can be used very often; $S(m)$ itself is easy to determine: For a determination that includes 12 periods, you must create 12 restricted key figures, each with a selection by period starting with the evaluation month minus m months (in BW, these key figures are referred to as S00 to S12).

In the next step, you must check the condition for m. Simplified, this looks as follows:

$$S(m) < A/R_p \leq S(m+1)$$

If the condition is fulfilled, the formula must be applied for the respective m; for DSO00, the formula then is:

NDIV0 (
((' AR /M00' > 0) AND (' AR /M00' <= 'S00'))
* 30 * ' AR /M00' / 'S00'
)

For the additional key figures, DSO01 to DSO11, you now have to add 30, 60, and so on in the calculation. For DSO01, the calculation looks like:

NDIV0 (
(('AR /M00' > 'S00') AND ('AR /M00' <= 'S01'))
* (30 * ('AR /M00' – 'S00') / ('S01' – 'S00') + 30)
)

For DSO02, the calculation is:

NDIV0 (
(('AR /M00' > 'S01') AND ('AR /M00' <= 'S02'))
* (30 * ('AR /M00' – 'S00' – 'S01') / ('S02' – 'S01') + 60)
)

DSO02 to DSO11 now follow the same structure. Finally, you must consider the case that the receivables are older than the history analyzed (one year in the example); therefore, DSO12 is:

NDIV0 (
('AR/M00' > 'S12')
* 360
)

At least at the details level, the gross sales of a single period can also be negative, that is, theoretically two or more formulas for DSO00 through DSO12 may not be equal to 0. In these cases, you must use the lowest value. This is done with the following formula:

(('DSO00' +'DSO01' + 'DSO02' + 'DSO03' + 'DSO04' + 'DSO05' + 'DSO06' + 'DSO07' + 'DSO08' + 'DSO09' + 'DSO10' + 'DSO11' + 'DSO12') <> 0)
*
MIN (MIN (MIN (MIN (MIN (MIN (MIN (MIN (MIN (MIN (MIN (MIN (
('DSO00' == 0) * 360 + ('DSO00' <> 0) * 'DSO00' ,
('DSO01' == 0) * 360 + ('DSO01' <> 0) * 'DSO01') ,
('DSO02' == 0) * 360 + ('DSO02' <> 0) * 'DSO02') ,
('DSO03' == 0) * 360 + ('DSO03' <> 0) * 'DSO03') ,
('DSO04' == 0) * 360 + ('DSO04' <> 0) * 'DSO04') ,
('DSO05' == 0) * 360 + ('DSO05' <> 0) * 'DSO05') ,
('DSO06' == 0) * 360 + ('DSO06' <> 0) * 'DSO06') ,
('DSO07' == 0) * 360 + ('DSO07' <> 0) * 'DSO07') ,
('DSO08' == 0) * 360 + ('DSO08' <> 0) * 'DSO08') ,
('DSO09' == 0) * 360 + ('DSO09' <> 0) * 'DSO09') ,
('DSO10' == 0) * 360 + ('DSO10' <> 0) * 'DSO10') ,
('DSO11' == 0) * 360 + ('DSO11' <> 0) * 'DSO11') ,
('DSO12' == 0) * 360 + ('DSO12' <> 0) * 'DSO12')

In the first part of the formula, we assumed that all formulas deliver zero as a result; this is especially the case when there are no open items.

Summary   This last calculation is much more effective than the two previous ones. The key figure responds fast if payment problems occur and can handle seasonal fluctuations quite well. If you keep in mind how much you could save here if you implemented good reporting, the relation of development effort and potential savings would be very positive.

The DSO determination example illustrated how you can perform complex calculations in the BW system, particularly countbacks.

9.2.5 Credit Management

The task of credit management is to monitor the credit limit for customers. Whereas you can always assign receivables to a company code, the organizational characteristic for credit management processes is the credit control area. A credit control area can include several company codes; however, each company code always belongs to only one credit control area. Reporting in SAP ECC is optimized for evaluating one customer; for a holistic view, it makes sense to use the analysis options in the BW system.

SAP's 0FI_AR_9 DataSource is a delta-enabled extractor for the credit management area, but it has one drawback: The DataSource merely provides data from the FI system, namely, from table KNKK. Credit management — and particularly the included dynamic credit review — is a comprehensive function including the SD module. For credit reviews, it is also important to know the value of the open orders, not just the open receivables. Without this information, the system cannot determine the credit limit used rate.

Dynamic credit review

The alternative is to add the SD fields to the Business Content extractor in the user exit. This SD information can then be read using the SD_CREDIT_EXPOSURE function module; the values delivered now correspond to the data of Transaction FD33 in SAP ECC.

Listing 9.7 shows the code in the exit.

```
FIELD-SYMBOLS: <F_DS> TYPE DTFIAR_9.

LOOP AT C_T_DATA ASSIGNING <F_DS>.

CALL FUNCTION 'SD_CREDIT_EXPOSURE'
    EXPORTING
*       FLAG_OPEN_DELIVERY          = 'X'
*       FLAG_OPEN_INVOICE           = 'X'
*       FLAG_OPEN_ORDER             = 'X'
*       HORIZON_DATE                = '99991231'
```

```
            KKBER                         = <F_DS>-KKBER
            KNKLI                         = <F_DS>-KUNNR
 *          T014                          = ' '
         IMPORTING
            OPEN_DELIVERY                 = <F_DS>-ZZO_DEL
            OPEN_INVOICE                  = <F_DS>-ZZO_INV
            OPEN_ORDER                    = <F_DS>-ZZO_ORD
            OPEN_DELIVERY_SECURE          = <F_DS>-ZZO_DEL_SEC
            OPEN_INVOICE_SECURE           = <F_DS>-ZZO_INV_SEC
            OPEN_ORDER_SECURE             = <F_DS>-ZZO_ORD_SEC.

     <F_DS>-ZZCMWAE = 'EUR'.

     ENDLOOP.
```

Listing 9.7 Customer Exit for Dynamic Credit Reviews

The delta mechanism doesn't consider changes in SD processes, that is, you can only load the enhanced source in Full mode. You can find additional information on the delta mechanism (for other AP, AR, and GL extractors as well) in SAP Note 1012874.

One more comment: The Business Content InfoObjects, 0REPR_GROUP and 0RISK_CATEG, are provided as exclusive attributes and are therefore not visible in other transformations. This setting is not useful and should be changed.

Summary   Business Content lacks information on dynamic credit reviews for credit management. SD data is required to determine the credit limit used. This section showed you how to enhance the Business Content DataSource.

9.2.6   Dunning History

Business Content does not contain key figures on the dunning history; instead, the SAP ECC table, MHNK, provides the relevant dunning data. The field LAUFD (date of dunning run) in table MHNK lets you set up a generic delta.

Figure 9.25 shows how a generic extractor is developed.

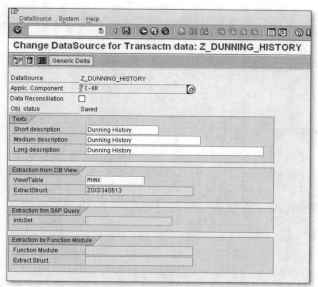

Figure 9.25 Generic Extractor for Dunning Data

Use the GENERIC DELTA button to enter the field LAUFD. The procedure now depends on the LSA strategy of creating one or more DSOs in the BW system that contain all fields or at least all relevant fields from the SAP ECC table. It is important, however, that the key of the default DSO corresponds semantically to the key of the table in SAP ECC. A critical addition for the InfoCube is a number key figure, that is, a key figure for the number of dunning notices. It makes sense to include this key figure in the DSO (DSO delta function).

Generic extractor

Eventually, you can set up an InfoCube with all of the relevant characteristics from table MHNK. You should then include this InfoCube in an overall AR MultiProvider, which lets you, for example, evaluate the number of dunning notices in other AR reports.

Now you have to check to see if InfoObjects exist for all of the required fields and whether InfoObjects in Business Content possibly exist for the table fields or if you have to create new InfoObjects. This is probably the most time-consuming task in this development process.

[+] **Generic Extractor for an SAP ECC Table**

If an SAP ECC table contains all of the relevant information, an enhancement is quite simple, because no ABAP code is required. You should be confident to set up the entire data model in a very short space of time.

9.2.7 Cash Reporting

Here, cash reporting refers to the analysis of the incoming payments from customers for products and services. Depending on the business model and strategy, this can be a very relevant key figure. It may even be the case that incoming payments are used as the basis for success bonuses or performance appraisals. A performance evaluation conducted based on the actually paid sales or service by customers might be a much more reliable figure than revenue or invoices issued. However, it's not that easy to establish the relation to reporting-relevant characteristics as it might seem to be at first glance. An incoming payment doesn't always clear exactly one invoice. There may also be payment and currency differences, and receivables can be allocated to payables, for example.

When a payment is cleared, open invoices are cleared, that is, incoming payments are identified by invoice document. Invoices make it much easier to import additional information, for example, from SD, than documents that refer to incoming payments. Therefore, a solution that uses balance movements is much more robust and easier to implement than a solution that uses incoming payments. You can thus determine cash as follows:

$$\text{CASH}_{Period=i} = \text{BILLSISSUED}_i - \underbrace{\left(OI_i - OI_{i-1}\right)}_{\text{Balance movements}} - \text{OTHER}_i$$

When a new invoice is issued, the open items (OI) increase; that is, the balance movements must be subtracted. If the balance movements is higher than the invoices issued, the customer must have cleared an invoice. Finally, you have to subtract all other transactions, particularly bad debt write-offs.

That means you need three key figures to determine cash: the invoiced amount, other transactions (that are not supposed to be paid as cash), and balance movements.

Invoiced amounts and other transactions are filters for the corresponding posting keys, and balance movements are changes of OIs.

When an item is cleared, the *status* characteristic changes from *open* to *cleared* in the InfoCube. The status changes because the line item DSO is used to create a change log with a before image having the *open* status, including all of the negative key figures, and with an after image having the *cleared* status, including all positive key figures. That means you can access the balance movements of the open items by manipulating the change log.

Balance movements through the change log

The before image contains the balance movements that is relevant here. For a time-dependent assignment, the clearing time is relevant; however, only the after image contains the clearing date, that is, you have to transfer the clearing date from the after image to the before-image record (ideally in the start routine).

Incoming payments that have not been cleared yet are also reported as balance movements. When an invoice is cleared, cash is assigned to this invoice, and the balance movements for the incoming payment is zero.

It depends on the image category and clearing status how the individual records from the change log are to be manipulated. The following sections describe which steps you need to perform.

You don't change the *new* image category for open items, and you create a history of two open items for the *new* image record for cleared items.

New, cleared

For example, a document was created on January 7. It was cleared on January 8. On January 7, however, no data was loaded — it is an invoice (see Table 9.13).

Image Category	Status	Posting Date	Clearing Date	Value
N	C	01/07	01/07	100

Table 9.13 "New, Cleared" Image Category

Now you have to create two new records for this record. The key figures that have been derived from the value (0CRE_DEB_LC) are now invoiced amount (R), balance movements (B), and other transactions (O) (see Table 9.14).

Image	Status	Date	R	B	O
N	C	01/07	100		
	O	01/07		100	
	O	01/08		−100	

Table 9.14 Modified Change Log for the "New, Cleared" Image Category

In the case of changed documents, you can distinguish between the following changes:

- ► 1: open to cleared
- ► 2: cleared to open
- ► 3: open to open
- ► 4: cleared to cleared

Field symbols In general, there are always before-image records for changed documents from a DSO change log. Because the values of the after image are supposed to be used to manipulate the data of the before image, you need a pointer (field symbol) to the before image (see Listing 9.8):

```
FIELD-SYMBOLS: <BEFORE_IMAGE> TYPE ANY.
... If before image:
    ASSIGN <SOURCE_PACKAGE> TO <BEFORE_IMAGE>.
```

Listing 9.8 Field Symbol for the Before Image

Open → cleared Change 1 is a normal clearing of a payment. The system updates the before image with the clearing date of the cleared document (after image). The change log for an invoice that was created on January 7 and cleared on February 2 looks like the one shown in Table 9.15.

Image Category	Status	Posting Date	Clearing Date	Value
N	O	01/07		100
B	O	01/07		−100
A	C	01/07	02/02	100

Table 9.15 Change Log for the "Open → Cleared" Change

Now you have to create two new records for this record. The key figures that have been derived from the value (0CRE_DEB_LC) are now invoiced amount (R), balance movements (B), other transactions (O), and non-cash (see Table 9.16).

Image	Status	Date	R	B	O
N	O	01/07	100	100	
B	O	02/02	−100	−100	
A	C	01/07.	100		

Table 9.16 Modified Change Log for "Open → Cleared"

If the incoming payment (Change 2) was registered in the system on January 31 but was cleared with the invoice on February 2, this leads to an entry of the incoming payment in the change log illustrated in Table 9.17.

Incoming payment, open → cleared

Image Category	Status	Posting Date	Clearing Date	Value
N	O	01/31		−100
B	O	01/31		100
A	C	01/31	02/02	−100

Table 9.17 Change Log for the "Open → Cleared" Change (Incoming Payment)

After the analogous manipulation, it looks like Table 9.18:

Image	Status	Date	R	B	O
N	O	01/31		−100	
B	O	02/02		100	
A	C	01/31			

Table 9.18 Modified Change Log for "Open → Cleared" (Incoming Payment)

In Change 2 (A in Table 9.19), an incoming payment was not assigned correctly and is now opened again. Because the document doesn't contain a date for reopening, you can use the system date of the load process.

Cleared → open

Image Category	Status	Posting Date	Clearing Date	Value
B	C	01/31	02/02	−100
A	O	01/31		100

Table 9.19 Change Log for the "Cleared → Open" Change

If we assume that the loading date is February 8, the modified change log looks like the one illustrated in Table 9.20.

Image	Status	Date	R	B	O
B	C	01/31	−100		
A	O	02/08	100	100	

Table 9.20 Modified Change Log for "Cleared → Open"

Due to the previous transaction, cash for the corresponding invoice is already displayed for February 2; by resetting the entries on February 8, the system displays negative cash for February 8.

Open → open

"Open → open" involves a change in the attributes of the characteristics. You can ignore this change for cash.

Cleared → cleared

The last case, that is, from cleared to cleared, should only occur if a document was opened and cleared on the same date, for example, with a new payment. In this case, you should set up a history similar to the *new, cleared* image scenario (see Table 9.21).

Image Category	Status	Posting Date	Clearing Date	Value
B	C	01/31	02/02	−100
A	C	01/31	02/08	100

Table 9.21 Change Log for the "Cleared → Cleared" Change

If we assume that the loading date is February 8, the modified change log looks like the one illustrated in Table 9.22.

Image	Status	Date	R	B	O
B	C	01/31	−100		
A	C	02/08	100		
	O	02/02		100	
	O	02/08		−100	

Table 9.22 Modified Change Log for "Cleared → Cleared"

Deciding whether a change is for an invoice or any other transaction is determined using the posting key. Usually, invoices include invoices, credit memos, and the corresponding reversal transactions (that is, the 1, 2, 11, and 12 posting keys).

Non-cash transactions are bad debts write-offs, for example. If we now assume that a receivable is written off on September 1, the change log looks like the one illustrated in Table 9.23.

Bad Debts Write-Offs

In addition to the change of the invoice document, a clearing document for the write-off was posted on September 1. You can identify that it is a non-cash transaction via the posting key (for example, 7 or 17) (see Table 9.24).

Image Category	Status	Posting Date	Clearing Date	Value
N	O	01/07		100
B	O	01/07		−100
A	C	01/07	09/01	100
N	C	09/01	09/01	−100

Table 9.23 Change Log for Bad Debts Write-Offs

Image	Status	Date	R	B	O
N	O	01/07	100	100	
B	O	09/01	−100	−100	
A	C	01/07	100		
A	C	09/01			−100

Table 9.24 Modified Change Log for Bad Debts Write-Offs

Transformation The best way to program the manipulation is to use the start routine of the accounts receivable line item DSO transformation for a cash Info-Cube. You should loop the SOURCE_PACKAGE and use the field symbols to refer to the respective item and before image as shown in Listing 9.9.

```
LOOP AT SOURCE_PACKAGE ASSIGN <SOURCE_PACKAGE>.
  ...
ENDLOOP.
```

Listing 9.9 Loop for SOURCE_PACKAGE

Furthermore, the key figure update is important. The *balance movements* key figure can only be updated by open amounts (see Listing 9.10).

```
IF SOURCE_FIELDS-FI_DOCSTAT EQ 'O'.
  RESULT = SOURCE_FIELDS-DEB_CRE_LC.
ELSE.
  CLEAR RESULT.
ENDIF.
```

Listing 9.10 Updating the Balance Movements

You can identify invoices and other transactions via the posting key. Listing 9.11 shows the corresponding logic.

```
IF SOURCE_FIELDS-POST_KEY EQ '01' OR
   SOURCE_FIELDS-POST_KEY EQ '02' OR
   SOURCE_FIELDS-POST_KEY EQ '11' OR
   SOURCE_FIELDS-POST_KEY EQ '12'.
  RESULT = SOURCE_FIELDS-DEB_CRE_LC.
ELSE.
  CLEAR RESULT.
ENDIF.
```

Listing 9.11 Updating the Key Figures Using the Posting Key

Summary The solution introduced here uses the change log from the DSO. You can also transfer the solution approach to similar problems. Since BW 7.0, the DTP lets you define that the initial load is supposed to be implemented from the change log and not from the active table. This allows you do use this solution also for historic data, given that the change log was not deleted yet.

9.2.8   Sales Reporting

Let's take a closer look at the basic posting record in Accounts Receivable (FI-AR) (see Figure 9.26).

Debit		Credit	
Customer	$ 12,000	Sales Revenues	$ 10,000
		VAT	$ 2,000

Figure 9.26   Posting Record — Outgoing Invoice

The sales revenues usually provide more details than the customer side. Normally, the sales side is not visible in the receivables extractor. In the following example, the system imports the cost center to the revenue line item.

Because multiple revenue items can exist, you may have to generate various entries. Like customers, lookups require a DSO with G/L line items. This kind of DSO is always necessary when the 0FI_GL_4 Data-Source (GL4 for short) is used, because this DataSource only provides after images in the delta, and a delta for the InfoCube update can only be created via a DSO.

Figure 9.27 illustrates an update concept. The G/L DSO is already imported to the transformation in the line item DSO for customers. If multiple entries exist, a flag is set in the DSO. If only one entry exists on the sales side, it is loaded to the DSO and then to the normal AR InfoCube. In addition, we will create a separate InfoCube for the various entries. This has a number of advantages, in particular, it leads to a clear and optimized data model. If you wanted to update the additional entries to the normal InfoCube, you would have to delete all of the other key figures. You must always consider these additional items, and you may have to add filters. The additional InfoCube, in contrast, can have a leaner design; it should only include characteristics that are relevant for this reporting scenario.

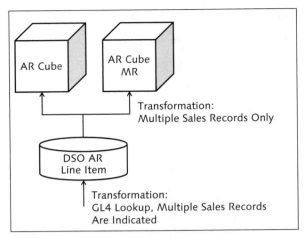

Figure 9.27 Logic for Updating Multiple Entries

Data model for
multiple entries

This section introduces the coding for this solution. In the transformation to the DSO, you have to import the G/L side, and multiple items on the offsetting entry side need to be selected. Listing 9.12 provides the declaration of the start routine in the DSO.

```
* Internal table for GL4-DSO
TYPES: BEGIN OF FIG4_TYPE,
  COMP_CODE TYPE /BI0/OICOMP_CODE,
  CHRT_ACCTS TYPE /BI0/OICHRT_ACCTS,
  GL_ACCOUNT TYPE /BI0/OIGL_ACCOUNT,
  FISCVARNT TYPE /BI0/OIFISCVARNT,
  FISCYEAR TYPE /BI0/OIFISCYEAR,
  FISCPER TYPE /BI0/OIFISCPER,
  AC_DOC_NO TYPE /BI0/OIAC_DOC_NO,
  ITEM_NUM TYPE /BI0/OIITEM_NUM,
  CO_AREA TYPE /BI0/OICO_AREA,
  COSTCENTER TYPE /BI0/OICOSTCENTER,
  DEB_CRE_LC TYPE /BI0/OIDEB_CRE_LC,
END OF FIG4_TYPE.

DATA: I_FIG4 TYPE SORTED TABLE OF FIG4_TYPE
             WITH UNIQUE KEY COMP_CODE
                             CHRT_ACCTS
                             GL_ACCOUNT
                             FISCVARNT
                             FISCYEAR
```

```
                        FISCPER
                        AC_DOC_NO
                        ITEM_NUM.

FIELD-SYMBOLS <FIG4> LIKE line OF i_fig4.

* Temporary auxiliary structure
TYPES: BEGIN OF TEMP_TYPE,
  COMP_CODE TYPE /BI0/OICOMP_CODE,
  CHRT_ACCTS TYPE /BI0/OICHRT_ACCTS,
  GL_ACCOUNT TYPE /BI0/OIGL_ACCOUNT,
  FISCVARNT TYPE /BI0/OIFISCVARNT,
  FISCYEAR TYPE /BI0/OIFISCYEAR,
  FISCPER TYPE /BI0/OIFISCPER,
  AC_DOC_NO TYPE /BI0/OIAC_DOC_NO,
  CO_AREA TYPE /BI0/OICO_AREA,
  COSTCENTER TYPE /BI0/OICOSTCENTER,
  DEB_CRE TYPE /BI0/OIDEB_CRE_LC,
  MULTI_REC TYPE /BIC/OIMULTI_REC,
END OF TEMP_TYPE.

DATA:
G_TEMP TYPE TEMP_TYPE.

DATA: I_TEMP TYPE TABLE OF TEMP_TYPE
          WITH KEY        COMP_CODE
                          CHRT_ACCTS
                          GL_ACCOUNT
                          FISCVARNT
                          FISCPER
                          AC_DOC_NO.

FIELD-SYMBOLS <TEMP> LIKE LINE OF I_TEMP.

Coding of start routine:
DATA:
I_COUNT TYPE I,
WA_SOURCE_PACKAGE TYPE _TY_S_SC_1.

* Always check if SOURCE_PACKAGE is empty, because
* the entire GL4-DSO will be read otherwise

DESCRIBE TABLE SOURCE_PACKAGE.
```

```
          IF SY-TFILL > 0.

          SELECT COMP_CODE
                 CHRT_ACCTS
                 GL_ACCOUNT
                 FISCVARNT
                 FISCYEAR
                 FISCPER
                 AC_DOC_NO
                 ITEM_NUM
                 CO_AREA
                 COSTCENTER
                 DEB_CRE_LC
             FROM /BIO/AOFIG_O0200
             INTO CORRESPONDING FIELDS OF TABLE I_FIG4
             FOR ALL ENTRIES IN SOURCE_PACKAGE
             WHERE COMP_CODE = SOURCE_PACKAGE-COMP_CODE AND
                   CHRT_ACCTS = SOURCE_PACKAGE-CHRT_ACCTS AND
                   FISCVARNT = SOURCE_PACKAGE-FISCVARNT AND
                   FISCPER = SOURCE_PACKAGE-FISCPER AND
                   AC_DOC_NO = SOURCE_PACKAGE-AC_DOC_NO AND
                   CHRT_ACCTS = SOURCE_PACKAGE-CHRT_ACCTS.

        LOOP AT SOURCE_PACKAGE INTO WA_SOURCE_PACKAGE.
          MOVE-CORRESPONDING  WA_SOURCE_PACKAGE TO G_TEMP.
          CLEAR: G_TEMP-CO_AREA,
                 G_TEMP-COSTCENTER,
                 G_TEMP-DEB_CRE,
                 G_TEMP-MULTI_REC.
          I_COUNT = 0.
          LOOP AT I_FIG4 ASSIGNING <FIG4>
            WHERE COMP_CODE = WA_SOURCE_PACKAGE-COMP_CODE AND
                  FISCVARNT = WA_SOURCE_PACKAGE-FISCVARNT AND
                  AC_DOC_NO = WA_SOURCE_PACKAGE-AC_DOC_NO AND
                  CHRT_ACCTS = WA_SOURCE_PACKAGE-CHRT_ACCTS AND
                  FISCPER = WA_SOURCE_PACKAGE-FISCPER.

            IF (  I_COUNT GE 1 ).
               G_TEMP-MULTI_REC = 'X'.
               EXIT.
            ENDIF.
```

```
   IF ( <FIG4>-COSTCENTER IS NOT INITIAL ).
     G_TEMP-CO_AREA = <FIG4>-CO_AREA.
     G_TEMP-COSTCENTER = <FIG4>-COSTCENTER.
     G_TEMP-DEB_CRE = <FIG4>-DEB_CRE_LC.
     I_COUNT = I_COUNT + 1.
   ENDIF.
  IF ( I_COUNT > 1 ).
    G_TEMP-MULTI_REC = 'X'.
  ENDIF.

  APPEND G_TEMP TO I_TEMP.
  DELETE ADJACENT DUPLICATES FROM I_TEMP.
  SORT I_TEMP.
ENDLOOP.
```

Listing 9.12 Start Routine for Importing the Revenue Side from GL4

The internal table, i_TEMP, contains document numbers with multiple entries on the revenue side. Listing 9.13 shows the update for the Multiple Entries flag (this data is loaded to a separate InfoCube).

```
READ TABLE i_TEMP
WITH KEY COMP_CODE = SOURCE_FIELDS-COMP_CODE
         FISCVARNT = SOURCE_FIELDS-FISCVARNT
         GL_ACCOUNT = SOURCE_FIELDS-GL_ACCOUNT
         AC_DOC_NO = SOURCE_FIELDS-AC_DOC_NO
         CHRT_ACCTS = SOURCE_FIELDS-CHRT_ACCTS
         FISCPER = SOURCE_FIELDS-FISCPER
  INTO G_TEMP.

IF SY-SUBRC = 0.
  RESULT = G_TEMP-MULTI_REC.
ELSE.
  CLEAR RESULT.
ENDIF.
```

Listing 9.13 Updating the "Multiple Entries" Flag

For multiple line items on the G/L side, you need an additional InfoCube that only contains this data. The MULTIPLE RECORDS flag lets you control whether the data needs to be imported from the normal InfoCube or from a separate InfoCube (see Listing 9.14).

```
TYPES: BEGIN OF FIG4_TYPE,
         COMP_CODE TYPE /BI0/OICOMP_CODE,
         CHRT_ACCTS TYPE /BI0/OICHRT_ACCTS,
         GL_ACCOUNT TYPE /BI0/OIGL_ACCOUNT,
         FISCVARNT TYPE /BI0/OIFISCVARNT,
         FISCYEAR TYPE /BI0/OIFISCYEAR,
         FISCPER TYPE /BI0/OIFISCPER,
         AC_DOC_NO TYPE /BI0/OIAC_DOC_NO,
         ITEM_NUM TYPE /BI0/OIITEM_NUM,
         CO_AREA TYPE /BI0/OICO_AREA,
         COSTCENTER TYPE /BI0/OICOSTCENTER,
         DEB_CRE_LC TYPE /BI0/OIDEB_CRE_LC,
       END OF FIG4_TYPE.

DATA: I_FIG4 TYPE SORTED TABLE OF FIG4_TYPE
         WITH UNIQUE KEY COMP_CODE
                         CHRT_ACCTS
                         GL_ACCOUNT
                         FISCVARNT
                         FISCYEAR
                         FISCPER
                         AC_DOC_NO
                         ITEM_NUM.

FIELD-SYMBOLS <FIG4> LIKE LINE OF I_FIG4.
```

Listing 9.14 Declaration Part of the Start Routine for Updating Multiple Posting Items on the Revenue Side

Because only data with multiple items on the revenue side is processed in this transformation, it is sufficient to enrich it with the GL4 information. You don't need any further lookups. Listing 9.15 now contains the coding for the start routine itself.

```
DELETE SOURCE_PACKAGE WHERE /BIC/MULTIPLE_RECORDS NE 'X'.

DESCRIBE TABLE SOURCE_PACKAGE.
IF SY-TFILL > 0.

* Multiple entries are first copied from SOURCE_PACKAGE to
* SOURCE_PACKAGE2, then SOURCE_PACKAGE2 to
* SOURCE_PACKAGE
```

```
DATA:
I_COUNT TYPE I,
SOURCE_PACKAGE2 TYPE _TY_T_SC_1.
CLEAR SOURCE_PACKAGE2.

DATA : WA_SOURCE_PACKAGE TYPE _TY_S_SC_1,
       WA_SOURCE_PACKAGE2 TYPE _TY_S_SC_1.

SELECT COMP_CODE
       CHRT_ACCTS
       GL_ACCOUNT
       FISCVARNT
       FISCYEAR
       FISCPER
       AC_DOC_NO
       ITEM_NUM
       CO_AREA
       COSTCENTER
       DEB_CRE_LC
    FROM /BIO/AOFIGL_O0200
    INTO CORRESPONDING FIELDS OF TABLE I_FIG4
    FOR ALL ENTRIES IN SOURCE_PACKAGE
    WHERE COMP_CODE = SOURCE_PACKAGE-COMP_CODE AND
          CHRT_ACCTS = SOURCE_PACKAGE-CHRT_ACCTS AND
          FISCVARNT = SOURCE_PACKAGE-FISCVARNT AND
          FISCPER = SOURCE_PACKAGE-FISCPER AND
          AC_DOC_NO = SOURCE_PACKAGE-AC_DOC_NO.

LOOP AT SOURCE_PACKAGE INTO WA_SOURCE_PACKAGE.

  LOOP AT I_FIG4 ASSIGNING <FIG4>
    WHERE ( GL_ACCOUNT BETWEEN ... ) AND
    COMP_CODE = WA_SOURCE_PACKAGE-COMP_CODE AND
    FISCVARNT = WA_SOURCE_PACKAGE-FISCVARNT AND
    AC_DOC_NO = WA_SOURCE_PACKAGE-AC_DOC_NO AND
    CHRT_ACCTS = WA_SOURCE_PACKAGE-CHRT_ACCTS AND
    FISCPER = WA_SOURCE_PACKAGE-FISCPER.

    CLEAR: WA_SOURCE_PACKAGE-CO_AREA,
           WA_SOURCE_PACKAGE-COSTCENTER,
           WA_SOURCE_PACKAGE-/BIC/CRD_DEB_LC2.
```

399

```
      WA_SOURCE_PACKAGE-CO_AREA = <FIG2>-CO_AREA.
      WA_SOURCE_PACKAGE-COSTCENTER = <FIG2>-COSTCENTER.
      WA_SOURCE_PACKAGE-/BIC/CRD_DEB_LC2 = <FIG2>-DEB_CRE_LC.

      APPEND WA_SOURCE_PACKAGE TO SOURCE_PACKAGE2.
    ENDLOOP.

ENDLOOP.

SOURCE_PACKAGE = SOURCE_PACKAGE2.

ENDIF.
```

Listing 9.15 Start Routine for Generating Multiple Entries

In the report, you then have to exclude the records with multiple entries from the normal AR InfoCube and import them from the InfoCube for multiple entries.

Rule Groups   Rule groups are a standard function for generating multiple entries in a transformation. When you execute a rule group, the SourcePackage is executed once more, whereas you can define different transfer rules here. However, rule groups would not work in this case study, because the number of offsetting entries is not always the same. Up to Release 3.5, you could copy the update process for individual key figures; this is no longer possible in the current version. This Release 3.5 function may be somewhat more flexible than the rule group function, but it also cannot fulfill all of the requirements of this example.

Summary   This case study demonstrated how you can generate multiple records for one source record, which is often necessary in real life. The solution approach described here is lean and easy to implement.

9.2.9   Overall View of AR Reporting

The AR reporting example illustrated which problem areas you can typically find in customer projects and how you can solve them. A lot of individual aspects were described, which similarly occur in other areas, too.

Figure 9.28 provides an overview of the overall data model.

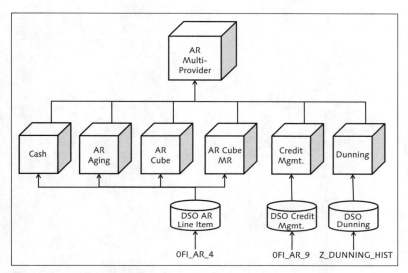

Figure 9.28 AR MultiProvider

This example demonstrated the advantages and disadvantages of Business Content. Business Content doesn't provide a satisfying sample solution in any of the fields described. This is different for extractors: The line item extractor is the central basis for most of the areas, the enhancement on the user exit for 0FI_AR_9 was quite easy, and the generic extractor for dunning data is created in one minute.

9.3 Conclusion

The first case study showed how you can implement the LSA in a concrete case. Following the basic principles is rather easy here, and it is particularly important that every project member follows them so that all of the benefits can be utilized.

The second case study showed the strengths and weaknesses of Business Content. The real benefits of Business Content are the DataSources, especially the delta-enabled line item extractors (this applies also to CO, Logistics, and Human Resources (HR)). This chapter introduced several interesting options for building up sophisticated solutions based on this raw data. In this context too, you should always consider the LSA.

In this chapter, you learn how to model a planning application and integrate it into an existing data model. The focus in this chapter is on Business Warehouse (BW) integrated planning.

10 Data Modeling for Planning Applications

When it released SAP NetWeaver 7.0, SAP provided a planning infrastructure that is fully integrated into BW called BW integrated planning. The term integrated in this context refers to technical integration; in other words, planning-specific objects are included in the implementation phase of a planning solution. However, data retention and, in particular, front-end components and input-ready queries and their integration into Microsoft Excel worksheets and web templates are modeled in the same environment that is used to create reports.

The integration of front-end tools is an innovation that differentiates BW integrated planning from the older product, SAP Business Information Warehouse — Business Planning and Simulation (BW-BPS). This innovation makes it easier for users to create planning applications, because they no longer have to create additional layout objects. SAP BusinessObjects Planning and Consolidation (BPC) is another new planning solution.

This chapter focuses on BW integrated planning. Because the planning application is defined solely in terms of BW objects, it is particularly suited for representing how data retention is modeled in a planning application. However, several aspects of modeling can also be applied to BW-BPS and, in part, to SAP BPC.

In Section 10.1, Planning System and Control System Requirements, we'll take a brief look at the planning processes supported by the product and at some of the planning tools provided by SAP. Section 10.2, Overview of BW Integrated Planning, is an overview of BW integrated planning. If you are already familiar with the material in these first two sections, you can skip ahead to Section 10.3, Case Study — Cost Planning on the Cost Center Level. In this section, we use a cost element planning example on the cost center level to present a real-world solution implementation. Other aspects that you need to consider in the context of data modeling for a planning application are dealt with in Section 10.4 Specific Modeling Issues.

10.1 Planning System and Control System Requirements

Planning processes

The planning process is an important component of enterprise management. Within this process, target values and standard values are defined that are used later on for a target/actual comparison with current key figures in the execution phase of the business processes. Thus, the planning process, in conjunction with the relevant monitoring processes, is a central tool for managing an enterprise and implementing an enterprise strategy. In turn, the success, or lack thereof, of implementing an enterprise's goals plays a significant role in determining whether an enterprise can achieve a competitive advantage.

Sample planning process

The planning process shown in Figure 10.1 is based on a sample enterprise operating in a buyers' market. You will notice that the overall planning process is divided into several subplans that are created step by step and in relation to each other. The revenue plan is created on the basis of an assessment of the target market in which the enterprise operates. There are two central factors when it comes to sales: The expected sales volume and the target price. Cost planning can be carried out once the sales quantity to be produced in the plan period is defined. The next and final step, then, is to carry out sales and profit planning, which is based on the sales and cost planning steps.

Balanced Scorecard

Recent years have seen a rise in the popularity of management techniques that let managers consider financial aspects in a more holistic way. These techniques also identify structural "early warning" indicators that could affect business success. These early warnings, which are used to create an integrated management system, are described in terms of key figures. In this context, the *balanced scorecard* (BSC) approach, pioneered in 1992 by Robert S. Kaplan and David P. Norton, analyzes not just the financial perspective, but also the customer perspective, and usually the process perspective and the potential or employee perspective as well. Note that these perspectives are only suggestions; the dimensions and relevant key figures in the BSC are intended to be tailored to suit the circumstances of the individual organization.

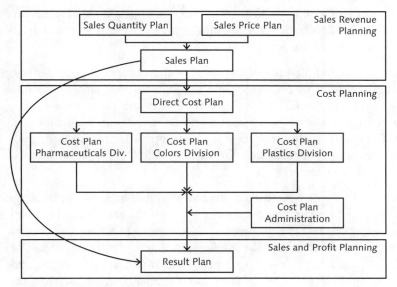

Figure 10.1 Sample Planning Process

Any information technology (IT)–supported planning process can be designed very differently, depending on the nature of the individual enterprise and the management methods in use there. It is possible to integrate separate plans with totally different time frames, different organizational structures, and different content.

Multilayered planning processes

An IT solution that is intended to support planning and management processes should be able to do the following:

IT requirements

▸ Optimally support every mapped subplan
▸ Be fully integrated in the sense that the plan figures can be seamlessly included in reports alongside the current figures
▸ Enable the smoothest possible data transfer at the interfaces to other (sub)plans
▸ Be sufficiently flexible to integrate new requirements into the existing solution

405

A range of IT solutions is available for each of the many operational planning processes. These solutions cover the specific requirements of a sub-planning process to more or less the same high standard. The available selection of tools that support strategic planning processes is smaller, keeping in mind that these tools have only recently come to the full attention of software manufacturers. Two challenges in this market are the lack of standardization for planning processes and the necessity to flexibly adapt planning processes.

Uses of BW integrated planning

The BW integrated plan that is the focus of this chapter is an infrastructure component. This plan is not a planning solution; rather, it is like a set of building blocks that we can use to create a planning solution. The potential uses of BW integrated planning range from self-contained, optimized planning applications to strategic, operational planning applications that are networked and coordinate interactions between the various areas of the enterprise.

Data model and planning model

Because no business content is delivered with BW integrated planning, the aim of the implementation project is to design a suitable data model and planning model. The data model has a special role here, as it determines the degree to which the above-mentioned requirements can be fulfilled. In particular, integrating plan figures and actual figures, and coordinating the data models of the various subplans are important tasks of the data model. A well-designed data model that follows the layer model described in Section 10.2.2, Diagram of a Planning Application, also offers the best level of investment protection in situations where the implementation of a (sub)plan has already started and more process steps will be integrated at a later stage. These points also apply to planning applications that are implemented using BW-BPS.

SAP Business Objects Planning and Consolidation

Unlike BW integrated planning and BW-BPS, SAP BPC, along with the Data Manager, has its own functionality for connecting to data sources and for data formatting, which gives company departments a degree of flexibility when it comes to data binding and data formatting. However, an integrated data basis is also the perfect prerequisite for an SAP BPC project.

The physical data models that are generated by SAP BPC to store actual and plan data are application-specific and therefore incompatible with a planned, cross-platform, logical data modeling approach within a data warehouse architecture.

We do not intend to recommend one of the alternative planning tools at this point, as the choice of tool depends on the individual project requirements. One central criterion in this choice is investment protection, as SAP maintains the solutions for varying periods of time. However, when selecting a solution, do not focus solely on the tool. A new or optimally integrated data model can make a central and highly valuable contribution within your Business Intelligence (BI) strategy and should be evaluated accordingly. In Section 10.2, you will become familiar with the components of a BW integrated planning application and find out what a typical underlying data model looks like.

10.2 Overview of BW Integrated Planning

BW integrated planning is an analytical planning tool. It uses the functions of SAP Business Explorer (BEx), a tool within BW. With it, you can create planning layouts using Excel or in the form of web applications. Thus, the tool lets you create a planning interface that matches your needs and those of your target user group. Data retrieval and data retention are carried out on the BW level. To do this, extra functionality was added to the Online Analytical Processing (OLAP) services to enable them to write data back to the BW system and to read data efficiently.

The modeling process for a BW integrated planning application is divided into two phases: data basis modeling and modeling the planning application itself. The data model delimits the content framework of the (sub) plans. In the data basis modeling phase, you have to define the levels on which planning will take place, and the characteristics and master data that will be accessed for reports and planning layouts. Planning-related requirements are just as important here as the requirements that are based on reporting targets.

If you already have a suitably modeled data basis, then you already have an important cornerstone of your planning application. In many cases, existing reporting data models serve as an initial starting point for data basis modeling (master data and transaction data) for a planning application. These reporting data models are usually implemented on the basis of a planning-specific, newly implemented InfoCube.

If a subplan is implemented as part of an overall enterprise planning process, each subplan is usually based on its own data mart. It is important

Selecting a tool

Modeling process

Link to layer architecture

in these situations that the subplan applications all share the main central objects. This is the only way of ensuring that the subplans are properly integrated with each other, either at all or with an appropriate level of resources. Therefore, this kind of planning application can be logically assigned to the Architected Data Mart (ADM) level of a layer architecture (for more information, see Chapter 8, Data Modeling in the Reporting Layer, and Chapter 9, Case Studies).

In addition to building an (integrated) planning application, BW integrated planning can also be used for recording and merging both plan data and actual data from subsidiaries, for example. In such cases, the recorded data can be logically assigned to the data retrieval layer. Quality assurance and release processes can be implemented as part of the process of updating data to superordinate layers.

An application for recording the number of hours of consulting services provided is an example of an application that only records actual data. You can see that integrated planning can be used to record data in different contexts with a high degree of flexibility. Similarly, the data models that form the basis of the plans can also be assigned to the various layers. The most common implementations are those on the data mart level.

In the next section, you will learn about the components that make up a planning application.

10.2.1 Components of a Planning Application

The implementation of a planning application is based on the data model and other planning-specific objects that are explained in the following sections.

Real-Time-Enabled InfoCube

A planning application is based on a new InfoCube type. InfoCubes that are known as real-time-enabled InfoCubes enable data to be written back and form the part of the data basis that stores recorded data.

Aggregation Level

Not all of the details of the data basis are relevant to every planning step. The aggregation level makes it possible for you to define the level on which plan data is recorded or modified. The aggregation level also usually provides a subset of the data basis characteristics. This level is simply another virtual provider rather than a physical data storage area.

Input-Ready Query

With BW integrated planning, you can record data using the front-end components from your reporting activities. If a query is based on an aggregation level, you can release it for data recording purposes. This query is then regarded as an input-ready query.

Planning Function

Manual input is not the only way of entering plan data; planning functions can also be used to manipulate data. There are predefined functions for this purpose, and you can also define your own functions.

Planning Sequence

In many cases, a simple planning function is not enough to complete more complex tasks. You can use a planning sequence to merge several planning functions into one logical entity.

Filters and Variables

You have the option of defining filters that restrict access to specific data. You can use filters in input-ready queries and when accessing planning functions. Filters do not always have to consist of fixed restrictions — they can also use variables. These are the same variables that are available for reporting purposes.

Data Slices and Characteristic Relationships

Data slices and characteristic relationships offer you even more design options. Data slices are used to partially protect your dataset from modifications, while characteristic relationships, on the other hand, give you the option of permitting specific combinations of characteristic instances for planning purposes.

In the following sections, we do not provide you with in-depth information on all of the design options; rather, we only describe them insofar as they are relevant to data modeling or for implementing case studies. In Section 10.2.2, we'll take a look at the structure of a planning application and its main components.

10.2.2 Diagram of a Planning Application

In this section, you will become familiar with a simple data model based on a typical planning application. The model is presented in diagrammatic form, which is intended to make clear the interaction between the components described in the previous section.

Step-by-step guide to a planning application Figure 10.2 illustrates the components of a planning application within the framework of BW integrated planning. The planning-specific objects ❷ are created in the Planning Modeler on the basis of the data model ❶. The front-end tool, SAP BEx, is used to create a plan query ❸. The plan query, for its part, can be used as a basis for implementing a planning application either on the Web (using the BEx Web Application Designer (WAD)) or in Excel ❹. Alternatively to the plan query itself, other planning-specific objects, such as filters and planning functions, can also be used to create the planning application.

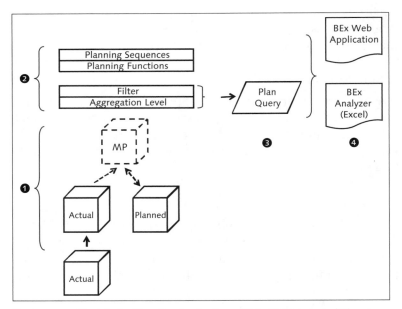

Figure 10.2 Model of a Planning Application within BW Integrated Planning

Step-by-step guide to a planning application Now let's take a closer look at the individual modeling steps required to implement a planning application within BW integrated planning.

Data Modeling

You create the data model in the Data Warehousing Workbench. In many cases, the actual data is obtained from an existing data set. For the following reasons, we recommend that you also create another, planning-specific InfoCube for storing the actual data:

▶ If all of the characteristics are not relevant to planning, the width of the data records and, thus, the data volume are reduced.

▶ The existing set of actual data is usually linked to a current data reporting run and as such is updated on an ongoing basis. However, several planning applications are designed in such a way that the actual data is loaded at a specified point in time and the next update only takes place once the planning stage is completed.

▶ It may be necessary to modify the actual data when it is transferred into the planning environment; for example, if there is a requirement to reassign characteristics or convert key figures.

The plan data InfoCube can initially be created as a copy of an actual data InfoCube. Subsequently, you can delete nonessential characteristics and add other planning-related characteristics, if necessary. Also, you can use the InfoCube settings to specify that it can function as a transactional InfoCube for storing plan data. The MultiProvider reproduces the structures of the actual data InfoCube and the plan data InfoCube.

Modeling Planning-Specific Components

You create the planning-specific components in the Planning Modeler. You can start the Planning Modeler in the web configuration interface, which runs with Java, using Transaction RSPLAN. In the Planning Modeler, you can define the aggregation level that is based on the MultiProvider. This level provides those characteristics that are relevant to specific planning functions and input-ready queries. In some cases, your requirements will be structured in such a way that you have to work with multiple aggregation levels. To do this, you can also define aggregation level–specific filters, planning functions, and planning sequences.

Defining a Plan Query

An input-ready query is created using the Query Designer, based on the aggregation level. The procedure for creating an input-ready query is the same as the procedure for creating a report query. You have access in the

Query Designer to previously defined filters, or you can create a new filter from scratch. The main thing you need to remember when creating an input-ready query is that such a query can once record data only you have set its "input-readiness" in the properties of the relevant elements *and* if you have designed the query in such a way that all of the characteristics of the aggregation level are unique (based on the sum total of the restrictions in the structures, key figures and filters). You can test your input-ready query straight away by executing it on the Web.

Structure of the Planning Application

A planning application usually contains other functionalities that you can subsequently extend in a web application or a BEx Analyzer Workbook by adding planning functions, displaying additional reports, or integrating a status administration function.

The data model presented in this section demonstrates a typical modeling approach; lots of other versions are also possible. To make sure that your informed enough to make a suitable choice, Section 10.2.3, modeling Alternatives, describes and evaluates three different modeling alternatives.

10.2.3 Modeling Alternatives

In the planning application model in Section 10.2.2, the aggregation level is defined on the basis of the MultiProvider. This variant corresponds to scenario ❶ in Figure 10.3. Scenarios ❷ and ❸ in the same figure illustrate alternative forms of modeling, which are described after the first scenario.

Comparing the alternatives

The central benefit of the first scenario compared to the second is that the aggregation level can be used to access both the current data Info-Cube and the plan data InfoCube. This is also the case for the query in the second scenario. However, you do have to consider the fact that planning functions are defined directly on the aggregation level. Therefore, you cannot access the current data InfoCube in this scenario. For example, if you want to implement planning functions that transfer current data to the plan data InfoCube, access to the current data InfoCube is still required. One sample scenario is the transfer of data from the previous year into an initial plan version.

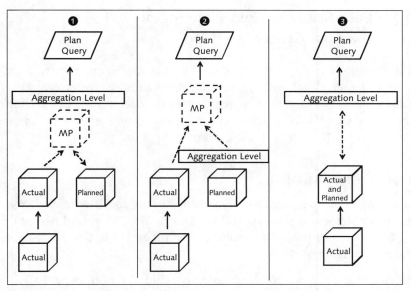

Figure 10.3 Modeling Alternatives to BW Integrated Planning

The first scenario also has another benefit over the second: If the planning application in question is a more complex one, you will need to use more than one aggregation level. In the second scenario, however, this means that you have to create a new MultiProvider for every aggregation level to enable repeat access to the current data.

The third scenario uses the same InfoCube to store both current and plan data. As a result, the loading procedure of the InfoCube (real-time loading) has to be changed before and after each loading step. This can be done automatically in process chains, but at the risk of further errors. We recommend that you keep current and plan data separate for other reasons, too. One is that data separation can lead to performance gains; another is that it simplifies administration.

Therefore, considering the preceding information, we recommend that you base your modeling on the first scenario.

The case studies in Section 10.3 give you the opportunity to follow the modeling process step by step.

10.3   Case Study — Cost Planning on the Cost Center Level

In the previous section, we introduced you to the elements needed to create a planning application, and you gained an initial overview of the various alternative modeling approaches for the data model. This section uses a case study — cost planning on the cost center level — to show you, step by step, how to create a planning application.

10.3.1   Initial Situation

Your company wants to plan cost elements on the cost center level. You plan to implement a planning solution using BW integrated planning and to follow the modeling scenario recommended in Section 10.2.3 (scenario ❶ in Figure 10.3).

This case study is based on the following technical requirements:

▸ Only value quantities (amounts) will be planned.

▸ The plan is based on one plan year, without further subdivisions.

▸ Planning is carried out on the basis of cost center and cost element. The origins of the various costs (internal orders, and so on) will not be considered.

▸ During the planning process, the planner will be able to access the current data from the previous three years.

▸ The current data will be transferred at the start of the planning round and will not be modified at any stage during the planning process.

Your company probably already has a current data InfoCube. This Info-Cube will provide the current data and serve as a basis for the structure of the planned data models.

To ensure that you can easily reproduce this case study, we are basing it on the standard InfoCube 0CCA_C11 (Costs and Allocations) and will explain the structure of the planning data model step by step. If you also intend to base your own work on this model, transfer InfoCube 0CCA_C11 from the content and load it with the appropriate current data.

10.3.2 Transferring Actual Data

First, make a copy of the existing current data InfoCube to create the current data InfoCube for the planning application. To do this, open the InfoProvider modeling view and click the InfoArea where you want to locate the new InfoCube. The EDIT INFOCUBE dialog opens, as shown in Figure 10.4. Enter the technical name of the InfoCube that you want to create ❶ and a descriptive name. Choose the standard InfoCube 0CCA_ C11 ❷ as a template, then click the Create button ❸ to create the new InfoCube.

Create the current data InfoCube

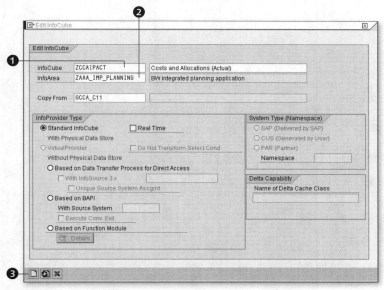

Figure 10.4 Creating the Current Data InfoCube

You can now reduce the scope of your planning-specific current data InfoCube by only using those characteristics that are relevant to planning, in accordance with your technical requirements. Figure 10.5 shows the characteristics and key figures that are relevant for our case study. Simply delete the characteristics and key figures that you do not need.

Reduce the scope

In our example, we have deleted the characteristics Partner Cost Center, Partner Order, Partner PSP Element, and Partner Object, among others.

The current data is aggregated when it is loaded. The various origins of the allocated cost quantities cannot be identified from this point on.

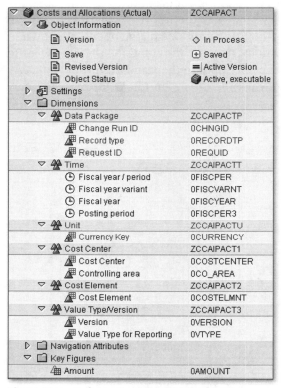

Figure 10.5 Defining the Current Data InfoCube

Data connection Now create the transformation required to transfer the current data (see Figure 10.6). The fields are mapped on a 1:1 basis, and make sure to set up the data transfer process (DTP) so that the data is loaded in "full" mode. Use the 0FISCYEAR filter to restrict the data to the previous year.

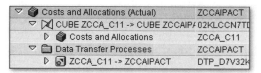

Figure 10.6 Transferring the Current Data

10.3.3 Modeling the Planning InfoCube

In most cases, including our present example, you can use the current data InfoCube as a template when creating the plan data InfoCube.

Create the plan data InfoCube

Create the InfoCube ZCCAIPPLA, using the InfoCube ZCCAIPACT (Costs and Allocations (Actual)), which we created in Section 10.3.2, as a template (see Figure 10.7). Make sure that you check the REAL TIME checkbox. This ensures that the new InfoCube can be used to store data. Because the plan data InfoCube does not get its data by means of updates, you do not need to create a transformation.

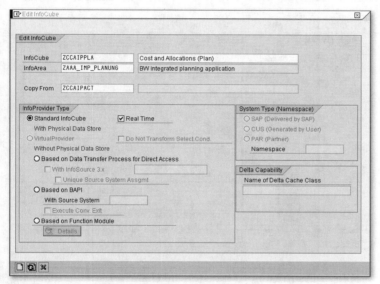

Figure 10.7 Creating the InfoCube for the Plan Data

10.3.4 Creating the Integrated Plan/Actual View

In our example, the current and plan InfoCubes have the same structure. This makes it very easy to create the MultiProvider. Create a new Multi-Provider called ZCCAIPMP (Costs and Allocations (Plan/Act)). Choose the InfoCubes ZCCAIPACT (Costs and Allocations (Actual)) and ZCCA-IPPLA (Costs and Allocations (Plan)) as the associated InfoProviders.

Create a MultiProvider

In the Edit MultiProvider view, transfer the following elements via drag and drop (see Figure 10.8):

▶ Transfer the time characteristics to the TIME dimension of the Multi-Providers ❶.

▶ Select and transfer the COST CENTER, COST ELEMENT, and VALUE TYPE/VERSION dimensions en masse ❷.

▶ Transfer the AMOUNT key figure to the KEY FIGURES directory. When you do this, the 0CURRENCY characteristic is automatically transferred to the UNIT dimension ❸.

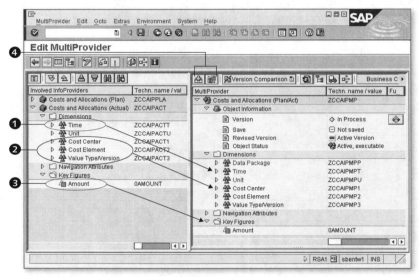

Figure 10.8 Structure of the MultiProvider

In our example, it is sufficient to transfer the characteristics and key figures of a *single* associated InfoCube, as they all have the same structure.

Identify characteristics and key figures

Once you have transferred the characteristics and key figures, you have to identify them ❹. In other words, you have to define which characteristics and key figures are to be obtained from which InfoCube. In our case, this decision is simple: We want to transfer all of the characteristics and key figures from all of the InfoCubes that contain the relevant characteristics and key figures. You also have the option of requesting the system to generate a proposal for identifying the characteristics (see Figure 10.9). Once you have done this for the characteristics and key figures, you have finished defining the MultiProvider and can now activate it.

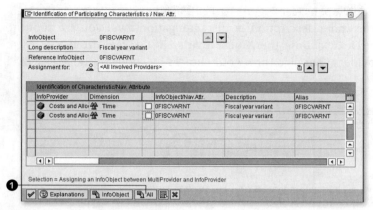

Figure 10.9 Generating Proposed Values

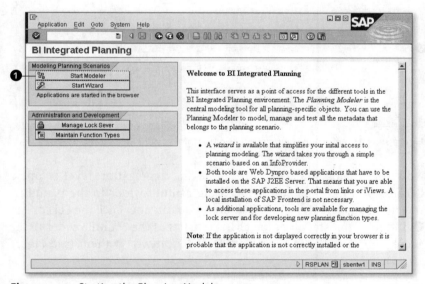

Figure 10.10 Starting the Planning Modeler

10.3.5 Defining the Aggregation Level

You will now create the aggregation level ZCCAIPAGG (Cost center planning), based on the MultiProvider you created in the previous section. To do this, click the Start MODELER (Transaction RSPLAN) button to start the Planning Modeler, as shown in Figure 10.10 ❶. In the Planning Modeler, open the AGGREGATION LEVELS tab and choose CREATE (see Figure 10.11)

Modeling in the
Planning Modeler

❷. A window opens (see Figure 10.12) that allows you to enter the technical name and a description of the aggregation level you are about to create ❸. Next, choose the MultiProvider ZCCAIPMP from the list of MultiProviders ❹ and confirm your choices by choosing TRANSFER ❺.

Figure 10.11 Creating an Aggregation Level in the Planning Modeler

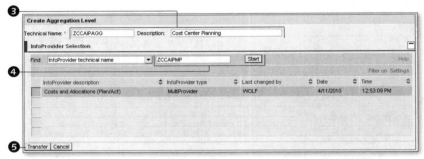

Figure 10.12 Creating an Aggregation Level — InfoProvider Selection

Create an aggregation level

Now, the dialog that lets you define the aggregation level is open. Because you have already reduced the MultiProvider to the planning-specific characteristics and key figures, you can now click the SELECT ALL ❻ button to transfer all of the characteristics of the MultiProvider to the aggregation level, and then SAVE ❼ and ACTIVATE ❽ them (see Figure 10.13).

Define content

It is more the exception than the rule that all characteristics of the underlying data model are transferred to the aggregation level. However, in Section 10.3.7, Extension – Data Formatting for Actual Data Transfer, as part of the material on model extensions, we will show you an example where this is not the case.

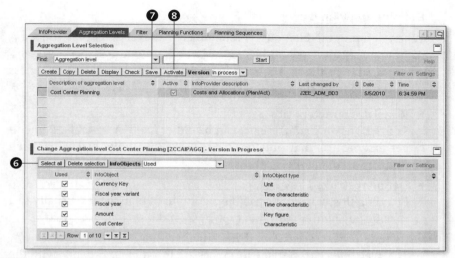

Figure 10.13 Creating an Aggregation Level — Selecting InfoObjects and Activation

In Figure 10.14, you can see the aggregation level and the associated components. This view is from the Data Warehousing Workbench. From there, you can go to the editing screen for the aggregation level, and double-click the aggregation level to go directly to the web interface for editing this component.

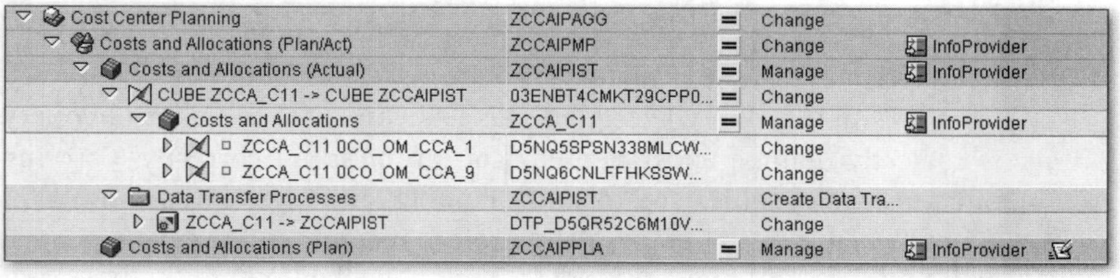

Figure 10.14 Aggregation Level for Cost Center Planning

10.3.6 Structure of an Input Layout

You have created the aggregation level and thus, you already have all of the backend components you need for our case study. What you still need to do for the planning application is define the plan query in the Query Designer and incorporate the query into either an Excel worksheet, using the BEx Analyzer, or into a web application, using the Web Application Designer (WAD).

Defining the Plan Query

When defining the plan query, remember that every cell that you want to be input-ready later on has to describe a unique instance for every characteristic on the aggregation level. You can ensure this uniqueness by doing the following:

▶ **Restrict characteristics**
Restrictions on characteristics can be either fixed or variable. Remember that the user may only be able to select one individual value when using a variable.

▶ **Define restricted key figures**
By doing this, you are restricting a column of plan values, usually to a specific key figure, the value type PLAN and a specific plan year.

▶ **Include characteristics in drill-down**
The available characteristic instances are listed in accordance with the settings and a unique instance that is specific to the plan value is output for each row or column.

To ensure that the query is input-ready at execution, you have to set the query properties for the plan query. You also need to set the column or cell that you want to be input-ready to READY FOR INPUT (LOCK-RELEVANT) and activate the START CHANGE MODE property for the query (both properties are located on the relevant PROPERTIES tab — either KEY FIGURE PLANNING or QUERY PLANNING).

If you want to test the plan query, you can execute it directly on the Web from within the Query Designer. This lets you check whether the query is correctly defined and whether data can be input correctly. Carrying out a test also enables you to start planning, although the save function is not available at this stage. We therefore recommend that you create a web template and make the save function available there (by means of a button, for example).

Example of a Web Planning Layout

Once executed, the planning layout looks like a completed report. If you have completed the characteristic restrictions and set the input-readiness properly, you will now see input-ready cells. Figure 10.15 shows an example of an input-ready plan query for recording cost elements for each calendar year. The column that contains empty cells ❶ is used to record the plan figures. The two columns to the right of it contain actual figures from the previous two years and provide the planner with comparison values for planning execution purposes. Once the plan data has been entered, it can be permanently saved to the plan InfoCube using the SAVE button.

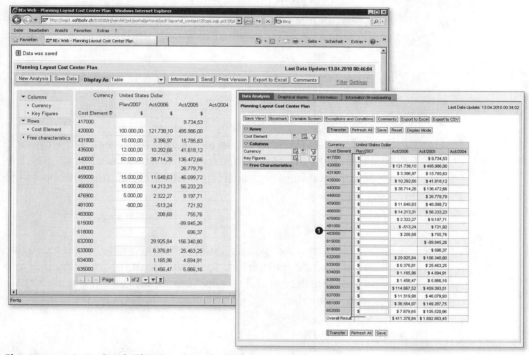

Figure 10.15 Input-Ready Plan Query on the Web

10.3.7 Extension – Data Formatting for Actual Data Transfer

Up to now, our planning model has imported actual data from the data source in the planning environment on a 1:1 basis. However, you will often need to format the data as the part of the DTP.

One frequently asked question is how to handle past changes to characteristic keys. A cost center restructuring process within an organization, for example, creates new cost centers and closes old ones. Only the current cost centers are relevant in the planning process, but actual legacy data still exists from the old cost centers. In this case, a suitable process

Characteristic
key changes

is needed to rebook the actual data to the current cost centers as part of the DTP.

In the following sections, we describe how you can make the required extensions to the model.

Defining a Transfer Table

The rules that define which old cost center is mapped to which new cost center can be easily described in a table with the following three columns:

▶ Old cost center number

▶ New cost center number

▶ Factor

The factor specifies the proportion of the old cost center that was transferred to the new cost center. The factor is also used as a basis for assigning the actual data that was transferred into the planning process to the new cost centers.

Mapping in the Model

To map the requirements, you need to extend the processing logic so that the actual data can be transferred. To do this, load the transfer table into BW and carry out the breakdown in accordance with the table entries when updating the data.

Loading the Flat File

Define DataSource   Proceed as follows to load a flat file. First, define a DataSource, choosing the flat file interface as the source system. Choose the conversion table (in CSV format) on the EXTRACTION tab page. Generate a proposal for the field format and overwrite the proposal as shown in Figure 10.16. Then assign a name to the DataSource and activate it.

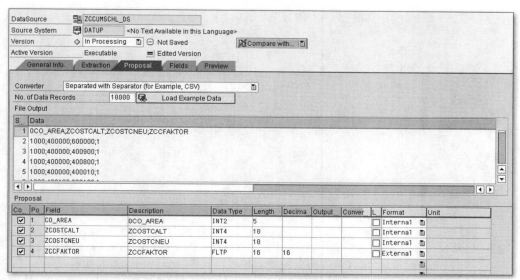

Figure 10.16 Formats of the DataSource Fields

Create the InfoObjects required to define the DataStore Object (DSO) as shown in Table 10.1. Make sure to create the cost center objects in the form of a reference to 0COSTCENTER.

Create InfoObjects

InfoObject	Description	Format
ZCOSTCALT	Cost center, old	CHAR 10 (reference: 0COSTCENTER)
ZCOSTCNEU	Cost center, new	CHAR 10 (reference: 0COSTCENTER)
ZCCFAKTOR	Cost center conversion factor (conversion factor)	Number (DEC, calculation field and amount field with comma)

Table 10.1 InfoObject Format

After creating the InfoObject, your next task is to create the DSO. Transfer 0CO_AREA, ZCOSTCALT, and ZCOSTCNEU to the key and transfer the key figure in the form of a data field. Figure 10.17 shows the result.

Create DSO

425

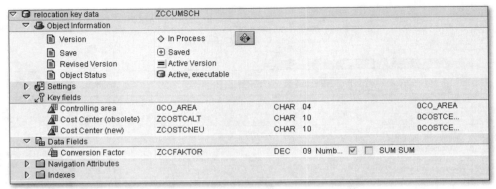

Figure 10.17   Defining the DSO for Saving Conversion Data

**Create
transformation**   Now all you need are the transformation and the DTP for loading the
data from the flat file to the DSO. The DTP allows you to directly access
the flat file. To do this, select FULL as the extraction mode and choose DO
NOT EXTRACT FROM PSA BUT ACCESS DATA SOURCE (FOR SMALL AMOUNT OF
DATA)) (see Figure 10.18).

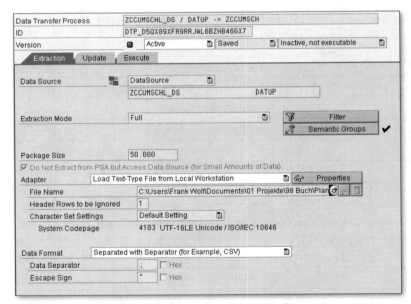

Figure 10.18   Defining the DTP for Loading Conversion Data

In this case, the flat file data is saved directly to the target rather than being temporarily saved to the PSA first. This technique is possible for smaller data volumes and makes the data flow more manageable. Now, execute the DTP to load the conversion table (see Figure 10.19).

▽ 🗂 relocation key data	ZCCUMSCH	=	Manage
▷ 📊 RSDS ZCCUMSCHL_DS DATUP -> ODSO ZCCUMSCH	06Z9ZJK8CH4KF28Y5ZQ3Y...	=	Change
▽ 🗂 Data Transfer Processes	ZCCUMSCH		Create Data Tra...
▽ 📊 ZCCUMSCHL_DS / DATUP -> ZCCUMSCH	DTP_D5QX89XFR9RRJWL6...		Change
🗺 DS Relocation Data	ZCCUMSCHL_DS	=	Change

Figure 10.19 Data Flow for Loading Conversion Data

Converting the Actual Data

The next step is to adapt the actual DTP so that the cost centers are converted during loading. The first thing to do is to create a start routine. This routine accesses the DSO content and reads the relevant factor. The key figure 0AMOUNT is multiplied by the factor and the result is posted to the new cost center. Figure 10.20 provides a diagram of this process, and Listing 10.1 contains the code for the start routine.

Create start routine

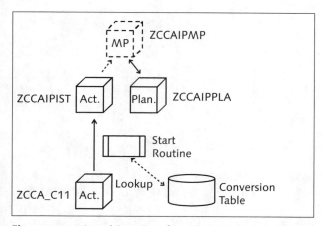

Figure 10.20 Actual Data Transfer with Conversion

Listing 10.1 shows the code for implementing the characteristic routine used to derive a business partner's rating score. The rating score is obtained from the DSO PXXBPD01 (business partner attributes) in the table with active data.

427

```
*$*$ begin of routine - insert your code only be-
low this line      *-*

    DATA: L_S_DATAPAK_LINE TYPE _ty_s_SC_1.

* Table for transferring converted records
    DATA: SOURCE_PACK2 TYPE TABLE of _ty_s_SC_1.

* Structure and table for transferring conversion rules
    TYPES: BEGIN OF comp,
              L_COST_ALT TYPE /BIC/AZCCUMSCH00-/BIC/ZCOSTCALT,
              L_COST_NEU TYPE /BIC/AZCCUMSCH00-/BIC/ZCOSTCNEU,
              L_FAKTOR   TYPE /BIC/AZCCUMSCH00-/BIC/ZCCFAKTOR,
           END OF comp.
    DATA: l_s_comp TYPE comp .
    DATA: l_th_comp TYPE TABLE OF comp.

    DATA: L_AMOUNT TYPE _ty_s_SC_1-AMOUNT,
          L_COSTCENTER TYPE _ty_s_SC_1-COSTCENTER.

* Data package loop
    LOOP at SOURCE_PACKAGE into L_S_DATAPAK_LINE.

*  Save source key figures
    L_AMOUNT = L_S_DATAPAK_LINE-AMOUNT.

    REFRESH l_th_comp.
    CLEAR l_s_comp.

* Read conversion rules for source cost center
    SELECT * FROM /BIC/AZCCUMSCH00
    APPENDING CORRESPONDING FIELDS OF TABLE l_th_comp
       WHERE /BIC/ZCOSTCALT = L_S_DATAPAK_LINE-COSTCENTER.

* Cost center is converted
    if sy-subrc = 0 .

*   Loop for conversion rules
    LOOP at l_th_comp into l_s_comp.

*     Convert cost center
        L_S_DATAPAK_LINE-COSTCENTER = l_s_comp-L_COST_NEU.
```

```
*        Convert source key figures with percentage factor
            L_S_DATAPAK_LINE-AMOUNT = L_AMOUNT * l_s_comp-L_
FAKTOR /
            100.

*        Transfer converted (and re-calculated) record to the
*        internal table
            APPEND L_S_DATAPAK_LINE to SOURCE_PACK2.

         ENDLOOP.
*  Check non-converted cost centers
       elseif sy-subrc <> 0 .

*  Error, cost center cannot be converted

       endif.
     ENDLOOP.

* Empty source data package
     REFRESH SOURCE_PACKAGE.

* Copy converted records to source data package that is
* processing now as target data package
     SOURCE_PACKAGE[] = SOURCE_PACK2[].

*$*$ end of routine - insert your code only before this line
```

Listing 10.1 Cost Center Conversion Start Routine

Alternatives for Mapping the Cost Center Reorganization Project

The definition of the planning layout that is included in the actual data conversion procedure described here is a simplified one. This is because the actual data has already been posted in a form suitable for a characteristic combination that is also used to record the plan data.

Alternative models

There are also other ways of dealing with changes that arise over the course of time. For example, what is known as a temporal join enables you to represent a time-based hierarchical breakdown. However, in our example, this approach would always assign one cost center to another in full; it would not allow you to distribute cost centers based on factors.

10.4 Specific Modeling Issues

In Section 10.3, you were shown how to implement a planning solution by means of the Cost Planning on the Cost Center Level case study. This section explains a variety of data modeling options for planning applications in more detail.

There are two different modeling approaches for key figures: The account model and the key figure model. Section 10.4.1, Key Figures and Account Model, describes these approaches. Subsequent sections provide information on how to log changes to a plan (Section 10.4.2, Tracking Changes to a Plan), how to set up status management and versioning management (Section 10.4.3, Status Management and Versioning Management), and how to transfer the plan results back to the operational application, where required, or alternatively, how to enable access to an adjacent subplan (Section 10.4.5, Transferring Subplans).

10.4.1 Key Figures and Account Model

As mentioned earlier, you have at your disposal two fundamentally different options for mapping key figures to your data model: The key figure model and the account model.

Key figure model

In the key figure model, the key figures are defined on the physical level, resulting in a wide fact table. In the account model, on the other hand, just one key figure is implemented physically, and its meaning is described by means of a characteristic. In other words, the unique meaning of a key figure in the account model is created through the additional restriction imposed by a characteristic.

You should always select the model that best matches your specific requirements. As indicated previously, the key figure model yields long data records. Therefore, if not all of the key figures are relevant, you may end up having to set aside very large amounts of memory, which in turn could have a negative effect on performance.

Account model

Assuming the same circumstances, the preceding problem does not arise in the account model. With this model, data records are only created for nonempty key figures. However, multiple data records are created to map multiple key figures. Because this contributes to the length of the fact table, decreased performance will result in this case, too.

One central difference between the two models becomes clear when you consider the maintenance requirement of the data model on the one hand and the planning application on the other. **Advantages and disadvantages**

It is easy to add a key figure on the data model level: simply load in a new characteristic instance. To add a physical key figure, on the other hand, you have to change the data model and then transport it.

This advantage is also reflected in the planning application. In the key figure model, when extensions are added, a new key figure has to be transferred to the aggregation level. In the account model, too, the physical key figure and the characteristic that describes the key figure are part of the aggregation level, and again, the addition of a key figure (in other words, a characteristic instance) has no effect on the definition.

The specific nature of each planning application will create additional advantages and disadvantages. Creating a key figure (retroactively) in the account model, for example, is simpler, as only one new characteristic instance has to be defined.

Table 10.2 juxtaposes the features of the key figure model and those of the account model, and describes the main differences between them.

	Key Figure Model	Account Model
Fact Table	Wide	Long
Performance	May be unnecessary if only a few key figures relevant to each data record; long records	Several times more data records than the account model
Adding Key Figures	Create new physical key figure, which leads to a change in the model	Re-define characteristic instance; no change to model
Key Figure in Planning Application	Explicitly change key figure	Define key figure by inserting a characteristic restriction (selection)
Maintenance Requirement for Planning Functions	High	Low
Planning Layout	Explicitly specify key figure as column or row	Restrict instance on the aggregation level
Possible to use variables?	No	Yes
Restrictions	Maximum 233 key figures; some functions unusable	—

Table 10.2 Comparison of Key Figure Model and Account Model

Select suitable
modeling approach

In conclusion, we recommend the key figure model if your key figures contain largely shared values, and the account model if the key figure model would create several initial key figures or if you expect that new key figures will have to be added retroactively to model on a regular basis.

In practice, you will rarely be able to make a global decision for all of the relevant key figures in the model. In such cases, you should consider modeling several InfoCubes, with the aim of being able to make an appropriate decision for every subdata model.

Comparison of
MM, PCA and
FI modeling

Both modeling approaches are used simultaneously in SAP's standard reporting content. The key figures in the Materials Management (MM) content area are also available as a key figure model, and the Profit center Accounting (PCA) and Financial Accounting (FI) key figures are available as an account model. You need to keep this difference in mind when defining a plan query that integrates "both worlds" (using a MultiProvider). In some cases, it makes sense to select a modeling approach in which only one model is used to define a plan query. This in turn can mean that the model has to be transferred (in a process known as "tipping" the data) for the sake of harmonization in the load processes for actual data.

10.4.2 Tracking Changes to a Plan

At first, it is not possible for you as the planner, using the standard tools, to track how a particular plan value came to exist. Regardless of whether you now get started with the planning layout or run a report, you will only see the result of the plan, but not how those values were arrived at (in other words, you will not have an insight into the planning process). You may well want to know whether the values were only input or changed iteratively multiple times; or you may wonder who made the changes, when, and in what order.

Additional fields
for plan data

Detailed plan data records can answer questions like these. To create detailed plan data records, you need to extend the planning application so that the user name, date and time, and a unique ID are saved automatically every time along with the plan data. If you do this, you will be able to easily generate a report that gives you an overview of every change made to the plan data. We will not go into further detail on the data protection aspects of this approach (monitoring of planning staff) at this point.

The following standard InfoObjects are suitable for making the required additions to the model:

- 0BBP_OBGUID — object GUID
- 0UNAME — creator's user name
- 0DATE — date
- 0TIME — time

Transfer the characteristics to the plan data InfoCube. The characteristics are not transferred to the aggregation level, as they are of no further relevance to the plan and are derived automatically by means of an exit when the data is saved. You have to specify this exit as an InfoProvider setting in the Planning Modeler.

To set up the derivation functionality, open the INFOPROVIDER tab page in the Planning Modeler. It is here that you will create a characteristic relationship. Proceed as follows (see Figure 10.21):

Define characteristic derivation

- Search for your plan data InfoProvider, select it, and click the CHANGE button ❶.
- Go to the CHARACTERISTIC RELATIONSHIPS area in the lower part of the screen and click the CREATE button ❷.
- Set WITH DERIVATION for the characteristic relationship ❸.

Next, select the class that provides the function for deriving characteristics ❹. You can either select the standard class CL_RSPLS_CR_EXIT_BASE as an initial template for a new class, or create a class of your own based on CL_RSPLS_CR_EXIT_BASE (in Transaction SE80, for example). Then enter the new class at this location.

Set the 0BBP_OBGUID, 0UNAME, 0DATE, and 0TIME characteristics, which you extended in the data model in this section, as target characteristics. Then select any other characteristic as the source characteristic. Actually, we do not need any source characteristic for our functionality, but this dialog requires one ❺.

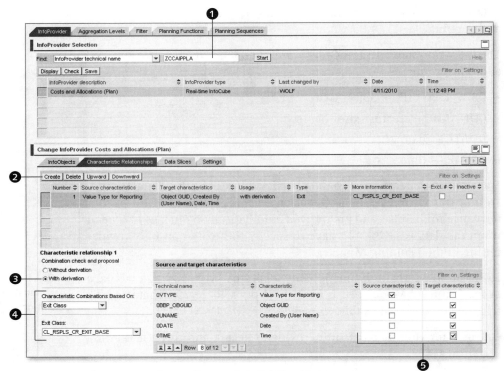

Figure 10.21 Create Characteristic Relationship

The important thing is that you implement the characteristic derivation method (see Listing 10.2) accordingly.

```
METHOD if_rspls_cr_methods~derive.
* implement your derivation algorithm here:
FIELD-SYMBOLS: <l_chavl> TYPE ANY.

* Identify GUID
ASSIGN COMPONENT 'BBP_OBGUID' OF STRUCTURE c_s_chas
TO <l_chavl>.
CALL FUNCTION 'GUID_CREATE'
IMPORTING
ev_guid_32 = <l_chavl>.

* User
```

```
ASSIGN COMPONENT 'USERNAME' OF STRUCTURE c_s_chas
TO <l_chavl>.
<l_chavl> = sy-uname.

* Date
ASSIGN COMPONENT 'DATE0' OF STRUCTURE c_s_chas
TO <l_chavl>.
<l_chavl> = sy-datlo.

* Time
ASSIGN COMPONENT 'TIME' OF STRUCTURE c_s_chas
TO <l_chavl>.
get time field <l_chavl>.
ENDMETHOD.
```

Listing 10.2   Deriving Characteristics in Method if_rspls_cr_methods~derive

The method we have shown you in this section for adding information to plan data records is not limited to the characteristics specified in the example — you can adapt it freely to your own requirements.

10.4.3   Status Management and Version Management

With the model extensions implemented in Section 10.4.2, you already know how to find out who made a particular change to the plan data, and when.

In many cases, plan data is planned on the basis of a multilevel consultation process rather than in a single step. A multilevel budget planning process is one example. Each planning step can only be undertaken once the previous planning step has been released.

If you are analyzing the results of the planning steps and want to create reports based on these results, it makes sense to save the data in the form of plan versions. You can do this by transferring another characteristic called *plan version* into the data model. To release a plan version, a planning function that copies the results of the last planning step to the new version in the form of source data is required. If you then integrate a status management function, you will be able to ensure that old plan

Versioning, status management

versions are automatically locked (that is, they cannot be changed), as only the current version is open for changes.

Copy plan data
In principle, it is possible to save the copies of the data directly to the planning InfoCube. However, we recommend that you set up a connection to another InfoCube where the finished versions can be saved. In this model, the plan version that is currently being worked on is located in the planning InfoCube itself. This approach has another advantage: Because they are saved in a separate InfoCube, the completed plan versions function as a kind of backup copy. Thus, if data is lost from the planning InfoCube, it is an easy matter to copy back the plan version that you need (by means of an update or a planning function). Figure 10.22 illustrates the model used to implement this approach.

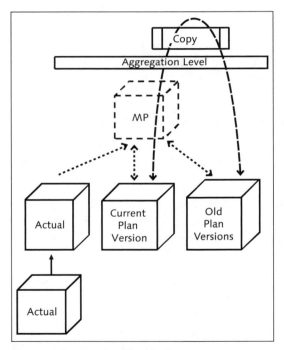

Figure 10.22 Copying Plan Versions

Status management
You can add a status management function to your plan by integrating a function that updates the relevant status to a table (for example, a DSO table or a table for an InfoObject that contains master data). You can inte-

grate this function at the status transition point, along with the function that copies the data.

As an alternative to this individualized solution, if you are using the Web as your planning environment, you can use the BW-BPS status and tracking system. However, with this system, you will have to make several wide-ranging settings (organizational structure, responsibilities, and so on). If your application is a relatively simple one, it is quicker to implement a lean, individualized solution.

Status and
tracking system

10.4.4 Retraction

The infrastructure component of the integrated planning approach lets you create a planning application that can be used to record and coordinate data. This plan data can then be used to manage operational processes. To set this up, you have to create an interface to the operational systems for data transfer purposes. Based on the process of extracting data from the SAP ERP system to the BW system, the process of sending data in the opposite direction is known as retraction.

The planning component BW-BPS has this kind of interface, which enables it to provide various components and structures for retracting data to SAP ERP. BW integrated planning, on the other hand, has no retraction mechanism. However, you can integrate the BW-BPS retraction mechanism into a planning application like ours; you will simply have to make the Customizing settings within BW-BPS.

Retraction with
BW BPS

If you do not required automatic data transfer or have already implemented an interface to the target system, it may be sufficient for you to make the plan data available as a flat file. This is easy to do in our cost center planning example. All we need to do is make a minor extension to the model.

Retraction with BW BPS

There are two categories of retractors in BW: pull retractors (such as CO-PA) and push retractors (CO-OM-CCA).

Pull retractors are SAP ERP add-ins that are set up and started there. Pull retractors need an interface to obtain data from the BW system. This interface is defined by means of a BW query. These retractors are there-

Pull retractors

fore independent of the planning tool and can be used equally well in the BW integrated planning environment or in the BW-BPS environment.

Push retractors

Push retractors are set up in the BW system and write data to the SAP ERP system via an interface. All of the retractors in BW-BPS are push retractors that are implemented in the form of planning functions. Therefore, they cannot be used directly in BW integrated planning. However, BW-BPS and BW integrated planning can access the same InfoCubes, which means that you can use BW-BPS to retract the data that you create in BW integrated planning.

Retraction steps when using BW-BPS

Make the following settings to enable cost center data retraction in our example:

- Create an InfoCube for retraction
- Maintain sender structure
- Define transfer rules for retraction (field assignment to UPS_RET_COPS structure)
- Create the planning area, planning level, planning function, and parameter group in BW-BPS (Transaction BPS0)

Figure 10.23 illustrates the interaction between the components.

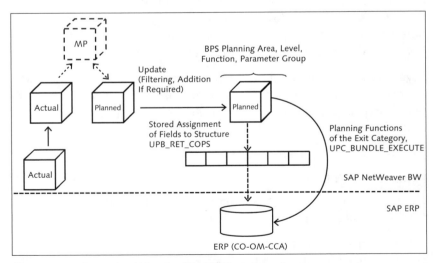

Figure 10.23 Retraction Using the BW-BPS Push Retractor

The first step — creating your own InfoCube for retraction — is optional. However, this approach to modeling has certain benefits. One benefit is increased flexibility, as more characteristics can be added, if needed, as the plan data is updated. Another is that with this approach, it is possible, under certain circumstances, to manage the scope of the transferred data, which is useful if you are using multiple plan versions but only one is relevant for retraction purposes, for example.

Once the planning process is complete, the retraction process runs as follows:

1. Planning activities are completed; a final plan version may be created.

2. In some cases, data is transferred to the retraction InfoCube.

3. A BW-BPS planning function is executed to retract the data. The planning function with the type Exit is started from within BW-BPS. This can either be done directly or by means of a batch job using program UPC_BUNDLE_EXECUTE. Business Application Programming Interfaces (BAPIs) are called in SAP ERP via a remote Function Call (RFC) connection to update the data.

Once these steps have been completed, you should check SAP ERP to make sure that all went according to plan (Transactions KP07 or KSBL).

Extracting the Plan Data as a Flat File

An alternative to using BW-BPS for retraction is to simply create a flat file and upload it to SAP ERP. Keep in mind, however, that directly extracting the data from an InfoCube is a little difficult to program due to the way the data is distributed across different tables. For the sake of flexibility, it makes sense to first transform the data in another DataProvider. Therefore, let us model this target as a DSO. The flat structure of a DSO can be easily read by a program. A file containing the plan data can be created on the application server, and this file can then be transferred to SAP ERP, either manually or automatically. Figure 10.24 shows the individual steps and components involved in transferring the plan data using a flat file.

Retraction by flat file

You can create a process chain to automate the process. The steps are as follows:

Retraction Steps for Extraction via DSO

1. Delete the content of the extraction DSO.

2. Close the request in the plan InfoCube so that the data can be extracted.

3. Load the data to the extraction DSO. You may also be able to filter out all of the data except the relevant plan version.

4. Extract the data to the extract file.

5. Change the plan InfoCube to suit the plan (if required).

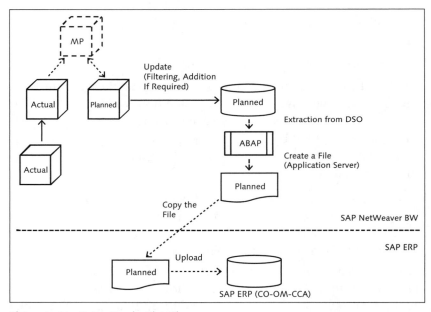

Figure 10.24 Retraction by Flat File

Export DSO content

Listing 10.3 contains a program for extracting plan data. It extracts the active data of a DSO to a flat file, and in doing so, exports all field content. The file thus created is saved on the application server. The file columns are fixed-length and are not comma separated.

```
REPORT Z_IP_EXTRACTION.
  DATA: l_s_PLANDAT_RET TYPE /BIC/AZPLA_RET00.
  DATA: l_th_PLANDAT_RET TYPE TABLE OF /BIC/AZPLA_RET00.
  DATA: l_f_FILE LIKE TSTRF01-FILE.
```

```
l_f_FILE = '/tmp/trans_i/PLAN_EXTRAKT.CSV'.
OPEN DATASET l_f_FILE FOR OUTPUT IN TEXT MODE ENCODING UTF-8.
SELECT * FROM /BIC/AZPLA_RET00
APPENDING CORRESPONDING FIELDS OF TABLE l_th_PLANDAT_RET.
LOOP at l_th_PLANDAT_RET into l_s_PLANDAT_RET.
  TRANSFER l_s_PLANDAT_RET TO l_f_FILE.
ENDLOOP.
CLOSE DATASET l_f_FILE .
END-OF-REPORT.
```

Listing 10.3   Program for Transferring Active DSO Data to a Flat File

Note that a license may be required to extract data from the BW system, depending on how you intend to use the data.

10.4.5 Transferring Subplans

In the previous section, we showed you a simple procedure for transferring plan data to a flat file so that the data could then be transferred to the operational system (SAP ERP).

If, on the other hand, the plan data is the result of a subplan and you intend to reuse it in another subplan, you have the task of transferring this data onto another planning application within the BW system. In this subsection, we assume that this planning application is also created using BW integrated planning.

Connecting subplans

In principle, transferring data by means of a transformation is not difficult; the source and target are modeled in the BW system. However, the work required to implement the plan data transfer can vary widely, depending on individual technical requirements and the way in which the data models are implemented in the IT system.

The following are some potential differences between the target data model and the source data model:

▸ The structure of the target data model is less detailed than the source.

▸ The target data model can contain other InfoObjects that the source does not provide (more details or different details).

▶ The target data model can be modeled in the account model, while the source uses the key figure model (or vice versa).

▶ Very different key figures may need to be planned in the target than in the source. However, it is possible to derive these from the source data using calculations of varying complexity.

The first point in the preceding list is usually straightforward; if you do not update the non-relevant characteristics, aggregation takes place automatically. Check that the totaling is correct in your case. You may have to map a different aggregation method.

Retrospectively reading data

If you want to add more InfoObjects to the data, you can do so by retroactively reading them as part of the update process. However, this is only easy to do if the relevant information is available in a 1:1 format. If the aggregation level of the data changes (to a higher level of detail), it is not always clear which characteristic instance is required. In such cases, you can either make no decision (assign #) or make a global assignment (for example, select one instance or opt for equal distribution across all instances).

[+] **Coordinating Data Models**

If you intend to set up an integrated planning scenario, we recommend that you pay particular attention to coordinating the data models. Otherwise, the models may well be insufficiently integrated, which makes it very difficult or even impossible to run global reports at a later stage. The crucial thing is that the same central objects are used to map the source and the target models, to the degree that is technically possible. You will also need to coordinate the level of detail of all of the interconnected planning models. This has two implications. One is that as many company departments as possible have to execute the same planning step in data models that use the same structure. The other is that even different subplans have to be coordinated in advance in such a way that enables them to be easily transferred to each other and that the results can be included in integrated reports.

Limits of unification

In the best-case scenario, you could create an enterprise data model (for our purposes, an InfoCube) to which all individual plans (and actual data, if required) are loaded and in which you could break down each key figure by all of the relevant characteristics. Although this level of full coordination is impossible to achieve in practice, it is useful to you as a theoretical ideal scenario when you are designing individual plans and want to lay the groundwork for subsequent planning steps ("start small, think big").

You should think carefully about which modeling approach (key figure or account model) you select. This is because the specific requirements of two sub-plans can lead to different models being used, and these will have to be integrated if data transfer is required. This can be done using the right algorithms without incurring any data loss.

Key figure model and account model

It is usually possible to further process key figures as part of an update process. Again, extensive programming may be required to derive the target key figure. In all cases, the aggregation behavior of the key figures has to be coordinated with the load procedure that you choose (see Chapter 4, Section 4.1.2, Key Figures, for more information).

Converting key figures

So what is the best way of designing the interface between two submodels so that the functionality required to transfer the subplans can be easily implemented? Figure 10.25 shows a possible solution.

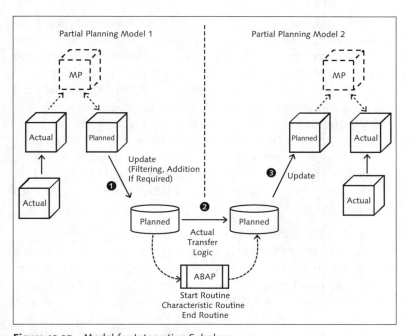

Figure 10.25 Model for Integrating Subplans

We recommend that you first load the data into a DSO rather than updating it directly from one InfoCube to another (except with very minor updates). This approach has the advantage that the update logic is divided into three clear steps:

▶ You have the opportunity in step ❶ to retroactively read data or filter out nonessential data in preparation of the actual transfer.

▶ When it comes to actually programming the transfer (step ❷), this approach gives you a simpler way (than if you were using an Info-Cube) to access the source data using a program. The logic can be distributed across the start routine, characteristic routine, and end routine in accordance with individual requirements.

▶ If there are any processing steps that need to be completed before the actual data transfer, these can be implemented in step ❸.

10.5   Conclusion

In this chapter, you learned how a data model is structured in BW integrated planning and how it can be integrated into the overall BW data model. We used fundamental modeling methods to separate data and to integrate it into a MultiProvider. The planning model is based on a BW data model. The more carefully you model the BW system, especially the master data, the less work is required to implement the planning scenario. If a specific area in your enterprise is already designed for actual data reporting, you may be able to implement an additional planning solution with comparatively little extra effort. The more subplanning processes that are to be integrated, the more work will be required, as the subplans have to be integrated with each other with varying degrees of automation.

If you are undecided about whether to use BW integrated planning or another tool, remember that BW integrated planning has the advantage that its planning projects will in all likelihood bring about an improvement in your BW data basis. This means that a (large) part of the investment creates benefits for more than just the planning solution. If you do decide to use another tool (for example, one with a user interface that you prefer) with its own data retention concept, the benefits of all your investment in data formatting may be restricted to that tool only. In this case, a better approach would be to format your data in BW, make the data available in the data propagation layer, and transfer it in this form to the third-party tool. You will still have to factor in the additional work required to write the externally created plan data back to the BW system, as only then can the plan data be used in BW reports.

The biggest advantage of BW integrated planning is its flexibility, as it is not confined to any one subject matter area; the content of the plan is what determines the underlying data model. Because there is no business content for BW integrated planning, the models (data model and planning model) have to be developed as part of the overall project. In some cases, the plan data model can be created on the basis of an actual data model of the Business Content.

You continuously need to optimize and enhance data retention and the data model to ensure the availability of information. This chapter shows you how to secure your investments in the SAP NetWeaver Business Warehouse (BW) data model for the long term, make them more economical, and adjust them to new requirements.

11 Optimizing Data Retention

Once you've completed your BW implementation project and put the system into operation, an enhancement or optimization requirement usually arises after a while:

▶ Due to the data growth, you must extend the disk space.

▶ The performance during staging or the query run exhibits a negative development.

▶ You want to implement new requirements that necessitate an adaptation of the data model.

When you structure a data model in BW you should consider the expected data volume. Frequently, it is not necessary to keep the data in BW for a very long time. The Information Lifecycle Management (ILM), which is described in Section 11.1, ILM, provides you with concepts for outsourcing data to various data media. In this chapter you will learn that you don't have to omit online availability, and how the outsourcing of data can result in savings and in improved performance in many cases.

To optimize performance, you usually have to make adaptations to the data model. Adaptations are also required if you want to align the data model with new requirements. To do this, BW includes tools that you can use to make adaptations and optimize the data model (see Section 11.2, Optimizing the Data Model).

11.1 ILM

Automated data administration

ILM doesn't refer to a specific product or technology. It rather entails a concept that strives to design processes and technologies of automated data administration in such a way that data can be managed according to specified guidelines, analog to its value and its intended use across its entire lifecycle on various storage media. The goal of ILM is to fully exploit the value of information that can be obtained from the data and minimize the costs associated with data storage at the same time.

High data volume

The amount of data stored in databases grows considerably every year. If you don't take any countermeasures, the considerable growth of the data volume in BW can result in problems. Examples include (see Schröder, 2009):

- ► Poor performance in staging (during data loading)
- ► Poor performance for the execution of queries (data analysis)
- ► A disproportionately increased time administration effort
- ► Growing requirements for the infrastructure (storage, backup, and so on)
- ► Continuously increasing costs for data retention

Countermeasures

Therefore, it is advisable to take countermeasures. BW comprises special functions that can be integrated seamlessly with the data model: the outsourcing of data to other (more cost-efficient) storage media while ensuring the online availability, the archiving, and, ultimately, the deletion of data.

Initially, Section 11.1.1, Data Lifecycle in SAP NetWeaver BW, presents the data lifecycle in SAP NetWeaver BW. In this context, different data require different strategies. Section 11.1.2, ILM for InfoCubes and DSOs, then considers the DataStore Objects (DSOs) and InfoCubes that are central in BW. Section 11.1.3, ILM for Master Data, outlines ILM for master data. Furthermore, Section 11.1.4, ILM for Change Log and Log Data, describes the change log and other log data, which involves data that continuously arises and needs to be managed. Finally, Section 11.1.5, ILM and LSA, discusses the modeling principles of Layered, Scalable Architecture (LSA) with regard to ILM.

11.1.1 Data Lifecycle in SAP NetWeaver BW

In a Data Warehouse (DWH) environment, data has a different meaning than in an SAP ERP system. The frequency of data access constantly decreases in the ERP system, while data in a DWH is relevant for a longer period of time. Most of the data accesses refer to the recent past, but an analysis of time series, trends, and strategic questions must access a longer history. Because the users can navigate freely within the scope of their authorizations and create their own analyses, it cannot be exactly defined later on which data was required when and by whom. Moreover, users frequently expect an ad hoc analysis so that data should not be needed to be re-imported due to the requirement of an archive. You must accommodate these specific requirements in an ILM concept.

Access frequency

Figure 11.1 illustrates that the appeal of data decreases considerably after some time. To answer special questions, data can still be significant enough that it must be accessed "occasionally." If a specific frequency of use for data is not maintained, cost/benefit considerations should lead to an outsourcing of the data.

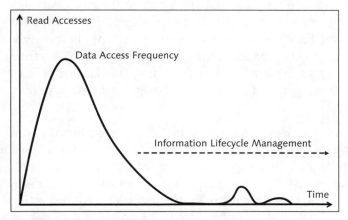

Figure 11.1 Time Line of Data Access Frequency

The time base is only one criterion based on which you can determine the (future) relevance of data. For example, consider the sale of enterprise parts: Here you have the task of finding a suitable storage option for data whose relevance has changed. In addition to analysis requirements, legal requirements can also dictate continued storage of data.

First phase in the relational model

The lifecycle of data starts with its transfer to the BW system. Already at this stage, phases are run that can be attributed to an enhanced data lifecycle: For example, you can delete data from the Persistent Staging Area (PSA) after you've completed quality assurance. Moreover, you can compress InfoCubes as soon as it is no longer required to access individual requests. The storage of data in the Reporting Layer can be implemented in various InfoCubes, for instance, organized by the age of the data.

Second phase — special storage solutions

You usually refer to ILM in the context of special technologies that let you outsource from the relational database. This outsourcing process should have two stages:

In the first stage, you can store data that is still occasionally accessed in a Nearline Storage (NLS) System. This can be followed by the archiving of data at a later time (second stage). The disadvantage of data archiving is that archived data first needs to be copied back to the relational database before you can analyze it.

Nearline storage

For the nearline storage of data in an NLS system, the data retention is outside the relational database; nevertheless data can still be accessed at any time. So data doesn't need to be copied back to the relational database prior to the analysis. NLS systems are provided by selected third parties. SAP has defined a standardized interface (NLS Application Programming Interface (API)) for connecting these systems. Such interfaces are used to integrate the various nearline storage media in BW. This enables an outsourcing of data to lower-cost storage media for InfoCubes and DSOs.

Archiving

In archiving, the system writes the data to a file system. Initially, you use the Archive Development Kit (ADK) to define which data is to be archived and how. Archiving objects are used for the exact description of the archiving process. This way, you determine which tables are supposed to be archived, how the data to be archived is selected, and where the archived data is supposed to be stored. The archived data can be transferred back to the BW System if required. However, this is not done automatically. Therefore, the archived data is not available to the end user initially.

Table 11.1 presents various ILM strategies.

Object Considered	Online Storage	Nearline Storage	Archiving	Deletion
Properties	Storage of data in the InfoProviders of BW	Storage of data in a nearline storage medium outside the database system	Storage of data outside the database system	Deletion of data without archiving
Storage medium	Database	Manufacturer-specific nearline storage media	Usually file system on the file server, tape backup, and so on	No medium required
Access type	Online	SQL access via API interface possible	Offline, no online access possible	Access no longer possible
Speed	Fast	Slower due to storage medium, also due to compression	Data must be loaded back to the BW system first	Recovery no longer possible

Table 11.1 Comparison of ILM Strategies (see Schröder, 2009)

11.1.2   ILM for InfoCubes and DataStore Objects

The significance of InfoCubes and DSOs for data retention in BW is very high; therefore, both the outsourcing to an NLS system and the archiving of data is possible for these InfoProviders. Beyond that you can also delete data. Usually, every outsourcing of data is followed by a deletion of data in BW.

You need to create a data archiving process as a prerequisite for archiving. This process forms the basis both for archiving and for the storage in an NLS system. You create the data archiving process using Transaction RSDAP. You first need to select the DataProvider (InfoCube or DSO) that is to be archived. Then, select EDIT to navigate to the maintenance of the data archiving process. Here, you specify whether it involves archiving (ADK) or storage in an NLS system (see Figure 11.2).

Data archiving process

If you select the ADK-BASED ARCHIVING option, the system generates an archiving object based on your specifications. By means of a SELECTION PROFILE you determine which characteristics are supposed to restrict archiving. Usually, you should select a time characteristic (see Figure 11.3), but other selection criteria are also possible. When you archive DSOs, you must ensure that only key fields are used as selection criteria.

Archiving object

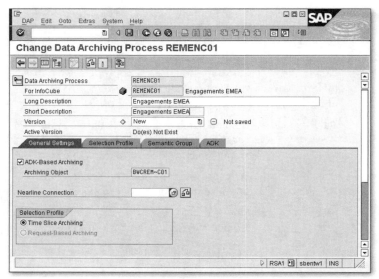

Figure 11.2 Create/Change Data Archiving Process

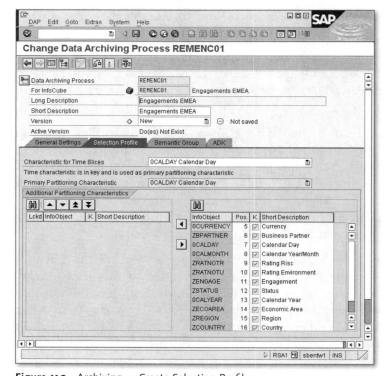

Figure 11.3 Archiving — Create Selection Profile

Via the SEMANTIC GROUP (Figure 11.4), you specify whether data is sup-   Semantic groups
posed to be stored with sorting. Sorting can be beneficial for the restore
if the restore is supposed to be performed partially selective.

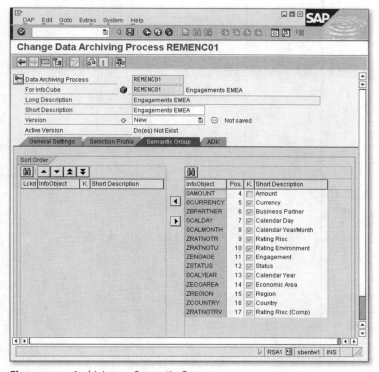

Figure 11.4 Archiving — Semantic Group

The last step for the definition of the ADK-based archiving specifies the
file storage (see Figure 11.5). Here, in the LOGICAL FILE NAME field, you
must enter a name that describes the archive files in the file server.

You can implement the archiving process in the ARCHIVING TAB, for
instance, in the InfoCube administration. This tab is only visible if you
created a data archiving process previously.

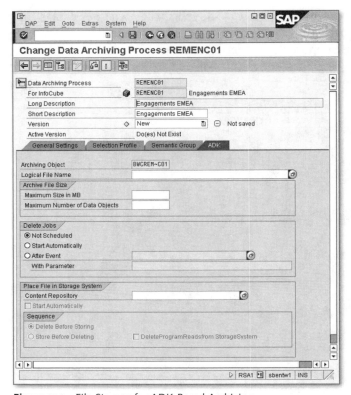

Figure 11.5 File Storage for ADK-Based Archiving

Deleting data The deletion of previously archived data is not automatic. After successful archiving, you can delete the data in Transaction SARA. To do this, specify the archiving object of the respective InfoProvider first. But the deletion via an archiving object in the context of archiving is not the only option for deleting data. As long as data hasn't been compressed yet, you can delete the InfoCube data separately for each request. In addition, selective deletion is also possible. You can find the SELECTIVE DELETION BUTTON with the function for selective deletion of data in the Content tab in the InfoCube administration. You can restrict the data to be deleted freely via the characteristics of the InfoProvider.

Restore Data that has been archived can be restored to the DataProvider of BW very flexibly (see Figure 11.6). The InfoProvider on which archiving was implemented is used as the logical data source for a data transfer process (DTP), which retrieves the data from the archive and writes it to a target via a transformation. This can involve the archived provider itself (restore in the original provider) or any other data target (restore in any targets). Therefore, the restore process doesn't correspond to a restore in the traditional sense because the data is not necessarily fully restored identically, that is, not exactly in the form as it was archived. Frequently, data only needs to be provided for a short period of time. In this case, it can be useful to provide them in the operational data store, for example. Because the restore from the archive is only possible if the InfoCube that was used for archiving is still available, you should check prior to deleting the InfoCube models to see if dependent archive data still exists.

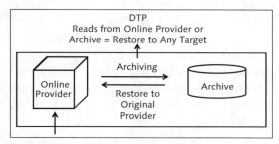

Figure 11.6 Integrating an Online Provider with Archiving in the Data Flow

11.1.3 ILM for Master Data

You can also delete the master data of an InfoObject. The prerequisite, however, is that the master data is no longer referenced by transaction data. To delete all master data, select the DELETE MASTER DATA menu item in the context menu of the InfoObjects. You can also delete individual data records in the master data maintenance. Hierarchies play a special role. Because they are not referenced directly, you can always delete them.

A concept for archiving the master data is not available in BW, however. If you also provide master data (in addition to the InfoObject) in DSOs, you can use the archiving function of the DSO to archive it.

11.1.4 ILM for Change Log and Log Data

Besides the actual user data (master and transaction data), which is stored in the various InfoProviders, in BW there are some additional datasets that must also be managed.

PSA and change log

You must interpret PSA and the change log as temporary datasets (the change log is also provided as PSA tables). If data was updated successfully, you can delete it. Accordingly, BW doesn't provide for an archiving of this data. You should therefore enhance your process chains by the appropriate deletion processes. To do this, use the process types, DELETE REQUESTS FROM PSA or DELETE REQUESTS FROM CHANGE LOG. You can also manually delete specific requests in the administration of PSA for a DataSource.

Monitoring information

With each extraction and loading process, you store monitoring information in the BW system. This information describes the status of the loading process and details about the parameterization and the status of the individual processing steps. The monitoring information is only of interest for a specific period of time until the corresponding request has been fully processed. Nevertheless, you cannot just delete monitoring information. At least the status information is repeatedly accessed at various occasions. Because the detail information is rather comprehensive, you have the option of archiving it. To do this, a predefined archiving object (BWREQARCH) is available.

Application logs

BW generates other logs in addition to the monitoring information. You can call the application log via Transaction SLG1. It enables events to be logged on an application or object basis. The logging, and therefore the evaluation, is implemented by objects and subobjects. You can only delete the application logs, not archive them. You delete them using Transaction SLG2. You can also use the SBAL_DELETE program.

Statistics data, Technical Content

The system stores statistics data in BW within the scope of data staging and for running queries. Technical Content of BW also uses this data (see Chapter 6, Business Content). Technical Content comprises extractors, data models, and reports. This way, you can conveniently evaluate the statistics data. An archiving of statistics data from the original tables is not provided, however. Therefore, you should delete it at regular intervals. If required, archiving is possible at the data models level of Technical Content.

11.1.5 ILM and LSA

The LSA presented in Chapter 5, 5
Reference Architecture for Data Modeling, already gives some clues on storing data and, consequently, for ILM as well.

At the Data Acquisition Layer, you store the data in PSA or in write-optimized DSOs. Usually, you immediately delete the data of this layer as soon as it is posted without any errors. In the Corporate Memory, this is different: Because data is supposed to be stored for the long term, it is recommended to use archiving or NLS solutions as alternatives. The prepared data of the Data Acquisition Layer is supposed to be available for the long term. Here as well the question arises as to whether archiving or another alternative storage option is supposed to be used.

Various requirements are possible at the Reporting Layer level. In most cases, these datasets include an appropriate history. Because data is supposed to be available ad hoc for reporting, it is recommended to use a nearline storage solution. In some scenarios, you can omit an outsourced storage. If the analysis horizon is not very large, you can store all relevant data in the InfoCubes. Moreover, if you model the Data Acquisition Layer appropriately, you can reload the data from this layer. However, such a strategy requires that the derivation rules of the Business Transformation Layer are stable and that the analysis doesn't need to be run ad hoc. If the data of the Reporting Layer must be provided for the long term and if the ad hoc availability is not a criterion, you can also use classic archiving.

Besides the reduction of the data volume in the DataProviders, an appropriate modeling of the DataProvider also contributes to an improved performance. There are special utilities for remodeling an existing data model that contains data. The following section discusses these utilities.

11.2 Optimizing the Data Model

It often becomes apparent after the fact that an actively used data model is unsuitable because either the functional requirements were not implemented optimally or they've changed. Performance problems are another reason for optimization. As long as a BW object doesn't contain any data yet, you can make changes without any problems. But if data is already loaded, many changes can no longer be implemented, or the data must be deleted and loaded again. In the production system, you must delete data before you import the corresponding transport including the changes because otherwise the transport would fail and changes cannot be made. But it is often no longer possible to reorganize the entire Info-

Cube or the system load would be too high to justify the changes. For this reason, BW also comprises a function for remodeling.

Besides this function, there are additional options to make data model changes. Table 11.2 provides an overview of these options.

Method	Advantages	Disadvantages
Deletion of data and re-initialize after change	Development effort is minimal, no adaptations to MultiProviders and queries necessary	System load due to re-initialization
Remodeling	Little development effort, no adaptations to MultiProviders and queries necessary	Must be run manually in all systems, otherwise risk of inconsistency; limited functionality in comparison to other options (for instance, for initial population of a new characteristic, only the characteristics of the same dimension are available — the level of detail cannot be changed)
New InfoCube: A new InfoCube is created in addition to the old InfoCube; data of the old InfoCube can be transferred via an additional transformation from the old InfoCube	Flexibility with regard to the amount of data of the old InfoCube that can be copied; all options are available, data doesn't need to be deleted (no reorganization required, validation can be designed flexibly)	Higher development effort, MultiProviders and queries must be adapted
Temporary auxiliary InfoCube: Data is loaded to a temporary InfoCube and deleted in the main InfoCube, changes to the data are implemented (transported) and data loaded back again	System load is possibly lower than in the reorganization from source data, possibly not all of the source data is still available, no adaptations to MultiProviders and queries necessary	Complex solution, corresponds to the remodeling functionality; however, it is implemented manually and without the restricted functionality

Table 11.2 Options for Implementing a Data Model Change

Out of these four alternatives, the deletion and reorganization of data is the standard method. In compliance with design guidelines, such as LSA, this flexibility should always be possible. Only if a reorganization is no longer possible due to data volume or the availability of the source data will you use one of the other alternatives. If a particularly high number of functional changes are necessary in the production system due to process changes, it may be useful to create a new InfoCube in BW.

11.2.1 Analyzing the Data Model

Besides changing functional requirements, data model changes can also be desirable due to a technical optimization. This primarily involves the data model of the BasicCubes and here, in turn, the level of detail and the dimension model.

You can obtain an initial overview of the data models of all InfoCubes using the SAP_INFOCUBE_DESIGNS program (see Figure 11.7).

Print a list of the cubes in the system and their layout

Print a list of the cubes in the system and their layout

0BWTC_C03	/BI0/D0BWTC_C031	rows:	2.664	ratio:	4	%
0BWTC_C03	/BI0/D0BWTC_C03P	rows:	3	ratio:	0	%
0BWTC_C03	/BI0/D0BWTC_C03T	rows:	32	ratio:	0	%
0BWTC_C03	/BI0/E0BWTC_C03	rows:	0	ratio:	0	%
0BWTC_C03	/BI0/F0BWTC_C03	rows:	63.673	ratio:	100	%
0BWTC_C04	/BI0/D0BWTC_C041	rows:	27	ratio:	23	%
0BWTC_C04	/BI0/D0BWTC_C04P	rows:	2	ratio:	2	%
0BWTC_C04	/BI0/D0BWTC_C04T	rows:	47	ratio:	39	%
0BWTC_C04	/BI0/E0BWTC_C04	rows:	0	ratio:	0	%
0BWTC_C04	/BI0/F0BWTC_C04	rows:	120	ratio:	100	%
0BWTC_C05	/BI0/D0BWTC_C051	rows:	2.144	ratio:	3	%
0BWTC_C05	/BI0/D0BWTC_C052	rows:	9.412	ratio:	15	%
0BWTC_C05	/BI0/D0BWTC_C055	rows:	13	ratio:	0	%
0BWTC_C05	/BI0/D0BWTC_C05P	rows:	3	ratio:	0	%
0BWTC_C05	/BI0/D0BWTC_C05T	rows:	536	ratio:	1	%
0BWTC_C05	/BI0/E0BWTC_C05	rows:	0	ratio:	0	%
0BWTC_C05	/BI0/F0BWTC_C05	rows:	63.083	ratio:	100	%
0BWTC_C09	/BI0/D0BWTC_C092	rows:	194	ratio:	101	%
0BWTC_C09	/BI0/D0BWTC_C09P	rows:	2	ratio:	1	%
0BWTC_C09	/BI0/D0BWTC_C09T	rows:	71	ratio:	37	%
0BWTC_C09	/BI0/E0BWTC_C09	rows:	0	ratio:	0	%
0BWTC_C09	/BI0/F0BWTC_C09	rows:	193	ratio:	100	%
0BWTC_C11	/BI0/D0BWTC_C112	rows:	401	ratio:	88	%
0BWTC_C11	/BI0/D0BWTC_C11P	rows:	2	ratio:	0	%
0BWTC_C11	/BI0/D0BWTC_C11T	rows:	48	ratio:	11	%
0BWTC_C11	/BI0/E0BWTC_C11	rows:	0	ratio:	0	%
0BWTC_C11	/BI0/F0BWTC_C11	rows:	457	ratio:	100	%
0TCT_C01	/BI0/D0TCT_C013	rows:	215	ratio:	1	%
0TCT_C01	/BI0/D0TCT_C018	rows:	31	ratio:	0	%
0TCT_C01	/BI0/D0TCT_C019	rows:	9.545	ratio:	50	%
0TCT_C01	/BI0/D0TCT_C01P	rows:	4	ratio:	0	%

Figure 11.7 Result of the SAP_INFOCUBE_DESIGNS Program

Dimension model
Due to the size of the dimension table, you must check the dimension model. You cannot avoid large dimensions in real life; but you should try to keep all dimensions as small as possible. Particularly avoid n:m relationships of characteristics within a dimension. Preferably, a dimension shouldn't exceed more than 10% of the records of the compressed fact tables. For larger InfoCubes with numerous characteristics, the distribution of characteristics in dimensions can be a tricky task, and due to the exponentially increasing number of options it is not possible to calculate the optimal design. Here, you simply require some knowledge of the data and the processes behind it — and some intuition.

Line items
When the ratio to the fact table reaches 20%, you should use a line item dimension. Line item dimensions can only contain one characteristic. Real line items, however, are usually compound characteristics — but compound characteristics are not permitted in a line item dimension either (compounds consist of several characteristics, and the individual characteristics are permitted; however, you then need several line item dimensions). It can be helpful to use a compound key instead of a compound. The most selective characteristics should be positioned at the beginning of a dimension, if possible. Only the first 16 characteristics of a dimension are supported via a B-tree index. Then the search of a DIM ID for a combination of SIDs is no longer supported via an index. So if a selective characteristic is used in one of the rear positions, this can have negative effects on the load performance.

Granularity
Furthermore, the performance is particularly influenced by the size of the fact table. With regard to content, this is referred to as granularity. For example, you could check to see if all characteristics were used in reporting or whether you could save some characteristics. You should check in particular whether single document characteristics exist in the InfoCube and whether you could also cover reporting via the DSO layer. Further improvement potential arises by omitting data to the day (0CALDAY).

You can also decrease the size of the fact table using an optimized key figure model, for example, by creating key figures for each currency instead of using the currency type. Cost element and accounts can be converted directly into key figures.

The compression removes the request ID from the data and it can have major influence on the size of the fact table depending on the data's nature. Therefore, you must also check in the analysis to see if compression occurs at regular intervals.

Logical partitioning is another option of optimization. Usually, data with very different characteristic values should not be merged into one InfoCube (for instance, planning and actual data). Moreover, you can achieve performance benefits due to the parallel query execution or due to lower data quantities. On the other hand, it is recommended to not add more than ten InfoCubes to a MultiProvider because the effort for linking the data would be too comprehensive.

Logical partitioning

| **Analyzing the InfoCube Data Model** | **[«]** |
| You can improve the data model by optimizing the dimension model and by reducing the granularity. | |

11.2.2 Changing the Fact Table

As long as an InfoCube contains data, various transformations are not permitted. It is necessary to either delete the data of the InfoCube or implement changes using the remodeling functionality. Deletion in this context means the deletion in the development system and then in the other systems respectively before the corresponding change is transported.

The following describes the various changes in the fact table:

▶ **Add characteristics**
It is always possible to add characteristics to a new or already-existing dimension. However, the new characteristic is initially for existing data. You can use the remodeling function to add a new characteristic to an existing table, which can be derived from the other characteristics of this dimension and whose granularity is not changed. To determine the new characteristic values, the options, FIXED VALUE, ATTRIBUTES, 1:1, and CUSTOMER EXIT, are available. In the customer exit, you must work with the SID values. The exit must be implemented as a class of the IF_RSCNV_EXIT interface (Transaction SE24). To convert SID values into characteristic values and vice versa, you are provided with the function modules, RRSI_SID_VAL_SINGLE_CONVERT and RRSI_VAL_SID_SINGLE_CONVERT. Examples for which the remodeling with new characteristic values seems useful include time charac-

teristics that have not existed in the InfoCube yet (for example, the quarter that can be derived from the month) or different accounts that are supposed to be compared with other accounts in a MultiProvider.

▶ **Delete characteristics**
The deletion of characteristics is not permitted in populated Info-Cubes. However, you can use the remodeling functionality to delete a characteristic even if the InfoCube is populated. If the granularity has changed due to the deletion of a characteristic, this results in multiple dimension records. These are not automatically deleted by the remodeling function. Therefore, you must run the repair in Transaction RSRV for MULTIPLE ENTRIES IN THE DIMENSIONS OF A (BASIC) INFO-CUBE.

▶ **Change navigation attributes**
You can activate and deactivate navigation attributes at any time. Their additional activation is basically completely harmless; nevertheless, some dependent objects are deactivated that should then be activated again. Removing navigation attributes can affect MultiProviders and queries if the navigation attributes are still required.

▶ **Add key figures**
You can always add new key figures. However, a new key figure is initial for existing data. Using the remodeling function lets you define a fixed value or populate the new key figure via a user exit. You must create the user exit just like the user exit for new characteristics. In the input structure, however, you are provided with the DIM IDs and not the SID. Alternatively, you can create a new transformation for a new key figure; this transformation only updates the new key figure, for example, recursive from the existing InfoCube.

▶ **Delete key figures**
Deletion of key figures is only possible for empty InfoCubes or via the remodeling function.

▶ **Change partitioning**
You should add partitions at regular intervals so that new data is not loaded to the marginal partition. However, if you forget to do so, you can retroactively change the partitioning via repartitioning (via the menu path INFOCUBE • OTHER FUNCTIONS • REPARTITIONING). Such changes are not transported and must be implemented manually in all systems.

▶ **Change clustering**
You can change the clustering using the reclustering function. Like remodeling, reclustering is not transported, and you must implement it in all systems otherwise inconsistencies will arise.

▶ **Retroactive zero elimination**
Zero values are usually removed in compression. However, you can set this option on or off. If zero values were not deleted at compression, you have the option of deleting them using the RSCDS_NULLELIM program.

Remodeling the Fact Table   **[«]**

Adding new characteristics without a re-initialization is only possible to a limited extent. The remodeling function is particularly useful for deleting characteristics and key figures.

11.2.3 Changing the Dimension Model

As was already described in Section 11.2.1, Analyzing the Data Model, the optimization of the dimension model is an essential task for the technical optimization of an InfoCube. The remodeling function always refers to individual dimensions or the fact table, that is, a redesign of the dimension model is not supported by the remodeling function. Section 11.2 presented the alternative options of remodeling.

The following describes the various changes to the dimension model:

▶ **Add a dimension**
You can always add a new dimension (until you reach the maximum number of 16 dimensions). This applies to both normal dimensions and line item dimensions.

▶ **Delete a dimension**
You can only delete a dimension in the case of an empty InfoCube and deletion is not supported by the remodeling function.

▶ **Change the order of characteristics**
You can always change the characteristic order within a dimension. This order is important because only the first 16 characteristics are indexed. It is recommended to position the most selective characteristics at the beginning.

> ▶ **Change dimension assignment of characteristics**
> In the case of populated InfoCubes you have the option of moving characteristics within a dimension (that is, the order of characteristics), but not to another dimension. This is the essential task of a remodeling. To do this, it is mandatory to delete the InfoCube content.
>
> ▶ **Change indexing of dimension tables**
> You can change the indexing of a dimension at any time. You set the indexing using the HIGH CARDINALITY flag. If you set this flag, the system uses a B-tree index instead of a bitmap index. Because you cannot use the B-tree index in star joins, you should only use it in exceptional cases.
>
> ▶ **Line item classification**
> It is not possible to turn a line item dimension into a normal dimension or vice versa if the InfoCube includes data.
>
> ▶ **Delete dimension entries**
> Due to deletion of requests, selective deletion, zero value elimination, and archiving, dimension entries can occur that are no longer required. These processes can also cause the dimension tables to become larger than the fact table itself. You can delete entries that are no longer required using Transaction RSRV. If this type of deletion process is supposed to be implemented periodically and automatically, you can use the RSDRD_DIM_REMOVE_UNUSED function module for this purpose.

[»]   **Remodeling the Dimension Model**

The remodeling of the dimension model is not supported by the remodeling function. Therefore, changes to the dimension model always require a re-initialization of the InfoCube data.

11.2.4 Changing DSOs

Also, for DSOs, it can be necessary to implement retroactive changes. Adding additional fields is often required. Unfortunately, for DSOs the system doesn't provide a remodeling function like for InfoCubes. This is particularly annoying for deleting fields.

The following describes the various changes of a DSO:

- **Add fields**

  You can always add fields — both in the key and in the data area. The fields are initial at first. But because data fields in the DSO are over-written anyway, you can still load these fields later on.

- **Delete fields**

  You can only delete fields if the DSO doesn't contain any data. So you should carefully consider whether deletion is absolutely necessary. If there are functional reasons why a field must be deleted, you should also think about setting the field to initial.

- **Change the key**

  If you determine that you've selected the wrong key of a DSO, you usually don't have to ask whether deletion is required because the data is incorrect from the functional perspective anyway. Adding is usually possible and applies after the change has been made. Because a change document (or a reposting) with a noninitial value of the additional key field would result in a new entry, a change without re-initialization only makes sense in very special cases. Deleting key fields and changing key fields to data fields or vice versa is only possible for empty DSOs.

- **Change order**

  You can also change the key and data fields if data is loaded.

- **Change type**

  You can only change the DSO type if the DSO doesn't contain any data.

- **Change SID generation**

  SID generation presents a high system load for large DSOs and you should only use it if a DSO is used frequently for reporting. You can activate or deactivate SID generation at any time.

Remodeling of DSOs

You cannot change the DSO type or the key for loaded data. But such changes are so fundamental that a reload is required anyway. The deletion of fields is the only change that is not supported but would be practical.

[«]

11.2.5 Changing InfoObjects

This section outlines changes to the InfoObjects themselves. If changes to the key figures and characteristics cannot be implemented, and if such a change is absolutely necessary in the InfoCube, you can replace a key figure or a characteristic using the remodeling function.

Key figures
To change a key figure, it is important to know if they've been used already (for instance, in an InfoCube). For key figures you can only change the exception aggregation later on, that is, after they've been used already.

Characteristics
You cannot delete characteristic data as easily as transactional data. To make all of the changes, the SID tables must be empty. This is only possible if you've previously deleted all of the InfoCubes and DSOs in which the relevant characteristic is used. But this is absolutely impossible for many characteristics. You can also make the following changes to characteristics if SID entries exist:

▶ **Change key**
You can extend the key retroactively and permit lowercase letters.

▶ **Attribute only**
You can deactivate the ATTRIBUTE ONLY setting retroactively.

▶ **Master data, texts, and hierarchies**
You can activate and deactivate master data, texts, and hierarchies retroactively.

▶ **Time dependency, language dependency**
You can retroactively activate the time dependency for attributes, and the time and language dependency for texts; however, a retroactive deactivation is not possible. The time dependency of navigation attributes must be assessed as very critical from a performance perspective. Because a retroactive change for active time and language dependency is not possible, you should think twice about making this setting.

▶ **Activate navigation attributes**
You can retroactively activate and deactivate navigation attributes at any time.

▶ **Change compound**
You can extend the compound retroactively, but you cannot remove a compound.

▶ **Change conversion routine**
You can always change the conversion routine; however, a retroactive change for some conversion routines that force an internal presenta-

tion can result in inconsistencies — this includes the following conversion routines: ALPHA, NUMC, and GJAHR. Previously, a special transaction existed to implement the data conversion (RSMDEXITON), which is no longer available since BW Release 7.

11.2.6 Remodeling Function

The remodeling function for InfoCubes lets you make changes to loaded objects that would normally only be possible for empty objects. The functional scope is rather concise in this context; moreover, you must take some general conditions into account. The following is supposed to present options, specific features, and the process flow.

You call the remodeling function via Transaction RSMRT (see Figure 11.8) or via the Data Warehousing Workbench (Transaction RSA1).

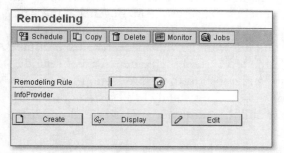

Figure 11.8 Initial Screen of the Remodeling Function — Transaction RSMRT

In Transaction RSMRT, you can create the remodeling rules; with a remodeling rule you can perform the following actions:

- Add a characteristic/key figure
- Delete a characteristic/key figure
- Replace a characteristic/key figure

You have the following options to derive new characteristics:

- Via a constant
- Via an attribute of another characteristic of the same dimension
- 1:1 from another characteristic of the same dimension

► Via a customer exit that can only process characteristics of the same dimension

You cannot increase the granularity here. If the granularity is decreased, this results in multiple entries in the dimension table, which must be cleansed.

New key figures can only be populated via a constant and a customer exit. Unlike characteristics, key figures are not key fields and there is nothing speaking against reposting an InfoCube in itself, whereas only the new key figures are updated and all other key figures remain unchanged. Technically, this is easier to implement than to work with the remodeling function, and it doesn't entail any of the disadvantages (for example, lack of transport support) which are described here for remodeling.

The remodeling rule can be scheduled as a job or executed directly. You can also transport the remodeling rule. However, you must schedule the implementation of the remodeling in every system. In general, the same strategy applies as usual, that is, development of the remodeling rules in the development system, unit test with individual data records, transport of the remodeling rules in the test system, implementation of remodeling and reconciliation tests, and transport to the production system. It is essential to implement the changes consistently in all systems otherwise inconsistencies would arise and the InfoCubes affected could no longer be transported.

To avoid errors during implementation, it is important to plan all of the relevant process chains in detail.

After the remodeling has been implemented, you must activate the deactivated objects again. To do this, you can use the activation programs, which are listed in Section 11.2.7, Activation Programs. You may need to adapt queries manually.

Summary — remodeling function
The most critical remodeling task, that is, the change of the dimension schema (by optimizing the dimension schema you can achieve considerable performance improvements), is not supported by the remodeling function. The option of deleting characteristics and key figures, in particular, is very handy.

11.2.7   Activation Programs

Retroactive changes (for instance, using the remodeling function) often have the result that dependent objects are set to inactive. Frequently, there is no comprehensible reason for this. Moreover, the changes that resulted in setting the objects to inactive cannot be determined easily. The activation usually requires a new transport; for a direct activation in the production system, you would have to open the system. By means of the activation programs, you can activate objects without a transport.

The following activation programs are used to activate InfoCubes, Info-Objects, MultiProviders, DSOs, DataSources, transfer structures, and transformations:

- RSDG_CUBE_ACTIVATE
- RSDG_IOBJ_ACTIVATE
- RSDG_MPRO_ACTIVATE
- RSDG_ODSO_ACTIVATE
- RSAOS_DATASOURCE_ACTIVATE
- RS_TRANSTRU_ACTIVATE_ALL
- RSD6_TRFN_ACTIVATE (see SAP Note 1408161)

11.3   Conclusion

The numerous optimization functions in BW offer manifold design options, whose usage should be scheduled and implemented in a targeted manner. You should think about the expected data volume at an early stage and systematically outsource data that is not used at all or only occasionally as appropriate (NLS or archive). This can also result in a considerable reduction of data retention costs.

You should test the data model with a larger, representative dataset before you implement it. In doing so, you can ensure that you don't have to implement a remodeling within a very short period of time. But you should reckon that you have to revise the data model in the medium to long term and in particular the dimensioning of InfoCubes. The most flexible way to respond is if you can re-initialize the dataset.

Here, the Data Propagation Layer within LSA serves as the data source. The remodeling function for InfoCubes can be used in special cases, and it can prevent you from having to reorganize the dataset. New InfoObjects can be derived from other characteristics or key figures. However, the function is not suitable for redimensioning. Remodeling of DSOs is not supported until BW Release 7.1.

This chapter deals with the special aspects of data modeling in Business Warehouse (BW) projects. It introduces the functional requirements to discuss which issues you must consider in the data model.

12 Specific Data Modeling Issues in BW Projects

The analytical data model is often considered the core of the Data Warehouse. It is not only about developing a system with a predefined quantity of reports but also about meeting the challenge of fully utilizing the analytical options for creating new reports and ad hoc queries.

You usually document the functional requirements for a data model in a technical concept. This chapter first presents the most important general conditions for BW projects and then demonstrates their relevance for the data model by clarifying some functional issues. Finally, some of the technical aspects are discussed.

12.1 General Conditions

This section introduces various general conditions that are relevant to the creation of a BW data model in BW projects.

While the implementation of an operational system involves a strict role distribution, the responsibilities in a BW project are less clearly defined. For operational systems, the end users usually define the requirements and the functional consultants carry out the Customizing and write specifications, which are then implemented by ABAP programmers.

Responsibilities in the BW project

The three main tasks for implementing a BW system are extraction/data staging, data modeling, and reporting. Because the tools for creating reports are easy to manage, it is common practice that the users create new queries themselves and even that the user departments are responsible for the entire reporting area. In this case, the data model (especially the MultiProvider description) is the actual interface between information technology (IT) and users.

Sponsorship and project initiative

The fact that most of the BW projects are implemented together with other SAP projects may indicate that the department representatives do not necessarily have to be the system's sponsors but that BW should be introduced in a larger overall project.

Even though the departments are not the direct initiators of the BW project (or of the subproject), it is critical to make sure early on that the necessary specialist knowledge for the project will be available to answer functional questions relating to the data model. This is not always the case.

Project organization

There are two basis ways to organize a BW project: a division into back-end and front-end areas or a division by subject areas. In this context, data modeling itself is the interface of the other areas and it is only organized as a specific subteam in very large projects.

Division into front end and backend

In some projects it can be useful to clearly separate reporting (Multi-Provider upwards) from data staging (InfoCube and DataStore Object (DSO)). In this case a subteam is responsible for data staging, from the extraction to the provisioning of physical InfoProviders, and another team is responsible for reporting, that is, from the creation of the Mul-tiProvider to the creation of reports. This kind of division requires good coordination and a detailed definition of the data model.

Division by subject area

You can also use a division by subject area to organize the project. In such cases, a BW consultant is responsible for a subject area, from extraction to reporting. This kind of project organization is usually the most effective because considerably less coordination effort is required than for the previously described division of responsibilities. For such a division of labor, the project lead must ensure an adequate documentation of the data model.

Figure 12.1 shows the various options for organizing the project.

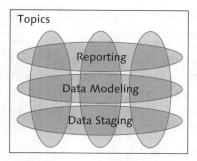

Topics

Reporting

Data Modeling

Data Staging

Figure 12.1 Options for Organizing the Project

When selecting the project organization type, bear in mind the following:

Criteria for selecting the project organization type

At the beginning of the selection process you have to make sure the technical capabilities of the individual developers are sufficient to cover all of the necessary subject areas. For example, complex extractors and transformations require good ABAP or ABAP Objects knowledge. For individual web reporting developments, developers with Java experience are required. In addition, some projects also require module knowledge in the operational system. Sometimes user departments want to develop the reports in their own department, that is, you have to distinguish between front end and backend.

A BW implementation doesn't just require developing new reports. Instead, it is also critical to sensitize the project sponsor and departments for the definition of the conceptual data models, because they determine the long-term options for developing new reports and power users can develop their own (ad hoc) queries.

The requirements for the quality of the data model's documentation depend on the division of tasks on one hand and on the departments' involvement on the other. Based on the initial technical situation, the following sections describe the issues affecting the data model.

12.2 The BW Functional Specification

The first step in the BW project is to prepare clear reporting requirements in cooperation with the departments within the requirements analysis.

These requirements need to be defined in the functional specification that lays the foundation for the definition of the data model.

Generally, you can write one functional specification for each report or one functional specification for an entire project. However, it makes more sense to write a functional specification for each subject area. In real life, this functional specification often corresponds to one MultiProvider or at least to a manageable number of them.

Content of the functional specification

The functional specification should contain the following:

► The process description and the identification of the business issues
► The content-related description of the transformation of characteristics
► The content-related description of the key figures
► The description of the data model
► The definition of reports or of the user interface (for example, for complex web developments)
► Time aspects of data load processes and data retention

Further subject areas in the context of functional requirements are authorizations and validation. In real life, you usually define authorizations in the authorization concept and the validation process in test case descriptions or in the system manual; both subject areas affect data modeling.

The following sections describe the individual subjects, which are relevant to data modeling in BW projects, in more detail.

12.2.1 Process Description and Business Issues

To ensure that the issues of the functional specification are understood by everyone involved in the project, you need a rough process description and content-related key figure description.

Documentation of the functional requirement

These descriptions are frequently only discussed and not documented in writing. The disadvantage here is that neither the departments nor IT can refer to clear statements. Apart from that, a functional specification is also a critical documentation for new employees, for further developments, or for support. If you don't document the business scenario, your only option is to deduce the aspects from the coding and data model. A missing process description can lead to conflicts and delays in implementation.

The functional specification, instead, doesn't require descriptions of the business case or similar — this kind of description is often used in real life but is not very useful in this context. A description should be concrete but not too detailed. The description should provide information on the target group of the reports and list the issues that need to be clarified. The process description should be very rough; however, it makes sense to include concrete transactions and table names, if required. References to specifications in the operational system are also very helpful.

If available, you may also include ER models (see Chapter 2, Basic Principles of Data Modeling) from the operational system in the description for a better explanation of the data basis.

12.2.2 Functional Description of the Transformation of Characteristics

BW imports characteristics from operational systems. However, this is not done on a one-to-one basis; instead, the characteristics are transformed first, for example, to compare data from different sources or create a format that is more appropriate for reporting purposes.

The functional description should also document in detail how the characteristics are supposed to be attained. You should document the following for all required characteristics (master data, texts, and hierarchies):

Documenting the characteristics

▶ **Source in the operational system**
You have to define from which source the system is supposed to read the master data for the respective characteristic or from which source the system is supposed to read the characteristic in the context of a transaction. In the simplest case, the respective characteristic is already available in the BW system, and the context is clear (for example, a default field in Business Content). In such cases, it is sufficient to design the definition as follows: "Use of an existing characteristic, update 1:1." If a characteristic is not available in the BW system yet, you should use a screenshot in the operational system to describe the context. You can also describe the table name and the table field. However, it may not be obvious to the user what this exactly means.

For master data, texts, and hierarchies, you should list the corresponding source.

▶ **Mapping the data**
In many cases, BW is supposed to map characteristics. Often, data from different systems is supposed to be converted into the same unit to compare the data in the report. Characteristics are frequently too detailed in the operational system so that they cannot be used in reporting, or you want to generate completely new characteristics, for example, by combining multiple characteristics.

You have to define the concrete mapping rules in the technical specification.

12.2.3 Functional Description of the Transformation of Key Figures

For key figures you must document the determination rules and restrictions. The logic of the transformation for key figures can be implemented at various places. This decision, however, is subject to the system-technical implementation and shouldn't be discussed in the functional specification in advance. As already mentioned in the context of the general conditions, the functional specification is the interface between IT and the user department if the reports are basically developed by the user department itself. In this case, you should define in the functional concept which key figures are supposed to physically exist.

Documenting key figures

You should document the following for all key figures required:

▶ **Source in the operational system**
Here, too, the simplest case is a one-to-one assignment of a key figure to a value from the operational system. You should also use screenshots (if it makes sense) to describe new values for key figures if these values can be interpreted differently.

▶ **Determinations and restrictions of the key figures**
A lot of key figures are either determined or derived from the various selections for characteristics. You should describe the determinations and restrictions in the functional specification independent of the logical and physical implementation.

An essential aspect in multidimensional modeling is the use of the account and key figure model. When describing the key figures in the functional specification, you shouldn't define any specifications for this purpose, that is, you shouldn't define if a key figure is supposed to physically exist or if it is supposed to be defined as a restricted or calculated key figure. A reason for a large number of key figures is often the fact that characteristic restrictions are already described as separate key figures. You can probably omit the description of key figures that are solely used to restrict characteristics and are thus not required for further calculations. On the other hand, a pure account model with just two physical key figures (value and quantity) is hard to describe from a functional perspective.

Often, key figures are also documented in a separate Microsoft Excel document. You should not only specify the source and determination of the key figures in a large table but also the MultiProviders that should contain the key figure and the characteristics that need to be available for these key figures.

12.2.4 Data Model in the Functional Specification

The functional specification should describe the conceptual data model. The description of the logical model in BW, however, differs from other Data Warehouse (DWH) systems due to the strict system specifications.

Although you don't usually use SAP terminology for logical descriptions, you should clarify if the logical level shouldn't be identical to the MultiProvider level or if you shouldn't describe the MultiProvider instead of the model.

MultiProviders in BW are virtual objects that combine data from various sources in the BW system and provide it for reporting. Therefore, MultiProviders separate the physical data retention from the logical user view.

MultiProvider

The MultiProvider level is the level that you have to use for creating reports. It is the level that report developers and backend developers have to define and the lowest level that should be specified by the departments. Technically, it is possible to develop BW reports directly at the physical level; however, this should only be done in exceptional cases, for example, for data validation purposes.

Other reasons for a comprehensive and high-quality description of MultiProviders are that the concrete definition of a MultiProvider takes place in the backend (that is, in the Data Warehousing Workbench), that a front-end user cannot normally access the backend, and that the definition of the MultiProvider is not clear from a front-end perspective (that is, the information from which physical source a characteristic or a key figure has been imported).

If the MultiProvider description is an essential interface in the project organization, you should also define this data model in the functional specification.

The conceptual data model is the description of the content-related level of a star schema. Therefore, it does not discuss the special aspects of BW, but describes the requirements in the real world. For this type of data model, you should use the ADAPT method, which was detailed in Chapter 2, Section 2.3, Modeling Methods. The creation of this kind of diagram is very complex, which is why it can be sufficient to alternatively list all characteristics and key figures for a reporting area and describe the special aspects.

MultiProvider description   For practical reasons, it seems to make sense to include the MultiProvider description instead of a conceptional data model. Because the departments are sometimes responsible for creating queries and because employees in the departments can often create their own queries, it is only reasonable to consider the MultiProvider definition a part of the functional specification. However, in real life you don't normally use a special description method. In most cases, you draw a simple star diagram with the fact table in the center and all dimensions around it or you settle for a list in tabular form.

12.2.5 Reporting/User Interface

An essential part of the functional specification is the description of all reports and of the user interface for complex front-end developments (for example, using web reporting).

Checking the front-end tools   The BW reporting tools are subject to some critical restrictions, which you should consider during the data modeling process. It is inevitable that an experienced BW reporting developer checks the report definitions against the suggested data models. Eventually, the data models must be enhanced in order to address the reporting needs. Otherwise, you run the risk that the reporting requirements are data-technically implemented but cannot be evaluated by the front-end tools (see Chapter 3, Section 3.2.2, Overview of Reporting and Analysis Using SAP NetWeaver BW). This can be a problem if the reporting development is organizationally separated from data provisioning and data modeling and thus described in its own technical specification. In this case, considerably more coordination effort is necessary, or the reporting development process requires comprehensive data modeling knowledge.

You must know the exact report definitions to create the data model and modify the data model in such a way that it fulfills all reporting requirements.

Checking concrete reporting requirements

12.2.6 Time Aspects of Data Load Processes and Data Retention

Already within the technical concept, you should address essential issues regarding the time aspects of data load processes and data retention. It is necessary to clarify the following issues:

▶ **Evaluation frequency and level**

▶ How often is the data supposed to be accessed and with which level of detail?

▶ Is it mainly data for ad hoc evaluations or do you expect accesses via standard reports at a very rough details level on a regular basis? Statistics data of an upstream system might provide information on the expected user behavior.

▶ **Data retention period**

▶ Do you mainly access the current year, or do you compare the years?

▶ How long is data supposed to be available even if it is rarely accessed?

▶ Can the level of detail be reduced for older data?

For planning data, you must also clarify how long it is supposed to be loaded for, how often it needs to be updated, and how long historical planning data is supposed to be available.

The data retention period management is discussed from a BW perspective using the term *data lifecycle* (see Chapter 11, Section 11.1, ILM).

▶ **Historical data**

Is historical data required? This refers to the data prior to the system implementation or system enhancement (particularly in the case of a combined implementation with an operational application) and not to the data retention period. You may have to develop specific extractors in a legacy system to do this, and additional data mapping is necessary. If it only involves a new reporting subject, historical data is transferred during the initialization of the data load process. Here, you also have to specify the extent of the history.

▶ **View of the past**

Is the view of the past supposed to be based on today's assignment? Are retroactive changes in operational processes possible, and if so, how are these changes supposed to affect reporting?

The different views of the historical data are a core issue of data modeling in BW.

▶ **Definition of the load cycle**

How soon must data be available? The data in the BW system is usually loaded every night. Critical data may also be required for immediate reporting. You can achieve this with short load cycles (in this case, however, data dependencies mustn't exist, for example, on master data) or with direct access to the operational system (real-time reporting). Nevertheless, there are critical disadvantages (performance, system load) to all of the options mentioned, which is why you should only use the options from the BW system for real-time reporting in exceptional cases. In general, you should implement such reporting requirements directly in the operational system.

It can be desirable that the user department itself can trigger the load process, for example, after the definition of planning or budget data or after closing postings. To do this, you can assign the corresponding authorizations for starting process chains to a limited user group. Unfortunately, BW doesn't deliver a user-friendly transaction for this function. That is, the respective user must deal with the very complex backend transaction. In projects, transactions are frequently written that only allow for starting individual process chains and indicate when a process is completed.

Weekly, monthly, quarterly, and even annual interfaces are also commonly used. Weekly interfaces, for example, can often be found for rarely changing, not critical[1] master data. The weekend is a generous time window. You should therefore try to implement load processes that are not necessarily daily but only required once a week. Monthly and annual interfaces are mainly used for data from external data providers, for example, market share data, economic data, or survey data.

Best Practices for Time Aspects   **[+]**

The following Best Practices have proven useful in real life:

▸ **Evaluation frequency and data model**
Evaluation frequency plays a major role for physical data modeling. However, it is difficult to make useful statements regarding the evaluation frequency in advance. Continuous system monitoring in the production system is much more important.

▸ **Data retention and data model**
In this context, a clear perception of the actual requirements and a sophisticated concept can lead to very good solutions, for example, a detailed month cube for the last months and separate cubes with tiered granularity for older periods. Chapter 9, Case Studies, and Chapter 11, Optimizing Data Retention, discuss the corresponding solutions.

▸ **Data model for historical data**
It usually makes sense to create specific cubes for legacy data, because this data often doesn't cover the entire range of characteristics and key figures.

▸ **Load cycle**
In BW, the data is normally loaded daily (overnight). But you always have to check with the departments if this is sufficient. You should implement real-time reporting requirements in the operational system if possible.

12.2.7 Authorization

In general, you distinguish between three authorization levels in BW:

▸ **Transactional authorization and usage**
Is BW supposed to be accessed via the Web, using Microsoft Excel, via SAP BusinessObjects, or with other tools, and which authoriza-

---

1 BW normally refers to critical master data as master data that must be available for lookups in transformations in subsequent data load processes. If such master data is missing, the data can no longer be validated, which often requires time-consuming reloading (or even reinitialization).

tions are the users supposed to have? In this context, you have to distinguish between power users and reporting users; power uses are usually authorized to create their own reports (locally, that is, directly in the production system).

▶ **Menu authorization**
In the menu authorization, the individual users are assigned the reports that are relevant for them. In BW, you can only control this via roles using Transaction PFCG under MENU; hence the term *menu authorization*. The first release of BW provided a specific Enterprise catalog and the issuing of reports was technically separated from general SAP authorizations, which definitely had its benefits. If you use BusinessObjects, this level corresponds to InfoViews and is therefore not included in the authorization management.

▶ **Analysis authorization (authorization for data)**
Which data view is the individual user supposed to have? You control this authorization type using Transaction RSECADMIN.

From a data model perspective, only the analysis authorizations are relevant. Most of the authorization requirements do not lead to data model adjustments. However, there are some requirements that necessitate specific modeling. The following sections discuss some examples of these.

Suppressing the details level
The most common requirement is the suppression of an evaluation at the details level. Basically, analysis authorizations work as follows: You define that a characteristic is relevant for the authorization and then assign either "*" (all), ":" (aggregated only), or concrete values. ":" is particularly important here. Without ":", you are authorized to view all of the values contained in the analysis authorization and evaluate them using this characteristic. You're not authorized to view all of the other data, that is, each report for the respective characteristic can be limited to authorized values only. Because it is a characteristic at the details level, this can include thousands, even millions of values, which leads to significant performance problems. With ":", you cannot carry out an evaluation for these characteristics but for all other characteristics. Let's assume that we are dealing here with the *employee* and *salary* characteristics. The user with the authorization for *employee* (":") cannot use the *employee* characteristic for evaluation purposes but can find information about the salaries of employees, which he is not supposed to view, by means of other characteristics.

Here, too, you need to bear in mind that the assignment of authorizations for higher characteristics (":") does not suppress the option of an evaluation at the details level. It is possible that names or number ranges enable the user to draw undesired conclusions. Furthermore, the user can also view display attributes. In most projects, however, no or hardly any authorizations for display attributes are assigned. Users can obtain detail data with display attributes and format it in Microsoft Excel (pivot tables).

A useful option for suppressing the details level efficiently is to use an additional data model (InfoCube) that no longer contains the desired detail information. This not only increases the performance but also enables you to mask detailed data that is supposed to remain confidential. This strategy is ideal if the volume of critical data is predefined (for example, critical orders, salaries of the executive board, etc.). That means you can assign a "*" authorization without any problems, because the detailed data does not exist or exists solely in an additional object that only a few employees can access.

Especially in Human Resources (HR) areas, the requirements for authorizations are frequently very complex and can only be fulfilled elegantly when being considered in the data model.

Another issue that you may need to consider in the data model is multidimensional authorizations. Multidimensional authorizations are authorizations for one characteristic respectively, depending on one or more other characteristics. For example, user X is authorized to view the sales figures for product 1 in region A and the sales figures for product 2 in region B. In real life, this kind of requirement often exists in relation to an organizational characteristic and a time characteristic, that is, authorizations are only supposed to be assigned for certain time periods and not for the entire past.

Multidimensional authorizations

An essential restriction of the Business Explorer (BEx) Query Designer is that it doesn't allow you to define OR links for restrictions (thus for different characteristics). Therefore, authorization variables don't work in this case, which leads to a critical restriction. A common alternative here is to introduce an additional characteristic with a composite key field. For example, the first four characters refer to the year and the following four characters to the company code. Because composite keys are mainly n:m relationships, you should monitor the growth of the respective dimension. The use of composite keys also lets you work with authorization variables. Authorization variables are variables that automatically read the authorized values in the analysis authorization. The artificial key ensures that the restrictions run in the background without the user noticing anything.

Different views For the data model, the demand for different authorization views that cannot be implemented in parallel or only with a lot of effort is relevant. For example, a user is not only supposed to view the times of his service employees but also the overall times required for his orders, regardless of whether the orders have been fulfilled by his employees or not. In such cases, you can create several MultiProviders that support the individual views (that is, times: employee view; times: order view).

Summary Authorizations can often significantly influence the BW data model; in this context, the restrictions for detail data are particularly important.

You can find more information on BW authorizations in John/Kiener (2010).

12.2.8 Validation

Validation concept BW is a standalone system, and complex transformation processes often make it difficult to understand the figures in the operational system. For data modeling, you should always keep in mind that a validation of the data must be feasible with an acceptable amount of effort. If a validation can solely be implemented at the details level, this level should also be available in BW (for example, in the consolidation layer). In the ideal case, you should already consider data validation aspects when you gather functional requirements. It may be possible that additional reports in BW or in the source system or even additional data models are necessary. Data validation processes may be discussed in separate test descriptions.

12.3   Specifications of the IT Department

Most of the issues described so far are part of the functional specification.

However, the BW data model is also influenced by non-functional aspects. The specifications of the IT department assume a major role for physical modeling. You should consider the following aspects in particular:

Specifications of the IT department

▶ Naming conventions (Chapter 5, Reference Architecture for Data Modeling, provides a concrete recommendation)

▶ BW architecture and strategy (for instance, for the global and local development)

▶ Enterprise Data Warehouse (EDW) architecture, that is, specification on the use of a layer model, such as the Layered, Scalable Architecture (LSA)

▶ General system-technical conditions (needs to be especially considered for live operation) and time window for data load processes

▶ Minimization of the support work

▶ Optimization of the reporting performance

▶ Optimization of the load performance

▶ Flexibility regarding enhancement and modifications

At this point, you should note that the definition of the data model also includes the following documents in addition to the technical concept:

Further documents

▶ **System specification (or DP specification)**
The system specification should describe the physical data model in particular, that is, not only the MultiProvider level but also the physical InfoCubes and DataStore Objects (DSOs). The description should be based on SAP application terminology and not on the database level, and the system specification must include a description of the data flow for which you can use flowcharts.

▶ **User documentation**
With the metadata repository, the BW system provides a user-friendly tool that lets you graphically map all of the data models. Therefore, you should limit the documentation to a very rough description without describing obvious logics and relations, for example.

▶ **System manual**
The system manual should document the time aspects of data retention and data load process in detail. In particular, it should provide detailed information on all process chains.

485

12.4 Conclusion

Conceptual data modeling is determined by the functional requirements. This chapter explained that in addition to the mere reporting requirements, further functional aspects, which are listed in the following, play a decisive role for data modeling:

▸ You must design the data model in such a way that the reporting requirements can be implemented using the options provided by the BEx application.

▸ Complex authorization requirements might only be implemented if they are considered in the data model.

▸ Time aspects assume a critical role for the design of the conceptual and physical data model.

▸ The data model must allow for data validation.

Finally, this chapter also addressed some technical aspects that are especially relevant to physical modeling.

13 Summary and Outlook

In this book, you learned how to structure information requirements and select a suitable description form for a logical data model and implement it in Business Warehouse (BW). The focus was on implementing requirements in BW. To successfully implement a data model, you must be able to select an appropriate storage form for data. Therefore, you learned which forms of data stores are used for data models in BW. An isolated view on the storage concepts is not sufficient, however. For this reason, the Layered, Scalable Architecture (LSA) was presented as a layer architecture that can serve as a reference architecture and be used to access SAP's wealth of experience, which has been gathered from many large BW implementations. This way, you can easily develop a future-oriented and flexible data model.

You should not underestimate the meaning of a custom architecture specification derived from the LSA, for example. Project experience has shown that a Data Warehouse (DWH) doesn't represent a standard solution. The DWH cannot be purchased and operated as a product, but is developed and enhanced step by step — usually iteratively — and the data model or architecture used has the task of setting standards to facilitate the integration of various topic areas.

Business Content has two major benefits: it supports the prototype implementation of a solution at an early project phase, and it provides valuable predefined modules (particularly InfoObjects and DataSources) for the implementation. The use of prototypes is often very helpful because you quickly get a basis for discussion to reconcile the requirements with the user department in a top-down approach. In most cases, however, you will adapt the Content's data model to your requirements. So it often makes sense to define MultiProviders, redimension data models, and implement additional layers. Even though the final implementation of a data model is only partially based on Business Content, it makes a valuable contribution. On the one hand, InfoObjects of Business Content can be used directly or can at least be reproduced on the basis of Business Content. On the other hand, for many topics there are standard extractors (that is, DataSources) that you can use directly or after enhancements. Unfortunately, most parts of Business Content are not based on the reference architecture provided by SAP so enhancements are required in any case. For the future, it would be nice to have abstracting reference models (for instance, in the form of Business Content) that are further developed with regard to content and include prepared business semantics.

At the beginning of this book, you got to know the Business Intelligence (BI) lifecycle model. The user department's involvement in BI/BW development was mentioned as an essential goal of this model. A lot of ideas that are based on LSA aim for better provisioning of user department-related or function-related data marts — by creating domains you can parallelize and accelerate data loading, for example. The Data Propagation Layer prepares "easily processible" data so that you can provide the data to the Data Mart Layer in a largely harmonized, quick, flexible, and historicized form. This way, you can easily meet your requirements with a reasonable effort and ensure the acceptance of the BW system.

In your analysis, you usually benefit the most if you interrelate the datasets and evaluate them comprehensively. InfoSets and MultiProviders enable this, provided that you create an overall picture at an early stage (from a functional point of view) and don't lose sight of the implementation's integration aspect. The prerequisite for comprehensively analyzing data is the harmonization of master data and the systematic use of identical or referencing InfoObjects. Therefore, it is important to identify central InfoObjects and to continuously use them in modeling. For additional requirements you must enhance the central objects, and you must avoid, by all means, creating new objects without due consideration.

We determined that, for example, creating domains leads to a rather "expanded" data model with many transformation steps. With SAP NetWeaver BW Release 7.3, SAP will presumably find a remedy here. SAP plans to supplement the modeling function in the Data Warehousing Workbench with another object, the Semantically Partitioned Object. This object provides the developers with special tools that support them in the semantic partitioning of DSOs and InfoCubes. These can be used to automatically generate the data transfer processes (DTPs) and present the data flow reduced to the key aspects.

Additional new developments with regard to data modeling and data retention are planned for SAP NetWeaver BW Release 7.3 (see SAP NetWeaver BW Solution Management, 2009).[1]

In the meantime, SAP has revoked Release 7.2, which is mentioned in this source. It will not be provided as a separate release as was originally planned. Instead, a consolidated Release 7.3 will be launched that combines the planned functions of Releases 7.2 and 7.3 (see SAP NetWeaver BW Solution Management, 2010). The ramp-up for SAP NetWeaver BW 7.3 is scheduled for the second half of 2010.

Some of the anticipated new developments in the data modeling environment include the following:

▶ Hierarchies are supposed to be integrated flexibly with the data flow.

▶ The remodeling function is supposed to be available for DataStore Objects (DSOs).

▶ The performance of DSOs will be optimized, for example, data activation.

▶ The integration of Nearline Storage (NLS) will be improved. At the query level, you will be able to specify whether the NLS archive is supposed to be included in the query. Furthermore, you will be able to look up data from NLS partitions in transformations.

▶ It will also be possible to archive uncompressed InfoCube data.

▶ In addition to the Semantically Partitioned Object previously mentioned, a tool will be provided that can copy entire data flows. Moreover, a tool for migrating data flows from Release 3.x to 7.x will be available.

▶ Hybrid Provider will constitute a new DataProvider type (see Chapter 4, Section 4.5.2, Real-Time Data Acquisition). It is supposed to integrate the transaction data from SAP ERP with reporting either via a Virtual Cube or via Real-time Data Acquisition (RDA) in real time. In this process, the essential components of the model will be automatically generated.

---

1 Note that the release has not been in the ramp-up yet at the time this book went to press and that SAP can withdraw any of the functions described here.

▶ The indexing for Business Warehouse Accelerator (BWA) doesn't need data loaded into InfoCubes in advance. The InfoCube's data model will still have to be created; but it will no longer be necessary to fill it with data. The data will be retrieved directly via an upstream DSO. Beyond that, BWA will also offer indexing of master data and hierarchies. An additional caching of data at the MultiProvider level will further accelerate cross-InfoCube queries.

As you can see, SAP has made major efforts to ensure a higher performance for data loading and running queries. The effort for the implementation and maintenance of partitioned data models (domain creation) will be reduced via the Semantically Partitioned Object, and the integration of RDA will be highly simplified via the VirtualProvider. Furthermore, a lot of minor changes will effect an even more efficient management of the system so that you can decrease the data retention costs and further increase system performance. You can see that many concepts that were presented in this book and deemed beneficial will be better supported by the system in the near future and can therefore be implemented more easily and at lower costs.

In addition to the further developments described, SAP BusinessObjects XI Release 3.2 also advanced the integration of BusinessObjects products. Data Integrator will be integrated more closely with the SAP NetWeaver BW data flow and in the future, loading processes can be scheduled using Data Integrator. Moreover, Metadata Manager will enable the user to trace a data flow in BW environments (data lineage) and implement change impact analyses. The front-end products will be further integrated as well.

All in all, the new options lead to very versatile design considerations that you must reflect on for the physical mapping of a data model. In the future, the transfer of an initially logically designed data model to an InfoCube structure will only be one part of the implementation process, and this transfer alone won't answer the questions regarding the overall architecture that is supposed to be implemented.

If you take a look at the future, where BI services will supplement every application with additional analytical components, even more users will expect high-performance access to an even larger amount of basic data. So the requirements on data modeling will increase in future. It is possible, however, that we will then discuss completely different implementation forms at the physical level. BWA provides initial indications about the direction the development could take. But the discussion of data modeling will remain active as long as we want to and have to describe and model systems for data retentions ourselves.

Appendices

A   Abbreviations

AP	Accounts Payable
AR	Accounts Receivable
AA	Asset Accounting
ABAP	Advanced Business Application Programming
ADAPT	Application Design for Analytical Processing Technologies
ADK	Archive Development Kit
ADM	Architected Data Mart (reporting level)
APD	Analysis Process Designer
API	Application Programming Interface
APO	Advanced Planning and Optimization
BAdI	Business Add-In
BAPI	Business Application Programming Interface
BEx	Business Explorer
BI	Business Intelligence
BPC	SAP BusinessObjects Planning and Consolidation
BPS	Business Planning and Simulation
BSC	Balanced Scorecard
BSP	Business Server Page
BW	Business Warehouse
BWA	Business Warehouse Accelerator
CAF	Composite Application Framework
CIF	Corporate Information Factory
CO	Controlling
CO-PA	Controlling – Profitability Analysis
CPU	Central Processing Unit
CRM	Customer Relationship Management
CSV	Comma Separated Values or Character Separated Values
CTO	Change and Transport Organizer

CURR	Currency field
DATS	Date field
DB Connect	Database Connect
DEC	Computed or amount field with decimal point and sign
DIM-ID	Dimensions ID (artificial dimension key)
DPO	Days Payable Outstanding
DS	DataSource
DSO	DataStore Object
DSO	Days Sales Outstanding
DTP	Data Transfer Process
DType	Data Type
DP	Data Processing
DWH	Data Warehouse
DWWB	Data Warehousing Workbench
ECC	Enterprise Core Components
EDI	Electronic Data Interchange
EDW	Enterprise Data Warehouse
EIS	Enterprise Information System
EMEA	Europe, Middle East, Africa
ER Model	Entity Relationship Model
ERP	Enterprise Resource Planning
ETL	Extract, Transform, Load
(F4) help	Input help in the SAP system
FI	Financials
FLTP	Floating Point Number
FTE	Full Time Equivalent
G/L	General Ledger
GUI	Graphical User Interface
GUID	Globally Unique Identifiers
P+L	Profit and Loss Statement
HCM	Human Capital Management

HR	Human Resources
HTML	Hypertext Markup Language
HTTP	Hypertext Transfer Protocol
HTTPS	Hypertext Transfer Protocol Secure
ICM	Internet Communication Manager
ID	Identifier
IDEFIX	Integration Definition for Information Modeling
IFRS	International Financial Reporting Standards
ILM	Information Lifecycle Management
IMG	Implementation Guide
INT4	4-byte integer
IP	Integrated Planning
IT	Information Technology
JPY	Japanese Yen
BOX	Box
KM	Knowledge Management
HI	Health Insurance
LID	Line Item Dimension
LIS	Logistics Information System
LOK	Local Key
LSA	Layered, Scalable Architecture
MDM	Master Data Management
MDX	Multidimensional Expressions
CHAR	Characteristic
MOLAP	Multidimensional Online Analytical Processing
MOSS	Microsoft Office SharePoint Server
MS	Microsoft
NewGL	New General Ledger
NLS	Nearline Storage
ODBO	OLE DB for OLAP
ODS	Operational Data Store

OEM	Original Equipment Manufacturer
OLAP	Online Analytical Processing
OLTP	Online Transactional Processing
OM	Organizational Management
OSS	Online Service System
PA	Personnel Administration
PC	Product Costing
PCA	Profit Center Accounting
PDF	Portable Document Format
PoS	Point of Sale
PSA	Persistent Staging Area
PY	Payroll
QA	Quality Assurance
QS	Quality Assurance
SSG	Source System Group
QUAN	Quantity field
RDA	Real-Time Data Acquisition
RDBMS	Relational Database Management System
RFC	Remote Function Call
RIG	Regional Implementation Group
ROLAP	Relational Online Analytical Processing
RRI	Report-Report Interface
SAS	originally for Statistical Analysis System
SCM	Supply Chain Management
SDN	SAP Developer Network
SEM	Strategic Enterprise Management
SID	Set ID (master data ID)
SKF	Statistical Key Figure
SL	Special Ledger
SOA	Service-Oriented Architecture
SP	Support Package

SPO	Semantically Partitioned Object
SPS	Support Package Stack
SQL	Structured Query Language
SUM	Total
THJ	Temporal Hierarchy Join
TIMS	Time field (hhmmss)
UD Connect	Universal Data Connect
USD	US Dollar
GAAP	Generally Accepted Accounting Principles
WAD	Web Application Designer
WB	Workbench
WBS	Work Breakdown Structure
XML	Extensible Markup Language
XMLA	XML for Analysis
XOR	Exclusive or
YTD	Year-to-Date

B Transactions

SAP NetWeaver Business Warehouse (BW) is not a transactional system. Therefore, transaction codes don't have the same significance as in SAP ERP. In particular, almost every backend task can be performed in the Data Warehousing Workbench (Transaction RSA1). Most BW transactions are usually shortcuts to navigate to the corresponding function faster than via the Data Warehousing Workbench. The following is a list of the most important transactions (from the SAP system for BW).

Transaction	Description
ABAPDOCU	Getting Started in ABAP, Documents and Examples
BALE	ALE Inbound IDoc
BPS0	Planning
CMOD	Project Management of SAP Extensions
DB02	Database Performance Analysis, View Tablespaces
FILE	Definition of File Paths, Logical File Names, Variables, and Syntax Groups
ICON	Icon Maintenance
LBW1	Extraction from LIS Structures
LISTCUBE	List Viewer for InfoCubes
LISTSCHEMA	View InfoCube Schema
MC23	Display Info Structure
MDXTEST	MDX Monitor for Testing
OLI1	INVCO Statistical Setup: Material Movements
OLI2	INVCO Statistical Setup: Stocks
OLI6	New Statistical Setup Plant Maintenance Information System
OLI7	SIS Statistical Setup: Orders
OLIM	Periodic Stock Quantity — Plant
OLIS	Implementation Guide LIS
OMO1	Update Maintenance: SIS

Transaction	Description
OMO2	Update Maintenance: PURCHIS
OMO9	Update Maintenance: INVCO
OOAP	Set Plan Version
OS06	OS Monitor
OSS1	Online Service System
PFCG	Profile Generator/Change User Profile, Role Maintenance
RRMX	Started Excel from SAP GUI
RSA1	DWH Administrator
RSA11	InfoCubes in DWH Workbench
RSA12	InfoSource in DWH Workbench
RSA13	Source System in DWH Workbench
RSA14	DSO in DWH Workbench
RSA15	InfoObjects in DWH Workbench
RSA3	Extractor Checker
RSA6	DataSource Postprocessing
RSA7	Delta Queue Monitor
RSADMIN	Maintenance RSADMIN
RSANWB	Analysis Process Designer
RSAWBSETTINGSDEL	Delete User Settings of DWH WB
RSBBS	Report-Report Interface
RSCUR	Manage Currency Conversion
RSD1	Maintenance of Characteristics
RSD2	Maintenance of Key Figures
RSD3	Maintenance of Units
RSD4	Maintenance of Time Characteristics
RSDCUBE	Introduction: InfoCube Processing
RSDCUBED	Introduction: InfoCube Processing (Content)
RSDCUBEM	Introduction: InfoCube Processing (M Version)
RSDDV	Maintenance of Aggregates

Transaction	Description
RSDIOBC	Introduction: InfoObject Catalog Processing
RSDIOBCD	Introduction: InfoObject Catalog Processing (Content)
RSDIOBCM	Introduction: InfoObject Catalog Processing (M Version)
RSDMD	Master Data Maintenance Basic Characteristic
RSECADMIN	BW Analysis Authorization
RSH1	Introduction: Hierarchy Processing
RSH3	Display of Hierarchies from Source System — Simulation
RSHIER	Hierarchy Maintenance without DWH WB
RSHIERINT	Hierarchy Maintenance without DWH WB
RSKC	Maintenance of Permitted Additional Characters
RSLGMP	Maintenance of the Source System Assignment after Transport
RSMO	Data Load Monitor (Complete): Start
RSO2	Generic Extractor Maintenance; see SAP Note 205986
RSPC	Process Chain Maintenance
RSQ02	Maintenance of InfoSets
RSQ10	Roles for InfoSet Query
RSRCACHE	OLAP Cache
RSRCATTTRACE	CATT Transaction for Trace Tool
RSRT	Query Monitor
RSRT1	Query Monitor
RSRT2	Query Monitor, New Version
RSRTRACE	OLAP Trace for Queries
RSRTRACETEST	Trace Tool Configuration
RSRV	Analysis and Repair Tool for BW Objects
RSSM	Maintain Authorization Objects (Old)
RST22	Short Dump Analysis

Transaction	Description
RSTT	Trace Tool
RSZC	Copy Query Objects
RSZDELETE	Delete Query Objects
RSZVERSION	Set Front-End Version
RZ01	Job Scheduling Monitor
RZ02	Network Graphics of SAP Instances
RZ03	Presentation and Control of SAP Instances
RZ04	Maintenance of the SAP Instances
RZ06	Alerts Thresholds Maintenance
RZ10	Profile Parameter Maintenance
RZ11	Profile Parameter Maintenance
RZ12	Maintenance of RFC Server Group Assignment
RZ15	Read XMI Log
RZ20	CCMS Monitoring/Alert Monitor
RZ21	CCMS Customizing Monitor Architecture
RZ25	Start Tools for a TID
S002	System Administration Easy Access (Administration, Monitor, User Maintenance, Transports)
SA38	ABAP Program Execution
SAINT	SAP Add-on Manager, for example, for SAP BW
SALE	ALE Configuration
SAPBWNEWS	News on SAP BW
SBIW	BW Customizing in the Source System
SCC4	Client Administration
SD11	Data Modeler
SE01	Transport Organizer (Extended View)
SE03	Transport Organizer Tools; Particularly for Unlocking
SE10	Customizing Organizer

Transaction	Description
SE11	Data Dictionary Maintenance
SE14	ABAP Dictionary Database Utility
SE15	Repository Information System
SE16	Data Browser (View Table Content)
SE30	Runtime Analysis of Queries
SE36	Create Logical Database
SE37	Manage Function Modules
SE38	Manage ABAP Programs
SE51	Screen Painter
SE80	Repository Browser
SE81	Application Hierarchy
SE84	Repository Information System
SE91	Message Maintenance
SE93	Transaction Maintenance Overview
SLG1	Evaluate Application Log
SM01	Lock Transactions
SM04	User List
SM12	Display and Delete Lock Entries
SM13	Asynchronous Update
SM21	Read System Log
SM30	Call View Maintenance
SM31	Table Maintenance
SM35	Batch Input Folder Monitor
SM36	Define Job
SM37	Batch Job Overview
SM38	Job Queue Management
SM49	External OS Commands
SM50	Process Overview
SM51	Instances/Process Overview
SM58	Transactional RFC

Transaction	Description
SM59	Setup Source System (RFC Destination)
SM62	Display/Maintenance of Event Names
SM66	Global Process Overview
SMICM	ICM Monitor
SMOD	Business Add-In Enhancements
SMX	Own Jobs
SNOTE	Import Corrections Automatically
SNUM	Number Range Object Maintenance
SO01	Business Workplace (Monitor Emails)
SP01	Spool Requests
SPAM	Support Package Manager
SPAU	Modification Adjustment
SPDD	Modification Adjustment in Data Dictionary
SPRO	Customizing Guidelines
SQ01	SAP Query
SSAA	Automated Administration Checks
ST01	System Trace
ST02	Overview System Utilization "Tune Summary"
ST03	Workload Statistics
ST04	Database Performance Analysis
ST05	Trace Requests
ST06	OS Monitor
ST11	Access to Error Log Files
ST22	ABAP Runtime Error Analysis
STMS	Transport System
STZBD	Time Zone Customizing
SU01	User Maintenance
SU25	User Profile Generator
SU53	Authorization Objects
SWU3	Consistency Check: Customizing

Transaction	Description
SXDA	Generate Batch Input Folders
TRANSFER	Maintenance of Data Package Characteristics
WE07	IDOC Statistics
WE20	EDI Partner Profiles
WE21	EDI Port Description
WE30	Development of IDoc Types
WEDI	IDoc and EDI Easy Access Basis

C   Programs

This appendix lists some important programs designed to facilitate your work with SAP NetWeaver Business Warehouse (BW). These programs also play a critical role because, unlike transactions, they can be used in process chains.

Program Name	Description
QUERY_CHECK	Checks a query through generation
RRHI_HIERARCHY_ACTIVATE	Activates a hierarchy
RS_CLIENT_COPY_BW	Implements the BW client after a successful Client_Copy
RS_ROUTINE	Auxiliary report for syntax checks of routines
RS_START_AWB	RS_START_AWB program
RSAGGR1	Aggregation of an InfoCube
RSAOS_DATASOURCE_ACTIVATE	Activation program for DataSources
RSC1_DIAGNOSIS	Diagnosis tool for DataSources
RSCDS_NULLELIM	Retroactive elimination of zeros
RSDELPART1	Deletion of requests; new job ID required (RSSM_UNIQUE_ID)
RSDG_AFTER_IMPORT_FOR_CORR	Starts the BW after-import routine for a job
RSDG_ATR_NAV_SWITCH_ON	Adds SIDs when a navigation attribute is activated
RSDG_CUBE_ACTIVATE	Activation program for InfoCubes
RSDG_CUBE_REORG_TEXTS	Reorganization of texts for InfoCubes
RSDG_DATS_TO_DATE	Sets the basic characteristic and references flag for characteristics of the DATS/TIMS type

Program Name	Description
RSDG_EXIST_ROUTINES_GENERATE	Post-generation of existing utility routines
RSDG_INITIAL_MD_INSERT	Inserts the initial entry in the master data table
RSDG_IOBC_REORG_TEXTS	Reorganization of texts for InfoObject catalogs
RSDG_IOBJ_ACTIVATE	Activation program for InfoObjects
RSDG_IOBJ_REORG	Reorganization for InfoObjects
RSDG_IOBJ_REORG_TEXTS	Reorganization of texts for InfoObjects
RSDG_LANGUAGE_AFTER_IMPORT	Postprocessing for the language import (copying texts to A/M)
RSDG_MEMORYID	Program for newly generating set/get parameter IDs
RSDG_MPRO_ACTIVATE	Activation program for MultiProviders
RSDG_ODSO_ACTIVATE	Activation program for DSOs
RSDG_SHLP_NO_LANGU_PRE_UPGRADE	Program for newly generating search helps for language-independent IOs
RSDG_SYS_IOBJ_TO_D_VERSION	Copies the fixed InfoObjects to the D version
RSDG_TADIR	Tadir interface
RSDMD_CHECKPRG_ALL	Check program for master data consistency
RSDMD_CLEAN_ATTRIBUTES	Cleanses the master data table
RSDMD_DEL_BACKGROUND	Auxiliary report for deleting master data in the background
RSDMD_DEL_MASTER_DATA	Deletes single master data records

Program Name	Description
RSDMD_DEL_MASTER_DATA_TEXTS	Auxiliary report for deleting texts in the background
RSDMRSDO	Calls the InfoObject generation
RSDPLIST	List of all InfoPackages
RSDRD_DELETE_FACTS	Program for performing selective deletion processes; you can also generate a program for selections or deletions, which can then be integrated in process chains.
RSDRD_INFORMIX_ROUTINES	INFORMIX: DB-dependent routines for deletion from the facts table
RSDRD_MSSQL_ROUTINES	MSSQL: DB-dependent routines for deletion from the facts table
RSDRD_ORACLE_ROUTINES	ORACLE: DB-dependent routines for deletion from the facts table
RSEXPORTFLATFILES	Exports CSV files
RSHIERARCHY	Calls the hierarchy maintenance
RSIC1	Initial screen of the InfoCube maintenance
RSIMPCONTENT	Imports applications and InfoSources from Business Content
RSIMPCURR	Imports exchange rates: selection
RSIMPCUST	Imports global settings: selection
RSKC_ALLOWED_CHAR_MAINTAIN	Maintenance of permitted additional characters in the BW system
RSMO1	Monitor report
RSMO1_RSM2	Monitor report
RSMO1A	Status output for monitor
RSMO1B	List output for monitor
RSMO2	Detail list output for monitor
RSMO3	Other detail output list
RSMOLIST	Status output for monitor
RSO_REPOSITORY_EXPORT_HTML	Exports HTML pages from BW Repository

Program Name	Description
RSREDITX_MESSAGE	Checks X_messages
RSRPR_BATCH	Main program for batch printing
RSRPR_PRINT_CONF_MAINTAIN	Starts the maintenance dialog for the print configuration maintenance
RSRPR_VARGROUP_MAINTAIN	Variant group maintenance for batch printing

D Function Modules and Includes

D.1 Function Modules

Function module	Description
CONVERT_TO_LOCAL_CURRENCY	Conversion into company reporting currency
FILE_GET_NAME	Conversion of a logical file name
RKE_TIMESTAMP_CONVERT_OUTPUT	Convert timestamp (parameter I_DAYST=X)
RRSI_SID_VAL_SINGLE_CONVERT	Conversion of SID into characteristic values
RRSI_VAL_SID_SINGLE_CONVERT	Conversion of characteristic values into SID
RS_BIW_ACTIVE	Determination whether it is a BW system
RS_TRANSTRU_ACTIVATE_ALL	Activation program for transfer structures
RSA_DEBUG_STATUS_GET	Determination whether debugging is permitted in this system/for this user
RSA_LOGICAL_SYSTEM_BIW_GET	Retrieve name of the logical system (for client)
RSA_PROFILE_LANGUAGE_GET	Retrieve activated languages of profile
RSAR_ODS_API_DEL	Delete DSO contents
RSAX_BIW_GET_DATA_SIMPLE	Template for a function module that can be used in a generic extractor
RSBB_URL_PREFIX_GET	Determination of WAS host name, WAS path, and WAS log
RSBX_BIW_GET_DATA	Data extraction API for InfoCubes
RSD_CUBE_GET	Returns information on an InfoCube
RSDDK_BIW_GET_DATA	BW statistics: transfer of transaction data
RSDDK_BIW_GET_TEXTS	BW statistics: transfer of texts

Function module	Description
RSDDK_STA_DB_TO_FILE	BW statistics: transaction and master data in files
RSDDK_STA_DEL_DATA	BW statistics: delete data in database tables (buffers)
RSDDK_STA_INFOCUBE	BW statistics: transaction data via interface directly in InfoCube
RSDRI_ODSO_DELETE_RFC	Delete data in DSO for direct writing (can be called remotely)
RSDRI_ODSO_INSERT_RFC	Insert data in DSO for direct writing (can be called remotely)
RSDRI_ODSO_MODIFY_RFC	Insert (if key not yet available) or change data in DSO for direct writing (can be called remotely)
RSDRI_ODSO_UPDATE_RFC	Change data in DSO for direct writing (can be called remotely)
RSDU_ANALYZE_INFOCUBE	Structure statistics for InfoCubes
RSDU_BUILD_BITMAP_INDEX	Structure bitmap indices for InfoCubes
RSDU_DROP_SECONDARY_INDEXES	Delete secondary indices of InfoCubes
RSKV_CHAVL_CHECK	Check for permitted characteristics
RSPC_ABAP_FINISH	Function module is to be executed for asynchronously run processes of the ABAP process type in process chains
RSPC_API_CHAIN_START	Start process chains (particularly if they can only be started otherwise via metachains)
RSPC_API_CHAIN_START	Start process chains (particularly if they can only be started otherwise via metachains)
RSSM_DELETE_REQUEST	Delete a request from an InfoCube (batch)
RSSM_EVENT_RAISE	Trigger an event in another system
RSSM_ICUBE_REQUESTS_GET	Read last request ID

Function module	Description
RSW_CURRENCY_TRANSLATION	Function module for currency translation

D.2   Includes

Include	Description
ZXKEXU01	Exit COPA
ZXRSAU01	Customer Function Call for transaction data provision
ZXRSAU02	Customer Function Call for master data provision
ZXRSAU03	Customer Function Call for text provision
ZXRSAU04	Customer Function Call for hierarchy provision
ZXRSRU01	Variable exits

E   Tables

This appendix lists the tables that are very helpful when you work with SAP NetWeaver Business Warehouse (BW).

Table Name	Description
AUSP	Classification definitions
ROMSDIOBJ	Assignment of master data attributes to InfoObjects
ROOSFIELD	DataSource Fields (ECC)
RSADMINS	Data import for administration settings
RSCOMPTLOGOT	Grouping component for TLOGO objects (for instance, for process chains (RSPC type))
RSCURTRT	Currency translation types
RSCURTXT	Texts for currency translation types
RSDATRNAV	Navigation attributes
RSDCHA	Characteristics catalog
RSDCHABAS	Basic characteristics (for characteristics, time characteristics, and units)
RSDCUBE	List of the InfoCubes
RSDDAGGL	List of aggregates
RSDDAGGRMODSTATE	Status of change run for aggregates
RSDDCHNGPROT	Table with InfoObjects whose master tables were changed
RSDDIM	List of dimensions
RSDICMULTIIOBJ	MultiProvider identification
RSDIOBJ	List of all InfoObjects
RSDIOBJCMP	Compounding (dependencies) of InfoObjects
RSDKYF	Key figures
RSDMTXTCHANGES	Last change of the text table of an InfoObject
RSDRDACTLOG	Logging of deletion activities
RSDTIM	Time characteristics

Table Name	Description
RSDUNI	Units
RSHIEDIR	Hierarchy directory
RSPARAM	System parameter
RSR_IC_READMODE	Default read mode for queries of an InfoCube
RSRHIEDIR_OLAP	OLAP-relevant information on hierarchies
RSRHINTAB_OLAP	Hierarchy intervals for OLAP processor
RSRLOGO	Logo settings for BEx browser
RSRWBTEMPLATE	Assignment of Excel workbooks as personal templates
RSRWORKBOOK	Where-used list for reports in workbooks
RSSOURSYSTEM	Table of source system IDs
RSSZTDIR	Directory of customer master data table
RSTHIERNODE	Texts of hierarchy nodes that cannot be posted to
RSZELTDIR	Directory of reporting component elements
RSZGLOBV	BW variables
RSZOPRATOR	Formula operators
RSZRANGE	Selection definitions for an element
RSZSELECT	Selection properties of an element
TSTC	All transaction codes

F   Delta Processes

Appendix F provides an overview of the most critical delta processes.

Delta Process	Description	New Image	After-Image	Before Image	Additive Image	Deletion	Reverse Image	Cube-capable
A	Master data delta		X					n/a
ABR	Complete delta with deletion indicator via delta queue	X	X	X			X	X
ABR1	Like ABR, but only serializable per request	X	X	X			X	X
ADD	Additive delta via extractor				X			X
ADDD	Additive delta via delta queue				X			X
AIE	After image via extractor		X					
AIED	After image with deletion indicator via extractor		X			X		
AIM	After image via delta queue		X					
AIMD	After image with deletion indicator via delta queue		X			X		
CUBE	Extraction of InfoCube				X			X
FIL0	Delta via file import with after image		X					
FIL1	Delta via file import with delta image				X			X
NEWE	Only new image via extractor	X						X

Delta Process	Description	New Image	After-Image	Before Image	Additive Image	Deletion	Reverse Image	Cube-capable
NEWD	Only new image via delta queue	X						X
ODS	Extraction of DSO	X	X	X			X	X

G   Posting Keys

Posting Key	Reversal	Sales	Payment	D/C	Account Type	S G/L	Description
0							Account assignment template
1	12	X		Debits	Customer		Invoice
2	11	X		Debits	Customer		Reversal credit memo
3	13			Debits	Customer		Expenses
4	14			Debits	Customer		Other receivable
5	15		X	Debits	Customer		Outgoing payments
6	16		X	Debits	Customer		Payment difference
7	17			Debits	Customer		Other clearing
8	18		X	Debits	Customer		Payment clearing
9	19			Debits	Customer		Special G/L customer/ debits
9						A	Reversal down payment
9						B	Bill of exchange receivable
9						C	IS-RE reversal rental collateral
9						E	Reversal individual value adjustment
9						F	Down payment request
9						G	Guarantee of payment
9						H	Rental collateral
9						I	Vendor debits
9						J	IS-RE advance payment receivable operating costs
9						K	IS-RE reversal advance payment operating costs
9						P	Payment request

Posting Key	Reversal	Sales	Payment	D/C	Account Type	S G/L	Description
9						Q	Remaining risk bill of exchange
9						R	Bill of exchange payment request
9						S	Check/bill of exchange
9						T	Reversal down payment
9						U	IS-RE reversal advance payment UM
9						W	Bill of exchange
9						Z	Interest receivable
11	2	X		Credit	Customer		Credit memo
12	1	X		Credit	Customer		Reversal invoice
13	3			Credit	Customer		Reversal expenses
14	4			Credit	Customer		Other payable
15	5		X	Credit	Customer		Incoming payment
16	6		X	Credit	Customer		Payment difference
17	7			Credit	Customer		Other clearing
18	8		X	Credit	Customer		Payment clearing
19	9			Credit	Customer		Special G/L customer/credit
19						A	Down payment received
19						B	Reversal bill of exchange receivable
19						C	IS-RE rental collateral
19						E	Individual value adjustment
19						F	Down payment request
19						G	Undo guarantee of payment
19						H	Reversal rental collateral

Posting Key	Reversal	Sales	Payment	D/C	Account Type	S G/L	Description
19						I	Vendor credit
19						J	IS-RE reversal advance payment receivable operating costs
19						K	IS-RE advance payment operating costs
19						P	Payment request
19						S	Reversal check/bill of exchange
19						T	Down payment
19						U	IS-RE advance payment sales-based rent
19						W	Reversal bill of exchange receivable
19						Z	Reversal interest receivable
21	32	X		Debits	Vendor		Credit memo
22	31	X		Debits	Vendor		Reversal invoice
24	34			Debits	Vendor		Other receivable
25	35		X	Debits	Vendor		Outgoing payments
26	36		X	Debits	Vendor		Payment difference
27	37			Debits	Vendor		Clearing
28	38		X	Debits	Vendor		Payment clearing
29	39		X	Debits	Vendor		Special general ledger vendor/debits
29						A	Down payment made
29						B	Down payment financial asset
29						D	Discount debits
29						G	Undo guarantee of payment
29						H	Reversal rental collateral

Posting Key	Reversal	Sales	Payment	D/C	Account Type	S G/L	Description
29						I	Investment down payment
29						J	Debits rental collateral
29						M	Down payment material asset
29						P	Payment request
29						S	Reversal check/bill of exchange
29						T	Down payment made
29						V	Down payment inventory
29						W	Reversal bill of exchange payable
31	22	X		Credit	Vendor		Invoice
32	21	X		Credit	Vendor		Reversal credit memo
34	24			Credit	Vendor		Other payable
35	25		X	Credit	Vendor		Incoming payment
36	26		X	Credit	Vendor		Payment difference
37	27			Credit	Vendor		Other clearing
38	28		X	Credit	Vendor		Payment clearing
39	29		X	Credit	Vendor		Special G/L indicator/ credit
39						A	Reversal down payment
39						B	Reversal down payment financial asset
39						D	Discount credit
39						F	Down payment request
39						G	Guarantee of payment
39						H	Rental collateral
39						I	Reversal investment down payment

Posting Key	Reversal	Sales	Payment	D/C	Account Type	S G/L	Description
39						J	Credit rental collateral
39						M	Reversal material down payment
39						P	Payment request
39						S	Check/bill of exchange
39						T	Reversal down payment
39						W	Bill of exchange payable
40	50			Debits	G/L		Debit posting
50	40			Credit	G/L		Credit posting
70	75			Debits	Fixed asset		Fixed assets debits
75	70			Credit	Fixed asset		Fixed assets credit
80				Debits	G/L		Initial entry of balances
81				Debits	G/L		Costs
83				Debits	G/L		Price difference
84				Debits	G/L		Consumption
85				Debits	G/L		Balance sheet change
86				Debits	G/L		GR/IR debit
89				Debits	Material		Stock receipts
90				Credit	G/L		Initial entry of balances
91				Credit	G/L		Costs
93				Credit	G/L		Price difference
94				Credit	G/L		Consumption
95				Credit	G/L		Balance sheet change
96				Credit	G/L		GR/IR credit
99				Credit	Material		Stock issues

H   Glossary

Data Warehousing Workbench
Central tool in the Data Warehousing process with functions for data modeling and for controlling, monitoring, and maintaining all tasks related to data retrieval, retention, and processing in BW. The Data Warehousing Workbench is available via Transaction RSA1.

Aggregate   Stores the dataset of an InfoCube redundantly and persistently in a summarized form in the database to enable faster access in reporting. Aggregates are maintained using Transaction RSDDV.

Display attribute   Can only be displayed in addition to the key or text of a characteristic, but cannot be used for navigation or as a filter. From a data model perspective, the difference of display attributes is that no SID table needs to be built for them.

Attribute   Master data of a characteristic. This can be characteristics or key figures. You can differentiate between display attributes and navigation attributes. Key figure attributes can only be display attributes, but you can reprocess them in the report via formula variables. Characteristic attributes themselves can also have master data, that is, attributes, which in turn can have master data, and so on.

BEx Analyzer   Reporting tool of BW with a Microsoft Excel front end. In BEx Analyzer, you can directly open the BEx Query Designer. BEx is particularly suited for IT-affine users, for instance, in CO.

BEx Broadcaster   Function for push reporting, that is, the distribution of precalculated reports, particularly for publishing on the Web or in portals. The function can also be used for caching queries.

BEx Query Designer   Tool for defining reports that provides functions to define queries on the InfoProvider. This way, you determine how data of the selected InfoProvider can be evaluated.

BEx Web Application Designer   Desktop application for creating web reports. The HTML pages generated can be tables, graphics, or maps.

Business Content   Preconfigured extractors and standard objects in the BW system for functional task areas ("business") and for system monitoring (Technical Content). Data models, queries, and roles are also delivered as content; but these should only be considered examples. BI Content and Standard Content are synonyms for Business Content.

Business Explorer (BEx)   All of the reporting tools of BW are officially called BEx: BEx Analyzer, BEx Query Designer, BEx Web Application Designer, BEx Report Designer, BEx Broadcaster, and so on. In day-to-day project work, BEx often just refers to the Excel front end (for instance, logon via BEx, Web, or GUI).

DataStore Object (DSO)   Flat structure that is used in data management. There are three types of DSOs. The most important form is the standard DSO, where you store changes to a document (key) via a change log. With this change log, you can perform a delta update in an InfoCube. In addition, the write-optimized DSO and the transactional DSO exist.

DataSource   A synonym for an extractor in the source system, that is, a program that prepares data for BW, provides it, and usually supports a delta process. On the BW side, this refers to a flat structure of fields that are offered for data transfer. The BW-relevant metadata of the DataSource is defined by replication or directly in BW depending on the source.

Data Warehouse   An integrated and topic-oriented "data store" that stores data from various data sources to provide it for decision support in the enterprise. BW is SAP's Data Warehouse, which offers functions for the integration, transformation, consolidation, cleansing, storage, and provision of data from SAP and non-SAP sources.

DB Connect   With DB Connect you can open further database connections in addition to the default database connection and use these connections for transferring data from tables or views to a BW system. This is usually faster and can be automated better than the loading process via files.

Delta process   Property of a DataSource, which specifies how the data is transferred. DataSources without delta process are only Full-enabled, that is, data must always be fully loaded. In particular, you must differentiate delta processes that can be updated directly in an InfoCube and those that initially require a standard DSO, that is, all after-image processes. Here, the delta for the InfoCube update is built via the

DSO's change log. Moreover, you must differentiate DataSources that form the delta via the extractor (for instance, via timestamp fields in the source tables) and those that populate a delta queue.

Dimension   Grouping of characteristics with related content under one superordinate. In logical and physical modeling (star schema, InfoCube) dimensions are tables that link all characteristics with the fact table via a generic dimension key. For physical modeling the structure of dimensions is based on technical aspects and characteristics may not be functional related.

InfoCubes   Central physical objects in BW that form the basis of reports and analyses. From a logical data modeling perspective, this involves an enhanced star schema.

InfoObject catalog   Folder for InfoObjects, or more precisely, for characteristics or key figures. InfoObject catalogs are only relevant in the backend. InfoObjects can be assigned to multiple catalogs. Dragging and dropping InfoObjects is not supported. The behavior of InfoObject catalogs in the transport system is not optimal — ideally you should only transport catalogs if all InfoObjects have already been transported. InfoObject catalogs are less significant today because InfoObjects can also be activated as InfoProviders and are then organized as InfoAreas.

InfoObject   Generic term for characteristics and key figures in BW.

InfoProvider   Superordinate for all data models that can be analyzed using BW reporting tools. Both physical objects (for example, InfoCubes and InfoObjects) and virtual objects (for example,

MultiProviders) are referred to as Info-Providers.

InfoSet Special form of an InfoProvider that lets you join BW objects. InfoSets (only the same name) also exist in the basis system, for example, you can create a generic extractor using an InfoSet. The unique feature of the BW InfoSet in comparison to the basis InfoSet is that it is not defined at the physical level but at application level (means you can work with InfoCubes and DSOs, and do not need to work an the database table level).

InfoSource Fixed structures that can be used for standardization. In particular, you can use InfoSources to implement central transformations that can be used multiple times, for example. InfoSources are also ABAP Dictionary objects. Up to Release 3.5, InfoSources used to be mandatory. Data of multiple DataSources were combined in one InfoSource and then loaded to InfoCubes or DSOs (which used to be called ODS back then) using update rules. InfoSources are still available in Release 7.x.

MultiProvider Merges the data of multiple physical BW objects. For example, a MultiProvider combines key figures from various InfoCubes with the same characteristics. Joins are not supported in MultiProviders.

Navigation attributes In reporting, they behave like characteristics in a cube, that is, you can use them for filtering an evaluation. However, the assignment of data is via the current (or also time-dependent) master data. In the BEx tools, you can recognize navigation attributes by the double "_" in the technical name.

OLAP Online Analytical Processing; serves for multidimensional consideration of data. In contrast to OLTP systems like SAP ERP, you use OLAP systems for complex analyses with a very high data volume.

Open hub service Function for the data export to another system.

Query A request to an InfoProvider that is created using the BEx Query Designer.

Persistent Staging Area (PSA)
Inbound storage area for data from the source system. The requested data is stored without any changes.

Safety interval Period where the system waits before data is retrieved in the delta process. The goal is to prevent the data that emerges during extraction from getting lost. For example: A security interval of 30 minutes means that only data that was posted at least 30 minutes ago is retrieved with the next delta. This is also referred to as the upper limit. In addition, you can also specify a lower limit. For example, a lower limit of 40 minutes and an upper limit of 30 minutes means that postings during the overlapping 10 minutes are transferred twice. This ensures additional security; however, the delta process must be able to handle duplicate data records.

Star schema Data model that is optimized for Data Warehouses and OLAP applications. The tables are arranged in a star formation: A fact table forms the center around which multiple dimension tables are grouped.

I   Literature

▶ Adamson, Christopher; Venerable, Michael: *Data Warehouse Design Solutions*, New York: Wiley 1998.

▶ Bauer, Eric; Siebert, Jörg: *New General Ledger in SAP ERP Financials*, 1st edition, Boston: Galileo Press 2007.

▶ Brochhausen, Ewald; Kielisch, Jürger; Schnerring, Jürgen; Staeck, Jens: *mySAP HR: Technical Principles and Programming*, 2nd edition, Boston: Galileo Press 2005.

▶ Brück, Uwe: *Praxishandbuch SAP-Controlling*, 3rd edition, Bonn: Galileo Press 2009.

▶ Bulos, Dan: *"A New Dimension,"* in: *Database Programming & Design*: 6/1996, pp. 33–37

▶ Chamoni, Peter; Gluchowski, Peter: *Analytische Informationssysteme*, Berlin, Heidelberg: Springer 1998.

▶ Chen, Peter Pin-Shan: *"The Entity-Relationship Model-Toward a Unified View of Data,"* in: *ACM Transactions on Database Systems*, Vol 1, No 1, March 1976.

▶ Eckerson Wayne W., *TDWI Benchmark Guide: Interpreting Benchmark Scores Using TDWI's Maturity Model*, 2007, *http://onereports.inquisiteasp.com/Docs/TDWI_Benchmark_Final.pdf* (last accessed on Feb 9, 2010).

▶ Egger, Norbert; Hastenrath, Klemens; Kästner, Alexander; Kramer, Sebastion; Stecher, Daniel: *Reporting und Analyse mit SAP BusinessObjects*, Bonn: Galileo Press 2009.

▶ Essl, Manuel; Oehler, Uwe: *The Developer's Guide to SAP xApp Analytics*, Bonn: Galileo Press 2007.

▶ Hahne, Michael: *SAP Business Information Warehouse: Mehrdimensionale Datenmodellierung*, Berlin Heidelberg: Springer 2004.

▶ Haupt, Jürgen: *Enterprise Data Warehousing mit SAP BW — Ein Überblick*, 2003, *http://www.sap.com/germany/media/500000.pdf* (last accessed on Feb 9, 2010).

▶ Heilig, Loren; Karch, Steffen; Böttcher, Oliver; Hofmann, Christiane; Pfennig, Roland: *SAP NetWeaver Master Data Management*, Boston: Galileo Press 2007.

▶ Herzog, Dirk: *ABAP Development for SAP BW -- User Exits and BAdIs*, 1st edition, Boston: Galileo Press 2006.

▶ Hess, Susanne; Lenz, Stefanie; Scheibler, Jochen: *Sales and Distribution Controlling with SAP NetWeaver BI*, Boston: Galileo Press 2009.

▶ Hilgefort, Ingo: *Integrating SAP Business Objects XI 3.1 Tools with SAP NetWeaver*, Boston: Galileo Press 2009.

▶ Inmon, William H.; Imhoff, Claudia; Battas, Greg: *Building the Operational Data Store*, New York: Wiley 1996.

▶ Inmon, William H.; Imhoff, Claudia; Sousa, Ryan: *Corporate Information Factory*, 2nd edition, New York: Wiley 2001.

▶ John, Peter; Kiener, Peter: *Berechtigungen in SAP NetWeaver BW*, Bonn: Galileo Press 2010.

▶ Knapp, Daniel: *Practical Data Modeling With SAP NetWeaver BW*, Boston: Galileo Press 2009.

▶ Knapp, Daniel: *SAP NetWeaver BW in der Personalwirtschaft*, Bonn: Galileo Press 2010.

▶ Lee, Stuart D.: *SAP FI/CO Interview Questions*, Riverside: Equity Press 2006.

▶ Mehrwald, Christian: *Data Warehousing with SAP Bw7 Bi in SAP Netweaver 2004s: Architecture, Concepts, and Implementation*, Santa Barbara: Rocky Nook 2009.

▶ Plattner, Hasso: *Trends and Concepts in the Software Industry*, Lecture 2007, *http://epic.hpi.uni-potsdam.de/pub/Home/TrendsAndConceptsI2007/06_-_Business_Intelligence.pdf* (last accessed on Feb 9, 2010).

▶ Rebstock, Michael; Hildebrand, Knut: *SAP R/3 Management: A Manager's Guide to SAP R/3*, Scottsdale: Coriolis Technology Press 1999.

▶ SAP NetWeaver BW Solution Management: *SAP NetWeaver BW — What's new with SAP NetWeaver BW 7.2 and in 2010*, 2009, *http://www.sdn.sap.com/irj/scn/go/portal/prtroot/docs/library/uuid/d0ea8b43-26af-2c10-f1b5-*

bbb69060de87?QuickLink=index&overridelayout=true (last accessed on Feb 9, 2010).

▶ SAP NetWeaver BW Solution Management: SAP NetWeaver Business Warehouse (BW) will be consolidated into SAP NetWeaver 7.3, 2010, *http://www.sdn.sap.com/irj/sdn/edw?rid=/webcontent/uuid/a0248a22-be02-2d10-c885-afafda4085ab* (last accessed on Mar 1, 2010).

▶ Schröder, Thomas: *SAP BW Performance Optimization Guide*, 1st edition, Boston: Galileo Press 2006.

▶ Staade, Michael; Schüler, Bernd: *SAP BI-Projektmanagement*, Bonn: Galileo Press 2007.

▶ Zinke, Matthias: *Remodellierung von Datenmodellen in SAP NetWeaver BW*, Bonn: Galileo Press 2010.

J   The Authors

Frank K. Wolf is an SAP NetWeaver BW and SAP BI Solution Consultant at Triple A Consulting GmbH & Co. KG in Eschborn, Germany. His consulting work focuses on data modeling, data warehouse architecture, and the implementation of complex reporting environments using SAP NetWeaver BW and SAP BusinessObjects. You are welcome to contact Frank at *frank.wolf@triple-a.de*.

Stefan Yamada holds a degree in Information Management from the Johannes Kepler University in Linz, Austria. In 1998, he started to engage in the data model of CRM and the integration of BW for SAP CRM consulting. Since 2000, he has worked for PricewaterhouseCoopers. Currently, he implements large, global SAP NetWeaver BW customer projects as a freelance consultant. His work focuses on backend development and data modeling. You are welcome to contact Stefan at *stefan.yamada@gmail.com*.

Index

C

L

M

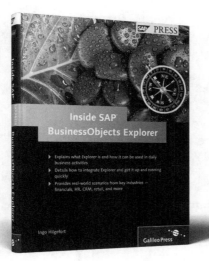

Explains what Explorer is and how it can be used in daily business activities

Details how to integrate and get Explorer up and running quickly

Uses real-world scenarios to show how it works in financials, HR, CRM, and retail

Ingo Hilgefort

Inside SAP BusinessObjects Explorer

With this book you'll learn what SAP BusinessObjects Explorer is, and find out how to install, deploy, and use it. Written for people who are interested in bringing Business Intelligence to business users, this book will teach you how to use it in your SAP environment and address specific questions about how it works with your existing SAP tools and data. After reading this book, you'll understand why and how to leverage Explorer to bring quick and easy access to data analysis to users throughout your company.

307 pp., 2010, 69,95 Euro / US$ 69.95
ISBN 978-1-59229-340-7

>> **www.sap-press.com**

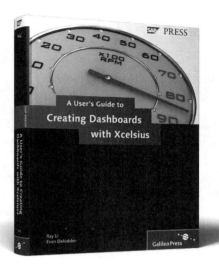

Explains how to use all of the
features in Xcelsius

Teaches you how to build and
customize interactive dash-boards to
effectively visualize your key business
data

Provides guidance on using Xcelsius
in an SAP environment

Evan Delodder, Ray Li

A User's Guide to Creating Dashboards with Xcelsius

Learn how to build your own Xcelsius dashboards, with this practical
book. It explains how to use Xcelsius in an end-to-end, linear "common
usage" manner, while highlighting typical scenarios where each feature
can be used to solve business problems. It also gives you detailed,
step-by-step guidance and best-practices for each feature, along with
hands-on exercises that will help you begin creating dashboards and
visualizations quickly. And if you're more advanced, you'll learn how to
customize the Xcelsius components, themes, and data connections so
you can use Xcelsius to the fullest extent.

approx. 620 pp., 49,95 Euro / US$ 49.95
ISBN 978-1-59229-335-3, Sept 2010

>> www.sap-press.com

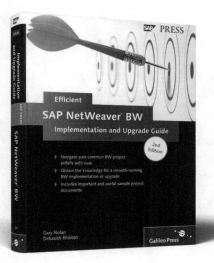

Explore the steps and components that ensure an efficient and smooth SAP BW implementation and upgrade

Learn about common practices and typical resource consid-erations for SAP BW projects

Leverage sample documents to help with your implementa-tion/upgrade

Gary Nolan, Debasish Khaitan

Efficient SAP NetWeaver BW Implementation and Upgrade Guide

This book offers a clear and easy-to-follow path for efficient SAP BW implementations and upgrades. The book starts by defining a typical NetWeaver BW project lifecycle, followed by an examination of proper project management and upgrade strategies, including understanding common mistakes, resource requirements, and project planning and development. The topics are presented in a linear, intuitive, project-based scenario, to help you navigate easily through all stages of the project, including pre-project considerations, actual project guidance, as well as the Go-Live and Post-Live monitoring and maintenance considerations.

532 pp., 2. edition, 79,95 Euro / US$ 79.95
ISBN 978-1-59229-336-0

Provides up-to-date, practical content for using Crystal Reports 2008.

Offers end-users and report designers targeted coverage for using Crystal Reports against SAP BW.

Written in an accessible, casual, very readable manner.

Mike Garrett

Using Crystal Reports with SAP

This book is a complete guide to the core functions of Crystal Reports, particularly as related to integration with other SAP data sources. The practical guidelines will give you the knowledge you need to create your own meaningful content using Crystal Reports with SAP BW as quickly as possible. And the end-of-chapter projects will help solidify and reinforce the reporting concepts presented and give you the foundation you need to begin creating your own formatted reports, sub-reports, alert reports, drill down reports, and more.

442 pp., 2010, 69,95 Euro / US$ 69.95
ISBN 978-1-59229-327-8

>> www.sap-press.com

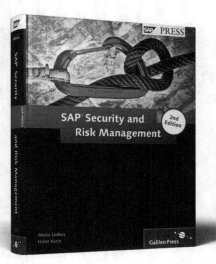

Describes system security for all SAP components

Contains new chapters on SAP GRC, SAP NetWeaver, SOA, J-SOX, and much more

Revised and updated with approximately 200 pages of brand new material

Mario Linkies, Horst Karin

SAP Security and Risk Management

With step-by-step instructions and numerous examples of proven methods, this book teaches you how to technically implement security in SAP NetWeaver. For all SAP applications, you'll learn where and how you can secure processes or improve the security of existing systems. To this end, you will learn the best practices of an SAP security strategy, as well as international standards. You will also learn how to integrate new technologies with your risk analysis. For this second edition, all parts of this book are updated to expand the description of new SAP products.

approx. 700 pp., 2. edition, 69,95 Euro / US$ 69.95
ISBN 978-1-59229-355-1, Sep 2010

>> www.sap-press.com

Interested in reading more?

Please visit our Web site for all
new book releases from SAP PRESS.

www.sap-press.com